hurricane-lamplight, sending me finally out into the alien night strangely haunted then and for long afterwards by that potent iconography.

After about a week of seesawing between cloud-hidden heights and lugubrious valley depths, we came to a particularly precipitous ascent. We started in the bowels of a deep gorge, passed up into cloud, and finally emerged into a new world of pure light, ultramarine sky and dazzling snow mountains. It was arrival – and it had happened, like the encounter with the hidden Buddha, suddenly and dramatically. Nearby was the notable Sherpa centre of Namche Bazaar.

Thereafter we delved on deeper among the bright peaks, finally venturing past the last human habitations to the sequestered heights where movement became difficult in the rarefied air, but

Solu Khumbu morning; Mt. Ama Dablam (LEFT) (1971)

where colours, undiminished by the usual atmospheric detritus, reached the eye with a primary intensity that lent the landscape a savage beauty from shimmering dawn till about mid-afternoon, when invariably the substantial world dissolved into a numinous mist.

My companion and I lost the true trail in such a mist somewhere up in the Solu Khumbu region, not far from Everest. Completely

THE SACRED MOUNTAIN

Travellers and Pilgrims at Mount Kailas in
Western Tibet and The Great Universal
Symbol of The Sacred Mountain

John Snelling

Revised and Enlarged Edition
including:
Kailas-Manasarovar Travellers' Guide

Forewords by
H.H. the Dalai Lama of Tibet
and Christmas Humphreys

London and The Hague:
EAST-WEST PUBLICATIONS
1990

For my daughter
S A R A H   S N E L L I N G
with all my love

First published 1983
Revised and enlarged edition 1990
Text Copyright © 1990 John Snelling
Illustrations © 1990 as Picture Credits—pages 456 & 457

Published by East-West Publications (UK) Ltd.,
8 Caledonia Street, London N1 9DZ.

ISBN 0 85692 173 4

The text and illustrations within this book are copyright
under the Berne Convention. No part may be reproduced,
stored in a retrieval system or transmitted in any way
without prior permission of the copyright owners.
Notwithstanding fair dealings for the purposes of review
as permitted by the Copyright Act 1956.

Designed by John Swain
Typeset in Great Britain by Gilbert Composing Services
Printed in Hong Kong by South China Printing Co.

CONTENTS

Kailas: the Great North Face

THE DALAI LAMA

FOREWORD

Amongst other sites of natural splendour, Mount Kailas and its environs have a special symbolic value for Tibetans. The region has been an undisputed part of Tibet since the emergence of the Tibetan nation, while the sacred peak has equally long been a focus of spiritual inspiration. For the early Tibetans who were Bönpos, the area represented the place where Shenrab Miwoche, the founder of their tradition, was born and gave teachings. Later it became an object of Buddhist veneration. Legends associate it with the Buddha and his immediate followers, with Guru Rinpoche, one of the pioneers of Buddhism in Tibet, and with Tibet's renowned saint, the yogi Milarepa. From the tantric view point too, many regard it as the abode of Chakrasamvara.

For centuries Tibetans have made arduous pilgrimages, sometimes the entire breadth of the country, to glimpse the holy peak and perform religious practices at its foot. The fact that Hindus and Jains from India, who hold Mount Kailas in equal respect, albeit for different reasons, were free to pursue their own pilgrimages, is indicative of the brotherly relations that always persisted between India and Tibet.

With the tragedy that overtook Tibet in recent years such practices became severely restricted and the surrounding temples and monuments were badly damaged, as in the rest of the country. However, lately, as conditions have been slightly relaxed and Tibetans permitted at least the outward trappings of religious practice, they have begun to journey to Kalias once more. Despite the hardships involved, the monasteries and stūpas are being rebuilt and people are again engaging in religious practices there.

These encouraging signs reveal the enduring fascination of the mountain, the indomitable spirit of the Tibetan people, and the continuing strength of their religious outlook.

Readers of John Snelling's book, *The Sacred Mountain* will find accounts of foreign travellers and pilgrims to Mount Kailas. From these they may gain some sense of the awe-inspiring physical presence of the peak itself, and the spiritual ideals that lead pilgrims to it.

November 2, 1988

FOREWORD TO THE FIRST EDITION

by Christmas Humphreys

When I was at school at Malvern, some sixty-odd years ago, the boys were turned out twice a week for a long walk round the countryside. But I, with a boon companion, would run from the College and race up the Beacon, the highest point in the Malvern Hills, through gorse and bracken, over rocks and holes, in a 900-foot scramble. At the summit, we would lie on our backs, with nothing above us but the sky and, when we stood up, a glorious view of seven counties.

This, I am sure, was more than a joyous form of exercise. Something happened in us beyond a mere climb for sturdy limbs. Already the mountain as such was calling us, and ever since, in the Alps, or later in the Himalayas, it was the non-stop scramble upwards of the heart and mind which I for one was seeking, and later found in the field of Buddhism.

And here is a book about the same phenomenon, beautifully produced and illustrated, and from an unexpected source. Mr. John Snelling, who has honoured me by asking for this Foreword, is the General Secretary of the Buddhist Society, London, and Editor of its journal, *The Middle Way*, a most sedentary pair of occupations. But ten years ago he made the Everest Trek from Kathmandu and in due course climbed to some 19,000 feet, which is higher than any mountain in Europe. This is an arduous and hazardous journey, and the clearly distinguishable stages of it were for him 'a series of hierarchic levels that suggested the graduated stages in the progress of the soul on the spiritual journey as described in traditional religious texts, both Eastern and Western'. He learnt the meaning of the mountains to both heart and feet, and much of Buddhism along the way. For these are truly *the* Hills, and those who travel in them are never the same afterwards. Even a single view, deeply seen and absorbed, can change one's inner being, as I found myself when I stood with Bhante Sangharakshita twenty years ago on a hill in Gangtok, Sikkim, and gazed on Kanchenjunga, forty miles away, and its sunlit peaks, which rise to some 28,000 feet above sea level.

It is therefore not surprising that many religions have sacred mountains at the heart of their cosmology, and Buddhism, a child of India, early accepted Mount Meru as the invisible yet ineffable Centre of all. It stands, as Mr. Snelling puts it, 'as heart and hub of a complex multidimensional system embracing both the spiritual and material realms', and he describes its symbolism in detail. But where is it to be found, for who is content with a cosmological symbol when sufficient search may reveal the physical fact? Seekers ranged the Himalayas for centuries, but eventually the mantle of Meru fell upon the crowning peak of a range in Western Tibet, a peak known as Kailas, which is some 22,000 feet high.

Only a few Western explorers and pilgrims have seen this remote and remarkable peak, and written of its wonderful symmetry and compelling spiritual presence. Giuseppe Tucci was there in 1935 and, in 1948, Lama Govinda, well known to us at the Buddhist Society in London, who talks of the 'joyful tension' felt by pilgrims as, after the rigours of the gruelling outward journey across the full width of the Himalayas, they begin the long circumambulation around the mountain which has been trodden by generations of devotees. I understand that for the time being, the Chinese, nowadays in political command of Tibet, will only allow access to the sacred mountain *via* Ladakh, and then to serious pilgrims only, travelling on foot. There may be merit in this decision, for the mountain is a supremely holy one, and difficulty of access protects its sanctity from the less pleasant aspects of tourism.

For millions this is Mount Meru made visible. From its environs rise four of the great rivers of India, with traditional names very similar to those accorded in ancient texts to the four rivers that rise from Meru. The mountain is venerated by the followers of four great religions, not only by Hindus and Buddhists but also by Jains and the indigenous Tibetan Böns. In its religious heyday, Kailas was crowded with monasteries and shrines, which lined the sacred peregrination route around it. Not even Olympus, or Fuji in Japan, can equal this ecstatic veneration.

To all who made pilgrimage to it, Kailas was the veritable Centre, both of the earth and of the universe and, more importantly, 'that conceptual point where sacred reality impinges upon profane reality, where time and eternity meet, and where all dualities are resolved'.

In his conclusion, where he attempts to unravel something of the great mystery that lies at the heart of the great symbol of the sacred mountain, Mr. Snelling reaches to China and quotes Hui Neng, the sixth Patriarch of the Zen Buddhist school: 'The idea of a self and of a being is Mount Meru . . . When you get rid of the idea of a self and of a being, Mount Meru will topple.' And so too, Mr. Snelling argues, Mount Kailas will topple, not necessarily the physical mountain (though that too, like all compounded things, must pass) but rather the mythical mountain lodged in the mind of the devotee, complete with its dense mantling of mind-made projections.

And what remains after that mighty falling? It would be improper to say anything further here, for if the end of a great pilgrimage could be so readily reached then there would be no virtue in the pilgrimage itself, and the sages all assure us that there is *every* virtue in the pilgrimage itself. (It is said in Buddhism to be better to travel well than to arrive.)

What lies ahead of the reader is a kind of literary pilgrimage to the sacred mountain, mainly conducted through an investigation of what was arguably the greatest of them all, Mount Kailas, in well-chosen words and magnificent pictures. It is replete with adventure, and many curious and absorbing things besides. Hopefully too, along the way, something of the power and magic of the sacred mountain will emerge from the pages and touch the heart of the reader.

London, 1982

Kailas as seen from Nyenri Gompa

AUTHOR'S PREFACE TO THE SECOND EDITION

A lot of water has passed under the bridge – if that's the right way to put it – since I originally wrote *The Sacred Mountain*.

In the first place – and as so often happens with books – much new information arrived after the book had gone to press. Particularly I met the widows of three Kailas travellers – (it's always the women who seem to survive, and often to an old age; the men die younger) – Lady Wakefield, the late Mrs Frederick Williamson and Mrs R. K. M. Saker. All kindly made available to me both written material, some of it hitherto unpublished, and pictures. I must register my sincere appreciation of their help. In the case of Mrs Williamson, the connection resulted in a fruitful collaboration on a book that recorded Frederick Williamson's life and career and her own part in it. I was also kindly lent Hyder Hearsey's autograph journal of his journey to Western Tibet with the great William Moorcroft by Hearsey's descendant, the late John Hearsey.

In the second place, dramatic developments in China in the early 1980s resulted in the opening up of Tibet to tourism and a whole new wave of visits to Kailas. In this new edition we therefore give account of a new generation of Kailas travellers, and I must sincerely thank many of them for either recording their reminiscenses or sending me in some cases very long and informative letters; also for lending photographs and pictures. I am particularly indebted to Bradley Rowe, the first European at Kailas since Lama Govinda; also Brian Beresford and Sean Jones, Naomi Duguid, William Forbes, Charlie Foster-Hall, Dr André Herold, Peter Overmire, Hugh Swift, Gilbert Levey, Richard Crane and Michael Henss.

Structurally, even though it was written at a time when Kailas-Manasarovar was closed to outsiders and was something of an enigma, the original text basically stands, though with revisions, corrections and the addition of supplementary material made available since publication. I have not, however, felt moved to change any of my original views on the spiritual significance of Kailas-Manasarovar or of the nature of sacred mountains and the practice of pilgrimage to them. However, I have tried to work out a standardized and more felicitous system of spelling for the Tibetan place-names in the Kailas-Manasarovar region, and for this as well as for much other invaluable advice I am indebted to Stephen Batchelor, author of the excellent *Tibet Guide* (London: Wisdom Publications, 1987), a person fully conversant with the arcane mysteries of both written and spoken Tibetan. I have also tried to give a more definitive survey of all the sacred sites around Kailas.

Other friends who gave much generous help, advice and support, and to whom much thanks is due, include Eva Hookway, who translated German language materials for me; Caille Golding, who read through the additional material and commented on it; and Martine Batchelor. I am also indebted to Hugh Richardson, the last British official stationed in Lhasa, who sent me several pages of close observations on the original text, of which I have taken full note in my revisions.

As to what has been added – i.e., material relating to the new wave of post-1981 travellers and pilgrims – this has been inserted near the end of the main text in form of an extra chapter. I have also suffixed new material relating to travel in the Kailas-Manasarovar region today and a few appendices that expand on matters raised in the main text.

Picasso used to say that, once a still life is arranged, the picture is painted. Something similar happens with books. Sometimes – all too rarely, unfortunately – a good subject arises that simply begs to be written about. It is almost as though it is hovering in the aether, waiting to be drawn down into concrete literary form. Such was the case with Kailas-Manasarovar. *The Sacred Mountain* was also my first book and, as with a first love, was in a way sweeter and more satisfying than the others that have come since. I will always harbour a special affection for it. It has won me many good friends and caused many good things to happen.

Ironically, however, I have not myself been able to visit Kailas-Manasarovar. Chronic ill health has prevented me from travelling for almost 15 years. But despite that, I regard myself as a devotee of the sacred mountain and all that it stands for. Furthermore, in the last analysis I don't believe one always has to visit a place, even a sacred place, to know what it's about. The creative imagination is endowed with quite wonderful powers; and there's also a sense in which we tune in to a deeper communal consciousness in which all the accumulated experience of the universe is available to us: something like Jung's collective unconscious. Guided by such hidden allies, one can, I believe, get closer to the reality of something like Kailas than, say, someone who goes there in entirely the wrong spirit.

In support of these views, I always cite the case of Arthur Waley, the doyen of all Western translators from the Chinese, who himself never went to China and never really wanted to go, believing that to do so might blunt rather than sharpen his understanding of its ancient culture.

Also I have one very powerful testimonial. I met Sean Jones shortly after he came back from Kailas at a slide show he gave at Manjushri London, a Tibetan Buddhist Centre run by Geshe Namgyal Wangchen.

"I read your book," Sean told me in his blunt way. "It was very accurate."

Sharpham,
August, 1988

List of Maps

New colour maps drawn by Chris Shaw

ERRATUM. On the Kailas Parikrama/Kora Map on p. 36, the mountain called Dharma King Norsang should in fact be called Palace of King Kuvera.

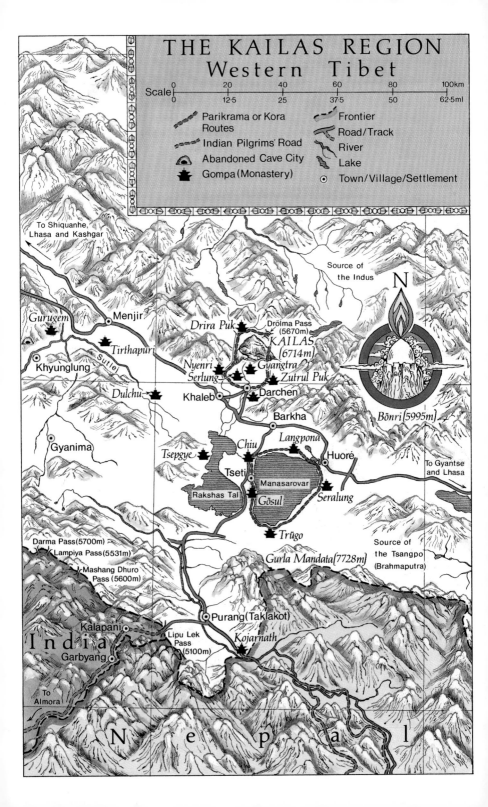

CHAPTER ONE

Himalaya

In 1971, I saw the Himalayas for the first time and like many before me was deeply affected. It was during the rainy season and I had gone up to the hill station of Mussoorie to escape the oppressive heat and humidity of the Indian plains. For weeks, dense monsoon clouds boiled out of the lower valleys, completely obscuring the surrounding mountain landscape. Then one evening I happened to go up to a rocky bluff a little above the new Buddhist temple built in a small Tibetan refugee community, and I found the world transformed. The usual mantle of cloud had suddenly and completely dissipated, and all around stretched a world whose vastness and beauty could not till then have been imagined. A dramatic sunset was also under way, and the sky looked as though the contents of a crucible of molten metals had been flamboyantly splashed across it.... And then, quite unexpectedly, I became aware of the jagged ribbon of the snow mountains. A hundred miles away on the utmost rim of the horizon, they were reflecting the rose light of the setting sun with icy brilliance. They were tiny – but magnificent.

Later, in Nepal, I made the Everest Trek, which had the feel of a religious pilgrimage about it. The earthen trail cut across the grain of the land with innumerable arduous ascents and descents, which, coupled to ancilliary hardships and hazards (like hunger, leeches and dysentery) all added up to a pretty substantial dose of salutary suffering for the two of us making the journey. Furthermore, in so far as we progressed from lush, green, terraced lowlands to barren rocky wastes at the heights, passed through cloud forest, topped the treeline and ventured beyond the critical 15,000 foot altitude level where the oxygen becomes thin in the air, this was also a journey that had a number of clearly-distinguishable stages. It involved passing through a series of hierarchic levels that suggested

The mantra OM MANI PADME HUM carved on a mani stone

the graduated stages in the progress of the soul on the spiritual journey as described in traditional religious texts, both Eastern and Western. There were even foretastes of the ultimate goal, in the form of glimpses of the snow peaks from the occasional high pass, that inspired us onward when our spirits flagged. And there were those soul-destroying phases when we just plodded on through endless, meaningless rain and mud, and felt we would never reach journey's end.

There was also copious evidence of Buddhism all along our route. *Stūpas** and *mani*† walls dotted the entire length of the trail; enormous *mantras*‡ were carved on the wayside rocks; prayer flags raked the wind along the heights; and there were *gompa*§ to stay at or visit in every village.

Entering one *gompa* cautiously, I found myself in almost total darkness. Then, as my eyes became habituated to the gloom (made more gloomy by everything being encrusted with the soot of butter-lamps), I was drawn to the far end by the dull glint of copper and gold. There I found a small shrine covered with the usual votive

---

*A type of Buddhist monument known in Tibet as *chörten*. (see p. 3).

†Walls composed of stones upon which the sacred formula *Om Mani Padme Hum* has been carved.

‡Religious formula, e.g. *Om Mani Padme Hum* (see above).

§Buddhist monastery or temple.

Buddhist stūpa or chörten at Cherkip, Lake Manasarovar

objects. . . .

Suddenly I was overtaken by a disconcerting sense of being watched. On checking, I found nothing to right, left or behind. Looking above, however, I discovered that I was being surveyed by an enormous gilded Buddha which occupied the interior of a commodious shaft cut up high behind the shrine. The Buddha was smiling, as though at my discomfort – a good-humoured smile to which I had to respond. . . .

On another occasion we sat till deep into the night with a bevy of *tsampa* – eating, *chang* – drinking* Sherpa villagers while two lamas – one small, stout and bald; the other gaunt, with long skeins of hair wound around his head – droned the sacred texts by the hour. As the night wore on, the benign and wrathful deities painted in vivid lacquers on the walls seemed to come alive and dance in the unstable

---

*Tsampa is a doughy dish made from roasted barley meal, sometimes mixed with butter tea. *Chang,* on the other hand, is a pungent barley beer brewed by Tibetans.

TOP LEFT: *Terraced rice paddies in Central Nepal (1971)*

LEFT: *The Author on the Everest Trek (1971)*

TOP RIGHT: *The summit of Everest (1971)*

disorientated, we wandered for hours in a mountain wasteland of moraine and scree, while the air rang with the threatening roar of distant waters plunging into unseen chasms.

As though by grace, in the last flicker of twilight we stumbled upon two isolated yakman's huts in a remote pasture-land amid the peaks, and took shelter there for the night. It was, we knew, only a temporary reprieve. We were in deep trouble, for which we alone

Thyangboche Gompa (1971)

LEFT, Cloud forest and, RIGHT, Approach to Everest (1971)

were to blame. We had in *hubris* trespassed upon the preserve of the gods, where human beings rightly should not go. With little food, and without either guide or compass, we had no certainty of ever finding our way out of that high labyrinth. Neither of us spoke that night. Sleep, when it came, was thin and fitful.

Strangely, however, the possibility of death in the near future from starvation or exposure had, in the final analysis, a liberating effect. All the mental and emotional baggage that entrammels us for most of our lives seemed to drop away during the hours of darkness, leaving us somehow clearer and freer and more in touch with the world. In short, close to death, we felt, paradoxically, very close to life.

We began to dehydrate in the thin air and I had to get up several times during the course of the night to go outside and slake my rampant thirst at a nearby stream. The veil of mist had miraculously lifted during the intervening hours of darkness; the night was clear and bright with flashing starlight. The great ice mountains, crowding huge and remarkably close all around, were picking up that light and reflecting it. They looked like great crystal cities of the future charged with vast protean energies.... And again, next morning, when we two potentially doomed men threw open the door of our little temporary shelter, we walked into a world bathed in brilliant sunshine – a world as fresh and as palpably god-given as on the first morning of creation.

In the event, *Nirvāna* was not for us on that occasion; nor did we perish in some uninhabited valley in the non-man's-land between Tibet and Nepal. Within about an hour of setting out, we recognized far below us the sky-blue lake which we had seen the previous afternoon. Then all was made clear. In the mist we had done the classic thing and blindly wandered in an almost perfect circle. The hut where we had spent the night was in fact hardly a stone's throw away from the moraine dump where we had originally gone astray. In a very short time, and with intense relief, we were soon following the main trail on up beside the cyclopean debris of the Khumbu Glacier. When we met two Sherpas, we did not hesitate to engage them to guide us to Base Camp on Everest and back. We were in no mood for any more misadventures.

Finally, next day, to stand in brilliant morning and see the world's highest mountains parading themselves in magnificent panoply to the farmost rim of the horizon. It was yet another demonstration of the infinite scope and beauty of things, which may so easily pass unnoticed as we pursue our blinkered concerns in the narrow confines of the cities of the plains. Would we, however, have been so sensitive to it all without the hard training of the difficult overland haul? The hunger, the blisters, the frustrations, the discomforts, and finally the culminating brush with mortality, had all helped to grind away a little of our usual arrogance and make us more humble and open – and consequently able to see the world a little more clearly.

However, it was just a taste – a little piece of paradise on account. Although we toyed with the idea of finding a cave and taking to the *yogic* life up there, it was not a viable possibility. We knew that we would soon be back among the cities of the plains, where we would have to struggle very hard to retain even a little of the clarity of vision that had been afforded us at the heights. The first spiritual insights may be given; the rest have to be earned through hard work.

Several weeks later, recrossing the Indian-Nepalese border at Raxaul, I was treated to a final parting glimpse of the Himalayas. It was a vivid evening and good to be back on the teeming, dusty plains, but those great mountains, disposed in full array and magnificence across the northern horizon, were again radiating the rich rose light of the setting sun.

Recalling this evocative scene at a later date, when the world had contracted to a tight knot, bereft of movement and magic, and when even the quality of light seemed to be deteriorating, I suddenly realized that total spiritual hopelessness – *damnation*, if you like – cannot be possible in a universe that affords sights of such beauty to its denizens; that whatever has charge of the disposal of things must be fundamentally benign and forgiving. That was a very great relief – and something that also has strong associations with Buddhism, for not so far from Raxaul, at Lumbini, just a few miles away across the Indo-Nepalese frontier, Gautama the Buddha was born, and such sights must have been familiar and influential for him. It may be a subjective thing, but the beauty of those mountains at sunset images very powerfully images the beauty of the religious way that the Buddha initiated – a way that itself leads from the morass of our human sufferings and problems to a true wholeness and harmony with that which *is*.

It is understandable that those who have inhabited the plains of India should have, from time immemorial, been similarly affected by those great mountains. The late Professor Junriro Takakusu, the eminent Japanese Buddhist scholar, has described the process whereby the invading light-skinned Aryans, who began to enter the subcontinent sometime during the second millennium B.C., at first pushed southwards in their march of victory – until they reached the tropical zone;

> Then, because of the severe heat, they chose to select their abode among the cool forests of the Black Mountains, which form the smaller range at the foot of the great Himalaya. Gradually they came to regard the forest as their ideal abode, and in time they acquired the habit of meditating with the great Himalaya as the object of their thoughts, for there was Himalaya, eternally magnificent, eternally unapproachable. During mornings and evenings the snows would glow in changing splendour as the rays of the sun struck them; in winter the glaciers in the valleys were frozen solid; but in summer the glaciers flowed along the winding valleys like giants coming to life after a year's sleep,
>
> (J. Takakusu, *Essentials of Buddhist Philosophy*)

On occasion, the Indians seem to have looked upon the Himalaya, the 'Abode of Snow', as a single, many-peaked mountain, personified as the god Himavat. A daughter of the mountain, by name Pārvatī Haimavati or Umā Devi, became the consort of the great Lord Shiva himself. Legend describes her playfully covering her Lord's eyes as he sat in meditation on a peak of Himalaya. Instantly all light and life were extinguished in the universe until, out of compassion for all beings, the god opened his third eye, which blazed like a new sun. So intense was its blazing that it scorched the mountains and forests of Himavat to oblivion. Only when he saw that the daughter of the mountain was properly contrite did he relent and restore her father to his former estate.

Many other legends relating to Lord Shiva and the goddess have the Himalaya for their setting. For instance, Dr. Tom Longstaff, the distinguished mountaineer, records an incident where a party of travellers were destroyed by an avalanche which local belief maintained had been hurled from the top of Trisul by Shiva himself, 'who was incensed at their approach to his veiled bride (Nanda Ghungti).' Indeed, one of his names is *Girisa*: 'Lord of the Hills'.

Nor is Lord Shiva alone in this. Hindu mythology records many gods having their abode in Himavat, together with all kinds of semi-divine and demonaic beings such as *rakshas* (demons) and *gandharvas* (celestial musicians). In these mountains the sacred river Ganges, personified as Ganga, another of Himavat's daughters, has its principal source. Here too are situated great shrines: Badrinath, consecrated to Vishnu; and Kedarnath, consecrated to Shiva, where once devotees hurled themselves bodily from the brink of an adjacent precipice – a reminder of the terrible aspect of the great god. In another of his aspects Lord Shiva is the Great Ascetic, and innumerable *yogis* and *rishis* are reputed to dwell in remote caves in the Himalayan fastnesses, performing their austerities. Withal, the virtues of Himalaya are supreme. To merely think of it is to gain vast merit, to see it is to have one's sins expunged as dew is evaporated by the morning sun.

Nor when Europeans came to India did they go untouched either. No less a luminary of the British Raj than Sir Francis Young husband recognized the fact that the mountains possess a unique capacity to affect the religious susceptibility in man and he wished this consciously exploited in order to awaken people to the truths of religion.

> Efforts should be made both in India and England to lead expeditions to the Himalayas to find the best view-points of the mountains and make them known to the outside world. When these best spots would be discovered, they would be turned into and preserved as places of pilgrimage.
>
> (quoted in: Swami Pranavānanda,
Exploration in Tibet, 1st edition)

During my time in northern India, as well as during the Everest Trek, I certainly felt deeply affected by this power. I also experienced the way in which a particular mountain can become charged with an almost inexorable magnet-like force capable of drawing one to it, like a fish hooked on a line, over miles and miles of the most inhospitable terrain. Certainly Everest became a sacred mountain for my companion and myself – as indeed it is for those who live in its environs, by whom it is called *Chomolungma*: 'Mother Goddess of the Land'.* Strangely this religious magnetism was apparent despite the fact that the mountain was invisible to us for virtually the whole of our journey, or perhaps the effect was heightened by our goal being obscured. Even when we were very close, looking across at it from the best vantage point – atop a 19,000 foot pile of rocks called Kalar Patar – it deigned to reveal only a portion of its summit. The rest of the great mountain remained withdrawn in seclusion behind its entourage of attendant peaks. What we could see of it was surprisingly snow-free and

---

* According to H. Hoffman (*Religions of Tibet*, London, 1961), 'The White Goddess of Heavn' (gNam-lha dkar-mo) also lives in the neighbourhood of Everest, together with five 'Sisters of Long Life', each of whom is endowed with a special pool of different-coloured water.

Everest from the North. The camp of one of the early mountaineering expeditions of the 1920s in the foreground.

regular – reminiscent of the top of the Great Pyramid of Gizeh. As solid and imperturbable as a great sage in deep meditation, it stood gloriously unmoved by the hurricane blast of the high-altitude wind that ripped a steady jet-stream plume of whiteness from its apex.

And what of those men who have attempted to climb this great mountain? One of the most sensitive responses by a mountaineer that I have come across is by the late G. H. Leigh-Mallory. He describes how Everest appeared to him more than fifty years ago as he approached it from the Tibetan side. Looking from a distance of about ten miles, at the bottom of the Rongbuk glacier:

> At the end of the valley, Everest rises not so much a peak as a prodigious mountain mass. There is no complication to the eye. The highest of the world's mountains, it seems, has to make but a single gesture of magnificence to be lord of all, vast in unchallenged and isolated

The Everest Trek: yak and driver (1971)

supremacy. To the discerning eye other mountains are visible, giants between 23000 and 26000 feet high. Not one of their slendered heads even reaches their chief's shoulder; beside Everest they escape notice – such is the preeminence of the greatest....

(quoted in: M. Ward (ed.), *The Mountaineer's Companion*)

In 1924, Mallory and his climbing partner Irvine were lost at over 28,000 feet while trying to scale this 'prodigious white fang excrescent in the jaw of the world'. As the search for the two climbers proceeded in vain, their colleague N. E. Odell reflected:

What right had we to venture thus far into the holy presence of the Supreme Goddess, or, much more, sling at her our blasphemous challenges to 'sting her very nose-tip'? If it was indeed the sacred grounds of Chomolungma, Goddess Mother of the Mountain Snows, had we violated it – was I now violating it? Had we approached her with due reverence and singleness of heart and purpose? And yet, as I gazed again another mood appeared to creep over her haunting features. There seemed to be something alluring in that towering presence. I was

Namche Bazaar (1971)

almost fascinated. I realized that no mere mountaineer alone could but
be fascinated, that he who approached close must be led on and,
oblivious of all obstacles, seek to reach that most sacred and highest
place of all.

Odell's tone is humble, even devout; he is obviously aware of the
hubris inherent in man's desire to conquer great mountain peaks.
This conquering spirit is very much a modern and a Western
phenomenon; other peoples do not on the whole display much
preoccupation with anything so inevitably bound to lead to
unnecessary discomfort and danger. Indeed, sensitive as they usually
are to the spiritual aspect of mountains, a desire to scale them would
in their eyes be often tantamount to outright sacrilege. Of course,
in recent years the inexorable spread of Western ideas and
influences, wedded to the power of Western money, have done a
great deal to erode such scruples. Nevertheless, it was religious
considerations that caused the Nepalese authorities to place the

Fish-tail Peak, Muchapuchare, out of bounds to climbers; and when, in 1956, Dr. Charles Evans led a British expedition to the world's third highest mountain, Kanchenjunga, which straddles the Nepal-Sikkim frontier, out of respect for Sikkimese beliefs his party left the top and its neighbourhood untouched, venturing no further up the mountain than was necessary to prove that its summit *could* be reached. Kanchenjunga, 'Five Treasuries of the Great Snow', so-called on account of its five majestic peaks, is personified as the highest god of the Himalayan state of Sikkim, and elaborate sword and mask dances are held to celebrate the god's feast in monasteries throughout the land.

Returning eventually from my travels to native ground in Britain, I worked on a B.B.C. radio programme about the religious connotations of mountains. Research revealed the surface of the earth to be liberally sprinkled with spiritually significant peaks: Fuji, Ontake, Wu T'ai, Omei, Chiu Hua, P'u T'o, Adam's Peak, Arunachala, Abu, Chomolhari, Demavend, Ararat, Ayer's Rock, Sinai, Moriah, Hira, Kilimanjaro, Athos, Olympus, Helicon, Parnassus, Popocatapetl, Shasta.... The list was apparently endless. Even in Britain we have our relatively modest but nevertheless spiritually evocative Glastonbury Tor, our enigmatic Silbury Hill, our various St. Michael's Mounts, not to mention many another mountain, hill, tumulus or tump clearly touched in some measure by the same magic.

One mountain, however, stands high above the rest, a sacred mountain overtopping the ranges of lesser sacred mountains, their epitome and apogee. This mountain is called *Kailas*. The present volume is principally concerned with Mount Kailas. Firstly, its spiritual and mythological associations are examined in some detail, together with their historical, religious, political and geographical contexts. The possibility of identifying Mount Kailas with Mount Meru, the *axis mundi* of many classical Eastern cosmologies, is also discussed. Then the narratives and reports of the relatively few Western travellers and explorers who managed to reach the remote Kailas are outlined with a view to discovering how the mountain impressed them, their purposes for going there and the adventures they experienced in doing so. This section of the book in fact represents a brief survey of the exploration of the part of Western Tibet in which Kailas is situated. Next, the accounts of the pilgrims, the men who travelled to Kailas primarily for spiritual purposes, are outlined with a view to discovering both how the sacred mountain and the long, difficult and dangerous pilgrimage to it affected *them*, especially, of course, from the spiritual point of view. Finally, the other sacred mountains of the world are reviewed, together with the ancillary kinds of religious and semi-religious associations with which mountains have been invested, and then an attempt is made to define the highest, fullest manifestations of the notion of the sacred mountain.*

The central thesis of the work is that sacred mountains – that is, mountains that are held in profound religious awe – participate in a universal symbol of archetypal power. In examining in depth the material relating to what is arguably the greatest of them, it is hoped that it might be possible to unravel the great mystery that this symbol enshrines.

---

* In the present Revised Edition, much new material has also been added, including accounts of journeys and pilgrimages made to Mt. Kailas in the 1980s.

Evening cloud formations over Kailas

Bronze relief now in the Institute of Ethnology of the University of Zürick depicting the Kailas-Manasarovar region and many of its gompa and auspicious sites. Milarepa appears in apotheosis on the summit while Naro Bön-chung clatters ignominiously down the south face having been trounced in the Great Contest of Magic (see pp. 31–38)

CHAPTER TWO

Mount Kailas and its Sacred Lakes

Had an enterprising cartographer ever been moved to draw a religious map of Asia, many of the thin red lines tracing the principal pilgrim routes would have been shown to converge on a remote and remarkable part of Western Tibet. Here, a little to the north of India, across the jagged rampart of the Great Himalaya, there is a sacred mountain called *Kailas*. For more than two millennia the faithful have made the arduous journey there: from all parts of India; from the Himalayan kingdoms of Sikkim, Bhutan, Nepal, Ladakh and Kashmir; from every quarter of the forbidden land of Tibet; and from far into the mysterious hinterland of Central Asia – and even from beyond.

Up to 1959, Tibet had for centuries been isolated both by its own sequestered situation on the Roof of the World and by the inwardly-directed religious preoccupations of a sizeable proportion of its population. Though *bona fide* pilgrims were always tolerated, foreigners were diligently debarred from crossing its frontiers, and no attempt was made by the government to have anything approaching normal relations with either its immediate neighbours or with the international community in general. By default, therefore, Tibet's political status went undefined and unguaranteed, and there was little that the Tibetans could do when, in the middle years of the present century, the Chinese, having carried through their own Marxist revolution, began to revive old claims that Tibet was an integral part of China and to advance these claims by force. In 1959, the monk-ruler of Tibet, His Holiness the Dalai Lama, fled to exile in India. Thereafter, the Chinese completed their takeover, and closed the borders of Tibet more inexorably than ever before to secular and religious traffic alike. It was not until the 1980s that the Chinese authorities finally relented and again allowed foreign pilgrims and travellers to visit Tibet.

The landscape of the corner of the great plateau of Tibet in which Kailas is situated is one of desolate beauty. In the high altitudes prevailing there – 13,000 feet and more – virtually no trees grow and little vegetation clothes the rugged terrain. Due to the transparency of the rarefied air, however, colours reach the eye with unfiltered intensity: rich reds, browns, yellows, purples – and in fine weather both sky and mirroring water are a deep, noble blue. Climate, on the other hand, is unpredictable, at times violent, and always prone to extremes of heat and cold. It is said that while a man's arm, exposed to the heat of the sun, may be being scorched, his feet, lying in shadow, may at the same time be suffering the ravages of frostbite. Not surprisingly, therefore, this has always been a scantily populated area.

The sacred Mount Kailas stands out of this elemental landscape, a compelling and uncannily symmetrical peak. Sheer walls of horizontally stratified conglomerate rock form a monumental plinth thousands of feet high that is finally capped by a cone of pure ice. Such is the regularity of the mountain that it looks as though it might have been carved by human – or more accurately, *super-human* – hands: those of the gods in fact. Kailas has been frequently compared to a great temple, a cathedral, or a *stūpa* – one of those characteristically Buddhist monuments known in Tibet as *chörtens* (see pp. 3 and 8). The analogy almost invariably has religious connotations, for in some mysterious ways Kailas seems to have the power to touch the spiritual heart of man; in the past this has been as true for hard-headed explorers as it has been for the more impressionable pilgrims.

The Religious Associations of Kailas

Kailas is regarded as a *sacred* mountain by followers of no less than four of the great religions of Asia: by Hindus, Jains, Buddhists and followers of the pre-Buddhist shamanistic religion of Tibet, the Bön-po.

Hindu Associations

Pious Hindus look upon Kailas as the Heaven or throne of

Shiva and Parvati at Mt. Kailas. Rock carving at Ellora in Central India

Mahādeva himself: the great god Shiva. Here he sits in perpetual meditation with his consort Pārvatī, the daughter of Himalaya. The situation is depicted in a carving in the great Kailasāntha temple at Ellora in Central India, with the demon Rāvana shaking the mountain in his vain attempt to unseat Lord Shiva and his mate. As the name suggests, Kailas was the prototype for the Kailasāntha Temple and indeed for other temples in India. (See p. 24). The appearance of the mountain is also strongly phallic, for which reason devotees of Shiva identify it with the *lingam*: the phallic symbol characteristic of Shaivism. In the *Mahānirvāna Tantra*, the 'Tantra of the Great Liberation,' a dialogue in which Lord Shiva expounds the principles of *Tantra* to his *shakti* or consort, Kailas is described in the following fulsome terms:

> The enchanting summit of the Lord of Mountains, resplendent with all its various jewels, clad with many a tree and many a creeper, melodious with the song of many a bird, scented with the fragrance of all the season's flowers, most beautiful, fanned by soft, cool, and perfumed breezes, shadowed by the still shade of stately trees; where cool groves resound with the sweet-voiced songs of troops of Apsara [heavenly

Mt. Kailas compared in side elevation with the Kailasantha Temple, Ellora, Central India (after E.B. Havell)

nymphs] and in the forest depths flocks of kolila [cockatoos] maddened with passion sing; where [Spring] Lord of the Seasons with his followers ever abide...; peopled by [troops of] Siddha [holy men of semi-divine status] Chāraṇa [celestial singers, dancers, bards or panegyrists of the gods], Gandharva [celestial musicians] and Gaṇapatya [devotees of the god Ganesha].

(trans. Arthur Avalon (Sir John Woodroffe)
The Tantra of the Great Liberation.)

Another Hindu belief can be found in the *Purāṇas,* a canon of popular traditional texts, which maintains that Kuvera, the god of wealth, ruled from a fabulous city called Alakā, which was situated on or near Kailas, and that eight lesser peaks nearby were his treasure houses. In Kālidāsa's classic Sanskrit epic poem, *Meghadūta* ('Cloud Messenger'), a lovelorn *yaksha* (a powerful spirit) banished from Alakā recruits a passing cloud to carry a message to his estranged wife, who still resides in Kuvera's city. The poet speaks of Kailas being used as a mirror by *Apsarases* (heavenly nymphs), the saddles of its ridges rent apart by Rāvāna's arms: 'With soaring peaks snow white as lotus blooms/Cleaving the sky, as stalwart as if they grew/Through heaping up day by day/The Three-eyed-One's [Lord Shiva's] o'erflowing laughter.'* Alakā itself is described as an exotic pleasure-city – a kind of celestial oriental Las Vegas – 'full of lovely girls and pictures;/Deep-toned tabors throb to dance and song,/Floors gem-inwrought, cloud-kissing roofs...'.

Finally, the great Hindu epics, the *Rāmāyana* and the *Mahābhārata*, have frequent recourse to Kailas as an analogy for anything of commanding height. It is said to be six leagues high, to be an assembly place for all gods and demons, and to be the site of a great jujube tree. In short, Kailas is the glory of the Himalayas:

> There is no mountain like Himachal, for in it are Kailas and Manasarovar. As the dew is dried up by the morning sun, so are the sins of the world dried up at the sight of Himachal.
> (Quoted C. A. Sherring, *Western Tibet and the British Borderland*. Arributed to the *Rāmāyana* but probably from the *Skanda Purāna*.)

Jain Associations

Kailas is also recognized as a spiritually significant peak by the followers of the Jain religion, a compassionate creed that arose in India at about the same time as Buddhism (around the sixth century B.C.), with which it has many affinities, including emphasis on the attainment of liberation from the painful round of worldly existence. In Jain writings Kailas is called *Astapāda*, and is reputed to have been the place where Rishabha, the first *Tirthankāra*, attained *Moksha* or Liberation. Although the actual and historical founder of Jainism was Mahāvira ('Great Man'), the 24th *Tirthankāra*, Jains in fact regard their creed as embodying timeless wisdom propounded

---

*In G H Rooke's translation, apropos the last line the commentary states that 'the whiteness of laughter has been adopted as a poetical convention.' (Rooke, p. 40n)

The Tantric Buddhist diety Demchog (Skt Chakrasamvara) in union with his consort Dorje Phamo (Vajravarahi)

in the world in all ages. The *Tīrthankāras* were the avatars of the present fallen age which has followed the golden age.

Buddhist Associations

Buddhists, meanwhile associate Kailas with a tantric meditational deity (*yidam*) called Demchog (*Skt.:* Chakrasamvara – 'Supreme Bliss') and his consort (*yum*) Dorje Phamo (*Skt.:* Vajravārāhī). This is not really the proper place to delve deeply into the great mystery of *yidams* but basically they figure as tutelary deities in Tantric Buddhism. While superficially they may be regarded as gods, and as such are represented in great and graphic detail in sacred paintings, initiates regard them more precisely as personifications of purified aspects of human nature, particularly of wrathful or passionate aspects which might ordinarily cause great suffering but which if properly transformed through spiritual training may produce true wisdom. 'The passions are the Buddha nature,' is a well-known saying in Buddhism. Demchog is an awe-inspiring figure, full of fierce energy. Depictions represent him as having four faces, each of a different colour (red, blue, green, white), each with three eyes. He wears a grizzly crown of human skulls and has a tiger skin draped around his waist. His body is blue and the twelve hands of his twelve arms each hold a symbolic object: a *vajra* (thunderbolt), elephant skin, cup, bell, dagger and so forth. Beneath his feet he tramples two prostrate figures. Dorje Phamo, meanwhile, with whom he unites in a glory of flames, carries a curved knife and a skull cup. Her naked body is red. She is associated with Tijung, a small pyramidal peak adjacent to Kailas, according to Swami Pranavānanda, who also maintains that Demchog is associated with two other Tibetan mountains besides Kailas: Lapchi, near Nepal, and Tsari, 200 miles east of Lhasa.

Swami Pranavānanda also asserts that the Buddha was thought to inhabit the sacred mountain with a retinue of five hundred *bodhisattvas* (realized beings who have deferred their own *Nirvāna* so that they may work for the salvation of all other beings), but this may not have been a generally held view, at least latterly, for in modern times the most important Buddhist association seems to have been with the great *guru*-poet Milarepa, who lived in the late eleventh and early twelfth centuries of the common era. He belonged to the Karma Kagyu school of Tibetan Buddhism, and was the pupil of Marpa the Translator, whom he succeeded as head of the order. He is often shown in Tibetan paintings with his right

A Bon-po pilgrim at Mt. Kailas (1926)

The Silver Castle of Khyunglung

hand cupped to his ear (like certain modern folk-singers when trying to get a note), his body a strange greyish or greenish colour as a result of his having lived exclusively on nettle stew at some time in his life. Legend holds that Milarepa was involved in a vital struggle for possession of Mount Kailas with Naro Bön-chung, a priest of the Bön faith.

Bön Associations

The word *Bön* is equivalent to the Tibetan word, *Chos*, which itself corresponds to the Sanskrit word *dharma*, a term that embraces such shades of meaning as 'religious teaching' or even 'Law of the Universe'. The origins of the Bön religion itself are unclear, but Bön myths speak of a western homeland called Tazik, possibly somewhere in modern Soviet Central Asia, where the teachings were first disseminated. Certainly Persian, Kashmiri, Indian and even Chinese influences can be detected in primitive Bön. After its transmission to Tibet, we can distinguish two distinct phases of further development:

Initially, before the arrival of Buddhism in the 7th century, the Bön-po were religious functionaries expert in the rituals concerned with the control of powerful spirits, death and burial, exorcism, divination and other occult matters. Their activities were not formalized and there was certainly a great deal of regional variation, but one of the most important centres of the early Bön cults was Zhang Zhung, an ancient frontier kingdom embracing mainly western Tibet but extending to include north and north-eastern parts of the plateau as well. Its capital was latterly at the 'Silver Castle' of Khyunglung just to the west of Kailas. Zhang Zhung was eventually incorporated into the centralized Tibetan state by King Songtsen Gampo in the mid-7th century A.D.

Later, there was a thrust to organize the Bön religion and to develop and systematize its teachings on a firm doctrinal basis so that it could hold its own against the usurping Buddhists. In the process Bön borrowed much from Buddhism, and some traffic also passed the other way. Shenrab Miwo, a partly mythical figure who was furnished with a life history and status similar to those of Shākyamuni Buddha, is credited with the systematization of the Bön religion (see p. 379).

Mountains were important power-points in the ancient Bön cults. They linked heaven and earth and so were endowed with powerful cosmogonic, theogonic and geneological associations, becoming the 'souls' of particular areas. Mount Kailas, called *Tisé*, was the Soul Mountain of Zhang Zhung. According to Prof. Giuseppe Tucci, who himself travelled in the Kailas region (see pp. 279–291):

> It towers under the heavenly sphere like a parasol with eight ribs . . ., and above the earth like an eight-petalled lotus, like a spread-out carpet. It is the navel of the world . . . seat of a sky goddess [the Goddess of Heavenly Grace, Sipaimen, one of 'the innumerable class of . . . female goddesses who enjoy great popularity in the folk religion of Tibet'] . . .
>
> [It] is the ladder which simultaneously ascends to heaven and descends from heaven . . .,and it thus has the same function as the 'heavenly cord' which links heaven and earth . . . The emanation-body* of Shenrab descended onto this mountain. The host of *Ge khod* gods has its palace there. According to tradition . . . there are 360 of these gods; the association of Tisé with the axis of the world, about which revolves the year with its 360 days, is obvious. The mountain is imagined as a great *chörten* made of rock-crystal, or a place where various families of gods reside. It has four gates: Chinese Tiger, Tortoise, Red Bird and Turquoise Dragon, which have the duty of guarding the four cardinal points . . .
>
> (G. Tucci, *The Religions of Tibet*†)

Various writers, including Namkhai Norbu Rinpoche, a married lama from Dergé currently teaching at Naples University (see pp. 376ff), have pointed out that the ancient Bön traditions also encompassed lofty spiritual teachings of the kind presently transmitted within the Dzogchen (lit. 'Great Perfection') tradition. Dzogchen is now regarded as the highest teaching of the Nyingma school of Tibetan Buddhism, the seminal school whose teachings were brought to Tibet in the 7th century by Guru Rinpoche; but there is also an ongoing Bönpo tradition of Dzogchen, in terms of whose symbology Kailas stands for the father-mountain, the active principle of skilful means, and Manasarovar for the mother-lake or passive principle of transcendent reality.§ Moreover, Dzogchen uses light symbolism extensively; indeed, the highest attainment on the path is the so-called Body of Light (alt. Rainbow Body). Prof. Tucci

---

*cf the *Nirmānakāya* of Shākyamuni Buddha, the body in which he appears in the world. This is not a 'real' body but a phantomlike appearance conjured up for compassionate purposes, to help suffering beings.

†For simplicity, certain changes of spelling, punctuation, etc. have been made here.

§For an account of a pilgrimage to Kailas by a Bön-po Dzogchen master, see pp. 431–3.

also writes of the 'apparition of light streaming from the snow of Mount Tisé and the waters of Lake Mapham' and points to its spiritual significance in terms of 'divine emanation' (*trulwa*). The intense struggle that was waged between the ancient Bön traditions of Zhang Zhung and the newly arrived Buddhism was focussed on Mount Kailas/Tisé and is mythically enshrined in the powerful legend of Milarepa's contest of magical powers with a Bön adept named Naro Bön-chung for possession of the sacred mountain.

The Great Contest of Magic

Apparently, when Milarepa went to Tisé (*Kang Rinpoche* or 'Precious Snow Mountain' is another name), he was met and welcomed by the local deities. He was not so cordially treated by Naro Bön-chung, however, whom he first encountered on the shores of Lake Manasarovar. He showed little respect for Milarepa, who already had a considerable reputation for mystical attainment, and told him that, as the Bön-po were in possession of the sacred mountain, he would have to change his faith if he wanted to stay and meditate there. Naturally, Milarepa did not accept this. He told Naro Bön-chung that the Buddha himself had prophesied that Kailas would one day fall under the sway of the followers of the Dharma and that moreover, as his own teacher, Marpa, had spoken of the mountain, it had become especially significant for him personally. He therefore invited the Bön priest to renounce his faith and become a Buddhist. Naro Bön-chung declined in his turn and suggested that they resolve their differences by holding a contest of magic. The loser should cede the sacred mountain to the winner.

Naro Bön-chung started the contest by straddling the lake and singing an inflamatory song which vaunted his own mystical prowess while deprecating that of his opponent. Milarepa replied by covering the lake with his own body *without at all enlarging his body*, and singing a counter refrain. Finally, for good measure, he put the whole of Lake Manasarovar on his finger-tip without harming any of the living beings in it.

The Bön priest was impressed and conceded initial defeat but insisted they hold another contest. He then betook himself to Kailas and began circumambulating the mountain in the anticlockwise manner that was later to become characteristic of the members of his faith. Milarepa and his disciples meanwhile began to do likewise in the contrary, clockwise direction that similarly later became

Thangka painting from Hemis Gompa, Ladakh depicting Milarepa and scenes from his contest of magic with Naro Bön-chung.

Milarepa's Rock at Zutrul Puk (1987)

established practice for Buddhists. They eventually met up on a large rock in the north-eastern valley of Kailas and began tugging each other to and fro. Milarepa, being the stronger, finally managed to drag the Bön priest off in the direction he wanted to go.

When they reached the northern valley of Kailas, Naro Bön-chung suggested a trial of strength. He promptly lifted a rock the size of a yak. Not at all disconcerted, his Buddhist opponent lifted both rock and lifter, then, as the latter still would not give in, he sat in the Lotus Cave (Pema Puk) on the west side of Castle Valley and stretched one leg clear across to the mouth of a cave on the east side where the Bön priest was now himself sitting. Naro Bön-chung attempted a similar feat but failed miserably, at which the 'Non-men spectators' watching from the sky began to hoot with laughter.

Despite intense shame and embarrassment, Naro Bön-chung declared his resolve to fight on. He began circumambulating the mountain again in his own mode. When he next encountered Milarepa, on the south side of the mountain, it had begun to rain.

Interior of Milarepa's Miracle Cave at Zutrul Puk (1935)

Morning light at Zutrul Puk Gompa (1985)

'We need a shelter to protect us,' the Buddhist said. 'Let's build a house. Would you prefer to lay the foundations and floor, or put on the roof?'

'I'd prefer to put on the roof', the Bön priest replied.

They set about the work but in no time it had turned into a competition as to who could split the biggest rocks. Naturally, Milarepa came out well ahead. He then rather unsportingly used his occult powers to make the roof stone too heavy for Naro Bön-chung to raise. In so doing he also cunningly prepared an opportunity for himself to demonstrate his own virtuosity yet again. He proceeded to dexterously manhandle the huge rock in various ways, leaving various prints of his hands, feet and head upon it. The cave thus made became famous and was called the Cave of the Miracle-Working (Zutrul Puk). Trounced yet again, Naro Bön-chung was obliged to admit defeat.

But still not final defeat. More contests took place between the two opponents until a final and deciding one was agreed. Possession of Kailas would fall to he who could first reach the summit of the mountain on the fifteenth day of the month.

Naro Bön-chung immediately got into training, applying himself assiduously to his Bön practices. Very early on the appointed morning, Milarepa's disciples caught sight of him flying through the sky. He was wearing a green cloak and playing a drum. As their own master had not yet got up, the disciples were understandably very upset. Their anxiety was intensified when, on being told what was happening, Milarepa showed little concern and made no move.

The disciples need not have worried, of course. At the very last moment Milarepa was able to halt his opponent's upward progress with a simple gesture. Then, as day broke, he snapped his fingers, donned his own cloak and soared towards the summit. He appeared upon it just as the first rays of sunlight touched it. Seeing him thus, the very apotheosis of victory, what could Naro Bön-chung do but fall ignominiously down the side of the mountain, his drum clattering after him?

Later, his spiritual arrogance finally subdued, Naro Bön-chung humbly asked Milarepa that his followers be allowed to continue to circumambulate the sacred mountain in their own fashion; also that they might be given a place from where they might be able to see Kailas. Milarepa granted the first request and in response to the second picked up a handful of snow and flung it onto the summit of a nearby mountain – afterwards called Bönri – thereby bequeathing it to the Bön-po.

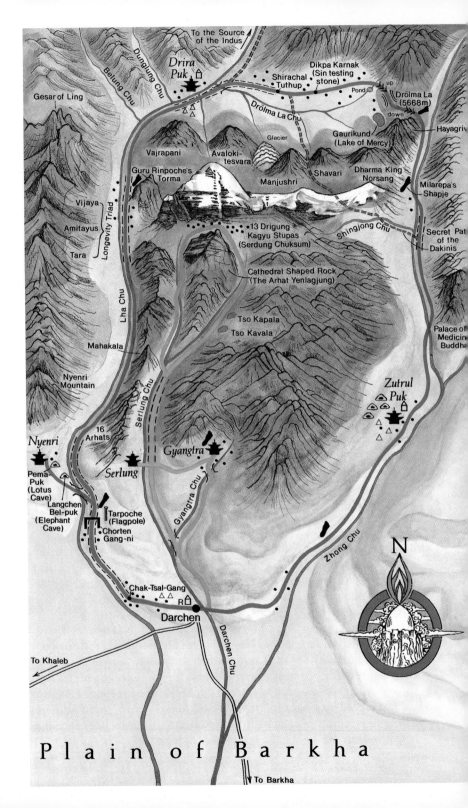

To the Source
of the Indus

Dunglung Chu

Belung Chu

*Drira
Puk*

Gesar of Ling

Shirachal
Tuthup

Dikpa Karnak
(Sin testing
stone)

Pond

up

Drölma La
(5668m)

down

Hayagriva

Drölma La Chu

Glacier

Gaurikund
(Lake of Mercy)

Vajrapani

Avaloki-
tesvara

Manjushri

Shavari

Dharma King
Norsang

Milarepa's
Shapje

Guru Rinpoche's
Torma

Vijaya

Longevity Triad

Amitayus

Tara

13 Drigung
Kagyu Stupas
(Serdung Chuksum)

Shingjong Chu

Secret Path
of the
Dakinis

Lha Chu

Cathedral Shaped Rock
(The Arhat Yenlagjung)

Mahakala

Tso Kapala

Tso Kavala

Palace of
Medicine
Buddha

Nyenri
Mountain

Serlung Chu

*Zutrul
Puk*

Nyenri

16
Arhats

Gyangtra

Pema-
Puk
(Lotus
Cave)

Serlung

Langchen
Bel-puk
(Elephant
Cave)

Tarpoche
(Flagpole)

Chorten
Gang-ni

Gyangtra Chu

Zhong Chu

N

Chak-Tsal-Gang

R

Darchen

Darchen Chu

To Khaleb

Plain of Barkha

To Barkha

KAILAS PARIKRAMA
(Kailas Kora)

Scale

0	1	2	3	4	5	6	7	8	9	10	11	12km
0		1		2		4		5		5		6		7	7·5ml

Inner Parikrama or Kora Route

Viewpoint of Summit

Road

River

Pass

Gompa (Monastery)

Shapje (Footprint)

Shrines

Guesthouse (IPGH)

Steep Gradients

Outer Parikrama or Kora Route

Track / Path

Village

Lake

Bridge

Gateway

Flagpole

Cave(s)

R Restaurant

△ Tents

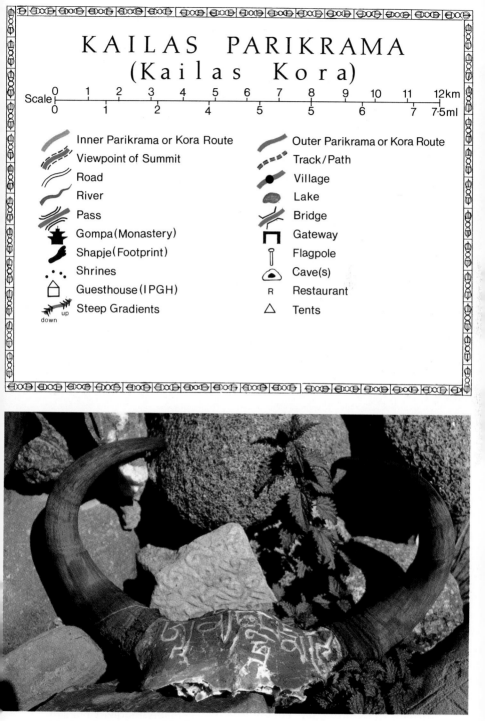

Mani on the Route around Kailas

Pile of yak bones at Langpona: Bönri, the Bön-po sacred mountain, in the background (1987)

Sacred Sites and Rites at Kailas

The principal purpose that any pilgrim of the classic age had in view when he undertook a pilgrimage to Mount Kailas was to perform ritual circumambulation of the sacred mountain. This is called *parikrama* in Sanskrit, *kora* in Tibetan. Buddhists and Hindus did it in a clockwise direction, the Bön-po went round anti-clockwise.

The orthodox Parikrama Route was 32 miles long and could be completed 'very comfortably in three days and two a bit hurriedly' (Swami Pranavānanda), though some especially athletic Tibetans strove to accomplish it in a single day and, at the other extreme, there were greater enthusiasts who performed it by means of prostration, measuring the full length of their bodies on the ground the whole way round. This slow and painful rite could take from fifteen to twenty days. Finally, the irredeemably indolent pilgrim could hire proxies to make the circuit for him.

Shapje (footprint) (1985)

The Kailas Parikrama began at Darchen in the south. Though basically just a tent settlement with only one or two permanent buildings, this was an important centre of the wool trade. A Bhutanese official (*Dashok*) was posted there, for the immediate area had been granted to the Maharaja of Bhutan by the King of Ladakh in the 17th century (see *Appendix 4*). The route then proceeded to the western valley, the valley of the Lha Chu or 'Water of the Gods', by way of the Gang-ni or Gateway to Kailas and Tarpoche, the great flag-pole where Buddhist festivals were celebrated. Beyond lay Nyenri, the first of the five *gompa* of Kailas, which, like Zutrul Puk in the east, fell under the aegis of Bhutan. Special sites in the western valley included Pema Puk ('Lotus Cave'); a pinnacle associated with Padmasambhava, the Tantric Master credited with the first succesful transmission of Buddhism to Tibet; and four minor peaks, three of which formed a triad symbolic of the Tantric deities Tara, Amitayus and Vijaya.

Beyond a place where three rivers converged lay Drira Puk Gompa. Opposite, the dramatic northern face of Kailas was flanked by three lesser peaks symbolic of Avalokiteshvasa, Vajrapāni and

Nyenri Gompa (1985)

The South Face of Kailas. RIGHT: The cathedral-shaped rock symbolic of the arhat Angi Raja (Yenlagjung) around which the Inner Kora runs. (1987).

The Great Rock on the Drölma-la. (1987)

Mañjushrī. The route now rose steeply towards the Drölma La, at 18,600 ft. the highest point of the circuit. It passed Dikpa Karnak, a tortuous rock where virtue (or lack of it) could be tested, and a peak associated with Kuvera, Hindu god of wealth. At Drölma La itself there was a huge boulder, festooned with prayer-flags, where it was customary to leave a personal memento: a lock of hair, perhaps, or a tooth. Beyond lay Gauri Kund, the so-called 'Lake of Mercy((*Tib.* Tukje Tso), where it was thought spiritually beneficial to bathe – hardly an inviting and often not a feasible prospect as it was usually frozen over.

Passing a peak associated with Hayagriva, the pilgrim then descended a staircase of rocks and boulders into the eastern valley, the valley of Zutrul Puk Gompa, the 'Miracle Cave' that featured in Milarepa's fantastic tussle with Naro Bön-chung. Nearby rose a minor peak called the Palace of the Medicine Buddha. The pilgrim then completed his Parikrama by returning to Darchen.

Alternatively, he could visit the sacred sites on the southern side. Besides Gyangtra and Serlung Gompa, the main feature here was the Inner Kora, a special circumambulation around a cathedral-shaped rock symbolic of the *arhat* Angi Raja. It passed two small lakes: Tso Kapala (or Rukta) and Tso Kavali (or Durchi); the water of one was said to be black, the other white. Pilgrims could take the soft alluvial soil of Tso Kapala as *prasad* (sacred gifts). The Inner Kora was strictly reserved for those who had already made thirteen rounds by the ordinary route. Immediately below the southern face of Kailas there was also a row of *chörtens* (Pranavānanda calls them Serdung Chuksum – 'Thirteen Chörtens') housing the remains of the masters of the Drigung Kagyu school of Tibetan Buddhism. This spot was notorious of rockfalls and avalanches; Pranavānanda talks of the air literally *whizzing* with falling debris.

Every inch of the Parikrama Route was replete with powerful symbolism, ritual significance and auspicious association. There were footprints (*shapje*) of the Buddha, Padmasambhava and other luminaries, sites where great masters had performed their spiritual practises, places where the pilgrim should prostrate himself or gather momentoes, and innumerable cairns to which a stone should be added in passing. There were rock formations in which believers could discern significant forms. One great boulder, for instance, was said to resemble Hanuman, the monkey god of Hindu mythology, while the great rock in the Inner Kora, when contemplated from Serlung, reminded Hindus of Nandi, Lord Shiva's bull mount.

Esoterically, the Mountain and its Parikrama Route amounted to a terrestrial projection of the cosmic *mandala*, so the circumambulation ritual was a kind of Tantric initiation (*see* pp. 307 and 354–5). Hindu devotees entered the Mandala of Shiva, Buddhists that of Demchog (Chakrasamvara). Also in a sense the circuit represented one turn of the Buddhist Wheel of Life (*see* p. 46): a progress from birth to death and on to rebirth, though in transmuted rather than in mundane form. Serious Tantric practice at Kailas would only be for the very few, however, most pilgrims merely seeking blessings and atonement for sins.

Tibetans often came from hundred of miles to Kailas, staying months or years away from home. Some brought their families and livestock with them. They aspired to make either three or thirteen circuits per visit, circumambulating either singly or in groups. As they went, they twirled prayer-wheels, muttered *mantras*, deposited

Buddhist Wheel of Life

Bön-po pilgrims prostrating around Kailas (1985)

mani stones and so forth, though the ritual was not *de rigeur* a solemn or self-mortifying rite and there would be opportunities for conviviality.

On the other hand, Hindus faithfully adhering to the stipulations laid down in their holy writ had a plethora of incidental observances to perform – shrines to visit, places to bathe, etc. – on *both* sides of the Himalayan crestline. The most dedicated would make a kind of Grand Parikrama, starting from Hardwar and taking in Bardrinath, Kedarnath and other Indian Himalayan *tirthas* before going to Tibet *via* the Niti Pass. Besides Kailas and the lakes, they visited Kojarnath, a monastery in the Karnali valley south-east of Taklakot, and Tirthapuri, north-west of Kailas, where there were hot springs and a cave associated with Padmasambhava. They would leave by the Lipu Lekh Pass.

Mount Meru, Axis Mundi

In discussing the religious and spiritual connotations of Mount
Kailas, it is interesting to speculate about the possible connexion
between the mountain and the mythical Mount Meru (alternatively, Sumeru, Sineru), the cosmic mountain or *axis mundi* of Hindu
cosmology and its Buddhist and Jain variants.

Early Hindu cosmological notions systematized in the *Purānas* has
Mount Meru standing at the centre of a complex multidimensional
system embracing both the material and spiritual dimensions. On
the one hand, the various heavens and underworlds are disposed in
due order of hierarchy along a vertical axis running through the
centre of Meru. On the other hand, the earth, the material
dimension, is disposed along a horizontal plane extending outwards
from the body of the mountain, rather below the median level. In
some versions, the seven continents are shown radiating outwards
in succession, each separated from the next by a sea of some exotic
liquid. A curtain wall of mountains forms the outer boundary,
beyond which is the Void. In other versions, the earth resembles a
great lotus flower, with the continents arranged like petals around
the great central pericarp of Meru. (see opposite)

Meru's reputed height is mind-boggling. A figure of 84,000
yojanas is often cited. It is difficult to give an accurate equivalent for a
yojana, estimates by scholars and translators varying from as little as
a league to as much as 9 miles. Probably the best way to view the
84,000 *yojanas* is as a figurative expression denoting sheer vastness
of altitude.

As for its other qualities like shape, colour and composition,
accounts also vary. Meru may be gold, or self-luminous, or multi-
coloured (red, white, yellow and 'dark'); it may be shaped like an
inverted cone, or saucer-shaped, or a parallelepiped; it may be
quadrangular, octangular, hundred-angled or even thousand-
angled.

What is certain, however, is that the sun, moon and other
heavenly bodies take their orbits around Meru, and that day and
night are in fact caused by the interposition of the bulk of the
mountain between the observer on earth and the luminaries in the
heavens. The Pole Star stands directly above its summit.

Meru is quite naturally the home and playground of the highest
of the gods – a kind of Hindu Olympus. It is principally associated
with Brahmā, the greatest of them all, and indeed his palace and
throne are situated on the summit. Other important deities have
their abodes elsewhere upon the mountain.

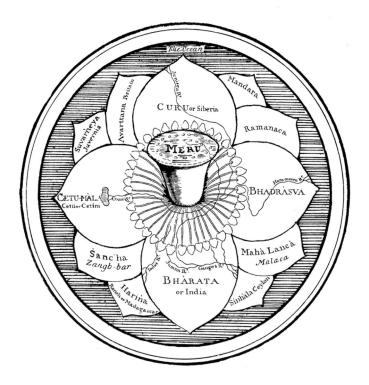

The Hindu Purānic view of the world as Great Lotus

Finally, Meru is the source of all the life-giving waters of the world. One Purānic myth describes the river Ganges issuing first of all from the foot of Vishnu, the Preserver, and thence descending onto the summit of Meru, washing the moon in its descent. It encloses the city of Brahmā on the summit and afterwards divides into four great streams which flow off in the four cardinal directions to water the four quarters of the world. These rivers are the Sītā, supposed to flow from an elephant's head; the Alakanada, supposed to flow from a cow's head; the Chaksu, from a horse's head; and, finally, the Bhadra, from a lion's head. There is another Purānic myth that describes the seminal stream as falling initially into the tresses of Shiva's hair, where it is detained until liberated by King Bhagīratha; it then divides into seven subsidiary streams: the Chaksu, Sītā, Sindhu, Hrādinī, Nalini, Pavani and Bhāgīrathī. The inevitable question is: can Mount Meru be identified with any actually existing mountain or mountain region? S. M. Ali, author of a substantial study of Purānic geographical notions, argues that there are five possible contenders for the mantle of original Meru:

1) The region covered by the Karakoram cluster of peaks.
2) The region covered by the Dhaulagiri cluster of peaks.
3) The region covered by the Everest cluster of peaks.
4) The Tibetan plateau enclosed by the Kun Lun and Himalayan arcs.
5) The Pamir high plateau enclosed by the snow-clad peaks of the Hindu Kush, Karakoram, Tien Shan and Trans Altai systems.

Having weighed up the respective qualities of each, he comes to the conclusion that the Meru described in the *Purānas* must be the Great Pamir Knot of Asia. Kailas, it will be noted, isn't even on the list of possibles. Whatever *earlier* classical tradition may have maintained, however, numerous writers are agreed that by modern times Kailas and Meru were regarded as one. Charles Sherring writes:

> In some accounts Mount Meru clearly indicates the mountains to the north and west of Cashmere, and in others those in the neighbourhood of Kailas and Lake Manasarovar. But whatever may have been the original meaning of the description, there is no question that all local traditions fix the spot as lying directly to the north of the Almora district; and this is the universal belief among all Hindus at the present time.
>
> (C. A. Sherring, *Western Tibet and the British Borderland*)

Sherring concedes that it could not be argued that the notion of Meru derived from some crucial formative experience at the time of the Aryan migrations, for the routes by which they entered India lie much further to the west. Once established on the plains as 'Hindus', however, it would have been quite natural for them to have been deeply awestruck by the majestic sight of the snowcapped Himalayas lying to the north and have come to regard them as the home of their gods. Finally, had they later dispatched explorers in search of the sources of the great rivers – all of which would be regarded as subsidiary streams of the great seminal river that descended from heaven – they might have been led to the Kailas-Manasarovar region. Sherring quotes the persuasive remarks of E. T. Atkinson, author of the encyclopaedic *Himalayan Gazeteer*:

> After traversing the difficult passes across the snowy range and the inclement table-land of Tibet, they discovered the group of mountains

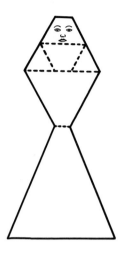

The Jain view of the world as Great Man

called Kailas, and the lakes from which flowed forth the great rivers to water and give life to the whole earth. The rugged grandeur of the scene, the awful solitude and the trials and dangers of the way itself naturally suggested to an imaginative and simple people that they had at length rediscovered the golden land, the true home of their gods....

(E. T. Atkinson, *Himalayan Gazeteer*)

The four great rivers that Atkinson mentions as rising in the Kailas-Manasarovar region are the Indus, Sutlej, Brahmaputra/ Tsangpo and Karnali. If indeed, as many maintain, Kailas and Meru came to be generally identified by Hindus in later tradition, then it was probably this important point of coincidence that sealed the matter. That Kailas was the source of four great rivers was quite simply too remarkable to be overlooked. Other factors, like the unusually regular shape of the mountain, would merely have lent extra weight to the identification.

The notion of Meru also appears prominently in Jainism. Jains display a singular preoccupation with cosmology, and cosmological diagrams are a prominent feature of their art. In the Jain view, the world resembles a great man (see above) . . . of three cups, placed one placed one above the other, with the lowest and topmost inverted. The disc of the earth lies in the lowest part of the middle or 'waist' section and is again dominated by the august presence of Meru, which, according to H. Jacobi, has grown to a dizzy 100,000 *yojanas* in

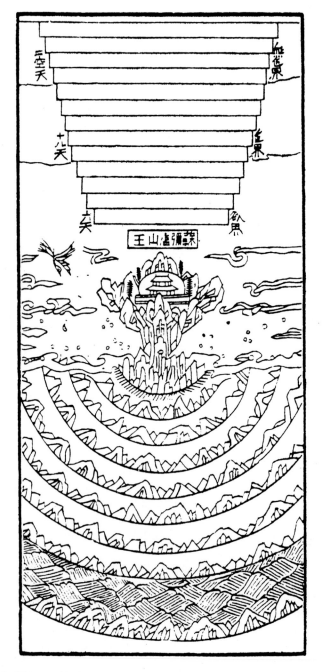

The Buddhist world view

height. The concentric oceans and continents radiate around it as in the Hindu view, though only two and a half of the continents are inhabited. Meru is finally also regarded as the centre around which the heavenly bodies – the Jains maintain that there are two sets of each – take their orbits.

Meru also figures in classical Buddhist cosmology (see opposite), towering as before at the centre of a multidimensional cosmic system 'like the handle of a mill-stone' (Wadell).* Again the fantastic height of 84,000 *yojanas* is specified, though in this case the mountain is also reputed to penetrate to a similar depth into the nether regions below the terrestrial plane, thus indicating a grand total of 168,000 *yojanas*. It is said to be mounted on the three-peaked Trikuta Rock, 'like a vessel upon a tripod' (Spence Hardy).* As regards its shape, descriptions vary, but one recurring view is that its summit is rather wider than its base, which accords with the old Hindu view. As regards composition and colouring, some Buddhist cosmologers maintain that the eastern face of Meru is silver or crystal (white), the southern face is sapphire or lapis lazuli (blue), the western face is ruby (red) and the northern face is gold (yellow). Finally, various kinds of sweet-smelling plants grow upon the mountain and spread their pleasant perfumes in all directions.

Seven concentric rings of golden mountains radiate out from the Buddhist Meru, each usually said to be separated from the next by an intervening sea. Between the last mountain range and the outer curtain wall of iron mountains (Chakravāla), there is a vast ocean in which bask the four great continents: Videha, Godānīya, Jambudvipa and Uttarakuru. Each is situated at one of the four cardinal points and is accompanied by a pair of satellite continents. Later Buddhist cosmologers have moved the continents in closer to the *axis mundi*, perhaps so that the abodes of men should not be exiled so far from the vital centre. Beyond the Chakravāla there is endless dark space in which float innumerable other world systems just like this one, each similarly founded on a two-layered basis of water and air, each with its constituent spheres arranged around a central Meru. All are subject to the Law of Impermancence (*anicca*), however, and thus are in process of coming into being and ceasing to be. Thus every Mount Meru, the hub of each world system and the symbol of all that is most fundamental and substantial, will eventually be destroyed:

> Worlds clash with worlds, Himalaya Mountains with Himalaya Mountains, and Mount Sinerus with Mount Sinerus, until they have

*See Bibliography.

ground each other to powder and have perished.

(trans. H. C. Warren, *Buddhism in Translation*)

In caverns beneath Mount Meru, well below sea level, there are four towns called 'Shining', 'Star-tassel', 'Deep' and 'Golden Town', each ruled by its respective king. In these towns dwell *asuras*, or titans: bellicose beings who often sally forth from their grim abyss to join battle with the gods (*devas*), their perpetual enemies, who inhabit the upper levels of Meru, the classic cause of their contention being the Great Wish-fulfilling Tree that grows half-way up the side of the mountain.

There are four upper terraces on Meru, separated from each other by 10,000 league intervals. The first three are inhabited by different kinds of *yakshas* (powerful spirits). The fourth is inhabited by the Four Great Kings, the guardians of the four quarters, who are ranked among the gods. They keep watch on the behaviour of human beings on earth and periodically report their findings to the gods on the level above them, who rejoice or lament accordingly. They also enjoy extensive retinues, which include *gandharvas* (celestial musicians).

Half-way up the side of Meru, Buddhist cosmologers maintain that the chariots of the sun, moon and stars are to be found. Then, on the summit, is situated the Heaven of the Thirty-three (Trāyastrimśa), so named because the sublime beings who dwell there are ruled by an élite of that number headed by Śakra, 'the Indira of the gods', highest of them all. According to mythology, at some remote period Śakra expelled the *asuras* who had originally inhabited the summit area. He flung them to the bottom of the mountain after having first, rather unsportingly, made them drunk. Thereafter he had to provide his new domain with extensive fortifications to protect it against an *asura* counter-attack. The splendour of the Heaven of the Thirty-three is a wonderful city called Sudarśana ('Lovely View': 'Belle View'). It boasts a thousand lofty gates, each guarded by five hundred blue-clad *yakshas*, all armed to the teeth. Like any other city, it has numerous streets of houses and several markets. It also has many distinguished buildings, the finest of which is Vaijayanta, a hundred-towered palace that the Venerable Mogallana, one of the Buddha's foremost devotees, thought to be the most beautiful of abodes. On each of the four sides of Sudarśana there is a great park containing a magic lake and a tower (*stūpa*) built over relics of the Buddha. On the north-east side of the city, meanwhile, there grows a great tree whose flowers give off a divine perfume, while on the south side lies a great preaching hall: Suddharma – 'Hall of the Excellent Law'. Here Śakra sits on his royal throne, flanked by the thirty-three, and listens to the reports of the Four Great Kings. Finally, Sudarśana is surrounded by 'districts, departments and hamlets belonging to the *devas'* (Spence Hardy), extending outward in every direction as far as the elaborate outer defences.

The gods who inhabit the Heaven of the Thirty-three are a most fortunate breed, endowed with every kind of personal advantage, living in commodious palaces made of precious materials, and enjoying almost unstinted pleasure and luxury. Still subject to the Law of Impermancence, however, their sojourn here, though long, is nevertheless of limited duration; the bitter season will inexorably come when their stock of merit is exhausted and they must die miserably. Gautama the Buddha is reputed to have visited this heaven to preach *Abhidharma* to his mother, who was reborn here as a *Devapūtra*. He is said to have covered the enormous distance to the summit of the world mountain in three huge strides, and also to have preached to eight million gods from Śakra's own throne in the great preaching hall.

Meru and Kailas

Tradition maintains that Buddhism took root in Tibet in the seventh century A.D., during the reign of King Songtsen Gampo. It came by various routes: roundabout *via* China and Central Asia, but principally and more directly from India and Nepal. Buddhist cosmological notions, and the concept of Mount Meru which they enshrine, would have been brought to Tibet with the rest. We know that Kailas was deeply venerated long before the advent of Buddhism and that later, in order to establish themselves in Western Tibet, it was vital for the Buddhists to displace the Bön-po and secure possession of the sacred mountain for themselves. What could have been more natural but that, once Kailas had become a manifestly *Buddhist* sacred mountain, the connotations of Meru should be transferred to it? And if such a development did gradually take place, would it not have been consolidated by the fact that over the course of the next thousand years or more the Hindus – who had been making pilgrimages to Manasarovar since time immemorial – began increasingly to venerate the nearby Kailas and endow it with, among other things, the connotations of Meru as laid down in their own traditions? Hinduism and Buddhism are not mutually opposed and contradicting religions but, rather, part of a single tradition and tend to accept and even adopt each others beliefs and practices with an open-mindedness that is hard for Westerners to comprehend.

What we are arguing here is not that Meru and Kailas were regarded as absolutely and definitively one at all times, which is the way the Western mind would like to have it, but rather that, in the more flexible, accommodating Eastern way, the notion of their identity over the centuries gradually gained a certain relative currency.

Finally, by way of closing the matter, it is interesting to note the Tibetan (one might say, *Tibetan Buddhist*) names for the four rivers rising in the Kailas-Manasarovar region as quoted by Swami Pranavānanda in his *Exploration in Tibet*. He cites as his reference a work he calls *Kangri Karchhak*, 'the Tibetan *Kailāsa Purāna'*, versions of which he found at the Drira Puk and Gyangtra Gompa. These would probably be the works which Professor Giuseppe Tucci found at the same places in 1935 and which he describes as pilgrims' guides to the sacred region outlining its historical, mythological and religious connotations. Tucci maintains that the versions he found were independent of each other. Pranavānanda's names for the great rivers are as follows:

In the West: the *Langchen Khambab* or Elephant-mouthed river – the Sutlej

In the North: the *Singhi Khambab* or Lion-mouthed river – the Indus

In the East: the *Tamchok Khambab* or Horse-mouthed river – the Brahmaputra

In the South: the *Mapcha Khambab* or Peacock-mouthed river – the Karnali

They are almost identical with the old Purānic names for the four waters that flowed from Mount Meru.

Other Manifestations of Meru

No consideration of the matter of Mount Meru would be complete without a word about the many ancilliary manifestations of the *axis mundi* in the various traditions. These exist by virtue of the fact that the ancient Oriental cosmologers were able to discern marvellous correspondences (or 'homologies') between the order of the universe or of its constituent world systems (macrocosm) and the structure of lesser entities, notably man (microcosm).

In the traditional Hindu Tantric view of the human body, for

The Hindu Tantric view of the human body and its chakras

instance, the median nerve which runs through the centre of the spinal column, and which is the chief channel for the psychic forces in man, corresponds to Meru. The practitioner of yoga seeks to divert the energy from the secondary nerves into the median nerve, where as *kundalinī* it rises by degrees from the perineum to the crown of the head, passing en route through the five *chakras* or vital centres. When *kundalinī* as *Shakti* (Divine Power) reaches the Thousand-petalled Lotus of the brain *chakra*, it unites with *Jñāna* (Divine Wisdom) and the yogi experiences realization. The brain *chakra* in this case corresponds to the summit of the world mountain (see above). Comparable notions are found in Buddhist Tantrism, though scholars would disagree about the degrees of sameness and difference between the two traditions, and about which ways influences travelled.

There is also a Meru of the *mandala* (see p. 58). Mandala are those cosmic diagrams used in connexion with certain meditation practices. C.G Jung called them 'magic circles'. That venerable authority on Tibetan Buddhism, L. A. Waddell, describes a mandalic ritual employing rice, where a portion of rice is set down in the centre to represent the world mountain, and the officiating lama chants: 'In the centre of the iron wall is *Hum* and *Ri-rab* (Meru), the king of mountains.' Another writer on Tibetan Buddhist practice,

Mandala

R. B. Ekvall, describes a simple substitute *mandala* that can be created by interlacing the fingers of both hands with the palms turned upwards and the two third fingers, back to back, 'pointing upward to represent Meru'. According to Professor Tucci,* the symbol of Meru in a *mandala* is the *brahmasūtra*, the 'thread of Brahmā', which effects the fundamental north-south, east-west divisions of the inner surface of the *mandala*. In initiations, the neophyte is conducted on a careful progress to the centre of the *mandala*; as he approaches it he must encounter the terrible guardians who protect the inner sanctum. The very centre of the *mandala* corresponds to the summit of Meru:

> Transformation from the plane of *samsara* to that of *nirvana* occurs in successive phases, by degrees; just as on the cosmic mountain and round the *axis mundi* are disposed, rank after rank, the Gods ever purer. Little by little one rises towards the peak and beyond the peak right up to the summit of all that becomes and has (*bhutakoti*), where takes place the passage to the other plane.
>
> (G. Tucci, *Theory and Practice of the Mandala*)

---

*Professor Tucci is disposed to see and indeed emphasize the common ground in the matter of the Hindu and Buddhist traditions of the *mandala*. As he writes in his Preface to *The Theory and Practice of the Mandala*: 'Dealing with the *mandala*, I have considered both the Buddhist as well as the Hindu *mandala*; there may be differences in expression and designs, there may be a different accent laid on the psychological and theoretical situations, but, as a whole, the spiritual background is the same: the same is the yearning to find a way out of time to eternity, to help the primaeval consciousness, which is fundamentally one, to recover its integrity.' Other scholars would perhaps prefer to stress the differences between the two traditions.

Mountains in general provided the prototype for the classical Hindu temple, Meru that for the most splendid type. Ideally, this should have six sides, up to sixteen storeys, be sixty-four cubits (*hastas*) high and thirty-two or fifty cubits in width; it may only be built with a member of the warrior (*kshattriya*) caste as patron and have as architect either a member of the priestly (*brahmin*) or merchant (*vaisya*) castes. Titus Burckhardt furthermore points out that every classic Hindu temple is built on mandalic or cosmic plan and so is symbolically pierced by the *axis mundi*, which emanates from well above the building, enters it through the cupola, proceeds downwards through the successively enlarging pyramidal super-structure to finally penetrate the womblike cavern at the heart:

> The axis of the world corresponds to the transcendent reality of *Purusha*, the Essence that passes through all planes of existence, linking their respective centres with unconditioned Being, situated symbolically at the highest point of the axis, clear of the pyramid of existence, the likeness of which is the temple with its many storeys.
>
> (T. Burckhardt, *Sacred Art in East and West*)

Similar symbolism is to be found in certain Buddhist buildings and monuments. The great Tibetan temple complex at Samyé was built on the cosmic plan by the Indian masters Padmasambhava and Shāntarakshita in the eighth century A.D., and it too has a token Meru at its heart. The notion of the world mountain is also implicit in that most characteristic of Buddhist monuments, the *stūpa*, by virtue of the fact that this too – as Lama Govinda puts it – has 'psycho-cosmic symbolism'. Of especial interest is the great eighth-century *stūpa*-temple at Borobodur in Java which, so the great historian of religion Mircea Eliade maintains, is nothing less than an artificial seven-storeyed world mountain: a man-made Meru (see (see p. 60). As the devotee approaches it, he believes that 'he is close to the centre of the world and on its highest terrace he breaks through into another sphere, transcending profane, heterogenous space and entering "a pure earth"' (M. Eliade, *Patterns in Comparative Religion*).

Borobodur irresistibaly calls to mind the seven-storeyed *ziggurats* of ancient Babylon – and indeed the many other world mountains, both man-made and mythological. For the notion of a great mountain, or alternatively a great tree, a navel or some such appropriate symbol standing at the centre of the world is by no means exclusive to Oriental tradition. It occurs, so Eliade maintains, in a multitude of cultures from Finland to Japan, and traces can be

Borobodur

found among primitives and in the symbolism of prehistoric monuments. It has archetypal power.

If, as we have argued, Meru became identified in later Hindu and Buddhist tradition with Mount Kailas, then all those pilgrims who directed their feet towards the sacred mountain in Western Tibet believed that in so doing they were venturing to the centre of the world, there to perform pious *parikrama* around the *axis mundi*, the essence that unites heaven, earth and hell, the vital Centre where spiritual transformation is possible.

The Sacred Lakes

Of the two lakes lying to the south of Kailas, the eastern Lake Manasarovar (*Tib.* Tso Mapham – 'The Undefeated' in honour of Milarepa's success in the encounter with Naro Bön-chung) is the better regarded, the more frequented and the more liberally

Gösul Gompa, Lake Manasarovar (1986)

endowed with both religious and mythological associations. Its beauties have been lavishly praised, in particular the rich colouring of its waters, which grade from a limpid blue near the shores to a deep emerald green as they approach the centre. It is an impressive foreground to the silver dome of Kailas shining away in the north.

At an altitude of 14,950 feet above sea level, Manasarovar is about 50 feet higher than its western neighbour, Rakshas Tal, from which it is separated by a narrow isthmus of land. It is also regarded as the highest body of fresh water in the world. In former times, eight *gompa* (Buddhist monasteries) surrounded its margins: Chiu, Cherkip, Langpona, Bönri, Seralung, Yerngo, Trügo, and Gösul. If the entire lake was seen as representing the Buddhist Wheel of Life (see p. 46), with the hub lying at its centre, then the eight *gompa* were situated at those points where the eight spokes intersected with the rim. As in the case of the Kailas Parïkrama, a complete circumambulation of the lake, passing by way of the eight *gompa*, was a single symbolic turn of the Wheel, with all the benefits that that implied. Swami Pranavānanda (see pp. 267 ff), who made no

less than nine Manasarovar Parikramas, said that they variously took him between two and four days to accomplish. A practitioner of trance running (*Lung-gom-pa*) could do it in a day. The length of the usual Parikrama Route was about 64 miles, while a circuit of the lake by way of its shores was about ten miles shorter, though this could only be performed in winter when the streams that otherwise made it impossible were frozen. All pilgrims had to be on the lookout for *dacoits* (bandits), who infested the area.

Some Buddhists, including Ekai Kawaguchi and Lama Anagārika Govinda (see p. 217, and p. 293), believed that Manasarovar was identical with the legendary Anotatta Lake. Prior to the birth of the Buddha, his mother, Queen Māyā, dreamt herself transported there by the gods and bathed in the waters. When her body had been thus purified and she was ready to receive him into her womb, the

Lake Manasarovar; the Gurla. Range beyond (1987).

Buddha appeared from the direction of Kailas (which was one of the five peaks surrounding Anotatta), riding a white elephant. A different legend describes the Buddha and many *bodhisattvas* sitting on lotus flowers floating on the surface of the lake. Yet another maintains that herbs capable of curing all the ills of mind and body abound in the earthly paradise that lies around Anotatta. The environs of Manasarovar have a similar therapeutic reputation, being endowed both with many kinds of curative herb and also with radioactive springs believed to possess healing properties. Thus the association with Anotatta is given added substance.

Nor is Manasarovar unvenerated by the Hindus. Their belief is

Pilgrims circumambulating Lake Manasarovar (1985)

that the lake was created by a mental effort on the part of the god Brahmā, the Creator. *Manas* means 'mind'. According to legend, Brahmā's sons, who were *rishis*, or holy men, repaired to Kailas, where they saw Shiva and Pārvatī, and they remained there for twelve years performing austerities. Lacking a convenient place to perform their ablutions, however, they appealed to their father for help. Brahmā obliged. While rejoicing at the creation of the lake, the Seven Rishis saw and worshipped a great *lingam* (phallus) that arose from its midst.

According to another Hindu legend, the Nāga King – the *nāgas* were a species of divine cobra – and his subjects live in the lake and feed on the fruit of a giant jambu tree that grows in the middle. Some of the fruit of the tree falls into the water and sinks, uneaten, to the bottom, where it is transformed into gold. Coincidentally – or perhaps not so coincidentally – gold has in fact been found near the north-west corner of Manasarovar, just south of Chiu Gompa.

Swami Pranavānanda says that it was mined for some time but that operations were eventually discontinued when small-pox broke out among the miners: a blight attributed to the wrath of the presiding deity. During the last mining operations a nugget of gold that was either the size or shape of a dog was found and a *chörten* built to mark the spot at a place afterwards called Serka-Kiro –' Gold Dog'. Another source suggests that the nugget was sent to Lhasa as a gift for the Dalai Lama but that the prelate regarded its extraction as sacreligious and ordered it returned to the earth from whence it was taken.

Besides the great *lingam* that the Seven Rishis saw emerging from the lake, Manasarovar has another connexion with Shiva: the god's swans are reputed to swim on its surface. Here again, reality helps substantiate legend, for in fact numerous species of aquatic bird do frequent the lake.

Finally – and demonstrating the continued veneration of Manasarovar by Indians up until comparatively recent times – some of the ashes of Mahātma Gandhi were taken and scattered on the lake near Tseti on 8th August, 1948, by a party of associates headed by Shree Surendra.*

In comparison, the western lake, Rakshas Tal (*Tib.* Langak Tso) has been far less generously treated. As its name implies – the *rakshas* were a class of demon – it was regarded as a haunt of demons and a place where one of the most notorious of them, Rāvana, the abductor of Sītā in the *Rāmāyana* legend, did penance to propitiate Shiva. Some visitors have claimed to have been able to detect a sinister quality in the atmosphere around the lake, although others have found it as beautiful as its eastern neighbour. Nevertheless, it can only boast a single *gompa*, Tsepgye, and no *parikrama* route. Why should this be so? The most plausible explanation is that, lacking the warm springs with which Manasarovar is endowed, Rakshas Tal and its environs are altogether colder and less hospitable in winter and in consequence were abandoned in favour of the more agreeable climes of Manasarovar.

Of the two lakes, Rakshas Tal is the smaller: around 140 square miles in area as opposed to about 200. It is also more irregular and indented; it is only in the matter of islands that it seems to have an advantage over its neighbour: it has two, Manasarovar none. One

---

*This is Swami Pranavānanda's account, but the 1967 edition of the *Encyclopaedia Britannica* gives the date as 1949.

ABOVE, Ganga Chu, the channel connecting the sacred lakes, with Chiu Gompa in 1986, and BELOW in 1984

of the two islands, Lachato, is a haunt of wild birds and hence a place visited by egg collectors when the ice of winter makes it accessible; the other island, Topserma, was at one time the refuge of a lama from Kham, who pursued his spiritual discipline there, alone, for about seven years some time at the beginning of this century.

Some writers have been disposed to see deep symbolical significance in the antithetical connotations of the two lakes. To them, Manasarovar represents the light, positive, masculine disposition; Rakshas Tal, the dark, negative, feminine. Like the *yin* and the *yang* of Chinese Taoist philosophy, however, they are not mutually exclusive but flow into one another by way of a channel that pierces the intervening isthmus. This is the Ganga Chu and was created, so legend would have it, as the result of a fight that took place between two golden fishes that once inhabited Manasarovar. In fleeing from his opponent, one of the fishes carved the channel to the adjacent lake. In doing so, it allowed the waters of Manasarovar to flow into those of Rakshas Tal, which were thereby sanctified and made fit to drink.

Visitors to the sacred lakes during the past two centuries have found water flowing in the Ganga Chu only occasionally. The flow, when it does take place, has sexual connotations for the Tibetans, who see it as 'intercourse between the 'bridegroom' Manasarovar and the 'bride' Rakshas Tal. This is a highly auspicious event, just as, on the other hand, prolonged absence of water in the channel bodes ill for the world.

Routes to the Kailas Region

Mount Kailas cannot be regarded as a mountain of the first rank in terms of altitude. Its summit is a modest 22,028 feet above sea level. Nor is it a peak of the Himalayas but rather belongs to a separate range that is variously called the Gangdisé or Kailas Range, or the Southern Transhimalaya.

Lying beyond the mighty wall of the Great Himalaya, Kailas is highly inaccessible for any wishing to reach it from the plains of India in the south. Up until the mid-twentieth century there was a choice of three general avenues of approach. The first, from the east, meant crossing the Himalaya somewhere to the east of Nepal, *via* the kingdoms of Sikkim or Bhutan. The traveller would then proceed to Kailas along the valley of the Yarlung Tsangpo/ Brahmaputra. The western approach, on the other hand, would be by way of Kashmir and Ladakh. The third and most direct route was straight up from the south, travelling slightly to the west of the

Nepalese border. This would involve trekking for upwards of two hundred miles* across the Himalayas and then crossing into Tibet by one of the high passes like the Niti, Lampkiya Dhura, Unta Dhura, Kungri Bingri or, the most popular and direct, the Lipu Lekh (16,700 ft.).

Conditions in the Kailas Region in Former Times

In the old pre-1959 lamaist days, once across the border the traveller found himself in Ngari or Western Tibet, a province ruled by the Dalai Lama's Viceroys or Garpöns presiding at Gartok in summer and at Gargunsa in winter. Local power was invested in

---

*The hill station of Almora, a very popular place from which to start a Kailas pilgrimage, is by Swami Pranavānanda's reckoning, 237 miles from Kailas.

Barkha (1987)

district governors or *dzongpöns*, who were stationed in some of the more prominent communities. There was a *dzongpön* at Taklakot, a community situated some eleven miles beyond the Lipu Lekh. This *dzongpön* bought his office. Lhasa, the Tibetan capital, was about 800 miles from Kailas and orders from the government there were relayed to local administrators along the high roads. The Lhasa-Gartok high road passed through a place called Barkha (alternative spelling, Barga), which was located on the marshy plain separating the sacred mountain from the twin lakes. An official called a *tarjum* presided over a staging post here, where the riders carrying the official mail could change their mounts.

Despite the prevalence of the noble teachings of the Buddha, old Tibet was a backward, even a barbarous place. That very

Nun and monks at Nyenri Gompa (1926)

exclusiveness that had kept the outside world at bay for so long and had protected the land from the worst aspects of modern development also effectively stood in the way of any advances that might have alleviated the poverty and generally advanced the lot of the ordinary lay population of what was in any case a very poor country. Certainly valuable religious traditions were thereby preserved and it was possible too for a large proportion of the population to devote themselves to the religious life, a great many of them as monks* and nuns. But critics of the old régime always maintain that such benefits were dearly bought at the expense of the underprivileged. Moreover, while great religious institutions and centres of learning flourished around the principal centres and there were also some fine exponents and teachers of Buddhism in the land, religious life in the more remote parts may not have been of a very high order. Dr. Sálim Ali, a self-confessed 'down-to-earth

---

*The term 'lama' is often used to describe any Tibetan Buddhist monk. In fact it is a term of respect used to refer to a teacher. Not all monks can be called 'lamas' by any means, and not all lamas are monks. A monk is more accurately called a *Ge-long.*

materialist' and hence a not very sympathetic witness, was in the Kailas region in 1945 and writes as follows:

> ...on the whole, I was repelled, and sometimes nauseated, by what passed for Buddhism in Tibet at the time of my visit and amazed at the profound reverence given to its philosophy in the outside world. There must doubtless be, and certainly are, some devout and deeply learned scholars of the prevailing brand of Buddhism in Tibet, but I could discern no spark of spirituality or enlightenment among the swarms of initiaties and young lamas who hung around every gompa and dzong. They seemed to me just a pack of dirty, lazy, ignorant louts leading a life of idle parasitism, who could have been more useful to themselves and to society as normal human beings....
>
> (letter to the author from Dr. Sálim Ali,
> dated 19th March 1981)

The defenders of the old régime, on the other hand, would no doubt contend that poverty, hard work and privation do not necessarily conduce to misery, and that, in fact, the ordinary lay people of old Tibet were happy with their spiritually-rich environment. Certainly many who have encountered Tibetans both before and after 1959 have been impressed with their general happiness and good nature.

Traditionally, the greater proportion of the secular population of Western Tibet have been nomadic herders (*dogpa*), scraping a subsistence living from flocks of sheep and goats. Yaks and horses are their beasts of burden, the wool trade their main economic activity. In former times, many found it difficult to make a living by fair means and consequently resorted to some form of *dacoity* or banditry. About a day's march beyond Taklakot, the traveller entered an area infested with *dacoits*, many of them armed with old muzzle-loading guns, who would have had few scruples about fleecing anyone they met, be he trader, traveller or pilgrim. Apparently, due to its extreme scarcity in the region, they were chiefly interested in stealing food. Local administration was rudimentary, to say the least, and policing virtually non-existent. The *dacoits* therefore had little fear of arrest. Those who were arrested, however, received the extremely draconian punishments usually dispensed in Tibet during this period: they might suffer some kind of painful mutilation or dismemberment, might even be put to death by being flung from a high place, or left out in the scorching heat of summer to slowly roast.

*Tibetan criminals
(1930 or 1932)*

Zorawar Singh's tomb at Toyo, near Taklakot (1926 – now destroyed)

Zorawar Singh's Invasion (1841)

Probably the most significant event in the nineteenth-century history of Western Tibet – and one said by some to exemplify the native cruelty of the Tibetans – was an invasion by a Sikh adventurer named Zorawar Singh, who was in the service of one of Ranjit Singh's former lieutenants, Gulab Singh, the master of Jammu, for whom he had already annexed Ladakh.

Zorawar forged into Western Tibet in May and June 1841, pillaging villages and *gompa* and destroying every *dzong* that lay in his path. At Barkha his comparatively modest force – some number it at 1,500 men – routed a far larger Tibetan force of 8,000 or 10,000 men (accounts vary). He then proceeded to Taklakot, where he established himself and behaved in a generally high-handed manner. Eventually, probably because he had heard that reinforcements were being sent against him and was anxious for his wife's safety, he left his main force under the command of his lieutenant, Bastiram, so as to conduct her out of the area. Returning from Gartok, however, he found himself cut off by a sizeable Tibetan force augmented with Chinese at a place called Toyo, some three miles from Taklakot. He was fatally wounded in the knee (the Tibetan equivalent of the Achilles heel?) by a gold bullet, the only weapon against which, so the superstitious Tibetans believed, this otherwise superhuman warrior was not proof.

Although he had invaded their territory, the Tibetans were inspired with deep respect for Zorawar, upon whom Swami Pranavānanda maintains they bestowed the heroic title of Singhi-Raja – 'Lion King.' Another writer, Charles Sherring, says that Zorawar's body was immediately dismembered and that the locals hung pieces of his flesh up in their houses for good luck. 'Rumour also says that the pieces sweated fat for many a long day, a sign which the most sceptical regarded as connected with the dead chief's bravery' (Sherring). An imposing *chörten* was also erected at Toyo over his other remains; this was regularly painted with red ochre. Swami Pranavānanda reports moreover that one of Zorawar's testicles – which he does not specify – was preserved under lock and key in the Simbiling Gompa at Taklakot but was brought out once every four years in the second month of the Tibetan calender (March–April) 'on the occasion of some special *Tantrik* rite called *Chakhar* (Iron Fort). One hand (wanting in two fingers) is preserved in the Sakya Monastery situated on the west of the Simbiling Gompa...' (Swami Pranavānanda, *Exploration in Tibet*, 2nd Edition).

Simbiling: The old hill-top gompa-cum-dzong at Taklakot (1926 – now destroyed)

As for the remainder of Zorawar's force of Dogra soldiers, these had already suffered badly from the exigencies of the Tibetan winter and it was said they were obliged to burn the stocks of their rifles for what small warmth this afforded them. Sherring reports that they were cut down with great brutality by the combined Tibetan-Chinese force; Swami Pranavānanda disputes this and imputes Sherring's charge to 'propaganda zeal to damn the Tibetans'. Whatever the real truth of the matter, however, it is certain that only a small and battered remnant of what had once been a glorious conquering army escaped across the high passes to the safety of British India.

Kirghiz-Kazaki Depredations (1941)

In 1941, eactly a century after the depredations of Zorawar Singh, three thousand Kirghiz-Kazaki nomads swept through Western Tibet, plundering and destroying as they went. They had left their homelands in Soviet Central Asia around 1938 and spent the intervening three years travelling in Chinese Sinkiang and Chinghai, before crossing the Kun Lun mountains and entering the Chang Tang, the barren northern plain of Tibet. Crossing the

Brahmaputra, an attempt was made to force an entry into Nepal, but this was resisted by Gurkha border guards and instead the Kirghiz-Kazakis proceeded westwards to the sacred region. Swami Pranavānanda stayed at Trügo Gompa on the shores of Lake Manasarovar from July to mid-September that year and to him we are indebted for information about the affair.

When the interlopers camped on the northern side of Manasarovar, their camp extended for some fifteen miles. By this time their herds had grown to large proportions, as had the quantities of silver and gold in their possession – much of it the spoils of plunder. They were also well armed, if estimates of five hundred guns and rifles are accurate. Nevertheless, they were discouraged from approaching Darchen or tampering with any of the monasteries of Kailas because the Bhutanese officer at Kailas had a fully-armed garrison. Instead, the Kirghiz-Kazakis moved on southwards between the two lakes, intending to push through Purang and into India by way of the Lipu Lekh. Again they were foiled, this time by the sharpshooting occupants of Tsepgye Gompa on Rakshas Tal, who shot dead two members of the advance guard, one of them the leader, a woman dressed in a red uniform.

The Kirghiz-Kazakis next withdrew north-westwards, still plundering and destroying wherever they did not meet with sufficient opposition. They passed through Tirthapuri, Khyunglung and Missar, and destroyed buildings at Gartok and Gargunsa, the summer and winter capitals of Western Tibet. Around November, they forced their way into Ladakh, where they were finally disarmed by British and Kashmiri troops before being allowed to proceed through Kashmir to the Hazara District of the North West Frontier Province, where they were subsequently settled.

Geography of the Sacred Region

The traveller of the classic era, standing in the full blast of the wind on the brow of the Lipu Lekh pass, would therefore have good reason to feel apprehensive about the land he was about to enter. It was indeed a very dangerous place. On the other hand, the overwhelming beauty of the landscape that presented itself to his eye if the day was clear might dispel his anxieties. Indeed, if he was of a religious turn of mind, he might well feel spiriutally exalted to know that, after the many rigours of the journey across the mountains, the sacred region now lay at his feet.

Below him, in the valley of the Karnali river, lay Taklakot, the

Amateur dacoit 'snapped' near Zorawar Singh's tomb (1926)

chief community of the populous Purang Valley. Here there would have been tents and houses, curious cave dwellings, a *gompa*, a *dzong* and a *mandi* (market).

Beyond Taklakot rose the imposing bulk of the snow-clad Gurla Mandhata (altitude: 25,355 feet). The traveller would have to cross one of the high ridges to the west of the mountain. Once up on the high pass, however, he would be treated to yet another visual feast: the two blue sacred lakes lying in the immediate foreground and beyond them, rising majestically out of the vividly-coloured ranges to the north, the snowy peak of the sacred mountain itself. Again, if he was a spiritual man, the sight would probably have him on his knees, making prostrations and offering thanks to the gods.

And so on to the shores of the sacred lakes, taking due care to steer well clear of *dacoits*. Once he had performed his business there, be it worldly or spiritual, the traveller would then continue north to Kailas, traversing on his way a flat marshy plain crossed by many streams flowing down from the sacred mountain. He would probably find many nomads camped here in their black tents, and might well also catch sight of herds of wild asses or *kyang*. Finally, he would arrive at Darchen where, if this was his purpose, he might begin the Kailas Parikrama.

CHAPTER THREE

Travellers in the Sacred Region: 1715–1850

Even before the Chinese takeover of Tibet in the 1950s, access to the Kailas region – and indeed to the whole of the country – had always been difficult for *Firinghis*, as the Tibetans called Europeans. The Lhasa government had for a long time maintained a total ban on their entry, a xenophobic policy that undoubtedly stemmed from a very realistic assessment of the dangers of allowing even ostensibly innocuous travellers like traders and missionaries to cross their borders. They had seen how commerce and Christianity had been a prelude to guns and annexation elsewhere – in nearby India, for instance. Officials in the frontier districts were therefore sternly enjoined to turn back any European whom they found in their territory. Penalties for failure to discharge this duty, even inadvertently, were draconian. We hear of the execution of comparatively important officials who were discovered to have fallen down in this respect.

For a time after 1904 things were slightly different. The guns of the Younghusband Expedition to Lhasa obliged the Tibetans to be rather more accommodating. During the brief ensuing period we find accounts of visits to Kailas and the sacred lakes written by comparatively relaxed travellers. They contrast with most of the earlier accounts, which were written by travellers who moved furtively and at speed across the desolate landscape, many of them disguised as *fakirs* (holy men) and living in fear of their lives.

Of the few Westerners who have set eyes upon the sacred mountain, the first were the Jesuit missionaries Ippolito Desideri and Manuel Freyre, who passed Kailas in the company of a charming Tartar princess *en route* for Lhasa from Kashmir and Ladakh in 1715. This initial encounter does not seem to have been

Padmasambhava (Guru Rinpoche) carved on a mani stone at Zutrul Puk (1987)

very auspicious – or representative:

> We left Cartoa [Gartok] in the second half of October, and arrived at the highest point reached during the whole journey in the desert called Ngari-Giongar on the 9th of November. This is held in much veneration by all of this people because of a certain URGHIEN [Padmasambhava, who brought Buddhism from India to Tibet towards the end of the 8th century A.D.], founder of the present Tibetan religion, of whom I shall speak later. Close by is a mountain of excessive height and great circumference, always enveloped in cloud, covered with snow and ice, and most horrible, barren, steep and bitterly cold [Mount Kailas]. In a cave hollowed out of the live rock the above-named Urghien is said to have lived for some time in absolute solitude, self mortification and continuous religious meditation. The cave is now a temple consecrated to him, with a rude, miserable monastery attached, where dwells a Lama, with a few monks who serve the temple [probably Nyenri Gompa]. Besides visiting the cave, to which they always bring offerings, the Tibetans walk devoutly round the base of the mountain, which takes

several days, and they believe this will bring them great indulgences. Owing to the snow on this mountain, my eyes became so inflamed that I well nigh lost my sight. I had no spectacles, and the only remedy, as I learnt from our escort, was to rub the eyes with snow.

(F. de Filippi, ed., The Travels of Ippolito Desideri
of Pistoia, S.J., 1712-21)

Disenchanted with the whole expedition, Freyre quickly returned to India, but Desideri remained in Tibet, mainly in the Lhasa area, for a number of years, manfully trying to convert the Tibetans from what he considered to be their misguided Buddhist convictions. Much to his disappointment, he was recalled by the Papal authorities and left the country in 1721.

The British encounter with Kailas and its environs stemmed from altogether more hardheaded motives. They wanted to know what was going on in the territories immediately adjacent to their prized Indian possessions; they were very interested too in the possibility of opening up trading connections; and, finally, they were concerned to improve their knowledge of the geography and other aspects of those areas. The twin lakes, Manasarovar and Rakshas Tal, interested them particularly, for it was known that some of the great rivers of the Indian subcontinent rose in or near them. At one time it was even thought that the Ganges had its source in Manasarovar, but this was finally disproved in 1808 when Lieutenant Webb, assisted by Captains Raper and Hearsey, fixed the principal source of the holy river on the southern side of the Great Himalaya.

The first Britisher to clap eyes on Mount Kailas was a veterinarian from Lancashire named William Moorcroft. Moorcroft was a great energizing and enterprising spirit – a man ahead of his time, whose ambitious schemes and projects were insufficiently understood in his own day, and whose reputation subsequently fell into undeserved eclipse.

Moorcroft was one of the pioneers of veterinary surgery in Britain and in his heyday he had a profitable London practice with premises in Oxford Street. Injudicious speculation in a scheme for manufacturing horseshoes with machinery ruined his finances, however, and in 1808, probably because it looked like the best way of recouping his fortune, he accepted the East India Company's invitation to become superintendent of its stud at Pusa near Cawnpore. In this capacity he advocated the notion of improving the quality of the Company's cavalry horses by interbreeding with Turkoman horses from Central Asia.

Moorcroft had not been long in India before he began to take a keen interest in the mysterious and little known lands lying beyond the Himalayas, and in 1812 he undertook an expedition to Lake Manasarovar. On this expedition, his interest in Central Asian horseflesh seems to have been subordinate to a concern with matters of greater commercial potential, principally the possibility of opening up to British interests the trade in *pashm*, the fine goats' wool from which the best quality Cashmere shawls are made. It is also clear from the precise and highly detailed scientific observations reported in his journal that he was very much a serious explorer. Finally, his journey may have had a political angle: among other things, he showed great interest in the activities of the Russians in Tibet.

A young Anglo-Indian adventurer was Moorcroft's companion on the expedition. This was Hyder Jung Hearsey – the same Hearsey who had been with Webb and Raper on the Ganges Expedition in 1808. Subsequently there had been unfortunate imputations of skulduggery to the man: that he had attempted to

LEFT: William Moorcroft and Hyder Hearsey disguised as Mahants at Kailas in 1812. Hearsey's own watercolour. RIGHT: William Moorcroft

appropriate glory for himself by cribbing Webb's map and passing it off to London as his own. Nothing untoward seems to have happened during the Manasarovar expedition, however; indeed 'Mr. H.' appears to have acquitted himself to Moorcroft's satisfaction.*

There was a strong air of irregularity about the whole project, however, which makes the fact that it miscarried during its closing stages not altogether surprising. For one thing, Moorcroft chose not to obtain the permission of the Nepalese authorities, then in possession of the Kumaon region, to cross their territory; for another, he elected to travel disguised as a Hindu *mahant* (holy man) making a pilgrimage to Kailas – a device which only partially worked and when it failed served only to arouse the worst suspicions against him.

*For Hearsey's view of the expedition and additional biographical material, see Appendix 2.

The outward journey across the mountains ran by way of the courses of the Rama and Alakanada rivers to Joshimath near Badrinath, then *via* Malari to Niti. The going was difficult, in parts so precipitous that Moorcroft had to crawl on his hands and knees for fear of falling to his death in terrible chasms; but these ordeals were to some extent redeemed by the wild and imposing majesty of the surrounding scenery: snowcapped mountains soaring above the cedars and cypresses that clothed the lower slopes, and rivers roaring in the hidden depths of valleys far below.

At Niti the expedition ran into its first setback. The size of the party and its possession of arms, allied to the fact that it was taking a highly unusual pilgrimage route to Manasarovar, gave the general impression that Moorcroft and Hearsey were in fact *Gorkhalis* or *Firinghis*, 'come with designs inimical to the *Undès*' – and measures were taken accordingly. They attempted to persuade the headman of Niti of their *bona fides*, and a letter and a present were forwarded to Daba, a major community on the other side of the border, addressed to an official whom Moorcroft called 'the Deba' – possibly a *dzongpön* or head man of some kind. He promptly replied, formally forbidding them to enter the country. It was also hinted that large numbers of troops had been dispatched to guard the high passes. Moorcroft was disappointed but not deterred. After much wheeling and dealing, during which large quantities of *timáshás* (a *timáshá* was 'the silver coin of Súnagar and Latakh') changed hands, he managed to get the exceedingly reluctant people of Niti to furnish him with the assistance he needed to proceed to *Undès*, as he called that part of Tibet which he proposed to enter, and so finally the expedition was under way again.

On reaching the high passes, Moorcroft was relieved to find only cairns and prayer flags: there was no sign of the troops with which he had been threatened. He was bothered, however, by a touch of altitude sickness, and experienced difficulty in breathing and 'a great oppression about the heart'. It was at this unpropitious moment that he obtained his first sight of Mount Kailas:

July 1st. – THERMOMETER at sun-rise 41; march at 5.35 A.M. At 3205 paces reach the summit where there is a heap of stones. Here we found two *Uniyas* [Tibetans], one of whom was busied in lighting a fire, into which the other threw some incense, which he had previously bruised on a stone. He then leisurely walked round the pile of stones, in the midst of which was a statue having a piece of cloth tied to it, and whilst walking, uttered a long prayer. To the East was the sacred mountain near the lake of *Manasarovar*, tipped with snow, and called *Cailas* or

Mahadeo ka Ling. Turning his face towards this mountain, and after raising his hands with the palms joined above his head, then touching his forehead, he suddenly placed them on the ground, and going on his knees pressed his forehead to the ground. This raising the hands, and prostration of the body and head, was repeated seven times; the other *Uniya,* less devout perhaps, contented himself with three salutations and a short prayer.

(Wm. Moorcroft, *A Journey to Lake Manasarovar,*
Asiatick Researches, Vol. 12, 1818)

The expedition then descended to the blasted plains of the great plateau and followed the road to Daba, where they presented themselves to the Deba. He was naturally very annoyed that the people of Niti had allowed Moorcroft's party to proceed in direct defiance of his orders. He was obliged to report the matter to the higher authorities in Gartok and await their instructions. Clearly the Tibetans were not convinced that Moorcroft and Hearsey were what they claimed to be. One of them noted that Hearsey's boots were of the European type (Moorcroft had taken the wise precaution of having his boots fashioned with turned-up toes and tags at the heels after the Oriental fashion); and there was the unusual redness of Moorcroft's complexion for which plausible explanation needed to be given. Nevertheless, relations seem to have been passably affable. A certain amount of palm-greasing may have helped in this, but in any case Moorcroft seems to have been a reasonable and diplomatic man (though a very determined one) and did nothing that might cause offence. On the contrary, he seems to have created quite a good impression. Indeed, actual warmth entered into his relationship with the local Chief Lama so that, when orders came that he must leave and present himself in Gartok, their parting was tinged with emotion.

Gartok, it transpired, was just a glorified encampment of black tents, with enormous herds of sheep, goats and yak together with some horses grazing on the desolate plain in which it stood. The interview with the Garpön (Viceroy) was not the ordeal it might have been, and in the event he allowed himself to be persuaded that the visitors were not *Firinghis,* though Moorcroft admits that the weight of his presents may have had a lot to do with this.

Much of Moorcroft's time at Gartok was spent in investigating the wool trade and especially the possibility of breaking the monopoly then held by Ladakhi merchants. He did in fact manage to obtain useful concessions from the Garpön and was allowed to buy quantities of wool on the spot. The authorities would not, however, accede to his request to be allowed to quit the country by a route

Darchen (1985)

Darchen (1926)

different from that by which he had entered; he must go as he had come – by the Niti.

Now enjoying official approval and support, the expedition proceeded south-east to Manasarovar by way of Missar and Tirthapuri. On the way Moorcroft was able to buy quantities of sheep, goats and yak, but he also began to suffer from bouts of fever and when he reached Darchen (he calls it *'Gangri* or *Darchan'*) he had to rest up for a whole day: August 4th. At Darchen he found four permanent houses and a number of tents; several merchants were staying at the place, including two Chinese tea merchants who claimed that their homes lay two months journey beyond Peking. The sacred mountain does not appear to have engaged his attention as far as one can tell from the edited published version of his journal. Perhaps commercial and scientific concerns kept his eyes focussed at a more mundane level.

During the inadequate two days that he was at Lake Manasarovar, August 6th and 7th, Moorcroft's chief concern was to determine whether any major rivers issued from it. Harballabh, the old *pundit* who was a member of the expedition, claimed that 'near the south-west corner, a river flowed from it, which flowing in a westerly direction, went along the *Rawanhrad* [Rakshas Tal] and escaping its Western extremity at the foot of the great mountain [Kailas?], formed the first branch of the *Setlej*'. Subsequent exploration, including a 25-mile walk by Moorcroft himself, albeit in adverse weather conditions and poor health, failed to prove the existence of this river and he was forced to conclude that, if it had ever existed, it had now dried up and its bed been filled in, possibly by an earthquake. His exploration had therefore shown – correctly, as later research was to prove – that Manasarovar gives rise to no major river. Its connecting channel with Rakshas Tal, the Ganga Chu, he failed to find, either through oversight or because it was dry that year and its bed perhaps shingled up.

In the case of Rakshas Tal, passing at a distance Moorcroft thought he saw a river issuing from it 'which probably communicates with the many streams which form the *Setlej*'. He was, however, prevented from actually going and confirming the matter by another bout of fever. The weather also changed abruptly for the worse, and a heavy fall of snow impressed upon him the urgency of returning to the high passes before they became impassable, thus preventing his expedition's timely return to the plains of India.

On 11th August, his retreat already underway across the marshy plain beyond the lakes where his yaks frequently sank up to their bellies in mud, Moorcroft was obliged by a hailstorm in mid-afternoon to halt beside a small river. He notes in his journal:

> *Cailas* mountain is supposed to be the favourite residence of MAHADEVA [Shiva], and is situated opposite to the great lake of *Rawanhrad*, and a little distant from that of *Manasarovar*. As its summit is always clothed with snow, it is but a cool seat: however this cold is said to be necessary on account of the poison which has heated his frame ever since he swallowed it at the period of the *Sankh Avatar*.
>
> *(Ibid.)*

Moorcroft passed through Tirthapuri and Khyunglung on his way back to Daba, and thence up to the Niti again. Once across the pass, however, difficulties began to pile upon the expedition until it was little short of a nightmare. In the first place it was exceedingly difficult to conduct the many animals they now had with them across terrain that was not only highly precipitous but also bedevilled by landslides, broken bridges and swollen rivers; and then soon afterwards the Nepalese authorities began to harrass them. Their failure to get permission for their trip, the size of their entourage of servants and bearers, the fact that Moorcroft and Hearsey travelled in disguise – all these factors had compounded the original suspicions of the Nepalese to the point where rampant paranoia broke loose. Rumours gained currency that an army of between 400 and 500 men had proceeded up to the Tibetan border to build forts and encourage the local people to rise up against their Nepalese masters.

The Nepalese were indecisive at first, merely trying to persuade Moorcroft to delay his journey while its motives were properly investigated. Moorcroft for his part doggedly refused to be delayed and concluded that the best course of action was to show a firm determination to proceed. Intransigence on both sides led to an inevitable confrontation and ensuing violence, which, due to their superior numbers, went in the Nepalis' favour. Moorcroft and his men were seized and detained under duress for some time. Eventually, however, all came out well: they were released on the orders of the Raja of Nepal and given safe conduct out of his territory.

This harrowing experience did not deter the enterprising Moorcroft from further adventures. In fact he was to go on to even more sensational ones. He eventually met his death in 1825 – some say he died of fever, others that he was poisoned – during the course of an audacious and equally pioneering expedition to

Bokhara by way of Ladakh, Kashmir, the Punjab and Afghanistan. He was accompanied on that occasion by a young geologist named George Trebeck, who himself died shortly after his mentor. By the time of his death Moorcroft's star had already sunk low. The East India Company had lost faith and interest in his great schemes for opening up commercial connections with Central Asia and had withdrawn its support and discontinued his pay.

There is a bizarre and implausible footnote to the story of William Moorcroft. In an account of his own travels in Tibet and other parts of Asia published in 1853, Abbé Huc recounts a more fanciful version of Moorcroft's death that he picked up in Lhasa. Far from meeting his end in the wastes of Turkistan, Moorcroft, it was claimed, had turned up in Lhasa in 1826 and lived there for more than a dozen years before finally dying in the Kailas-Manasarovar region while travelling back to Ladakh.

Nearly thirty-five years were to elapse before the next Englishman set eyes on the sacred mountain. In September and October, 1846, Lieutenant Henry Strachey of the 66th Regiment, Bengal Native Infantry, made a journey to Lake Rakshas Tal, which he believed to be of more immediate geographical interest than its neighbour, Manasarovar, because it had been less visited and studied.

As Strachey was a military man, and his narrative suggests quite a typical one, it is not surprising that his journey was altogether different in character from that of his great precursor, Moorcroft, who served John Company. Strachey in fact portrays his foray as having all the pace and urgency of a lightning strike into enemy territory. His tight, economical party moved with speed and secrecy across the alien landscape, studiously avoiding all contact with the local people and giving all habitations a wide berth or else passing them under cover of darkness. It was, in short, a concentrated military-style operation. In the matter of disguise, however, there was a major point of similarity with Moorcroft. Before crossing into Western Tibet, or *Hundes* as he called it, Strachey donned native costume – 'just enough to pass muster' – though he refused to go to the length of darkening his skin.

During his outward journey across the Kumaon region, Strachey followed the course of the Kali river upstream to its confluence with the Kunti Yakti. He paused at the village of Kunti to exchange his plains servants for mountain people – Bhotias and other Kumaonis – then continued on his way to Hundes with stern warnings resounding in his ears of the perils he might meet at the hands of the Khampa brigands infesting that land. The Khampas are, literally, the inhabitants of the province of Kham in eastern Tibet. They are the most martial of the Tibetans and, apparently, in the old days were much given to banditry, notably in the Kailas-Manasarovar region, where the many pilgrims were easy prey for them.

Strachey, his servants and baggage animals – yaks, dzos and ponies – crossed into Tibet by the Lampkiya Dhura Pass. It was a difficult transit for both men and animals, through deep snow. Strachey chose the pass because he thought it would give him the most direct line of approach on Rakshas Tal, but in fact it brought him over the border much too far to the west and it took him four days, rather longer than he had calculated, to reach his objective, having travelled a considerable way round through Lama Chörten.

Strachey, it would seem, was far more sensitive to the beauties of the Tibetan landscape than Moorcroft and there is a touch of poetry in his descriptions that is entirely lacking in the earlier explorer's record. He felt that what he saw on the northern side of the Himalayas exceeded in aesthetic appeal anything he had seen on the southern side. Rakshas Tal was a sheet of water of the clearest, brightest blue reflecting with double intensity the colour of the sky, except at its northern extremity where it took on the deeper purple hue of the wall of mountain that overshadowed it. Across the low hills in the middle of the opposite bank, he could just make out Manasarovar – 'a streak of bright blue'. The lakes themselves were bounded by low hills which in places plunged deeply into the water. These hills were bare of vegetation and 'tinted with many shades of red, brown or yellow'. Above them in the south-east rose 'the snowy mass of Momonangli' [Gurla Mandhata]; to the north on the other hand, was 'a green grassy plain from the back of which the Gangri Mountains rose in dark steep slopes'. Here 'the main peak of Kailas, now fully developed to its very base, was seen on the extreme left of the range'.

Shortly afterwards, having rounded the northern horn of Rakshas Tal, he was to get a closer and more impressive prospect of the sacred mountain:

> The most remarkable object here was Kailas, now revealed in full proportion to its very base, rising opposite [northward] straight out of the plain only two or three miles distant. The south-west front of Kailas is in line with the adjacent range, but separated on either side by a deep ravine; the base of the mass thus isolated is two or three miles in length perhaps; the general height of it, I estimate to be 4250 feet above the plain, but from the west the peak rises some 1500 feet higher, in a cone

LT. COLONEL HENRY STRACHEY,

Henry Strachey

or dome rather, of paraboloidal shape; the general figure is not unlike that of Nanda Devi, as seen from Almora. The peak and the upper part of the eastern ridge were all covered with snow, which contrasted beautifully with the deep colour of the mass of the mountain below; the stratification of the rock is strongly marked in successive ledges that catch the snow falling from above, forming irregular bands of alternate white and purple; one of these bands more marked than the rest encircles the base of the peak, and this, according to the Hindu tradition, is the mark of the cable with which the Rakshas attempted to drag the throne of Siva from its place....The openings on both sides of Kailas disclose only more mountains in the rear; the Western ravine appears to be two or three miles deep; the back of the eastern recess is occupied by a fine pyramidal mass rising in steps of rock and snow, with a curious slant caused by the dip of the stratification (to the eastward).

(Lieut Henry Strachey, *Narrative of a Journey to Cho Lagan, etc.*, Journal of the Asiatic Society of Bengal. July, August and September 1848)

His final judgement is that 'in picturesque beauty Kailas far surpasses the big Gurla, or any other of the Indian Himalaya that I have seen; it is full of majesty, a King of mountains'. Proceeding in due course to geographical matters, Strachey was unable to locate a visible channel connecting Rakshas Tal with the Sutlej and apart from the possibility of the lake periodically overflowing, 'the only effluence is by filtration through the porous soil of the intermediate ground'. He was, however, successful in locating a channel connecting the two lakes with each other, and a broad stream was flowing through it. This was two or three miles west of Chiu Gompa, near the old gold workings.

The morale of Strachey's Kumaoni servants was low throughout their time in Tibet. They lived in continual fear of either falling into the hands of Khampa bandits and being brutalized by them, or of being caught by the Tibetan authorities – in which case they fully expected to be hung. Unexpected meetings with indeterminate Tibetans invariably put them in a state of funk, which on one occasion a disgusted Strachey was to describe as 'little short of rank cowardice'. Discontent and distrust fomented by these not altogether unreasonable fears were bound to grow worse the longer the expedition was delayed on Tibetan soil. They came to a head when, proceeding southwards along the shores of Manasarovar, Strachey mooted the idea of doing a complete circuit of the lake. His men not only reacted with the anticipated lack of enthusiasm but, ominously, baggage ponies and later even some of the men themselves began to mysteriously stray from the party and not return. His 'discontented and dispirited companions' were clearly intent on putting a spoke in the wheel of his *parikrama*; therefore Strachey decided that it would be wiser to forget the notion – it promised to yield little useful knowledge anyway, he consoled himself – and return with all possible dispatch to the other side of the border.

His exit route took him along the north-west slopes of Gurla Mandhata to Taklakot, which he passed at night, and so up to the Lipu Lekh Pass, the crossing of which was an altogether easier proposition than the earlier crossing of the Lampkiya Dhura.

Two years later, in 1848, Strachey's brother Richard visited the Kailas region with a certain Mr. J. E. Winterbottom. Richard Strachey was a military engineer with keen scientific interests who was to have a distinguished career in the Indian Army, finally retiring from it in 1875 with the rank of Lieutenant-General. He and his companion crossed the Great Himalaya even further to the west than his brother had done. Starting from Milam, they went

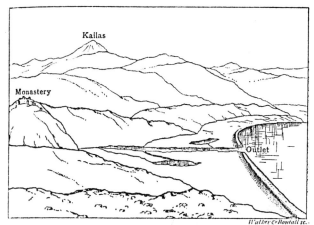

SKETCH OF OUTLET FROM MANASAROWAR, SEEN FROM THE SOUTH.

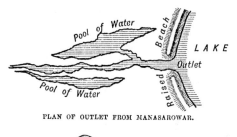

PLAN OF OUTLET FROM MANASAROWAR.

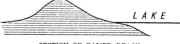

SECTION OF RAISED BEACH.

over by the Unta Dhura Pass (17,590 feet) and descended to the Plain
of Gu-gé. They then took the unusual course of proceeding
northwards to touch the Sutlej before turning to approach the
southern shores of the lakes from the north-west. They skirted the
southern shore of Rakshas Tal and then proceeded in the opposite
direction to Henry Strachey up the isthmus separating the two
lakes. They wanted to prove the existence of the channel joining the
two lakes which Henry had observed in 1846. This they were fully
able to do.

Afterwards they made their way back over the Himalayas at their
original crossing point, though they employed a somewhat more
southerly route to get there. Their expedition was significant for
the valuable geological and botanical information that Richard
Strachey collected, in addition to information of glaciers and
snowfall.

Mani stones at Lake Manasarovar (1987)

CHAPTER FOUR

Travellers in the Sacred Region: 1850–1900

During the second half of the nineteenth century the trickle of travellers to the sacred region continued, though their object changed somewhat. Instead of serious-minded explorers and surveyors, we find a motley brigade of sportsmen and adventurers, who no doubt found heightened excitement in flouting the strictures of the Tibetan authorities to gate crash the 'Forbidden Land'. Unfortunately for some – and also for hapless Tibetan scapegoats – this excitement was not without cost.

In 1855 or 1860 – the date given varies – a certain 'Mr. Drummond' committed the terrible sacrilege of sailing an indiarubber boat on Lake Manasarovar. Subsequent rumour had it that the local *dzongpön* was decapitated for allowing this enormity to take place in his territory.

The German Schlaginweit brothers, Adolph and Robert, both protégés of the great Alexander Humboldt and highly professional in their explorational techniques, planned to visit Manasarovar in 1855 but were intercepted by the Tibetans just short of Daba and diverted north-westwards to Gartok. Along their route, however, they were able to see and sketch part of the Kailas Range.

Then in June, 1864, a party of British sportsmen set off from Almora for the 'Land of the Huns'. It included Thomas W. Webber, Late Forest Surveyor for the North-West Provinces and Deputy Conservator of Forests in the Central Provinces and Gorakhpur; Lieutenant E. Smyth, Inspector of Schools, North-West Provinces; Henry Hodgson; and Hon. Robert Drummond, I.C.S., son of Viscount Strathallan and brother of the Lieutenant-Governor of the North-West Provinces. This last-named must be the self-same 'Mr Drummond' whom a later writer, Charles Sherring, identifies as the one time Commissioner of Bareilly and the person whose sailing interlude on Manasarovar had such dire consequences for the local *dzongpön*.

The party crossed into Tibet by the Nepalese Tinkar Pass, fully expecting to be stopped by the Tibetans, but determined to browbeat and bluster their way through to their Tibetan hunting grounds by sheer force of numbers – they had sixty Bhotia servants and many yaks with them – and their formidable array of firepower. They appear to have been, and indeed to have considered themselves, nothing short of a modest private army. The anticipated confrontation took place just outside Taklakot. About sixty Tibetan horsemen bore down upon them and began 'wheeling in picturesque confusion right in front of our line of march'. This display was no doubt meant to strike fear into their hearts, but the Tibetans had seriously underestimated the fibre of these British intruders, who merely stood their ground and roared with laughter. So infectious was this laughter, in fact, that the Tibetans were obliged to abandon their attempt at looking ferocious and joined in themselves. Finally they began sticking out their tongues, which Webber understood to be a recognized form of friendly salute among them; also that the correct response was to do likewise and touch tongues – 'a part of the ceremony we felt inclined to omit'.

At Taklakot the party was met by about 200 footsoldiers, some of whom grovelled on the ground begging the Britishers not to proceed while the others drew their hands rapidly across their throats. It was unclear whether the latter was 'a threat or a freemason's sign'. When the British party made a push towards the bridge across the Karnali, however, the Tibetans broke up its timbers before they could reach it. This led to stern remonstrations:

> We held forth by our interpreters that we were friendly travellers...; at the same time that, if any violence was attempted, we were well armed and prepared to defend ourselves and our property. That in pulling down the bridge and preventing us from reaching our camping ground they had committed an unfriendly act, to atone for which they would be required to bring us fuel and supplies, for which we would pay.
>
> (Thos. W. Webber, *In the Forests of Upper India*)

The next day, the British sportsmen were honoured with a visit from the *dzongpön* and the chief lama of Taklakot, accompanied by some soldiers. Drummond received them seated on a chair within a tent – 'the symbol of the Indian Sirkar'* – with his companions

---

*The Indian Government

ranged around him. The Tibetans were obliged to sit on the ground in order to explain their fears to the interlopers, who plied them with Jameson's whiskey to weaken their opposition. Nothing was decided that day, but next day word came from the *dzongpön* that they could make a month's trip to the north-east as long as they would give a firm undertaking not to go near the sacred lake. They also had to pretend to have had a great fight so that if his Lhasa masters called him to question, the *dzongpön* could claim that he had been overwhelmed by sheer force of numbers.

So the party proceeded north-eastwards, crossing the high ridges east of Gurla Mandhata *via* a snowbound pass and thence descending to the valleys and plains beyond, where they split up to pursue their various sporting interests. Drummond went to the east and Smyth to the north after antelope and ovis ammon (one of the largest species of wild sheep); Webber and Hodgson restricted themselves to seeking wild yak – especially 'big bulls'. These ferocious beasts turned out to have more wit and cunning than their awkward, shaggy appearance suggested, but eventually a fine pair were tracked down. Webber describes a kill:

> The first shot awoke the echoes from the rocks above, and the bullet thud was clearly heard. The great hairy bulls, with bloodshot eyes and heads in the air, faced around and made some startled runs, grunting savagely, but stopped short to reconnoitre for their concealed enemy. Five more barrels were emptied, and still they came on, almost up to the rocks where we were crouched, frantically loading up and cramming in bullets and ramming them down, for the rifles were old-fashioned muzzle-loaders, 14 and 16 bore, loaded with conical bullets and four drachms of powder. The biggest bull had been hit four times, but seemed none the worse, while his companions, also getting a bullet in the chest, thought it wise to retreat up the valley. But the first, discovering his enemy, staggered on, foaming with rage, and fell to the last two barrels, which struck him in the head within a few yards of the moraine. He was game to the last, and was only stopped by weight of lead – a grand beast, seventeen hands to the shoulder and weighing as much as any prize short horn.
>
> *(Ibid.)*

During their sporting travels Webber and Hodgson were also able to get an imposing view of Mount Kailas away to the west:

> On one occasion we crossed another lofty divide, and found ourselves suddenly out on the northern slopes of another watershed, none other than that of the mighty Indus. Far beneath us, some miles away, lay the

most brilliantly beautiful blue sea, the celebrated Manasarovar lake, as it proved, which we had promised not to approach. The foreground was flat, rolling hills and ridges sloping gradually towards the lake, all bare and tinted in the most crude colours – reds and pinks and orange – while hundreds of miles to the north and west in the violet distance there stretched range after range of low, jagged hills, all alike, and succeeding one another in endless succession. Conspicuous, and towering above them all, was the snowcapped summit of the sacred Kailas. We sat down for a while and munched our biscuits and enjoyed the wonderful and expansive panorama, and sketched it in watercolours as a record of our tramp.

(Ibid.)

Having enjoyed good sport, the party were reunited and returned together to Taklakot. After exchanging presents and farewells with their friend, the *dzongpön*, they proceeded back towards the high passes leading to India. No doubt the *dzongpön* was highly relieved to see them go. His relief would, however, have been premature. Smyth and Webber dodged back across the border further west for a spot of shooting on the Plains of Gyanima.

A year later another pair of sportsmen made a similar trip: Captain H. U. Smith and Mr. A. S. H. Harrison. They left Naini Tal in June 1865 and by 31st July had reached 'Shib and Chillum: two camping grounds well known to traders and the turning point for all sportsmen'. It would therefore seem that by this date the border was fairly crawling with British sportsmen eager to slip across into Tibet and to start blazing away at the exotic game roaming the great plateau. The Tibetan authorities kept a keen eye out for them and could usually pick out any planning a long foray across the border by the number of their yaks and the quantity of their provisions. To dupe them, therefore, Smith and Harrison forwarded their main provisions in the care of a trustworthy trader with orders to meet them in due course at 'Kylas'. Meanwhile they themselves proceeded towards the border with only minimal supplies.

They were intercepted at 'Shib' by a party of 'Tartar' guards who tried to turn them back but who eventually conceded that they might proceed to 'Idyum', though they wisely insisted that they accompany them. Smith and Harrison were, however, by dint of guile and devilish cunning, able to give these unwanted chaperones the slip and then proceeded post haste, marching day and night, to their rendezvous point. At 'Kylas', or more exactly 'the village of Darchin', they were able not only to reclaim their extra gear but they received a warm welcome from the 'high priest'. They had already met this dignitary at 'Shib', where he had gone to trade, and he had assured Smith and Harrison that he would help them if they for their part could successfully spirit themselves to his small domain. This was 'a little territory held by the priests, who were quite independent of the Chinese authorities'. The 'high priest' was as good as his word for the two sportsmen found that preparations had been made for their stay. They gave their benefactor gifts of brandy and an air gun as a token of their appreciation. He returned the gesture by furnishing them with two guides who knew the best shooting grounds thereabouts.

Smith claims to have fished in the holy Manasarovar – surely another terrible sacrilege for which someone's head might have rolled! Afterwards he and his companion, Harrison, applied themselves to slaughtering the game in the areas to the east and north of the lake. Smith claims to have bagged a black wolf – 'the first ever shot in that part of the world'.

Later they returned to Darchen to take their leave of the benevolent priest and then travelled east by easy stages towards Gartok, their principal object now being to trace the source of the Sutlej. Their subsequent venture into the field of hydrography was somewhat disastrous for their reputation. They were foolish enough to cast doubt on the Strachey brothers' findings by denying both the existence of the channel joining the two lakes and of the old watercourse connecting Rakshas Tal with the Sutlej. When Smith propounded these notions at a meeting of the Royal Geographical Society, a Dr. Thomson leapt up and staunchly defended the Stracheys. Perhaps it would have been better if Smith and Harrison had confined themselves to plain *shikar* (sport) and not ventured into areas where they were not so well qualified.

If trepassers were going to continue to make such incursions into Tibetan territory in defiance of the authorities, it was more or less certain that eventually one of them would come unpleasantly unstuck. The unlucky head upon which the brunt of Tibetan annoyance was to fall was that of Arnold Henry Savage Landor, the grandson of the distinguished writer and himself the author of such gems of travel literature as *Corea, or the land of the Morning Calm* and *Alone with the Hairy Ainu*.

It is, however, hard to feel sympathy for this victim, for he seems to have brought his ordeals upon himself by his arrogant, foolhardy and often downright outrageous behaviour. From the pages of the account of his Tibetan travels, *In the Forbidden Land*, Landor comes across as a caricature Victorian imperialist: a braggart, bigot and bully.

His contempt for the Tibetans was absolute from the start. In his

Arnold Savage Landor
before his Tibetan ordeal

view, not only were they superstitious, insanitary and degenerate
in their customs but, worse still, they were spineless cowards to a
man; with blood duly boiling, Landor was forever having to teach
them salutory lessons. For instance, while still in Bhotia territory,
he describes encountering an impudent Tibetan who had a few
disparaging things to say about the English:

> This remark was too much for me, and it might anyhow have been
> unwise to allow it to pass unchallenged. Throwing myself on him, I
> grabbed him by his pigtail and landed in his face a number of blows
> straight from the shoulder. When I let him go, he threw himself down,
> crying, and implored my pardon. Once and for all to disillusion the
> Tibetan on one or two points, I made him lick my shoes clean with his
> tongue, in the presence of the assembled Shokas (Bhotias). Thus done, he
> tried to scamper away, but I caught him once more by his pigtail, and
> kicked him down the front steps which he had dared to come up
> unasked.
>
> (A.H. Savage Landor, *In the Forbidden Land*)

Ludicrous as it may seem, this is not at all unrepresentative of the
attitudes expressed in *In the Forbidden Land*. The book is little more
than an inflated example of the boys' adventure stories of the era,
heavily laced with all the characteristic prejudices and posturings.
In his own eyes, Landor is always indubitably *right*: he is the noble

English hero and the Tibetans just villainous savages.

Also slightly ludicrous is Landor's stance of being a proper scientific observer. He travelled with mandatory surveying equipment, and was forever making highly precise calculations and dutifully noting them down. Such was his dedication to enlarging the province of scientific knowledge, in fact, that when a prisoner of the Tibetans and denied access to writing materials, he noted his findings in his own blood – and in cypher too. He even claimed to have been the first Englishman to visit the northern source of the Brahmaputra and, trusting that he would not be thought immodest, promptly named it after himself.

Sven Hedin, the great Swedish explorer who was in the same region a few years later, makes short shrift of these pretensions:

> The extraordinary Munchausen romance which an English newspaper writer named Landor narrated and which quite set aside all the conscientious reliable descriptions of Moorcroft, Strachey and the pundits, had no effect whatsoever. Among the uncritical, sensation-loving public Landor had a certain temporary success; but among geographers, especially in London, he was received with justifiable suspicion.
>
> (Sven Hedin, *Transhimalaya*)

Tom Longstaff also furnishes further reason to doubt Landor's credibility. He once retraced Landor's ascent of a mountain in Nepal, accompanied by Landor's own guides. He found the cairn beyond which Landor had definitely not proceeded. It lay at an altitude of about 16,500 feet – definitely not at 23,000 feet as Landor had claimed. 'Landor had taken artistic licence', Longstaff concluded – surely an understatement.

Landor undertook his expedition to Tibet in the spring, summer and autumn of 1897. During the early stages of his journey he followed a route similar to that of Henry Strachey. He penetrated into Tibet by the Lampkiya Pass and from there proceeded to Lama Chörten, where he got his first view of Kailas:

> To the north the clouds had dispersed, and the snow-capped sacred Kelas [sic] Mount stood majestic before us. In appearance not unlike the graceful roof of a temple, Kelas towers over the long white-capped range, contrasting in beautiful blending of tints with the warm sienna colour of the lower elevations. Kelas is some two thousand feet higher than the other peaks of the Gangir [sic] chain, with strongly defined ledges and terraces marking its stratifications, and covered with horizontal layers of snow standing out in brilliant colour against the

South-west view of Kailas

dark iceworn rock....

My men, with heads uncovered, their faces turned towards the sacred
peak, were muttering prayers. With joined hands which they slowly
raised as high as the forehead, they prayed fervently, and then went
down on their knees, with heads bent low on the ground. My brigand
follower, who was standing close by me, hurriedly whispered that I
should join in this act of prayer....

'You must keep friends with the gods,' he said; 'misfortune will attend
you if you do not salaam to Kelas; that is the home of a good god!' And he
pointed to the peak with the most devout air of conviction.

To please him I saluted the mountain with utmost deference, and taking
my cue from the others, placed a white stone on one of the hundreds of
Chokdens or *Obos* [cairns] erected by devotees at this spot....
                                                        (Landor: *Ibid.*)

The Tibetans were hot on his trail by now – as indeed they were to
be throughout his time in their land. They were to try the full
gamut of approaches to get him to leave: gentle ones initially, like
trying to reason with him, begging him, even offering him bribes;
only when these failed did they resort to threats and, ultimately,
probably in sheer desperation, to direct physical violence. All except
the last were of no avail. Landor simply would not be deflected from
his intention of pushing right through to Lhasa. Such blind
tenacity, if not merely a pose for the benefit of the readership, is
hard to credit. Landor himself suggests that the thought of failure
was always too galling to bear contemplation. There was moreover
always the lure of doing the forbidden. Though he does not
mention it himself, there was probably an element of realistic
calculation there too: he was banking on the fact that the Tibetans
would not dare to do him any harm for fear of provoking a punitive
expedition. The British, after all, were extremely powerful and
situated just over a couple of hundred miles away on the plains of
India – much nearer than Lhasa.

The first confrontation came at Gyanima. The Barkha Tarjum
came in person to ask the Englishman to turn back. Finding Landor
obdurate, however, he first recanted and granted him unofficial
permission to proceed with a small party to Lake Manasarovar, then
retracted and insisted that the whole expedition return directly to
India by the way it had come. As there were large numbers of armed
soldiers blocking the way, it would have been unrealistic to proceed,
so Landor decided to resort to skilful means. Outwardly obeying
the *tarjum's* injunction, he seemed to be making his way back

towards the Lampkiya Pass; but once out of sight he stopped and divided his party into two groups. The larger group would return to India with Dr. Harkua Wilson of the American Episcopal Mission, who had accompanied the expedition so far. The other, a tight, picked team led by Landor himself and carrying only minimal supplies and equipment, would attempt a commando-like dash across 'unfrequented wilds' to the lakes and afterwards on to the Tibetan capital itself.

After 'adventures and escapes far too numerous to relate here' Landor's group arrived on the southern shores of the sacred lakes, where they obtained another fine prospect of Kailas:

> To the N. of the lakes stood the magnificent Tize, the sacred Kelas mountain, overtopping by some two thousand feet all other snowy peaks of the Gangri chain, which extended roughly from N.W. to S.E. From this spot we could see more distinctly than from Lama Chokten the band round the base of the mountain, which, according to legend, was formed by the rope of a Rakas (devil) trying to tear down this throne of the gods.

> Tize, the great sacred peak, is of fascinating interest, owing to its peculiar shape. It resembles, as I have said, the giant roof of a temple, but to my mind it lacks the gracefulness of sweeping curves such are found in Fujiama of Japan, the most artistically beautiful mountain I have ever seen. Tize is angular, uncomfortably angular, if I may be allowed the expression, and although its height, the vivid colour of its base, and the masses of snow that cover its slopes, give it a peculiar attraction, it nevertheless struck me as being intensely picturesque, at least from the point of view from which I saw it, and from which the whole of it was visible. When clouds were round it, toning down and modifying its shape, Tize appeared at its best from the painter's point of view. Under these conditions, I have thought it very beautiful, especially at sunrise, with one side tinted red and yellow, and its rocky base standing majestic against a background of shiny gold. With my telescope, I could plainly distinguish, especially on the E. side, the defile along which the worshippers make the circuit of the base of the mountain, though I was told that some pilgrims actually march round it on the snowy ledge directly over its base, and just above the darker band of rock described before. On the S.W. side can be seen, on the top of a lower peak, a gigantic Obo.

> *(Ibid.)*

Landor was having trouble with his servants by now – not surprisingly, for they had been discovered by the Tibetans and, openly hunted and miserably equipped, they had every prospect of

Mansing, Landor, Chanden Singh

suffering a great deal when their pursuers finally caught up with them. Their brave leader was incensed at all attempts at defection, however, and, in true Victorian schoolmasterly style, liberally administered punitive thrashings to those who showed such intolerable 'disloyalty' – or merely threatened to shoot out of hand any man who tried to desert. Nevertheless, by the time he had reached Trügo Gompa on the southern shore of Manasarovar, he admits to being down to nine men. Five more left him at the lake. Three marches further on all but two had deserted.

No Victorian schoolboy romance is complete without its complement of faithful native servants ready to follow their great white leader to the the death. Landor's devoted duo consisted of an ex-policeman named Chanden Singh, whom he had hired back in Almora, and a leper named Mansing. Together they forged eastwards, over the 16,900 foot Maium Pass and down into the valley of the Tsangpo/Brahmaputra. They were now under constant surveillance as well as desperately badly equipped and provisioned. The journey became increasingly difficult. Finally, during a river crossing, one of their yaks went under the water and, although the animal was saved, a great deal of the food, money and equipment that it was carrying was irrecoverably lost. This was a disaster; from now on they had to live off the land.

On 19th August 1897 they reached a place which Landor calls 'Toxem'. The villagers received them well and promised to supply them with food and horses. The next morning, however, as they were inspecting the horses offered for sale, they were seized from behind in the most treacherously underhand fashion. Naturally, men of Landor's calibre do not give in without putting up a fight, and his two trusty retainers gave (almost) as good as their master, but eventually all were overpowered by sheer force of numbers:

> All was over now, and bound like a dangerous criminal, I looked round to see what had become of my men. When I realised that it took the Tibetans five hundred men all counted to arrest a starved Englishman and his two half-dying servants, and that, even then, they dared not do it openly, but had to resort to abject treachery; when I found that these soldiers were picked troops from Lhassa [sic] and Sigatz [sic], despatched on purpose to arrest our progress and capture us, I could not restrain a smile of contempt for those into whose hands we had fallen.
>
> (*Ibid.*)

And now came the hideous Oriental tortures – or so Landor luridly depicts them. Having been tightly bound and subjected to preliminary humiliations, he was made to ride a horse sitting on a spiked saddle, which savagely gouged his back. The Tibetans also took pot shots at him into the bargain. Then he was introduced to a group of 'the most villainous brutes I had ever set eyes upon. One, a powerful repulsive individual, held in his hand a great knobbed mallet used for fracturing bones; another carried a bow and arrows; a third held a big two-handed sword; while others made a display of various ghastly instruments of torture'. Next he was bound to the sharp edge of a prism-shaped log and told by his principal tormentor, the fiendish *Pombo* – Landor defines him as a 'Grand Lama. . . or governor of a province, with powers equivalent to those of a feudal king' – who had worked himself into a frenzy and was foaming at the mouth, that his eyes were going to be put out. In the actual event, although a red-hot iron was flourished in his face,

*Arnold Savage Landor
after his Tibetan ordeal*

Landor suffered nothing worse than a scorched nose and temporary disturbance of vision. But this was not the end. Afterwards, the butt of a matchlock was placed against his forehead and the weapon discharged. Landor received an unpleasant blow, but he merely laughed in order to tantalize his tormentors and demonstrate the absurdity of their every attempt to break his spirit. Not surprisingly, this spurred the Pombo on to greater excesses. He now produced a vicious two-handed sword. After carefully measuring its keen edge against his victim's exposed neck, he raised it aloft. The first swing swept short of its mark. And the second. Landor still had his somewhat inflated head on his shoulders when he was at last led off to meet his next ordeal: being stretched on a rack-like device.

In the end, for all their cowardice and cruelty, Landor assures his reader that the Tibetans could not help being impressed by the native English fortitude with which he bore all. Even the evil Pombo was obliged to concede respect and after a while even became passably affable. Clearly the Tibetans had no real intention of killing him but were just mounting an elaborate display to put the wind up him and get him out of their country.

Eventually Landor and his two servants – who had probably been brutalized as much if not more than their master – were led back to Taklakot, where they were conveniently allowed to escape and reach the search party led by Dr. Harkua Wilson, which had been sent out when news of Landor's misfortunes had reached the authorities on the other side of the border. More substantial help was also on its way. The Government of India had dispatched a magistrate named Mr. J. Larkin. Landor ran into Larkin's party after he himself had got back across the frontier. Although severely depleted by his ordeals, he insisted on accompanying the magistrate back to the Lipu Lekh Pass, where they waited for the Taklakot Dzongpön to obey their summons and present himself to answer for what had taken place. The Dzongpön did not appear though he did return a good part of Landor's property, which had been confiscated.

And so, filthy, ragged, vermin-ridden, though apparently very little the wiser, Arnold Henry Savage Landor returned to the plains of India. At Bombay he took ship for Italy, where his family home was situated. In due course, without stint of space or hyperbole, he was to tell the world the story of his remarkable adventures *In the Forbidden Land* – adventures in which he had acquitted himself in a manner befitting an English explorer and gentleman.

Much of the serious surveying work that was done in Tibet during this period was performed by members of the Corps of Pundits, a group of undercover native surveyors recruited to work in the territories beyond the British frontiers by Major T. D. Montgomerie of the Survey of India. They were given a thorough technical grounding in their work, and when in the field – where they travelled often in disguise – they might use the accoutrements of the peripatetic holy man (prayer-wheel, rosary and so forth), suitably modified, to help them in their surveying. Two who were active in the Kailas-Manasarovar region were Nain Singh, the doyen of them all, and Kalian Singh.

The man who selected the young Pundits for training at the Engineering College at Roorkee was the self-same Edmund Smyth who had been in Tibet with Webber, Hodgson and Viscount Strathallan's son, Robert Drummond, in 1864. Before joining the Indian Army, Smyth had been a contemporary at Rugby School of Thomas Hughes, who immortalized him in his classic *Tom Brown's Schooldays* as Crab Jones, 'the queerest coldest fish at Rugby'. A later Kailas traveller, Tom Longstaff, wrote warmly of 'my old friend Edmund Smyth', whom he believed could fairly claim to be the first European at the source o the Brahmaputra – 'which was conveniently ignored by Sven Hedin when claiming its first discovery'. Longstaff goes on: 'He was a grand old man with an enduring affection for the beauties of landscape. A notable *shikari*, he

was the first European to explore many of the remote byways of
Kumaon Garhwal and... -this is particularly interesting-"...in
1851 and 1853 he had visited the adjacent parts of Tibet."
Unfortunately, Smyth published no accounts of these clandestine
forays, which is not surprising, since in making them he was not
only cocking a snook at the Tibetan authorities but at his own
masters in British India as well. However, there are letters and
these show that his companion on those journeys was no ordinary
mortal but John Hanning Speke, the great Richard Burton's
succesful adversary in the search for the source of the Nile. In the
early 1850s Speke was, like Smyth, a young and hot-blooded Indian
Army officer. In a letter of 1853, Smyth wrote that he and Speke
'travelled for months together in Chinese Tartary to the North of
the Himalyah mountains from the Manasarovar Lake to Askardo
(Little Tibet).'*

CHAPTER FIVE

Travellers in the Sacred Region: 1904-1911

Around the turn of the present century, British suspicion of increasing Russian influence in Tibet developed into virtual paranoia. This, allied to impatience with the continuing refusal of the Tibetan authorities to regularize their diplomatic and trading relations with their Indian neighbour, finally tipped the Viceroy, Lord Curzon, into direct action. Thus, in 1904, the guns of the Younghusband Expedition to Lhasa temporarily cowed the Tibetan government into modifying its rigidly exclusive attitude towards the outside world.

One of the concessions conceded and duly enshrined in Article Five of the Treaty signed between the two principal parties allowed for the establishment of three trade marts in Tibet. One was to be situated in Gartok in Western Tibet, and a British expedition was promptly assembled and dispatched from Central Tibet to inspect the place. As a survey of the country through which it was to pass was also to be carried out, the expedition included two surveyors among its four officers: Captains C.H.D. Ryder and H. Wood of the Royal Engineers. Ryder had already done sterling survey work in Western China, Burma and along the Indian frontier, as well as distinguishing himself as a first-rate field engineer at Gyantse during the recent Anglo-Tibetan hostilities. Lieutenant F. M. ('Eric') Bailey of the 32nd Pioneers also went as Interpreter and Assistant to Captain C. G. Rawling of the Somersetshire Light Infantry, who

Captain C.H.D. Ryder

was placed in general control*. Surbordinate members of the
expedition included Sub-Surveyor Ram Singh R. S.; Hospital
Assistant Hira Singh; three military surveyors; five Gurkha sepoys;
five survey Khalassies; seven pony-drivers; two Hindustani and
two Tibetan servants; and finally a Ladakhi named Mohammed Isa,
later to meet his end in the service of Sven Hedin, who acted as
Caravan Leader. Transport consisted of twenty-six baggage-
ponies, seventeen riding-ponies and some one hundred yaks; these
were to carry the Expedition's considerable supplies and equipment.

When it set off from Gyantse on October 10th, 1904, the
expedition was accompanied by an official of the Lhasa government
and carried a 'very strongly worded permit signed with the seal of
the Lhasa government and of the three great Lhasa monasteries,
and directing all officials along the route to render every asistance'
(Ryder). These were unique and highly privileged conditions of
travel – ones which would surely have made those earlier travellers
who had ventured into the hostile wastes of western Tibet highly
envious. The expedition leader, Captain Cecil Rawling, was fully
aware of the great significance of the undertaking: this was the first

---

*For additional biographical material on Rawling, Ryder and Bailey, see
Appendix 3.

Captain Cecil Rawling

time that 'British officers, with only a nominal escort, were going to traverse Tibet with the cognizance and assistance of the Tibetan authorities'. Nevertheless, being no stranger to Tibet himself – he had done fine explorational work in remote parts of Western Tibet in 1903 – he was also aware of the many uncertainties that hung over the whole venture, and that it was bound to meet considerable difficulties. Two problems loomed largest: the impossibility of knowing how the provincial Tibetans would treat the expedition and whether they would render the required and necessary assistance; and secondly the fact that the Tibetan winter – an adversary more formidable than the most hostile Tibetans – was advancing fast. Not only could the members of the party expect to bear at least some of its rigours during the course of their thousand-mile journey, but there was the distinct possibility that the high passes back to India would be blocked by the time they reached them, in which case they would have to resign themselves to the prospect of seeing the winter out somewhere in the desolation of Western Tibet.

Rawling need not have vexed himself on the first score. In complete contrast to the experience of his precursors, he and his colleagues were to encounter cordiality, gifts and warm hospitality

The Panchen or Tashi Lama (1904/5)

wherever they broke march. Regarding the winter, however, his
apprehensions proved well-founded, though not to the point of
realizing the worst possibilities. As the expedition progressed
westwards it met with progressively more severe weather
conditions. Apart from the occasional sunny days, when it was
pleasant enough out of the shade, biting cold was the norm,
frequently exacerbated by fierce winds, often reaching hurricane
force, which made surveying both difficult and painful. By the time
the travellers reached the high country towards Kailas the breath
froze in their beards and their faces were covered with ice.

The first leg of the eight-hundred mile stage to Gartok ran
through the valley of the Nyang Chu – 'one of the richest and most
prosperous valleys in Tibet, – to Shigatse, where the expedition
paused for several days. An army of tailors was employed in making

warm clothing for everyone: sewing lambskins into their coats, for instance, and fitting them out with fur hats and gloves. There was also time to visit the great Lamaist theopolis at nearby Tashilhunpo, seat of the august Panchen Lama, second only in the Tibetan hierarchy to the Dalai Lama himself. The monastery complex housed some four thousand monks; it was not so large as some of the great Lhasa monasteries but was rather more richly endowed. The monks entertained their British visitors cordially with tea (usually undrinkable), cakes and dried fruit; they also showed them around:

> The bulk of the buildings, the residences of the monks, were of the usual type – narrow paved roads with high houses on each side, dirty, and not picturesque; but we also enjoyed the sight of the tombs of the five previous Tashi Lamas, each a separate building with its golden roof and highly ornamented interior, filled with a wealth of turquoises, gold bowls, and rare old jade and cloisonné, the effect being somewhat marred by a foreground of small vessels holding lighted tapers fed by very evil-smelling butter.
>
> (Capt. C. H. D. Ryder, 'Exploration and Survey with the Tibet Frontier Commission', etc., *Geographical Journal*, Vol XXV, October 1905)

There was also an audience with the Panchen Lama himself, then a young man of only twenty-three or thereabouts but nevertheless endowed with a quiet dignity that made a lasting impression upon his visitors. Indeed, his personality and the low lighting of the room in which the encounter took place together combined to make the whole proceeding seem like a religious ceremony. It concluded with the traditional presentation of silk scarves (*khata*) and a blessing.

After Shigatse, the expedition's route broadly followed the course of the Brahmaputra/Tsangpo upstream to its headwaters just east of the Kailas-Manasarovar region. On occasions, members of the survey team split off from the main party to pursue their trigonometrical work in the surrounding hills and valleys. During the initial stages, the country through which they passed was comparatively populous and benign – scattered with pleasant villages surrounded by outlying patches of cultivation, and here and there an imposing *dzong* or *gompa* perched on a rocky pinnacle like a stork's nest. Later on, however, it became increasingly arid, harsh and thinly populated. There were no trees then, not even the occasional oasis of cultivation, and such settled communities as existed were isolated, mean and dirty. This was the domain of

View near Saga on the Southern Route to Kailas (1987)

Nomad tent between Parayang and the Maium La (1987)

nomadic herders (*dogpa*) and even they were not numerous.

There were compensations for the harshness of weather and terrain, though. Game became more plentiful as the expedition progressed westwards and its members were then able to indulge in the occasional spot of *shikar*. Wild sheep and antelope were among the more plentiful quarry, but Rawling was proud to be able to bag a large and obviously predatory wolf. Wood, on the other hand, was fortunate enough to catch a glimpse of that rarest of carnivores: the snow leopard. Other visual treats included a series of views of the northern side of Mount Everest – the members of the expedition were the first Westerners to see the world's highest peak from this aspect:

> We had a magnificent view from a hill a few hundred feet above the pass of the main Himalayan range. Mount Everest stood up towering above the rest of the range in its neighbourhood in one isolated peak, a continuous drop of some 8000 feet separating it from the rest of the range east and west of it.
>
> (*Ibid.*)

The expedition eventually reached the watershed range from the valleys of which issue the many streams that give rise to the

The South Face of Kailas at sunset

Tsangpo/Brahmaputra. After a few days of bright sunshine, the weather took a turn for the worse here and the pass of Maium La (16,900 feet) was under a foot or two of snow when the party crossed it. Beyond, after crossing several more, rather lower passes and traversing expanses of undulating ground, they came in sight of the sacred lakes.

Naturally, the members of the expedition applied themselves to the perennial and fascinating hydrological problems of the area. They managed to confirm the existence of the channel connecting the twin lakes, though found it dry. No water was running between the western shore of Rakshas Tal and the course of the Sutlej either, and it was doubted whether it would ever flow again.

And so to the sacred mountain. One might have expected military men to be unimpressed but, as in the case of Henry Strachey half a century before, this was not so. Rawling showed himself highly sensitive to the beauties of Kailas:

Kailas Parbat is by far the largest and highest of the many pinnacles that tower up in the sky from the range of mountains which lies to the north of the Manasarowar Lake; its summit rises over 22,000 feet above sea-level, or some 7,000 feet above the surrounding plain. Figures, as a rule, convey but a vague idea to the general mind, and it is indeed difficult to place before the mental vision a true picture of this most beautiful mountain.

In shape it resembles a vast cathedral, the roof of which, rising to a ridge in the centre, is otherwise regular in outline and covered with eternal snow. Below this so-called roof, the sides of the mountain are perpendicular and fall sheer for hundreds of feet, the strata horizontal, the layers of stone varying slightly in colour, and the dividing lines showing up clear and distinct. The layers are again divided or split by perpendicular cracks, which give to the entire mountain the appearance of having been built by giant hands, of huge blocks of reddish stone.

At the foot of these Titanic walls a number of caves are said to exist, and dark and gloomy ravines lie on either side, while from the neighbouring and lesser hills rise numberless pinnacles and slender spires of rock.

Wonderful is the appearance of this mountain in the early morning, when its roof of spotless snow is touched by the rising sun and changed in hue to a soft but vivid pink, whilst the ravines below still hold the blackness of the night. As the light increases so do the mighty walls brighten in colour, and form a happy contrast to the blue waters of Manasarowar rippling in the morning breeze, changing gradually, as one gazes, from purple to brightest blue.

No wonder then that this spot is believed by Hindus and Mahomedans [Not so – author.] alike to be the home of all the gods, that of the waters of its holy lake they drink, and that it is *the* Holy Mountain, and the most sacred spot on earth, a pilgrimage to which ensures both sanctity and renown.

(Capt. C. G. Rawling, *The Great Plateau*)

Rawling and his party visited Barkha, the staging post on the main Lhasa-Gartok highway which crossed the lush plain at the southern foot of Kailas, where they were entertained by the *tarjum* or presiding officer. The building they entered consisted of about nine rooms arranged around a courtyard. Despite having been cleaned in their honour, it was still very dirty – all travellers in Tibet stress the ubiquitous dirt – though the general atmosphere was made cheerful by the Manchester and Indian cotton prints that covered the smoke-begrimed walls. Large quantities of Chinese brick tea were stored here, for which, apparently, the Tibetans had an inordinate thirst. By preference they took it mixed with butter – a rank and souplike concoction that would make even the most gross and long-standing brews of British cafeterias and buffets seem delicate. This tea was exported to Tibet pressed into blocks of about five pounds weight each and finally sewn inside skins for protection in transit. It cost a fair amount on the Western Tibetan market although it was pretty rough stuff; Rawling aptly calls it 'the leavings and sweepings of the Chinese crop'. Superior quality Indian tea could certainly be had at more modest cost but the Tibetans were firmly set against it. Wily Chinese tea merchants had put about the rumour that it induced unpleasant headaches.

After Barkha, the expedition crossed the Indus-Sutlej watershed by way of a 16,200 foot pass called the Jerko La and reached Gartok on December 9th. This was the official summer residence of the Garpöns or Viceroys, but they travelled up from their winter residence at Gargunsa some thirty miles away in order to treat with the British. The members of the expedition were exceedingly unimpressed with Gartok; Ryder dismisses it as 'one of the most dreary inhabited places that we had struck in our journey', and continues:

> A long broad plain, absolutely bare, with a dozen wretched hovels in the middle, constitutes at this time of year what is in summer the chief trading centre of Western Tibet. The wind howled round the hut we were in continuously, and, the weather looking threatening, we were not anxious to stay a minute longer than was necessary for Captain Rawling to settle up trade questions with the Garpöns.
>
> (Ryder, *Ibid.*)

Rawling was able to discharge his duties in a single day, and then the sprint for India was on. The expedition had first to cross a number of high passes, however, where they encountered blizzards and scathing winds; then they entered the bizarre canyon lands of the Upper Sutlej Valley:

> We were now in the most cut-up country I have ever seen; it must resemble the loess formation of China. The bottom of every nullah [side-valley] was some hundreds of feet below the general level of the valley, with their edges so cut and worn into fantastic shapes that it was difficult to believe that one was not looking on the ruins of old castles. There are also innumerable caves in which the inhabitants live.
>
> (Ryder *Ibid.*)

Rawling and Bailey took off to visit the ruins of the ancient city of Thöling. These were situated on the summit of an isolated plateau of sandstone, and the sole means of reaching them was by means of funnel-like holes carved in the solid rock. Although largely deserted by modern times, Thöling continued to enjoy its traditional status

The Senior Garpon of Western Tibet (1926)

Charles Atmore Sherring

as the spiritual capital of Western Tibet and was the seat of the *Khenpo* or regional patriarch. Nearby was another remarkable relic: an ancient iron chain cantilever bridge reputed to date back to the time of Alexander the Great.

Rawling's party crossed the Great Himalaya by the Shipki La, a 15,400 foot pass. It was Christmas by now and three feet of snow bedevilled their progress. Their privations were soon to be over, however. After only eighteen more marches they were once again enjoying the pleasures of civilization in that doyen of hill stations: Simla.

Within months another member of this new generation of privileged travellers was making his way towards Western Tibet; not a military man this time but a representative of that other face of the official British presence in India – a civil servant.

In 1905, Charles Atmore Sherring,* I.C.S., Deputy Commissioner of Almora, was sent on a tour of the Bhot Mahals, which was subsequently extended to include an official mission to Gartok, to check the functioning of the new trade arrangements. His line of approach was the most direct and convenient one: up the course of the Kali river, close along the Nepalese border, passing through centres like Ascot and Garbyang, and so on up to the benign Lipu

---

*(1868–1940); arrived in India (U.P.), 1899; retired, 1914.

Lekh Pass by way of the totally unbenign Nerpani Trail. He travelled in appropriate style, lacking nothing in the way of equipment, and accompanied by a sizeable retinue of staff. As he progressed unhurriedly across the landscape, he scrutinized it with a pragmatic eye: noting prevailing conditions of trade, bandying figures of volume and value, devising schemes to expedite traffic. He discerned where new roads or railway connections might be developed and finely calculated what the repercussions might be in terms of intangible political realities like *influence* and *interest*. He had a keen nose for the machinations of rival powers, and could even detect a suspicious Russian aroma on the rarefied air of Western Tibet – and had not his great precursor Moorcroft sensed much the same thing as far back as 1812?

Yet this was not all there was to the man. Behind the professional persona seems to have lain something of the scholar* who took a keen and compassionate interest in the culture and traditions of the indigenous people. Notable among these were the Bhotias, a mountain people of Mongolian stock, though lately espousing Hinduism, who lived in the area adjacent to the Tibetan border. Sherring extended this same humane curiosity to the Tibetans once across the high passes. Indeed, he seems an example of the better type of British servant of India: a responsible man aware that power and privilege entailed a corresponding debt of duty and concern for the people of the land – the very antithesis of a Landor. There was in fact a tradition of service to India in his family; his father, Rev. Matthew Sherring – also a writer of books – had lived and died as a missionary out there, although originally trained as a doctor.

But what makes Sherring even more significant in terms of the central theme of the present book is that he was the first of our Kailas travellers to be really awake to the extensive religious connotations of this rare quarter of the world:

This part of Western Tibet and the British Borderland is a country most sacred to the Hindus and Buddhists, and appealing as it does with its awful solemnity and weird grandeur of landscape to all that is romantic in the human soul, it is clothed the while to the eye of faith with a garment of mystery that makes it the fit abode of the great gods of Hinduism and Buddhism.
(C. A. Sherring, *Western Tibet and the British Borderland*)

On a broader level he takes full cognizance of the spiritual power of

*Sherring had been a Queen's Scholar at Westminster before going on to Trinity College, Cambridge, where he graduated with an M.A. in Classics.

the Himalaya in general – there being 'no place in all this fair earth of ours which can compare with the marvellous beauty of these everlasting snows'. Above all, however, Kailas* rears up pre-eminent, the crowning apex of this whole upward spiritual urge and the seal of the sanctity of the entire region.

Sherring is depicted in photographs taken during his venture into Western Tibet as dapperly clad in Norfolk jacket and plus-fours, and wearing a compact topi on his head. He regails us in his account of his journey with some vivid descriptions, in splendidly Augustan prose, of the beauties of the passing scene. Beyond the major Bhotia community of Garbyang, his way led along the dizzy Nerpani Trail – *nerpani* meaning literally 'no water'. Here the traveller had to gird up his courage and march boldly along narrow stone ledges flashed into the sides of sheer precipices. The final ascent to the Lipu Lekh Pass (16,780 feet) was broad and gradual: it could happily accommodate a cart road. Finally, at the top of the pass, there was a revelation:

> The first view of Tibet from the Lipu Lekh Pass is magnificent as, amidst all the other beauties of the landscape, the centre of the picture is occupied by four peaks, all over 22,000 ft., which are quite close together, the highest being Gurla Mandhata, 25,350 ft. This solid mass lends a grandeur to the whole which is quite awe-inspiring, and on all sides the most beautiful coloured rocks heighten the effect, so that the impression on the beholder is that the scene before him is truly one of nature's grandest handi-works. There are no trees or verdure to relieve the severity of what he sees, and the almost total absence of animal life adds to the feeling of intense desolation prevailing everywhere.
>
> These divers colours among the rocks are quite a feature of the country all the way to Taklakot, and of the landscape round that fortress. There are sepia, burnt sienna, raw sienna, violet, all shades of yellow and many lovely shades of red. The brilliancy of the sunshine and the intense sharpness of all lines, added to the clearness of the air, which makes the most distant objects appear close, while all around is a penetrating glare, make one liken the landscape to nothing so much as that part of Arabia which one sees near Suez.
>
> (*Ibid.*)

And so to Taklakot, just a few miles over the other side of the border, where there were the inevitable meetings with the leading local citizenry: the acting *dzongpön*, and his coquettish wife, who

---

*We have already noted in the first chapter that Sherring also discussed the latterday identification of Mounts Kailas and Meru in some depth.

The representatives of the Dzongpön of Taklakot (1926)

insisted on being photographed – alone; and the head lama of the
Simbiling Gompa. Sherring tried to impress his hosts with his
knowledge of Tibetan Buddhism by showing them his copies of
L. A. Waddell's illustrated books on the subject. The stand-in
dzongpön was rather more impressed, however, with the European
magazines that were also shown him, especially with the
advertisements for hair-restorers and beauty preparations. All in
all the social side of the visit was a great success and their parting
was on the very best of terms. Indeed Sherring seems to have
generally liked and in many ways admired the Tibetans – in all but
one particular, where for a moment his usual open-mindedness fails
and he cannot forebear lapsing into classic Victorian prudishness.
Having discussed the prevailing instituition of *polyandry*, he writes:

> The result of domestic life as described above is that a most
> unsatisfactory state of things exists in the society of this part of Tibet,
> which leads to very general impropriety between the sexes, and which
> forms a curse to a nation boasting so many qualities of endurance and
> manliness which cannot but otherwise call forth our admiration.
>
> *(Ibid.)*

For part of his journey Sherring was accompanied by the
distinguished mountaineer, Dr. Tom Longstaff, who was planning

an assault on the hitherto unscaled peak of Gurla Mandhata, and who had brought along with him two professional Alpine guides, the Brocherels, for the purpose. Although they reached heights of 23,000 feet or more, the climbers were denied the summit due to their inadequate knowledge of the topography of the mountain. They also narrowly escaped death twice: firstly, on the mountain itself, when an avalanche swept them down for about three thousand feet; and secondly, having left the mountain and failing to meet up with Sherring's main party at the appointed place, they found themselves alone in inhospitable, *dacoit*-infested wastes without food, shelter, money or arms to defend themselves.

Sherring had meanwhile passed down from Taklakot, past Toyo where the tomb of Zorawar Singh lay, and so on up to the Gurla Pass (16,200 feet), where another stunning panorama greeted him:

> The view as one surveys this holy place, venerated alike by Buddhists and Hindus, is one of the most beautiful throughout the whole of this part of the country. The Mansarowar Lake, forty-five miles in circumference, on the right, and Rakas Tal, of equal size and more varied contour, on the left, make with their lovely dark blue a magnificent foreground to the range of the Kailas mountains at the back, while the holy Kailas peak, Tise of the Tibetans, the Heaven of the Hindus and Buddhists, fills the centre of the picture, full of majesty, a king of mountains, dominating the entire chain by 2000 feet. The colouring of the rocks and the hue of the water, softened by the green of thousands and thousands of acres of verdant pasture-land, form a setting to the landscape which is indescribably charming, and although one misses the foliage of the forests, the colours are so esquisite in their brilliancy that they clothe the austerity of the mountains with a mantel that veils all their harshness. As one reaches the heaps of stones (each traveller should cast a stone on the crest according to universal custom) and see the monuments [*Chörtens*] erected by pious hands which mark the top of the pass, and the view bursts upon the sight, prayers and ejaculations break forth on all sides from the weary travellers, giving place later to a feeling of absolute contentment that they have been blessed to see 'what kings and mighty men have desired to see and not seen'.
>
> (*Ibid.*)

Tom Longstaff and friends, much the worse for their ordeals, rejoined Sherring on the shores of Lake Manasarovar, having been lucky enough to meet up with Thakur Jai Chand, a Kunawari then acting as Trade Agent for the British in Gartok, who happened to be travelling the same route and gave them assistance.

Passing along the isthmus between the two lakes, Sherring was able to photograph the controversial channel connecting them. No

Gurla Mandhata (1985)

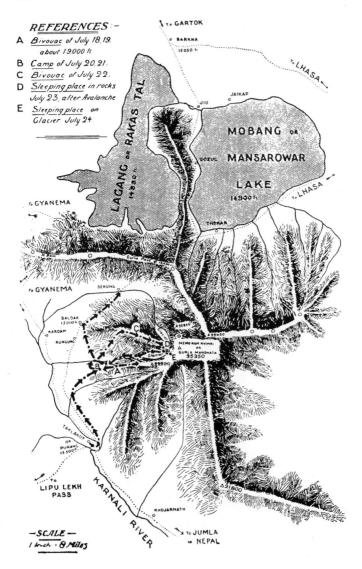

Sketch map illustrating Longstaff's assault on Gurla

Dr. Tom Longstaff

water was flowing through it at the time, however, because the mouth was blocked by a bank of sand. The last occasion when it had flowed had been during the exceptional rains that fell eleven years before; it was clearly remembered because it had been the year of the Khumb Mela Fair at Kailas.

Sherring found his next destination, Barkha, not at all easy to locate. He describes it as lying 'on an enormous plain, viz., the plateau of 15,000 ft., which extends for many miles, and until one actually reaches it is very difficult to see, being concealed on the east by a bank. The approach is over hummocks of sand and juniper bushes, and it is impossible to travel fast.' The presiding official was absent from the staging-post at the time of Sherring's visit: he had been called to Gartok to stand trial for the murder of a servant of the Simbiling Gompa in Taklakot. His stand-in was also absent, so Sherring had to be content to be entertained by a minor functionary called a *goba*. Afterwards, he journeyed on to Darchen, the starting-point for the Kailas Parikrama. The journey was across a 'wilderness of bog, morass and sand hummocks'.

Despite being deeply fascinated by all the lore and mythology surrounding the sacred mountain, Sherring does not seem to have been tempted to circumambulate it himself. He was particularly amused by the fact that proxies were allowed to go round on behalf of indolent or indisposed devotees, thinking this good evidence that 'the element of humour is rarely wanting in Tibet'.

After Darchen, Sherring proceeded to Gartok to discharge his official duties, which having been duly accomplished he was free to return to India *via* a more westerly route than that by which he had entered Tibet. He crossed the high Balchh, Kungri Bingri and Unta Dhura passes to Milam and thence returned to base. Once more upon home ground, with its forests and hamlets and fertile valleys, he writes:

> ... we could not but help comparing this homely sight with what we had just left behind on the other side of the great barrier of the Himalayas, where desolation is boldly written across a treeless landscape, where, with few exceptions, cultivation is unknown, and a nomad population living in tents is so scattered over the barren wilderness that the traveller can travel for days and see no human being, while the absence of houses makes desolation more desolate; and we felt that, however pleasant our trip, the return home was good.
>
> *(Ibid.)*

Sherring eventually returned to roost in England in 1914. In later life he was a magistrate for Surrey and a director of the newspaper wholesaling house of Wm. Dawson and Son. He died of a heart attack in East Sheen, in 1940, at the onset of German bombing. His work in India was carried on by his successors at Almora, of course, and indeed their records show that the British took their new political and trading connections with Western Tibet most seriously. Showers of bureaucratic communiqués transmigrated across the Great Himalaya detailing any and every event of significance, and several times in succeeding years important British officials again ventured over the high passes to make personal contact with the Tibetan authorities.

In July 1907, W. S. Cassels, Assistant Commissioner, Almora, went to Gyanima by way of Taklakot and the Southern shore of Rakshas Tal; and in July 1911 , N. C. Stiffe went to Gyanimia *via* Barkha, accompanied by Captain A. D. Stewart.

British political interest in Western Tibet had now advanced so far that Cassels in the official report of his visit of 1907 openly discussed the problems that would attend on administering the area, and came to the conclusion that these threatened to be so large that the British might account themselves lucky not to have to bear this particular white man's burden. He was also disconcerted to see indications of increasing Chinese interest in the affairs of Western Tibet, and duly noted that the Tibetans seemed favourably disposed to the influence of China. 'Perhaps the effects of the Russo-Japanese War', he concluded.

Trade-wise, on the other hand, the persistent rub was the interference of the Dzongpön of Taklakot in the Bhotia wool trade – the Bhotias were sponsored by Cawnpore Woollen Mills and large sums were involved – by imposing levies of his own. Neither Cassels nor Stiffe looked forward to much change in the situation while the *dzongpön* purchased his office and would naturally expect a good return on his investment: 'men would hardly exchange the luxury of Lhasa for the bleak exile of Western Tibet for nothing'. This aside, the British were also very eager to promote other forms of trade – and in both directions. Cassels was very taken up with the possibility of introducing Indian Berenag tea and Indian cigarettes into the Western Tibetan market. He saw the matter of roads as vital in trade and argued that investment should be made in their improvement with a view to thereby stimulating economic activity. Sherring's old belief that pilgrims would be the pioneers in matters of trade prompted him to the following fascinating comments, however:

Kunwar Kharag Singh tells me that at the present time about 150 faquirs visit Kailas in an ordinary year. When the Khumb Mela takes place every 12th year, the number of pilgrims from India rises to 400. At present the pilgrim traffic is very small. I myself met three faquirs in Tibet. One of them accompanied my camp from first to last. He bathed in Manasarovar and contemplated Kailas from a distance of 15 miles, has uttered the word 'Kailas' in an ecstatic way ever since, and will no doubt always claim to have visited Kailas. When I was in Gyanema I met a faquir from Delhi. Kailas is visible from Gyanema, and this faquir told me that the sight of it was good enough for him; he was not going there because it was too cold and the discomfort too great. I met a third faquir. He spoke excellent English and was a tahbildar in Jaipur state before he resolved to forsake the things of the world and become a sadhu. He went from Gangutri as far as Gyanema. He fell ill in Gyanema and returned thence to India without visiting Kailas or Manasarovar. He told me that the *pujari* in Kailas were ignorant; that there were no religious devotees in Kailas learned in Indian philosophy and religion; and that nothing was to be gained by a visit to the place. I conclude, therefore, that many of the faquirs who claim to have visited Kailas have gone no further than

Sven Hedin and his party

Taklakot or Gyanema. On paper the journey to Kailas appears easy. In practice it is difficult and attended by great discomfort. The pilgrim must take his own food with him; the climate is bleak; the wind is a blizzard; there is the fear of dacoits; the road is very bad, and the country eerie and almost uninhabited.

It will be many years before the pilgrim trade from India becomes considerable....

> (Report by W. S. Cassels, Assistant Commissioner,
> Almora, on a visit to Western Tibet in July 1907,
> India Office Library, L/P&S/7/207/No 1873)

Cassels could also claim fame as the first disc-jockey in Western Tibet. During his journey, he held little gramophone concerts and delighted the Tibetans with such period pieces as Harry Lauder's *Stop Your Tickling, Jock!* and Dan Leno's *Red Poppies.*

If anyone can be said to have played the part of a Richard Burton or a John Hanning Speke in the search for the sources of the great rivers of the Indian subcontinent, it must be Sven Hedin (1865-1952), the distinguished Swedish explorer. During the course of a long and highly successful career of Central Asian exploration, Hedin chalked up a number of claims to geographical 'firsts', including claims to have discovered the sources of both the Indus and Brahmaputra rivers. He was also the first Westerner to make the Parikrama or Circumambulation of Mount Kailas.

In 1901-2, Hedin had penetrated deep into the heart of Tibet, only to have been turned back by the authorities. A man of remorseless determination and will, he returned to India in 1905 with his heart set on exploring those areas of the Forbidden Land which appeared on the maps of the day as a great amorphous white patch bearing the summary legend 'Unexplored'. In Simla he was lionized by the luminaries of British India: Viceroy Minto, Kitchener, Younghusband - they were all behind his new Tibetan project to a man. The India Office in London was not so acquiescent, however, and refused to lend its sanction. In consequence, it looked for a while as though the whole enterprise was in jeopardy.

Hedin had managed to obtain a Chinese passport, however, and eventually the British authorities allowed him to proceed to Kashmir and Ladakh on the understanding that he would visit Turkistan. In Ladakh, he assembled a considerable caravan of some thirty porters and servants, one hundred and thirty animals, and bought provisions sufficient for a very long march. He had brought special equipment with him from Europe: the usual surveying and photographic gear, a collapsible boat made of oiled canvas, and a fabulous cornucopia of medical resources contained in a splendid case of burnished aluminium, supplied courtesy of Messrs Burroughs and Wellcome. When all was complete, the caravan moved off towards the high passes.

Of course, Hedin had no intention whatsoever of going to Chinese Turkistan. The directives of the bureaucrats meant little to him. He was a man whose thinking was cast in the old heroic mould; his obsession was to win fame and glory through explorational achievement; anything that did not work toward this end was trivial, not worthy of consideration. Once he was into the high country where the borders of Ladakh, Tibet and Turkistan blur into each other, therefore, he quite cynically pointed his caravan in the direction of his only real objective: Tibet.

Hedin's route took him across the awesomely barren Chang Tang; Capt. C. G. Rawling (1903) was one of the few Westerners who had ventured there before him. For over eighty days, Hedin saw no other human beings besides the men of his own party. Biting winds and withering sub-zero temperatures decimated his pack animals. Both caravan and supplies were seriously depleted by the time they at last encountered the first nomads, from whom they were able to buy replacement animals and a few spare supplies. Money was about the only thing that was not in short supply during the expedition. Hedin carried sacks containing thousands of rupees with him, a high proportion of them supplied by Nobel, the dynamite millionaire.

Outstanding adventures during the first leg of the route included two dramatic lake interludes: one at Lake Lighten, where Hedin sailed his collapsible boat and nearly came to grief in a terrible night storm; the other at Ngangtse Tso, which was frozen and in consequence explored by sledge. There were also perilous encounters with wolves and crazed yaks.

Despite all hardships and crises, Hedin pushed doggedly on. He seems a deeply lonely figure, more emotionally involved with his favourite animals than with the people with whom he travelled. An amusing incident with a favourite puppy or horse will warrant several sentences in his journal, and he is deeply moved when one dies. People do not command the same space or depth of sentiment. Thrust back on his own resources, partly by circumstances, partly by choice, he seems to have fortified himself spiritually by constantly meditating on notions of heroic achievement. The Swedish hero, Marcus Curtius, who ended his life in a glorious horseback leap into an awesome abyss, was frequently in his thoughts. To Hedin, geographical 'firsts' were quite simply the contemporary counterpart of the legendary feats of the heroes of old.

The whole time he travelled, Hedin was bedevilled by uncertainty as to how the Tibetan authorities would treat him when they eventually got wind of his presence in their land. Would he be simply turned back as in 1902? As encounters with Tibetans became more frequent, it did look as though this was what might happen. Then ironically at Ngangtse Tso, Hlaje Tsering, the self-same provincial governor who had done the honours in 1902, turned up in person to repeat the old routine. As luck would have it, however, no less a person than the brother of the Panchen Lama turned up at precisely the same time, carrying Hedin's mail from Shigatse. Seeing that the old interloper had friends in high places, Hlaje Tsering allowed Hedin to proceed to Shigatse to have his fate determined there.

To get into the Tsangpo Valley, where lay the principal routes to Shigatse, Hedin had first to cross the great mountain system which he subsequently named the *Transhimalaya*. On those sequestered heights, his spirits soared, for he realized that he was on one of the great watersheds of the world and could in fact lay claim to a highly significant 'first':

> It was delightful this evening to sit at length in the warmth of the camp fire. In silent meditation my eyes swept from the rocky crests, brightly lighted by the moon, down to the dark shadowy depths of the valley, where there were only wolves crouching in their holes. It seemed as though all belonged to me; as though I had marched into this land a conqueror at the head of victorious legions, and had crushed all opposition. Oh, what splendid legions! Five-and-twenty ragged fellows from Ladakh, ten lean jades, and about twenty worn-out yaks. And yet I had succeeded! Marcus could not have been prouder of the triumphs he achieved in the war against Jurgurtha than I was when I had won my victory over the 'Trans-Himalaya' at Sela-la, that Sela-la which, now bathed in moonlight, seemed to us the extreme outpost on the limits of boundless space.
>
> (Sven Hedin, *Transhimalaya*)

Hedin arrived at Shigatse at a timely moment. Thousands of pilgrims had arrived from all parts of Tibet and from adjacent Buddhist countries to witness the new year celebrations at Tashilhunpo, the Panchen Lama's theopolis. Hedin witnessed the celebrations, and also met the Panchen Lama. The young prelate's palpable spirituality impressed the Swede as strongly as it had impressed the British group led by Rawling. Hedin also took the opportunity of visiting and sketching – he was an accomplished

Tashilhunpo, from a drawing by Sven Hedin

draughtsman and watercolourist – the temples, mausolea and inhabitants of Tashilhunpo, and he studied Tibetan Buddhism closely, sometimes with a sympathy that suggests that he may himself have had leanings towards the spiritual life, at other times with rather less sympathy and indeed a certain admixture of Christian prejudice against 'false faiths.'

All the time Hedin was at Shigatse the usual battle of wills was going on. On the one hand, there was the Swedish explorer doggedly set on doing what he had a mind to do. On the other hand, there were the Tibetan authorities, equally determined to uphold their own policies and have the foreigner obey them. The Tibetans wanted to send Hedin back the way he had come – this was their usual course with foreigners who succeeded in illegally entering their country. The whole notion was anathema to Hedin, however, because it would be to retrace old ground and thus give him no opportunity for new geographical discoveries. An alternative possibility was that the Tibetans, in order to achieve a quick riddance, might insist that he leave the country by the most immediate route: that is, the direct southerly one back to India *via* Gyantse, Sikkim and Darjeeling. This would also take him through much-travelled and therefore geographically uninteresting territory. What Hedin wanted was a chance to get into some more of those blank spaces on the map, and he was prepared to use any trick, tactic or ploy to swing things his own way. He would stall, bluster, threaten, bargain, lay red herrings.... Where discoveries were concerned, he was utterly without morals.

Eventually a compromise was agreed – and it says a great deal for the stature of the man that even in the heart of alien territory he could yet contrive to get a large measure of his own way. He *should* return to Ladakh, but by a route rather to the south of his outward one: a route that would in fact take him up the Tsangpo Valley to Gartok – broadly the same route taken by Rawling's party. At every stage, however, Hedin conspired to dodge the restraints of the officials who were meant to control him and strayed off his ordained route into unfrequented byways where he could make fresh explorations.

In mid-July 1907, Hedin located what he claimed to be the true source of the Tsangpo/Brahmaputra on the main glacier of the Kubi-gangri Mountains, at a height of 15,958 feet. A few days later:

> ...we rode over the Tage-tsangpo, where its valley opens into the flat basin of Manasarovar – a new chapter in the chronicles of our journey. Again, Gurla Mandhata showed itself in all its glory, and in the northwest Kang-rinpoche or Kailas, the holy mountain, like a great *chörten* on a lama's grave, rose above the jagged ridge which forms the horizon in that direction. On seeing, it, all our men suddenly jumped out of their saddles and threw themselves on the ground. Only Rabsang, a confirmed heathen, remained seated on his horse, and was afterwards well scolded by Tsering.
>
> (*Ibid.*)

Hedin was to top the Drummond sacrilege of 1855/60. Not only did he sail his collapsible boat on Lake Manasarovar, but he also sailed on the neighbouring Rakshas Tal as well, though there were no subsequent reports of decapitations. When he initially proposed his Manasarovar venture to his guides, Hedin was told the whole thing would be quite impossible. As the lake was the home of the gods, they told him, any mortal who ventured upon it must surely perish. Moreover there was a practical problem deriving from the fact that the lake was said not to be flat at all but formed like a transparent dome. If anyone succeeded in sailing a boat up one side of it, they would only come to grief when their craft came shooting down the other side!

Nevertheless, the days on the lake were idyllic. Hedin tacked to and fro on the turquoise waters with the great crystal dome of Kailas looming up to the north, complemented by that of Gurla

Mandhata in the south. He did not neglect his scientific duties, of course, but took innumerable soundings and generally made close study of the lake before going to Rakshas Tal to do likewise.

Naturally Hedin also visited the channel connecting the two lakes. He found it dry, though it was reported that water had flowed through it four years earlier. He went on to the old dry bed of the Sutlej discovered by Henry Strachey in 1846, and, though he found no water there either, was convinced that there was subterranean filtration between the western lake and the main stream of the river. If this were the case, the source of the Sutlej could then be traced back to Rakshas Tal and, further still, *via* the connecting channel, back to Manasarovar, and finally to streams flowing into that lake from the highlands to the east. This theory in fact upheld local tradition and also a thesis advanced in Chi Chao Nan's *Hydrography*, an eighteenth century Chinese work, which maintained that the upper headwater of the Sutlej was the Tage-tsangpo, a stream arising from the Ganglung Glacier, which lay not many miles north-west of the source of the Tsangpo/Brahmaputra. Hedin insists that this assertion would be good even though many of the channels were dry for most of the time, and he dismisses as 'prognostication' the notion that the hydrography of the area might have changed permanently and that water would never flow through these old channels again.

During his sojourn at the sacred lakes, Hedin repeatedly observed, admired and sketched Kailas:

> The sun sets and we sit still and wait, confused by the rush of the spirits of the air and water. This time they have played a pretty trick, and we have been caught. To the north rises Kang-rinpoche, lofty and bright as a royal crown. Its summit is like a *chörten* on the grave of a Grand Lama. Snow and ice with vertical and slightly inclined fissures and ledges form a network like the white web of a gigantic spider on the black cliffs.
>
> (*Ibid.*)

It was, however, seen to be best advantage from a distance:

> The nearer we came to the holy mountain, the less imposing it appeared; it was finest from Langak-tso [Rakshas Tal]. In form it resembles a tetrahedron set on a prism. From the middle of its white top a belt of ice falls precipitously down, and below it stands a stalagmite of ice, into which a thick stream of water pours from above. The stream splits into glittering drops of spray and thin sheets of water – a grand spectacle, which one could watch with pleasure for hours.
>
> (*Ibid.*)

Hedin seems to have had no doubt that this was truly a *holy* mountain - the most famous in the whole world. This being the case, he was prepared to join with the other pilgrims - Buddhists, Hindus, Bön-po - who were engaged in making the Kailas Parikrama. On 3rd September 1907, laden with only minimal supplies and accompanied by a single servant, a Buddhist named Rabsang, Hedin gave the slip to the 'Gova of Barkha' who was keeping him under surveillance, and rode north from his camp at Khaleb, a few miles due west of Darchen, to the mouth of the Dunlung valley. Three other servants had already gone on ahead - Tsering, Namgyal and Ishe. Hedin rejoined them at the first moraines and the whole party proceeded in close column across the undulating, debris-strewn ground. To the east they could see a party of pilgrims from Kham resting on the banks of the Dunlung river, their horses grazing on the fresh grass, their tents nearby.

Riding on up the valley, they soon found themselves hemmed in by solid walls of hard green and violet conglomerate rock, at the foot of which lay cones of scree debris. The main pilgrim road lay on the left bank of the river, where there were also several rows of *manis* and *chörtens* and a small cubical house. As the party went on, the cliffs assumed 'ever wilder forms, falling perpendicularly to terraces and pebble screes, forming steps and ledges, fortifications, battlements and towers, as though built by human hands'. They were composed of sandstone conglomerate and appeared horizontal to the naked eye, though in fact there was a 10° dip to the south.

They passed another pilgrim group, which was crossing a small bridge that spanned the river. Hedin's party held to the right bank, however. On the sheer rock face above them was a ledge where a hermit lived and nearby a terrace where the first *gompa* (monastery) of Kailas was situated: Nyenri Gompa. The perilousness of the *gompa's* situation had been demonstrated some five years before when a huge boulder had fallen and shattered half the building. Dominating the cliff was a prayer-flag called *Nyandi-kong*.

Hedin was well received at the *gompa*, which, like Darchen and Zutrul Puk, fell within the aegis of the Maharaja of Bhutan. He was told that pilgrims flocked to Kailas in especially great numbers every twelve years. That year, 1907, five thousand had already called at the *gompa*, most of them being from Ladakh. Among the treasures of Nyenri were a huge copper vessel, said to have flown from India long ago, and a fine pair of elephant's tusks set up before the altar. Hedin found the view from the roof magnificent.

After three hours, Hedin's party left Nyenri and descended a steep, zig-zagging path running through boulders and scree. 'At

The West Face of Kailas and Guru Rinpoche's Torma (1987)

Kailas Kora: the Western Valley (1985)

every turn I could stand still in astonishment,' he writes, 'for this valley is one of the grandest and most beautiful wildernesses I have ever seen.' The right-hand precipice was divided into two stages, separated by a gaping ravine; the left hand precipice was a single vertical wall of rock carved into forms of rococo intricacy. Melted ice-water cascaded from the heights above, dousing the rock walls as it fell and turning to spray when whipped up by the wind.

Hedin noticed that the members of the next two pilgrim groups he encountered were not socializing with each other at all but grimly murmuring the sacred *mantra, Om mani padme hum,* as they hurried on their way. One pilgrim from Ghertse was said to be on his tenth circuit. There were numerous cairns about the place at this point; apparently it was customary to add a stone to them in passing. The icy peak of Kailas, meanwhile, had vanished from view but became visible again a little later through a gap in the ubiquitous rock walls. The sun also broke occasionally through such gaps to dispel with bright yellow light the shadow trapped in the tight, enclosed places.

At Dunlung-do three valleys converged: the Chamo-lung-chen, the Dunlung and the Hle-lungpa. Hedin's party ascended the last. They now found that granite was the prevailing rock; and the summit of Kailas, turning a sharp edge to the north, appeared more like a tetrahedron than ever.

Drira Puk was the next *gompa*; it stood on a slope to the right of the valley. The sacred *mantra* was carved on a huge block of granite that stood beside the path that led up to it. There were also long *manis*, streamers and cairns. The *gompa* itself was full to capacity because all the pilgrim parties encountered during the day had stopped there for the night. Accommodation was free and extended even to members of the Bön religion. Hedin pitched his tent on the roof amid the pilgrims' luggage, and was able to enjoy a fine view of the dramatic north face of the sacred mountain. The temperature was decidedly cool, however, and an uncomfortable wind was blowing.

When he discovered from the monks at Drira Puk that the source of the Indus – the river that according to mythology issues from the mouth of the lion – lay just three days' march to the north, he was sorely tempted to abandon his *parikrama* and repair there immediately. After holding a council of war, however, it was decided that it was not an opportune time to make the trip: money was in short supply and, anyway, things were too uncertain back at Khaleb for any more risks to be taken for the moment.

Accordingly next morning, 4th September, Hedin's party took their leave of the monks of Drira Puk, crossed the river again and began the ascent of a rough, boulder-strewn slope. This became progressively more steep as they proceeded eastwards until they reached the brow of the first ridge, after which the ground levelled out for a while. Here they enjoyed a splendid view of a short, truncated glacier that was fed from a sharply-defined, trough-shaped firn basin lying on the north side of Kailas. From the sacred mountain itself, a sharp, jagged ridge ran off to the east. It had a furrowed appearance due to alternating belts of snow and stone. From all parts of the ice-mantle and snow fields, streams cascaded down to the river that flowed to their right. To their left, north-wards, the mountains consisted of vertical, fissured granite sculpted into 'wild pyramidal forms'. The summit of Kailas rose above this 'sea of wild mountains' like a 'mighty crystal of hexagonal form'.

A party of impoverished women and children were toiling wearily up towards the next pass, at the summit of which Hedin met an old pilgrim who had already completed nine of the thirteen circuits he intended to make. With this kind of experience to his credit, he clearly knew his way around the sacred mountain, so Hedin sensibly secured his services as guide. At Tutu-dapso they encountered literally hundreds of votive cairns.

The ascent to the next pass was the most arduous of the whole *parikrama* so far. The path was cluttered with a proliferation of granite boulders which ranged in colour from pink to light-grey and off-white. Between two such boulders a pathethic heap of rags was found. This turned out on closer examination to be the clothing of an emaciated pilgrim who had collapsed. A little later they encountered Dikpa Karnak: the famed test-stone for sinners. If a person could scramble through the narrow passage beneath the rock here, then he showed himself innocent of sin. A sinner, on the other hand, be he ever so lean, would surely get stuck. The servant Ishe attempted the test and was promptly exposed as a sinner. His companions left him to kick and struggle for a while by way of penance before releasing him. A little later Ishe was able to redeem himself by triumphantly passing at the next test-stone: a double passage formed by three huge stone blocks, where the candidate had to creep through by the left and return by the right. His master was not very impressed by this achievement, however, as he estimated that the passages were wide enough to accommodate small yaks and thus did not constitute a particularly rigorous test of virtue.

The enthusiasm which the *parikrama* clearly inspired in Hedin caused him to write at this point:

> Our wanderings round Kang-rinpoche, the 'holy ice mountain' or the 'ice jewel' is one of my most memorable recollections in Tibet, and I quite understand how the Tibetans can regard as a divine sanctuary this wonderful mountain which has so striking resemblance to a *chörten*, the monument which is erected in memory of a deceased saint within or without the temples. How often during our roaming have I heard of this mountain of salvation! And now I myself walked in pilgrim garb around the path between the monasteries, which are set, like precious stones in a bangle, in the track of pilgrims round Kang-rinpoche, the finger which points up to the mighty gods throned like stars in unfathomable space.

> From the highlands of Kham in the remotest east, from Naksang and Amdo, from the unknown Bongba, which we have heard of only in vague reports, from the black tents which stand like the spots of a leopard scattered among the drear valleys of Tibet, from Ladak in the mountains of the far west, from the Himalayan lands in the south, thousands of pilgrims come hither annually, to pace slowly and in deep meditation the 28 miles round the navel of the earth, the mountain of salvation.

> (*Ibid.*)

He goes on to imagine the innumerable winding roads and paths, starting in the remotest regions of Asia, and converging inexorably

THE KAILAS FROM N

THE KAILAS FROM S.W.

Views of Kailas by Sven Hedin

on Kailas. He compares them to the migratory flight-paths of wild geese: that they exist is known, but not their precise courses, or how they would look on a map.

The *parikrama* path now snaked downhill between boulders to the Dung-shapje: a basin of rock with a stone the shape of a yak's cloven hoof lying in it. The established practice here was to strike the hoof-shaped stone against the wall of the basin, and then run it around the inside like a pestle, thus helping deepen it. Beyond, a stream flanked either side of the path that ascended to the next ridge. There were cairns on every rock flat enough to serve as a base for one.

Straight ahead now lay the Drölma La (pass), which gave access to the eastern valley of Kailas. The Drölma La was the highest point on the *parikrama*, and was generally thought to mark its half-way stage. It was crowned by a huge boulder, the mass of which Hedin estimated to be anything up to ten thousand cubic feet. This was topped by a grim profusion of cairns, bones, horns and prayer flags.

The custom was for pilgrims to daub this rock with butter as they passed, and then stick some momento of themselves – a lock of hair, perhaps, or a tooth, or fragments of clothing – to the surface. In consequence, the great rock had something of the appearance of a bedraggled wig. It was permissible to take a relic from the rock as a talisman – Hedin's old guide had many such relics hanging around his neck.

Hedin sketched the scene from the pass, although the summit of Kailas was not completely in view at this point. As he was engaged in this work, a lama appeared who was doing the *parikrama* with a sick child slung in a basket around his neck. Later he was also to encounter those especially enthusiastic circumambulators who made their circuits by measuring the length of their bodies on the ground the whole way round. Hedin gave the lama alms to help him with his holy work; the lama then began chanting *mantras* and the last the Swede saw of him he was prostrating himself before the great rock with its matting of rancid butter and human remains.

Hedin next seems to have left the usual *parikrama* route and cut across country in a south-westerly direction to join the route that came directly northwards from a place he calls 'Draxhan',* up the valley of the Serlung-Chu to the southern foot of Kailas. He visited the small, circular lake of Tso Kavala, which he was told was permanently frozen. He could not linger there as time was pressing so he and his party went slipping and sliding down into the Serlung valley. Through the large valley which entered on the right, called Khandro Sanglam ('The Secret Path of the Dakinis'), he could again see the summit of Kailas – 'which has a sharp edge towards the north-east, and again looks like a crystal'. Here also two *manis* marked the place where the prevailing granite gave way once more to conglomerate; thereafter the way was choked with boulders of conglomerate.

Hedin now cut back to the main *parikrama* route to bivouac for the night on the roof of the Zutrul Puk Gompa. He had heard *Om mani padme hum* chanted so much that day that the rhythms of the sacred *mantra* went on echoing round and round in his brain as long as he remained awake.

As Zutrul Puk Gompa did not contain anything of particular interest, it did not detain Hedin long the next morning. His party was therefore soon riding down the gradually widening valley, past more *chörtens* and *manis*, until, at the boulder-choked entrance, they caught their first glimpse of Rakshas Tal and the Gurla group since

---

*Darchen?

Pilgrim doing the Kailas Kora by the prostration method (1988)

setting off on their circumambulation. They duly ended their
parikrama at Darchen, where they left the pilgrim road to cut back to
Khaleb, catching sight on the way of the fourth monastery of
Kailas – probably Gyangtra Gompa – which was perched high upon
a terrace in the valley immediately below the sacred peak.

On his return to Khaleb, Hedin told the Gova of Barkha – 'who
had the hopeless and thankless task of watching my proceedings' –
that he intended to visit the source of the Indus. The Gova retorted
that he could in no way countenance this, but, after a great deal of
haggling, a skilful solution to the dilemma was devised. If Hedin
would like to divide his caravan into two parts, the main portion
could proceed in a proper manner to Gartok along the high road.
Hedin, meanwhile, could go off with the remainder for a brief
excursion to the north – provided he understood that he was doing
so entirely at his own risk.

Needless to say, this suited Hedin perfectly, and on 8th
September, accompanied by only five companions, he again set off

up the western valley of Kailas for Drira Puk. From there he crossed the Transhimalaya by way of the Tseti pass and so on down to the source of the Indus at Singhi Khambab. This was another exploration 'first' which, with the earlier one gained at the source of the Tsangpo/Brahmaputra, made a neat pair that gave Hedin no inconsiderable satisfaction.

Hedin subsequently met up with his main party at Gartok as arranged and thereafter, for the moment becoming uncharacteristically compliant, proceeded in a more or less straightforward way back to Ladakh.

This was all a cunning pose, however. The lure of those beguiling blank spaces on the map had not yet loosened their grip on Hedin's imagination. On reaching Ladakh, he threw up an elaborate smokescreen of false reports and rumours to mislead *all* parties while at the same time covertly re-equipping himself and establishing a new caravan. He then turned east into Tibet once more to make a second and far more secret transit of the blank area, adopting a route rather to the south of his earlier ones. He himself travelled in disguise, acting the part of a servant whenever Tibetans were encountered. However, all this subterfuge put a terrible strain upon him, and to make things worse Hedin had not seen another Westerner for two years; so when the inevitable discovery came it was rather a relief. Nevertheless, even then the Tibetans were to find Hedin still dogged and slippery, and he made several more crossings of his beloved Transhimalaya before they were eventually able to get shot of him.

Hedin's final exit route took him to the south. A year after his initial visit, he was back in the Kailas-Manasarovar region *en route* for Simla, *via* the Upper Sutlej Valley and the Shipki La. In India, Minto, Kitchener and other of Hedin's auspicious Raj friends turned out to welcome the conquering hero in fitting style. Yet the man who had braved the worst hazards of the great plateau not once but twice still suffered the pangs of stagefright as he went before a glittering social gathering to lecture upon his travels. This was no real cause for shame. He had, after all, proved himself thoroughly worthy of his idol, Marcus Curtius.

After days of rest and recuperation whiled away amid the civilized amenities of Simla, first as the guest of the Viceroy and Lady Minto, then of Lord Kitchener, Hedin returned to Europe fully expecting to receive the acclaim his great achievements merited. Sadly for the old lion of Central Asian exploration, the final act was not to be all laurels and honourable tranquillity. That very high-handedness and remorseless drive for personal achievement that had taken him thrice into Tibet against all the odds had also alienated many, including influential people at the Royal Geographical Society in London. A number were out to dispute his claims to geographical 'firsts', notably that young upstart, Tom Longstaff, who instead was advancing the claims of Edmund Smyth and his sporting comrades to have been the first Europeans at the source of the Brahmaputra and those of the Pundit, Nain Singh, to have discovered the Transhimalaya. Longstaff, among others, didn't like the name that Hedin had given the range either, and he was moreover in favour of Henry Strachey's location of the main source of the Sutlej at the head of the Darma Yankti. He would only concede to Hedin that he might claim 'the distinction of being the first traveller to reach the ultimate source of the Indus.' Despite diplomatic attempts to smooth the situation, the public debate* grew heated and ugly and eventually the Swedish explorer, his massive ego badly mauled, withdrew to the Continent in high dudgeon. A subsequent knighthood conferred through the good offices of Lords Curzon and Morley failed to salve his resentments and he turned to Germany for that appreciation that the perfidious British had denied him. Open support of Kaiser Wilhelm in the First World War and of Adolf Hitler in the Second lost him respect not only in this country but in his own as well, and it was a sad and largely forgotten man rather than a revered conqueror who passed away in Stockholm in 1952.

---

*For a full account, see Charles Allen, *A Mountain in Tibet*, London 1982, final chapter.

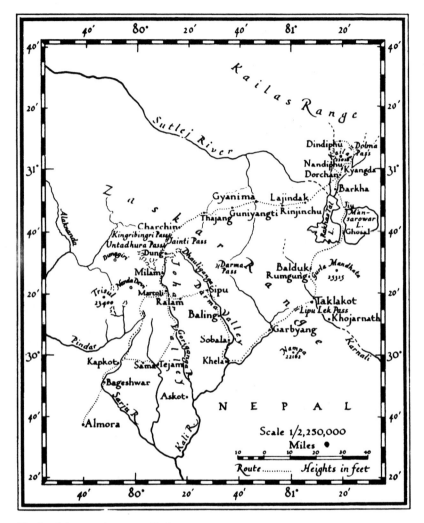

The Ruttledge party's route to Kailas

CHAPTER SIX
Travellers in the Sacred Region:
1926–1932

By the 1920s, Mount Kailas was under threat. European travellers had already committed the sacrilege of sailing on the sacred lakes, and, in 1905, Tom Longstaff had made a mountaineering assault on the summit of Gurla Mandhata. Clearly, it would not be long before mountaineers were setting their sights on the summit of the sacred mountain itself and, perhaps, if they were successful, trampling on the throne of the gods in their Alpine boots.

In July 1926, the gods might well have felt especially uneasy. Two distinguished mountaineers had arrived in Darchen. One was Colonel Commandant R. C. Wilson, D.S.O., M.C., of the Indian Army; the other, Hugh Ruttledge of the I.C.S., lately appointed Deputy Commissioner for Almora. Ruttledge had begun his mountaineering career in the Alps, while on leave in 1921. He would later go on to lead two notable, though unsuccessful, Everest expeditions: that of 1933, when a height of 28,000 feet was reached on the first assault, and that of 1936. He was primarily in Tibet on official business on this occasion, however: reports had been received from Bhotia traders complaining of infringements of their trading rights in Tibet and it had been considered advisable in official circles that these reports should be investigated.

At Barkha, Ruttledge discovered that the newly-appointed senior Garpön of Gartok, whom he was hoping to meet, was not expected to pass through *en route* for Lhasa for several days more, so he decided to put the spare time to advantage by making the Kailas Parikrama with his wife, who was accompanying him. Accordingly, on 21st July, they travelled north to Darchen with Colonel Wilson. Of Darchen Ruttledge writes:

*Colonel R.C. Wilson, Hugh Ruttledge, Mrs Ruttledge and their party after their
1926 Tour of Western Tibet*

The place was full of interesting types: nomads from the north, one of
them a smartly dressed youth armed with an old but well-kept Russian
Army rifle, and accompanied by an equally smart wife whose fur toque
was the admiration of us all; pilgrims from Kham on the Chinese
frontier; big hulking Nekarias; soi-disant traders, but obviously of
doubtful respectability; beggars of every description; and three devoted
Hindus from the Central and United Provinces, recently robbed, and
miserably cold and underfed, requiring assistance. One cheerful party of
Tibetans was busily engaged in performing the parikarma [*sic*] a distance
of 28 miles, once a day for twelve consecutive days, thereby acquiring
sufficient merit to last a lifetime. The altitude of Dorchan [*sic*] is about
15,200 feet.

(Hugh Ruttledge, 'Notes on a Visit to Western
Tibet', *Geographical Journal*, Vol. LXXI, May 1928)

At 7 a.m. on 22nd July, the main party set off westwards along the
pilgrim route. Colonel Wilson and his Sherpa, Satan [*sic*],
meanwhile struck up the nearest valley with the intention of
reconnoitring approaches to Mount Kailas. Wilson's account of his
experiences casts an interesting light on the topography of the
sacred mountain.

The mountain is best seen from a distance and has the appearance of a somewhat lopsided white bowler hat placed on a square plinth of considerable steepness. As one approaches [from the south] the summit is more and more concealed until one can only get an occasional glimpse of it between ridges running down from the snow cap. This cap ends abruptly at the plinth and forms little or no glacier.

It [Kailas] stands up prominently in a massif of its own, projecting S. from the Kailas Range of the Himalayas, to which it is joined by the Dolma pass ridge.

(Col. R. C. Wilson, 'Kailas Parbat and Two Passes in the Kumaon Himalaya', *Alpine Journal*, Vol. 40, 1928)

The following sketch map accompanies his account:

KAILAS

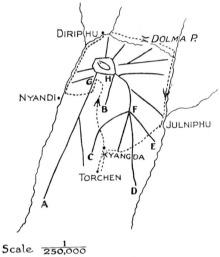

Scale $\frac{1}{250,000}$

Dotted lines indicate the writer's routes.

Having passed close to Gyangtra Gompa, Wilson and Satan emerged from the valley by a col to the north, and thence reached the foot of Point B without loss of altitude. They then kept on up the valley, maintaining the ridge HB on their right. This valley was deep and dark, and proved to be a cul-de-sac. When they reached the end, they found the perpendicular plinth towering before them 'black and forbidding'. On the right, at Point H, where the long ridge marked HF sprang from the plinth, there was a small glacier which reached the valley in the form of fragments of ice and snow.

On their left, leading up to the gendarme marked G, there was a shale slope as steep as anything Wilson had hitherto encountered in his mountaineering career. Meanwhile, straight ahead, at the foot of the plinth, there was a fan of snow which had fallen from the gulley that was so prominent a mark on the middle of the summit cap. To the right of this fan, between it and the debris of a tiny glacier, there was a small niche, partly natural, partly man-made, in which a row of clay votive tablets had been placed, probably, Wilson felt, by the lamas of Gyangtra Gompa. From this point, Wilson noted a very marked flattening of the south-east ridge of the snow-cap. There was also a flat continuation of that ridge, which could be gained by a short but steep climb at Point H.

'Sahib, we can climb that!' Satan exclaimed, as he too saw that this represented a feasible route to the summit.

Time, however, was against them. They had to look for a way down, though this was not easily found. The shale slope to their left proved impossibly unstable. Then, to make matters worse, snow began to fall as well. Finally, a brilliant flash of lightning and a shattering crash of thunder heralded the breaking of one of those violent storms for which Kailas is notorious. Clearly, the gods of the sacred mountain were showing their displeasure at this impertinent intrusion upon their sacrosanct domain. There was nothing to be done but to place their ice-axes at a safe distance and sit it out.

An hour and a half later, Wilson and Satan achieved the col between Gendarme G and the plinth. Above them, the mountain towered almost perpendicularly; below them lowered a pitch-black abyss of forbidding depth and steepness – 'quite the most awesome place I have ever looked into'. The sides were composed in part of slatey black shale, in part of snow. Descent by this way was not to be contemplated.

The south-west ridge offered the only viable alternative. They attained this by climbing up a steep shale slope from Point E only to find that the other side was perpendicular. Or almost so. Looking back, however, they could see a slight bend in the ridge about a mile away, which might indicate a more reasonable slope on the west side. A hole was poked in the snow overhang on their side and they forced their way up. Once through, they found that they had been correct in their supposition and now had a comparatively easy (though visually sensational) descent into the western valley ahead of them. That night, they met up with the Ruttledges at Drira Puk.

Wilson drew the following conclusions from his day's reconnaissance:

Should fate again take me to Torchen [*sic*] with a couple of days to spare, I should make for the ridge HF, moving either round the foot of D or via Kyangda [*sic*] and over ridge FD. I should expect to get on the ridge HF about point F and to have an easy passage to the foot of the final ascent. A reasonably comfortable camp could be made here and the carriers sent down again to the foot of F for the night.

Next day the carriers could return to H and remove camp to the foot of F, whilst the climbers went on to the top and back. As regards altitudes, Torchen is probably about 15,500 feet, point H about 20,000 and the summit is 22,028.

The photograph shows the final slope to be reasonable, though the snow might be found powdery and treacherous.

Should the route suggested above prove impracticable, an alternative line to point H would be to leave C and the ridge HB on one's right and to trust to finding a way up on to H from near the foot of the mountain where the small glacier falls into the valley and the niche with the images has been made.

In this event one would have to be content with a light camp, as the climb to H might prove too much for laden carriers.

Finally, there remains a third possible route: to get on up the long N. ridge somewhere near the Dolma Pass [*sic*].

(Wilson, *Ibid.*)

Meanwhile, the Ruttledges had passed up the western valley of Kailas and called in at Nyenri Gompa before going on to Drira Puk, where they arrived in the evening and met up with Wilson and Satan. At Drira Puk, they admired the imposing view of the north face of Kailas, which Ruttledge estimated to be a sheer precipice of 6,000 feet, 'utterly unclimbable'. Near the summit there was some snow and ice, but the rest of the face was composed of limestone slabs of brown and chocolate colour that were entirely unbroken and far too steep to hold snow.

Next day they went on to the Drölma La, passed the great boulder with its bunting of human and other relics, and proceeded to the Gauri Kund lake, the surface ice of which had melted a little in the heat of the sun, enabling pilgrims to perform token ceremonial ablutions.

From this point Ruttledge contemplated the north-east ridge and, impressed by its mountaineering possibilities, was tempted to try an ascent, but was unable to do so due to lack of time. The north-east ridge rose steeply for about a thousand feet and then carried on at an easy angle for about two miles until it articulated with the

Kailas: the North Face (1985)

Drölma La (1926)

north-east arête leading sharply to the summit.

A steep descent down execrable boulders led the party into the beautiful green eastern valley, which was watered by a river and stood in sharp contrast to the savage grandeur of its western counterpart. Although the summit of Kailas was then obscured by cloud, Ruttledge was of the opinion that angles on the eastern side were less severe than those elsewhere and might offer other viable lines of approach for future mountaineers. The permanent snow-line seemed to be mainly around the 19,000 foot mark.

Having spent the next night at Zutrul Puk, the party left the usual pilgrim route and cut across country, hoping to see more of the sacred mountain from the south. Cloud obscured their view, however. They visited Gyangtra Gompa, where the head lama seemed none too pleased by their visit, though he did consent to show then around. One of the things they saw was a suit of chain armour said to be a relic of Zorawar Singh's army.

On their return to Darchen, Ruttledge's party found that the Garpön had already arrived and himself set off on a *parikrama*, so they had to sit tight and await his return. The interview with him, when eventually it did take place, was both interesting and pleasant, for he was the scion of a good Lhasa family and possessed both quick perceptions and charming manners. Afterwards, Ruttledge and him companions journeyed to the market centre at Gyanima by way of Lejandak, where the Sutlej properly begins to flow as a continuous stream. Ruttledge was of the opinion that Rakshas Tal must be the true source of the river as there was a long chain of pools stretching between the two. At Gyanima, they met both the British Trade Agent and the Tibetan Government Trader, the *Shung tsong*, who proved to be a 'most amusing and sagacious person fully alive to the iniquities of his traffic'. After three days of official business, they set off for the Kungri Bingri, Jayanti and Unta Dhura passes, and thence returned to base at Almora – 'after some 600 miles of enjoyable trekking, performed entirely on foot to the scandal of right-thinking Indians and Tibetans'.

For Mrs. Ruttledge this was an outstanding achievement. She was, so far as research has revealed, the first Western woman to visit the sacred mountain and perform the 32-mile Parikrama.

The next British official visitor to Kailas was in time to rise to the heights in public life. In fact, when Sir Edward Wakefield died in Ireland in 1969, the obituary columns were stretched to accommodate all his achievements. He had for a start been the first High Commissioner to Malta. He had also served as Tory MP for West Derbyshire (1950–1962), and been a government whip. Earlier, between 1927 and 1947, he had served firstly in the Indian Civil Service and later in the Political Department.

Teddy Wakefield was born in 1903, very distantly related to that enlightened colonialist, Edward Gibbon Wakefield. He was educated at Haileybury, a public school that specialized in turning out servants of the Indian Empire, from where he went up to Trinity, Cambridge to take a First in the Classical Tripos. His past-times included *shikar*, and he was schooled in mountaineering by the notable climber, Geoffrey Winthrop Young.

It was in 1929 that Wakefield had the good fortune to be elected to the select club of Kailas travellers. That year he was deputed, among other things, to inspect the Trade Agency in Gartok and to 'report on the suitability of the present trade marts'. He set off from Simla on June 4th. His party included a bearer, a cook and a Gurkha escort of one Havildar and four riflemen. The Gartok Agency Doctor, Kanshi Ram, with more servants, Gurkhas and mules, had left a fortnight earlier; they waited for Wakefield to catch them up at Sarahan.

When he got to Sarahan, Wakefield was hospitably received by the Rajah of Bashahr; he and his party then proceeded to Pooh.

E.B. Wakefield and Gurkha Escort

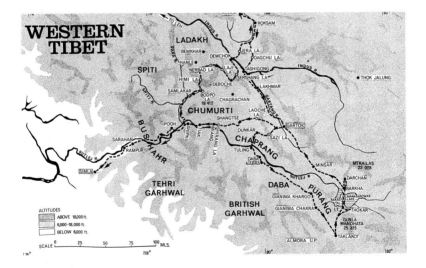

Map of E.B. Wakefield's 1929 Tour of Western Tibet

Electing now to apply a 'liberal interpretation' to his instructions, he sent the Agency Staff and baggage on directly to Gartok across the Shipki Pass, while he himself led a compact party along the Spiti Khad route into the Tibetan province of Chumurti, where he was detailed to speak to the 'Pon' about dealing more firmly with local *dacoits*. Hearing *en route* that the 'Pon' was away on pilgrimage, however, he decided to bypass the capital, Chagrachan, and to follow 'the route normally taken by traders travelling to Demchok', which went *via* Deboche. He was later to discover to his chagrin that 'there was no Deboche-Demchok route'. By then his party had dragged itself through a tangle of trackless mountain wastes and across high passes at a cost of much suffering and one dead Gurkha, who had succumbed to mountain sickness.

Eventually, Wakefield found his way down into the Indus Valley. He forded the great river and, after several long but not easy marches, came in sight of Rudok itself on July 17th. Next morning, in the brilliant light of the new day, 'this rugged eminence of rock, crowned by the Jongpen's palace, white and brown against a background of blue sky, seemed yet more beautiful and impressive and worthy of sanctity ... than Lhasa ...'

A messenger now rode out from Rudok, bringing a note. Scanning it, Wakefield was astonished to find it penned in immaculate English copperplate handwriting:

Dear Dr. Wakefield, [it ran]

I am glad too hear you've arrived. Please let me know at what time I may come to see you.

Yours sincerely,

K. K. Möndo

Möndo, an ordained monk, was the local *dzongpön*. He also boasted another distinction, then most rare in Western Tibet: he had received an English public school education at Rugby. In 1913, four Tibetan boys had been sent to England by order of the XIIIth Dalai Lama, who at the time was endeavouring, much to the disgust of the powerful conservative factions in the great monasteries of the Lhasa district, to introduce a modest measure of modernity into Tibetan life as insurance against the erosion of his country's precarious independence.

After Rugby, Möndo trained at a mining college and later put his skills to use when he began prospecting for gold to the north of Lhasa. Unfortunately, the local lamas feared his excavations would

E.B. Wakefield

upset the presiding earth spirits and he was forced to desist. He then hoped to be allowed to retire to a monastery but was obliged to become a monk-policeman in Lhasa instead. For some obscure crime he was later disgraced, degraded and exiled to the desolate wastes of Western Tibet: tough punishment indeed for a Lhasa sophisticate with a pukka education. His misfortunes may have had something to do with the fact that he brought a motorcycle back from England and was wont to roar through the streets of the holy city, belching exhaust and, on one occasion, causing a high dignitary to be pitched from his mule.

Wakefield found Möndo, who was then about 30, quite charming. He showed his guest over the *dzong* and entertained him to dinner – like all Lhasa gentry, Möndo favoured Chinese food, which he obtained from Lhasa – 'with a grace and courtesy which were unexceptionable.' His English was a bit rusty, but 'it was perfect English when it did arrive'. They reminisced nostalgically about English public school life: cloistered quadrangles and perfectly mown lawns and playing fields – about the natural inverse of the conditions that surrounded them up there on the Roof of the World.

Surprisingly, for all his social graces and though apparently well-liked by British (i.e. Indian) traders, among his own Tibetan subjects Möndo 'was regarded as the most oppressive of a succession of tyrannical Jongpens... No method by which money can be extracted from empoverished subjects has not been put into practice,' Wakefield wrote. However, there was one despotic abuse of power in which Möndo did not indulge. Having himself been whacked at Rugby for failing to do his prep, he refrained from meteing out corporal punishment, though fully empowered to do so.

Wakefield left Rudok on July 21st, Möndo having parted from him with fulsome protestations of eternal friendship. Moving south-east, the British party then forded the Indus opposite Tashigong, and from there travelled to Lakmar, where they visited some borax mines, and so on to Gartok.

Wakefield, like many of his predecessors, was neither impressed with Gartok nor with its Garpöns. The place itself was bleak and the Senior Garpön was a liar who had made such a principle of falsehood that he only deviated from it on those rare occasions when the truth might serve his purposes better.

From Gartok, Wakefield went on to Daba *via* Thöling in the Upper Sutlej Valley. He crossed the Sazi Pass on the way, and climbed the adjacent Sazi Peak with Raghu Das, the interpreter that he had hired at Sarahan on the recommendation of the Rajah of Bashahr. Raghu Das went down so badly with snow-blindness afterwards, however, that he 'had to be held by several men from attempting to knock his brains out against the rocks.' A cocaine solution administered by Dr Kanshi Ram brought him some relief.

There being no traders at Daba, Wakefield went on to visit the trade marts at Nabra, Shibchilam, Gyanima Khargo and Gyanima Chakra, and Taklakot. His account of those visits throws up interesting facts about trading affairs between Western Tibet and British India, particularly relating to the wool trade, which as we have noted elsewhere was an old and important commercial connection. At Nabra, for instance, a lonely grazing ground near Daba used by Niti traders, he had to adjudicate on a point arising out of the 'Arat or Mitr system of trade'. By this system, an Indian party would make 'Gambiya Satta' with a Tibetan party, whereby the latter would pledge to trade only with the Indian party and his family for generations to come. The agreement would be solemnly sealed by drinking a draught of *chang* (Tibetan barley beer) in which a little gold dust had been mixed. At Gyanima Chakra, on the other hand, 'the mart of the Darma traders', he spent four days settling disputes. 'The Darma men are a dissolute set of drunkards, but endowed with unexpected tenacity of purpose; and they prosecute with vigour, when sober, the quarrels they have started in their cups.' Finally, Wakefield's judicial work at Taklakot, the biggest of

Chiu Gompa, Lake Manasarovar (1987)

the marts, took a full six days to settle because of 'the reluctance which traders and Tibetans alike displayed to telling the truth.'

Now Wakefield turned north, intending to visit Lake Manasarovar and the trade marts at Trügo, Barkha and Darchen. All of his party bathed in the 'cold but holy waters of Lake Manasarowar' and collected many 'sacred treasures', viz.:

> (i) pebbles from the shore . . which are sewn up in a bag and hung round the necks of ponies before they are left to graze on the mountains, so that they will not stray, or be attacked by wild beasts, or stolen; (ii) parts of fish . . . which, when burnt, relieve by their smell all pain, whether of man or beasts, and are a sure remedy in every case of sickness; (iii) water . . . , which, drunk by the dying, ensures their immediate entry into Heaven; and (iv) sand . . . , which is placed in the mouth of a dead man to prevent him being re-born in the body of an animal.
>
> (E. B. Wakefield, "A Journey to Western Tibet, 1929," *Alpine Journal*, Vol. LXVI, No 303)

Passing near Chiu Gompa, he found 'deep and fast-flowing' water in the Ganga Chu. Then, while staying at Barkha, he strolled over to Darchen with several members of his party who were anxious to see the monastery there:

> It is normally administered by a Bhutanese official known as the Dashok, but the post has been vacant for the last two years and control of the mart as well as the monastery is now in the hands of an elderly Lama. This Lama, a handsome, well-built man with a refined face and a short beard slightly touched with grey, entertained us with real grace and courtesy. I presented him with Rs. 4/- the price of a sheep, on my account; and the other members of the party also gave him small sums of money. Thereupon, having lit candles in front of the shrine, he said prayers for each of us individually as well as for the benefit of the Government of India.
>
> (*Ibid.*)

From Barkha, Wakefield planned to follow the main Lhasa-Leh trail back to Gartok. On the first day, however, there was a nasty incident. Dr Kanshi Ram was riding ahead with two unarmed *chaprassies* (grooms), when a bullet whistled past his head. Then a rough-looking Tibetan came up. He was carrying a gun.

'Who are you?' the Tibetan asked in his native tongue. 'What have you got with you?'

'You'd better be careful,' Ram cautioned. 'I'm a member of the

British Trade Agency staff. The rest of my party, with soldiers, is coming up behind.' This seemed to cut little ice with the Tibetan, who began reloading his matchlock. The doctor thereupon wheeled his pony round and rode off at speed, followed by the *chaprassies*. The Tibetan gave chase; but then, thinking better of it, turned aside to look at a *kyang* that had been pulled down by his ferocious dogs.

Belatedly remembering that he had a revolver, Ram recovered his courage and stealthily crept up behind the *dacoit*, who instantly spun round and raised his matchlock. The doctor fired first and, though he aimed to miss, scared the *dacoit* so much that the scoundrel allowed himself to be disarmed.

Wakefield handed the *dacoit* over to a servant of the Barkha Tarjum and in due course he was punished with 200 stripes. Apparently, more serious in Tibetan eyes than sniping at the doctor was the fact that he had killed a *kyang*. Recently an edict had been issued in Lhasa forbidding tobacco smoking and the slaughter of wild animals. Both these practises were thought to shorten the life of the reigning Dalai Lama! – (he in fact died four years later).

Wakefield was back in Gartok in time for the annual fair, the highlight of which was a spectacular horse-race. This was run, using boy jockeys, 'after the moon has set and before the sun has risen over the neighbouring hills.' Quite unconcerned with alien values like sportsmanship, the Garpöns blatantly resorted to foul means to ensure that one of them secured the handsome prize donated by the Lhasa Government. Not content with having their own horses start off before the others and their lackeys impeding the competition further along the course, they also browbeat the hapless owner into leasing them the favourite for the race day each year.

Besides this horse-race there were shooting and archery displays; also dance performances. A host of officials were present, dressed in their most picturesque and colourful costumes. Many of them, as well as visiting traders, called on Wakefield. He was particularly interested to meet the Sarpön, who was in charge of the local gold fields, and the Chumurti Pon, with whom he discussed *dacoit* problems. Among the traders, he was fascinated by an enterprising Ladakhi, whose agents in Khotan and Yarkand obtained jade cups for him, which he subsequently traded in Lhasa.

A heavy fall of snow delayed Wakefield and it was not until September 27th that he finally led his party to the Shipki Pass by

Feeder stream flowing from Kailas to Manasarovar, east of Barkha and north of Langpona (198?

way of Chaprang, Shangtse, Miang and Tial, a village on the banks of the Sutlej. Having crossed the high passes, they had to negotiate the rugged and precipitous Hupsang Ravine but, with only minor mishaps, they arrived safely back in Simla on October 19th. Wakefield had been away for five months and covered a distance of 1,300 miles – 'excluding all divagations in pursuit of game or mountains tops.' He was proud too that he had walked on foot throughout and, as a result, 'suffered less than the rest of the party from colds and headaches and those other bodily ailments which are inevitable in a country where fruit and vegetables are unobtainable.'

Three years later, two more Englishmen travelled to the Kailas-Manasarovar region: Frederick Williamson and Frank Ludlow.

Frederick Williamson I.P.S.

*Ludlow (LEFT) and
Williamson
(RIGHT) in Bhutan
(1933)*

Williamson (1891–1935) was brought up in England and Australia. After Cambridge, he entered the I.C.S. (Indian Civil Service) and saw service in Orissa, Bihar, Mysore and on the North-West Frontier. During World War I he served with the Middlesex Regiment and the Gurkhas in Palestine. Back in India after the War, he transferred to the Political Service, whose 150 or so members worked in the self-governing native states and in lands beyond the frontiers of India. Williamson's first posting (1924–6) was to Gyantse and Yatung in southern Tibet as B.T.A. (British Trade Agent). Many British officers and men found the climatic rigours, extreme remoteness and scant comforts of southern Tibet hard to take, but not Williamson. He was by nature a quiet, conscientious man, a keen photographer, and endowed with a love of nature and *shikar* (sport). He fell completely under the spell of Tibet.

In 1923, Frank Ludlow (1885–1972) of the Indian Educational Service went to Gyantse to become headmaster of a short-lived school run on English public school lines. He was a tall, lanky, unassuming man. He rarely spoke, Margaret Williamson told me, but when he did 'it was always well worth listening to'. As a student at Cambridge, Ludlow had read Botany under Prof. Marshall Ward, father of Frank Kingdon Ward, the well-known Himalayan and Transhimalayan plant-hunter. Ludlow never married; plants and birds were the principal loves of his life.

Meeting in Gyantse, Ludlow and Williamson found that they had a much in common. A longstanding friendship was forged but it was soon interrupted when in 1927 Williamson was posted to the Consulate at Kashgar. In that lonely outpost on the northern arm of the Silk Road in Chinese Turkistan, he promptly found himself embroiled in the intrigues and general skulduggery that went with what Rudyard Kipling dubbed 'The Great Game': the Anglo-Russian contest for influence in Central Asia. But despite all the underhand tricks that his Russian opposite numbers – men with melodramatic names like Doumpiss and Posnikoff – played on him, Williamson never lost his cool. In his dispatches home, the strongest epithet he used was 'tactless'.

In 1927, Ludlow retired from the I.E.S., and from then on, in the words of Sir Basil Gould, he 'lived the good life, giving scope to his love of Kashmir and the Himalayas, and studying their botany and birds'. His first move was to take up Williamson's invitation to spend the winter of 1929/30 in Kashgar, and there he met George Sherriff, Williamson's Vice-Consul. It was a fateful meeting, for despite certain fundamental differences of temperament the two men shared a common love of nature and of the outdoor life. The friendship they forged in Kashgar was to last twenty years and formed the basis of a number of highly-successful specimen-collecting expeditions in the Himalayan region and southern Tibet. As with so many Englishmen of the period, however, they were never able to take the difficult step from surname to first-name terms.

Against the subzero temperatures of that Sinkiang winter, Williamson, Ludlow and Sherriff huddled close to the giant Russian stove in Chini Bagh, the British Consulate in Kashgar, and debated future plans. Williamson confessed his devotion to Tibet and his earnest desire to be posted back there. 'I too had fallen in love with Tibet.' Ludlow wrote; '...and Sherriff had also come under its spell... So we extracted a promise from Williamson that when he had obtained the coveted post of Political Officer in Sikkim, Bhutan and Tibet, he would do all he could to obtain permission for us to travel in that country.'

In 1931 Williamson did achieve his dearest wish and became Acting Political Officer in Sikkim. After a period of leave in Europe, he returned to the East in 1932, when his first official task was to go to Western Tibet to look into a boundary dispute that had flared up between Tibet and the native state of Tehri. True to his word, he asked his friend Ludlow to go along too.

Williamson and Ludlow set off from Almora on 14th August 1932. They were fully supported by the Government of India, and carried 'a large and cordial' passport from the Tibetans. The only stipulation that restricted them was that they should not shoot in the vicinity of sacred sites. 'We shall interpret it exactly,' the conscientious Williamson declared.

Thirty-one coolies carried their baggage. Williamson had his faithful manservant Samdup with him too, and his trusty gun-dog Bruce; also a clerk named Lobsang and a Lepcha cook. Ludlow, on the other hand, took along his 'general factotum and bird-skinner', a Kashmiri named Ramzan Mir. With his help, Ludlow was able to put together a small ornithological collection in Western Tibet which, according to the noted Indian ornithologist, Dr. Sálim Ali, 'the late Hugh Whistler pronounced...to consist of typical Tibetan Plateau forms, not differing from those occuring in Ladakh on the one hand or in the neighbourhood of Lhasa on the other'.

It took the party seventeen days to cross British (now Indian) territory, but long before then Williamson was gloomily noting in his journal:

> Ludlow says (and I agree with him) that 'travelling is difficult in the Kumaon. Coolies are thoroughly bad, animal transport is outrageously expensive, while rain falls unceasingly. When, by chance, the sun happens to shine, it is most infernally hot...'
> (Frederick Williamson. *Western Tibet.*
> Unpublished autograph journal.)

They had travelled by way of Ascot, Berenag, and Sirthang. At the last place, they had encountered another Kailas traveller, the enigmatic American missionary Steiner. Sadly, the meeting was neither a memorable nor an inspiring one:

> Steiner, the German-American Padre, who went to Kailas in 1930, very kindly invited us to stay with him. We are glad we did not, as we called this evening and found him very talkative, and very dull. We had hoped to get a lot of useful information from him, but could not even get in a question!
> (*Ibid*)

The date given here for Steiner's first visit disagrees with Swami Pranavānanda's date of 1931. The *swami* also adds that there was a second visit in 1942. Both visits, during which the Parikramas of both Kailas and Manasarovar were performed, were naturally for the purpose of 'missionary propaganda work'.

Having paused at Garbyang on August 29th to rest, dry kit, wash clothes and lay on new transport, Williamson and Ludlow set off for the Lipu Lekh. Williamson, still apparently disconsolate, registered himself in stiff disagreement with Charles Sherring's dictum that the scenery thereabouts was some of the finest in the Himalayas.

At Taklakot, Williamson had both social and business meetings

View of the Himalayas above Kalapani. Lipu Lekh on the left (1926)

Cave city at Taklakot (1984)

with the local *dzongpön*, whose father, he was surprised to learn, had been Tibetan Trade Agent in Yatung when he himself had been B.T.A. Later, having stocked up with Nepalese rice and obtained transport for the next stage, the British party proceeded along the main route up over the ridges of Gurla Mandhata and thence down to the shores of Rakshas Tal, which looked quite beautiful in Williamson's eyes despite the dullness of the weather. On the road they met an English-speaking *sadhu*, who was in anything but a spiritually equanimous mood:

> He said he could not understand why we came to such a country as there was nothing here but suffering, and nothing beautiful or attractive. He himself had found no spiritual benefit. He was limping and asked for medicine to cure a wound in his foot. We told him we could do our best if he came to camp, but he said he could not turn back. He also asked for water and seemed little able to look after himself.
>
> *(Ibid)*

Their camp that night was 'the most horrible we have yet struck'. They pitched their tents in the teeth of a howling gale, then managed with great difficulty to fetch water from the lake and to cook a meal from tins over a yak-dung fire. 'A nasty night...'

Next day they passed along the isthmus separating the two lakes. They observed some tempting bar-headed geese, but sadly had to refrain from taking pot-shots at them in deference to the Tibetan Government's ban. They camped that night beside the 'miserable pile' of Chiu Gompa. There was water flowing in the nearby Ganga Chu, and abundant shoals of fish – 'But the place is sacred!' Williamson lamented.

Making their way to Barkha next day across level ground covered with thorny scrub and scattered grass, they saw more bar-headed geese. The twin peaks of Kailas and Gurla Mandhata were obscured by low cloud, however: 'as coy as ever...we saw only the bases of them...' At Barkha itself, there were many sheep belonging to the nomadic *dogpas*. On the scratchy, erratic cine film that Williamson shot there, Ludlow stands amid the many fleecy denizens of the place, smiling shyly in a floppy tweed hat. Firewood was plentiful thereabouts, and the people helpful, so they made a pleasant camp that day, though Williamson, like a good thrifty Scot, lamented the high cost of their transport as he paid it off: 'This is very different from our expenditure in British territory. We paid Rs. 38/- plus Rs. 8/- *bakshish* among 4 men...'

On September 9th they reached Darchen, over which the

The western shore of Lake Manasarovar

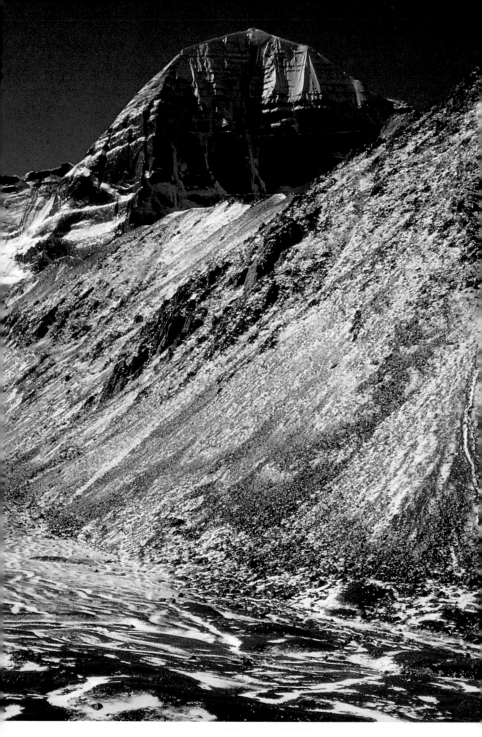

Kailas: The North-east Face (1987)

Tibetans and the Bhutanese were at the time in contention. Recently, the local Bhutanese officer (*Dashok*), one Tobda-la, had been driven out and replaced by a Tibetan, who proved at first 'friendly and helpful', but next day, when Williamson applied to him for help mustering transport, did a complete *volte face* and became cussedly awkward. As a result, Williamson had to send his servant Lobsang back to Barkha to scrounge a few ponies, a mule and four coolies for the next leg of the journey.

'A miserable hovel, not worth any trouble let alone the ill feeling between Tibet and Bhutan about it,' Williamson noted grimly of Darchen. Later he was to meet some Tibetans who had been caught in the cross-fire of the dispute. They had apparently once been Bhutanese subjects but, when the fracas blew up, had been beaten by the agents of the Tibetan Government, who then, adding insult to injury, promptly doubled their tax burdens too. (*The full text of Williamson's official "Note on the Darchin Monastery Dispute" is given in Appendix 4*).

And so to Kailas Parikrama, which for Williamson and Ludlow began at 9.40 a.m. on 11th September. They travelled till 3 p.m., covering in all some eleven miles of rugged ground. At the end of the day, though they took two tents, they did not use them for they were able to find accomodation in Drira Puk Gompa, where they were kindly received by the occupants: one monk and two child novices. Here they were also able to catch a fleeting glimpse of the great 6,000 foot northern face of Kailas – and hastily snapped and filmed it before the veil of cloud again descended.

The next day they covered some seventeen miles, travelling from 8.45 a.m. to 5 p.m. Starting from Drira Puk, they panted and scrambled up to the Drölma La, suffering the adverse effects of the altitude all the way. Had they not been able to borrow three yaks from the *gompa*, their servants would have been sorely tried. Breathless, the party reached the summit at last, where they encountered four or five pilgrims, plus the usual cairns and wind-tattered bunting of prayer flags.

Proceeding, Williamson and Ludlow dutifully washed their faces and hands in the purifying waters of the sacred Gauri Kund before dropping steeply into the eastern valley, which they found stony and marshy, hence much more difficult to negotiate than its western counterpart. Sadly, the negative tenour and adverse weather conditions that had prevailed throughout their tour of Tibet so far were maintained, so they hurried past "Ziripu" Gompa (Zutrul Puk) without pausing in their haste to get back to Darchen. 'A nasty day', was Williamson's verdict. They had not so much as

The Citadel at Tsaparang (1985)

glimpsed the pristine cone of the sacred mountain even once. Things improved at Darchen next day, however. The weather was "perfect, almost cloudless", so cameras clicked and whirred to make up for lost time and opportunity. Ludlow and Samdup also took baths, while the servants generally tidied up in preparation for the next leg of the journey. This took them on to Gartok, where they met the Junior Garpön, the British Trade Agent (an Indian national), British and local traders and the Dzongpön of Tsaparang, who had come to meet Williamson in order to discuss the Tibet-Tehri Boundary Dispute.

Four days later, they moved on again, travelling south in company with the Dzongpön of Tsaparang towards the area at issue between Tibet and Tehri. Now well away from sacred sites, the Tibetan Government's injunction against *shikar* no longer applied, so Williamson and Ludlow could discharge their guns freely. They visited Tsaparang and Thöling, the ancient cities of the lost Kingdom of Gu-gé, and then tramped through the dusty, dessiccated canyonlands of the Upper Sutlej Valley. Their gateway through the snowy mountains was the 18,300 foot Pula La.

When he eventually reached the disputed area, Williamson realised that the problem could not be resolved on the spot by local officials, but he gained useful insights into its particulars that served him well when he later discussed the matter with government officials in Lhasa and Bumthang, the Tibetan and Bhutanese capitals, which he visited officially on his 1933 tour. He and his party finally arrived in Tehri on 23rd October, having traversed a total of 592 miles. After so much slogging footwork across rugged terrain, it was strange to see a chauffeured motor car coming to drive them to the local guest house. Williamson noted: 'Somewhat unwillingly we went across the river, got into the car and were motored there'.

A few days later they were in Narendranagar with the Political Agent, Stubbs, and his assistants, who took them for a 'so-called shoot' before motoring them to Hardwar to catch the night train for Delhi.

A few months later, Williamson found to his delight that he had been elevated to the full status of Political Officer in Sikkim. In that capacity he paid three official visits to Tibet with his young wife: in 1933, 1934 and 1935. Sadly while in Lhasa on that last visit, in the midst of delicate and important negotiations concerning the return to Tibet of the exiled Panchen Lama, he was struck down with a kidney complaint. The possibility of bringing a plane in to fly him down to hospital in Calcutta was mooted. One did not arrive. He sank lower and lower. His young widow was at his bedside when he died. A few days later she took his body south for burial in the small cemetary reserved for Christians and Muslims at Gyantse. She then returned home to Britain. She had been married for a mere two-and-a-half years.

Ludlow lived on for another thirty-seven years. During World War II, he and his friend George Sherriff (who had by then acquired a wife, Betty) represented the British in Lhasa. Ludlow then tried to persuade the neutral Tibetans to allow shipments of war supplies to pass through their territory between British India to China; he was not successful. However, his and Sherriff's good work on behalf of the Natural History Departments or the British Museum – and gardeners everywhere – is still remembered – with much appreciation.

CHAPTER SEVEN

Travellers in the Sacred Region 1936–1945

In the mid-1930s, Herbert Tichy (1912–87), then a young geology student at the University of Vienna, was growing restless in the cloistered academic life. A previous trip to India had afforded him an unforgettable taste of freedom and adventure, and his imagination was brimming with visions of the East. One in particular haunted his hours in the enervating lecture halls. He had come upon it in a book on Tibet by Sven Hedin: 'a bare rocky countryside out of which the summit of a snow-clad mountain rose up like a glittering pyramid of silver'. Reasoning with inexorable Germanic logic that it was senseless to merely sit and dream of such marvels, Tichy determined to see this wonderful far-off mountain for himself.

Accordingly, he conjured out of the ether a noble undertaking called 'The Austrian Central Asian Expedition', whose imposing letterheads were soon bearing requests for support and sponsorship to numerous newspapers and commercial concerns. In due course, the Expedition – or rather Tichy himself, for he *was* the Expedition – was receiving quantities of free supplies and equipment, which included a motorcycle from the firm of Puch. Solid financial support arrived in the form of an advance paid by a newspaper editor to his 'Special Correspondent in Asia' – Tichy again, of course. Finally, as this was in the Thirties, the young adventurer did not intend to abandon his academic career, so with characteristic initiative he persuaded his professor to allow him to make the Himalayas the subject of his doctoral thesis.

With everything thus neatly arranged, Tichy sailed for Bombay. His expedition was to take him to various parts of India, as well as to Burma and Afghanistan, before he was to make a brief foray into Tibet to realize his ambition of seeing Sven Hedin's sacred

Setting off from Almora (1936)

Herbert Tichy and Chatter Bhuj Kapur chatting with a sadhu en route for Kailas in 1936

mountain with his own eyes. He had three companions with him on
the last adventure. There was an Indian friend, a student of law at
the University of Lahore, whom he had met on his first visit to
India: Chatter Bhuj Kapur. There was a sixteen-year-old Hindu
bearer named Ranschid. And finally there was a Sherpa porter from
Darjeeling named Kitar, a veteran of many Himalayan mountaineering expeditions, whom Tichy had engaged because he was
himself planning an assault of Gurla Mandhata.

Starting from Almora early on the morning of 4th May 1936,
Tichy's little expedition followed the Kali river across the Kumaon
region. Being on the main pilgrim route, they met many yogis and
ascetics: men ready to brave icy winds and snow in order to realize a
spiritual ideal. Perhaps the most unlikely encounter was in a small
cave, to which Tichy was attracted by the sound of muttered
mantras. Inside, he discovered an ancient sage swathed in blankets,
who addressed him in fluent German. Apparently, this ascetic had
been sent in his youth to study in Europe. On his return to India,
however, the spiritual had presented its higher claims to him, and in
the classical manner he had renounced all his worldly goods in
favour of the solitude and discomfort of a cave in the Himalayas.

Tichy and his friends reached Garbyang in pouring rain on the
evening of 20th May. It was still early in the season, and many of the
inhabitants had not yet returned from their winter quarters in the
lower valleys. Thus the Austrian found the place largely
deserted – but spectacular: surrounded on all sides by imposing
snow-clad peaks. He also found the Bhotia girls very attractive – and
surprisingly liberated – but he was not able to realize his full
romantic potential with them because his friend Kapur had put it
about that he was an idiot. This was not an underhand move
designed to gain the Indian law student a monopoly of the girls'
favours; rather it was an attempt to offer some kind of plausible
explanation of why his companion was unable to speak Hindustani
when to all intents and purposes he looked a thoroughgoing Hindu.

During the course of their march Tichy had in fact been
progressively slipping into disguise, for, as an unofficial European
traveller, he could not expect sanction for his journey from the
Tibetan authorities. He therefore resorted to the long-established
device of masquerading as an Indian *fakir*: dying his hair and beard
jet-black, and allowing them to grow long and unkempt. He also
donned a greasy old turban and other Hindustani articles of
clothing, and to perfect the effect restricted himself entirely to
eating native fare, its very liberal hot chillie content notwithstanding. Kapur, on the other hand, as an Indian, could readily gain

entry to Tibet as a *bona fide* Hindu pilgrim.

Unable to get baggage animals because the high passes were still snowbound, Tichy engaged a couple of coolies in Garbyang to carry his party's luggage into Tibet. He also obtained the services of a Tibetan-speaking guide named Nan Singh. This company duly set off from Garbyang around 23rd May, and two days later camped at Synchum just below the Lipu Lekh pass. The snow lay thickly all around and, laden with heavy packs, the travellers sank deeply into it at every step. They therefore had to bivouac at Synchum, cowering for shelter from the bitter wind behind a small stone wall

*Tichy in disguise
(1936)*

until the early hours of the next morning, when the snow had frozen hard enough to bear their weight. Then, having toiled upwards for many hours, they at last saw, in the grey light of dawn, the prayer flags and *chörtens* that marked the summit of the pass, and when the sun rose a little later they were presented with a splendid view of the great treeless plains of Tibet:

> We seemed serenely apart from the noisy turmoil of humanity, and, bathed in the healthy morning sunlight, I was able to drink in all the spirit of loveliness around me.
>
> (C.B. Kapur, 'A Pilgrimage to Mount Kailas',
> *Modern Review*, August 1936)

They proceeded directly to Taklakot – with some trepidation, for they knew that they must, like all pilgrims, present themselves to the local *dzongpön*. In addition, a high official from Lhasa was also paying a visit to the place, which might lead to embarrassing complications. Initially, Tichy was tempted to try to slip past without declaring himself but eventually decided that this would be foolish because they had already met several Tibetans and their presence in the country would soon be widely known. Alternative strategems were therefore devised. His party timed their arrival at Taklakot very precisely so as to appear in the failing light of evening. Then, just outside the place, Tichy began to feign sickness. The locals who witnessed his pantomine sagely diagnosed 'mountain sickness', a commonplace malady even among the Tibetans themselves. He was hurried to the shelter of the local *dharmasala* or guest-house, where he remained in a pitiful condition while his companions dutifully went to see the local officials, who were so completely satisfied that they did not require to see the sick member of the party.

At Taklakot they also had their first experiences of real Tibetans. They were not impressed. Chatter Kapur describes his impressions of them thus:

> They were all awfully dirty and wore greasy clothes. Men and women looked very much alike, for in Tibet men (except the lamas) do not cut their hair and very few have hair on their chins. They all smelled profusely and touched nearly all the things we wore or carried with us, like children. They have never seen the things which we had, modern material civilization not having reached their country yet.
>
> (*Ibid*)

Finally, pack horses and a driver were engaged at Taklakot to replace the Garbyang coolies, and when all preparations were complete, Tichy and company marched to their next camping place near the village of Rungong. This was to be their base camp for the long-projected assault on Gurla Mandhata.

Tichy had prepared his attempt on the mountain very carefully, studying Tom Longstaff's account of his own attempt. He planned to employ the 'rush' method, whose principal exponents at the time were Eric Shipton and Longstaff himself. Accompanied only by the Sherpa, Kitar, and carrying only minimal supplies and equipment, Tichy grappled with the snow and storms of the great mountain for five days and forged to a creditable altitude of 23,500 feet, before sheer exhaustion obliged him to return to base camp. He fully intended making a second attempt, but back at Rungong ominous developments were afoot. The local people had seen the two climbers on the mountain and had leapt to the conclusion that they were looking for gold and silver. They had decided to report the matter to the officials at Taklakot, and were even debating whether to arrest these trespassers on sacred ground themselves. Fortunately, Kapur had been able to make them believe that Tichy and Kitar had really been inspired by more lofty motives: had, in fact, gone to the snowy heights to be nearer the gods. The pious people of Rungong naturally found such motives quite understandable and let the matter drop. Tichy and his friends therefore quickly struck camp and proceeded northwards in respectable pilgrim fashion before the villagers were disabused of their false impressions.

The party was now well and truly into *dacoit* country. Their guide, Nan Singh, was very put out that they had no arms to defend themselves, so before leaving Rungong he had skilfully wrapped their ice-axes in pieces of cloth, leaving only the ends exposed. They carried these imitation guns throughout their time in Tibet, and they served them well. Not long after they had crossed the Gurla Pass – where they obtained their first imposing view of the sacred region – they were approached by a gang of fearsome-looking *dacoits*, armed with spears, who wanted to know why they carried their guns in such an unusual fashion. Nan Singh explained that they were exceptional weapons of their own manufacture which could fire fifty rounds without reloading and therefore required special protection. The *dacoits* were appropriately impressed and passed on without causing trouble.

It was not long before the party were on the shores of Lake

Manasarovar. Here they performed the ritual ablutions, though Tichy and Kapur, being rather less pious than their companions, did not prolong their stay in the icy waters. They subsequently found accommodation at Trügo Gompa, which, like all the *gompa* they visited in Tibet, was exceedingly dark and dirty, though it contained a wealth of ancient books and ritual objects. They frequently heard the lamas chanting the *mantra*, *Om mani padme hum*: the monotonous rhythm building up towards a crescendo to the accompaniment of drums, cymbals and thigh-bone trumpets, then dissipating into a formless cacophony and finally into silence – the characteristic sound of Tibetan Buddhism. Tichy was very impressed with the *gompa*, which seemed to ride on the waters of the sacred lake like a vessel, commanding a fine view of Kailas in the distance. It was so far removed from the hurly-burly of 'civilized' life, a place of 'rest, peace and adjustment' – yet, of course, he had to admit that in the last analysis all that was really pure supposition: who could really tell what was in these lamas' minds?

After Trügo, they journeyed up the narrow isthmus separating the two lakes; they passed Chiu Gompa on its eminence, the connecting channel and the old gold fields, then over the lush pasturelands to the north of the lakes, and so to Barkha, which they found hard to locate as it lies in a hollow. Here they were entertained by the *tarjum*, the staging-post official, and also witnessed the Tibetan method of slaughtering a goat: the beast's mouth and nose were closed for about two minutes until it suffocated.

They finally arrived at Darchen, which they left at 6 a.m. on the morning of 2nd June to commence their *parikrama* of Mount Kailas, despite the fact that it had snowed heavily the night before. They also knew that no less a person than one of the Garpöns of Ngari (Western Tibet) was engaged in making several *parikrama* at that time, which also occasioned a certain trepidation. The first leg of the circumambulation passed off without mischance, however, and it looked as though the whole thing might pass off safely, but at Drira Puk Tichy blundered. Up until then he had assiduously maintained his cover, augmenting his physical disguise by playing the part of a pious idiot, suffering the abuse and impositions of his companions with apparently boundless good nature and avoiding all conversations by diligently twirling his prayer-wheel and intoning his *mantra*: *Ram, Ram, Ram* . . . Now he was suddenly overwhelmed by the beautiful spectacle of a group of lamas coming out of the *gompa* and bowing to the sacred mountain as its great northern face reflected the

radiance of the sunset. He could not resist trying to capture the scene in a photograph, and had to grovel at full length on the ground in order to compose both mountain and lamas in the viewfinder. Nothing was said at the time, but later, when he and his friends were taking their evening tea in their own quarters in the *gompa*, a lama entered and announced that the Garpön, who was also lodging there, wished to see them immediately.

The interpreter, Nan Singh, who had hitherto represented himself as a man of invincible courage and fortitude, blanched

Looking south from Gyangtra Gompa to Rakshas Tal and the Himalaya (1987)

horribly. Still, there was no way out – though before answering the
Garpön's call they took the precaution of hiding their Leica among
some rocks.

The Garpön received them in an open, well-illuminated room. He
was a tall man, slightly on the stout side, but clean and better
dressed than any Tibetan they had hitherto seen. Everything about
him, in fact, indicated his being of high rank and used to obedience.

Tichy and his companions duly prostrated themselves. The Garpön motioned them to rise from the floor and fixed them with a penetrating gaze. This particularly upset Nan Singh, who turned a sickly green and seemed on the point of fainting. When called to translate the Garpön's questions, he could hardly stammer out the words. The Viceroy was not, however, interested in Nan Singh; Tichy was the real object of his curiosity.

'Take off those glasses,' he ordered the Austrian.

Tichy was obliged to obey, though to do so might well be to give himself away by showing the Garpön his blue eyes, the unmistakable hallmark of a European. Nevertheless, he tried to maintain a brave façade, and once the glasses were off returned the Garpön's gaze as squarely as he was able.

'Take off the turban,' was the Garpön's next command.

Tichy again obeyed without demur, and the greasy cloth was removed to reveal long tangles of neglected and – most importantly – jet-black hair. He noted with satisfaction the good effect this had on the Viceroy; it seemed to offset the bad impression made by his blue eyes. Tichy and Kapur were in fact passing themselves off as Kashmiris, who may indeed have comparatively light skin.

Then the Garpön fired the inevitable question: 'What were you doing in front of the *gompa* with a camera?'

So he knew . . . . Tichy felt trapped. There was nothing for it but to try to bluff his way out. Nan Singh translated his phonily innocent retorts:

Camera? What a strange idea! What could have led the lamas to think he had such a thing . . .?' He paused for a moment to reflect. *Ah, yes: he had it. They must have seen him looking through his telescope – the one given him by the English sahib whom he'd served so faithfully. . . .*

A really desperate game – but, played with conviction, somehow it worked. The Garpön was swayed. The atmosphere lightened. Even Nan Singh's nerve revived, and soon he was translating away with his usual panache. The telescope was produced and presented to the Garpön, who took it and focussed it on the summit of Kailas. He became instantly chastened to see the abode of his gods brought so unbelievably close. *Would it be possible to actually see the gods themselves through this wonderful instrument?* he wondered. Tichy assured him it would; explaining that he and his friends had been graced with such a sight themselves, though it had taken a great deal of patience; and anyway, they were men whose unusual piety had gained them a great deal of spiritual merit. Naturally, as the Garpön was so taken with the telescope, he was made a present of it. The awkward

Pilgrims at Kailas (1986)

questions did not end there, however. The Viceroy next wanted to know what had brought them to Tibet so early in the season. The main pilgrim influx was not expected until August, when the high passes would be completely free of snow.

To this Kapur supplied an astoundingly inventive reply. 'We have come so early because we are mad with love,' he explained. 'A year ago we saw our neighbour's daughters – girls of such ravishing beauty . . .' And here he proceeded to go into juicy detail about the girls' charms, amplifying his description with extravagant curving gestures. 'Their parents are so pious, however, that they would not allow us to marry them until we had purified ourselves of the sins of our youth by making a pilgrimage to Mount Kailas,' he continued. 'Naturally, we set off at once. What is a little snow on the passes to we who care only to be in the arms of our beloved beauties . . . . You understand?' And he concluded by smacking his lips lasciviously, a sound that Tichy tried to imitate, but unsuccessfully, as his mouth was dry with fear and excitement.

The Garpön understood only too well. He also expressed himself very interested in hearing more about these girls' finer parts, but here the travellers had to invoke the claims of honour and discreetly drew a veil over their already over-exposed imaginary sweethearts. Tactfully, the Garpön did not press the matter further.

Their friendship now seemed sealed and the atmosphere to have relaxed sufficiently for the ensuing conversation to range comparatively freely over a variety of topics. Emboldened, Tichy asked through his interpreter whether European mountaineers might attempt the sacrilege of climbing Mount Kailas as they had already begun to commit comparable enormities in Kashmir.

The Garpön smiled indulgently. 'Only a man entirely free of sin could climb Kailas,' he replied. 'And he wouldn't have to actually scale the sheer walls of ice to do it – he'd just turn himself into a bird and fly to the summit.'

And why were the Tibetans so reluctant to allow Europeans into their land?

'I have seen many Europeans, and many Indians who are ruled by Europeans,' the Garpön said. 'They all seemed very unhappy to me. We have our gods and we are content. If the Europeans came, however, they would drive the gods away and bring us nothing in their place. That's why we prefer to be left alone.'

He went on to sum up the situation in Tibet. 'In your country, Kashmir, you may be a great lord, a tax-collector or a substantial landowner. Here, you are nothing. Even I, the ruler of this whole province, am nothing. *Only the gods rule here.'*

The sun had now fully set; it was night. The Garpön rose and bowed deeply to the sacred mountain. Tichy followed his example; and as he did not feel that he was dissembling. At that moment he was as completely sincere in his salutation as any pious Indian or Tibetan pilgrim. He was simply overawed by the overwhelming sanctity of the sacred mountain. Afterwards, he squatted on the floor in an attitude of prayer and stared up at the luminous peak, absorbing its image into his soul.

Next morning, when they awoke, the travellers found that the Garpön had already left to continue his *parikrama.* They took their time over their breakfast and then set off themselves, toiling up the steep ascent to the still-snowbound Drölma La. On the way, they passed a group of prostrating pilgrims, and again Tichy was tempted to use his camera – much to the consternation of Nan Singh, who prudently thought it unwise to risk another crisis when they had so narrowly wriggled their way out of the last.

A little beyond the frozen Gauri Kund lake they met up again

Tirthapuri and the Sutlej (1987)

with the Garpön and his party, who were resting on the grass of the agreeable green eastern valley. He motioned Tichy to join him, apparently pleased to see him again, and plied him with butter tea and *tsampa*. He was very amused at Tichy's ineptitude in eating this typical Tibetan fare with his fingers. Then the questions started again. Rather than risk giving himself away by transmitting his answers through Nan Singh in faltering Hindustani, Tichy opted to recite rousing passages of German poetry and leave it to the interpreter to make up his own plausible answers. This device worked excellently, and the Garpön later proceeded on his way apparently completely satisfied.

That night, that of 4th June, Tichy and his friends returned to Darchen, their *parikrama* completed. Now all that remained was to slip out of the country without further trouble. The plan was to go out by a different route from that by which they had entered. This involved making a wide detour to the west, following the course of the Sutlej for the first lap of the way, passing near Tirthapuri and Khyunglung, then veering south for Chitichun and so to the Kungri Bringri Pass. They were repeatedly told that this pass would still be snowbound and impassable but, being young and adventurous, they were prepared to chance their luck that way rather than face the monotony of retracing their former route.

It took them six days of enervating, waterless marching to reach Chitichun. For some of the way they had Tibetan travelling companions – nomads for the most part. They also had another brush with *dacoits* – three of them this time: young men armed with muzzle-loaders. They openly declared their profession and even seemed to think it a perfectly respectable means of livelihood. To discourage them from discharging their professional duties, Nan Singh concocted a fanciful tale about their being agents of the Maharaja of Kashmir sent to survey the land in preparation for a pilgrimage that their master was to make to Mount Kailas in the following year. Should any mischance befall them, the Maharaja would most certainly dispatch an entire army to wreak the most terrible revenge. Duly warned, the *dacoits* took themselves off quite meekly. Had they sought to rob them, however, their main concern would have been to steal food, which was at a premium in that arid, barren region, where markets were only held once a year.

As the party approached the towering white chaos of the Great Himalaya, it became clear that they might not find it at all easy to locate their chosen pass. Nan Singh, who had assured them that he could point them straight to it, turned out to have a far less exact knowledge of the land than he had claimed, and in any case he intended to leave them at Chitichun in order to make his own way back to Garbyang, his home, *via* Taklakot and the Lipu Lekh. The horse-dealer whose animals had carried their baggage since Taklakot was also scheduled to split off from the party at the same place. Tichy was therefore in something of a dilemma. Faced with the possibility of being without guides or transport in an inhospitable and bewildering area, he decided to act summarily, threatening to withhold Nan Singh's pay until substitute guides had been found. This Nan Singh managed to do and duly went on his way with the horse-dealer, but the new coolie-guides – a pair of Tibetan nomads – were unreliable and temperamental, and it was only by dint of much cajoling and *baksheesh* (handouts of cash) that they were kept to their original undertaking to guide the party across the high passes.

Tichy and his friends did finally reach the Kungri Bingri

Pass (18,300 feet). It was indeed still snowbound, so they had to cross it at night when the snow was frozen hard. No evocative moonlight illuminated their high transit: cloud obscured the moon, and scything winds sliced up from the glaciers far below.

They pushed on over moraines to the next pass, the Jayanti (18,500 feet), where their guides left them, though by mutual agreement. The view from the head of this pass was tremendous: Nanda Devi, Nanda Kot and other ice giants soared magnificently around. Tichy also cast one last look at Tibet over his shoulder. Despite the rigours that that inexorable, primordial land had imposed upon him, the Austrian knew that it had worked a potent magic. The sheer scale of the landscape, its rarefied and impossible beauties, would always linger in his memory, calling him back. And if he had any choice in the matter, he would choose to die within sight of Mount Kailas rather than anywhere else.

The way ahead was quite straightforward now: over the final pass, the Unta Dhura (17,950 feet), and on to the village of Milam, from where the route back to Almora would be no more difficult than that up to Garbyang. One final and potentially insuperable obstacle barred their way. A crucial bridge across a torrent had been dismantled by the people living on the Indian side to prevent marauders coming into their territory from Tibet. Tichy and his friends had two options: to return to Tibet and make their way round to the Lipu Lekh, or somehow to get across the torrent. Tichy eventually decided on the latter course, so he and Kapur stripped off, armed themselves with a rope and braved the turbulent waters. They made it to the far side, where they roped up the dismantled timbers and hauled them back into place so that Ranschid and Kitar could come across with their gear.

No sooner was this crisis over than someone started shooting at them. It turned out to be Captain John Locke, a British sportsman, who claimed to have mistaken them for game. Appropriately apologetic, he invited them back to his camp for a slap-up meal complete with wines and spirits. He also filled them in on the latest news: the Italians had attacked Addis Ababa, and the Japanese had bombed Manchuria. The travellers were back to 'civilization' with a vengeance!

Not long afterwards, Tichy and Kapur took leave of their friends Kitar and Ranschid on the platform of the railway station at Kathgodam. It was a sad parting. A few moments later, through the window of the departing train, they saw the mountains sliding into the distance. Finally, they disappeared.

The infant Sutlej between Gurugem and Khyunglung (1987)

Herbert Tichy's later life continued the pattern set in his youth: he travelled widely and wrote many books about his travels. He passed the Second World War in China, where he lived for some eight years in all. True to his resolution, he returned many times to the Himalayas, and among his many achievements can be counted the first ascent of Cho Oyo, which is probably the seventh highest mountain in the world. Herbert Tichy died in Vienna in 1987.

As for his friend, Chatter Bhuj Kapur, he is also still alive and lives in London, in a street behind the Exhibition Hall at Olympia. I have met him a number of times and recalled with him his remarkable journey to Mount Kailas. He was surprised that anyone should be taking an interest in it at all. Retired now, he left his native Punjab at the time of Partition and spent several years in Delhi before coming to London, where he worked first as a teacher and later as an educational administrator. He is a sensitive person, unobtrusive in manner. When asked what his motive in going to Kailas was, he answered, 'It was an adventure!' Even though he does not claim to be a religious person, he admits that Kailas had a deep spiritual effect upon him which has remained alive and fresh during the intervening forty years. He is in no doubt that there is something intrinsically sacred about the mountain. When asked where the particular spiritual potency of Kailas might reside, he simply raised both arms till they were horizontally presented across his chest then raised a simple pyramid with his flattened hands. It lay in its unique and unusually symmetrical shape, he explained, and in the fact that it stood out as a single snow-clad peak in an otherwise snowless desolation.

The fate of the third member of Tichy's party, Kitar, was not so fortunate. Shortly after returning from Tibet he fell ill and died while serving the Anglo-American Expedition that successfully climbed Nanda Devi in 1937.

Of young Ranschid, all that remains is a blank.

After the mountaineers, the scientist; after the ice-axe, the geologist's hammer strikes the sacred rock of Mount Kailas.

Also in 1936, during an expedition with his colleague Arnold Heim, the Swiss geologist Augusto Gansser found himself in the village of Kuti, where the local inhabitants were preparing for their festival of the dead. For this to be properly performed, two sheep reared at the foot of the sacred Kailas were required; therefore, on 28th July, two sturdy Bhotias were dispatched to procure them. They travelled with two additional companions: a Sherpa porter named Paldin, and a rather paunchy, bearded lama wearing a heavy

Paldin (1936)   *Augusto Gansser (1936)*

red sheepskin caftan and fur cap. The lama's obesity was not due to body fat, however, but to the fact that beneath his robes he carried a small armoury of scientific gear: sketchbook, hammer, aneroid, field-glasses, Leica, and even a bottle of hydrochloric acid. It was Gansser himself, who, denied proper credentials, was continuing the tradition first established by William Moorcroft of disguising himself in order to penetrate the Kailas-Manasarovar region.

The four men crossed into Tibet by the Mangshang Pass and then made their way to Darchen by the western shore of Rakshas Tal, where Gansser came to several important conclusions concerning the present hydrography of the lakes region:

> The domain of these mighty lakes is undergoing depression, and it has long been known that the Sutlej has ceased to derive any of its waters from them. They have no outlet now, and I can find plain evidence of changes in the direction of the flow – very recent changes in the course of the rivers that rise in the Transhimalaya.
>
> (A. Gansser and A. Heim: *The Throne of the Gods*)

During the journey the travellers slept rough: either under the stars, or in the tents of nomads, where adults children and animals all lived together in atmospheres made acrid by the smoke of yak-dung fires.

At Darchen, Gansser and Paldin embarked upon the Kailas Parikrama. The Sherpa first performed the ritual prostration, then looked at his employer to see his reaction – 'No, Paldin ... the mountain is just as sacred to me as it is to you, for I too am a pilgrim,' Gansser reassured his porter. 'Just as those two lamas who passed a moment ago. Like you, like them, I am in search of the beautiful, the sacred in this wonderful mountain.'

But if the pilgrim in Gansser had been awakened, the geologist had not fallen into abeyance. He realized that the remarkable position of Kailas presented fascinating geological problems for solution:

> Strangely enough, it consists of horizonally stratified conglomerate masses with erratic admixture. In the course of geological aeons, these strata have been elevated many thousands of feet without any change in the horizontal lay-out.
>
> *(Ibid.)*

As the collection of specimens would, however, be regarded as sacrilege by pilgrims and lamas alike, he had to proceed with extreme caution and employ what he calls 'peculiar methods'.

Having marched up the western valley of Kailas between high walls of conglomerate rock, he at last reached the northern side, which was of far greater interest from a geological point of view. Here he examined closely the granite pediment upon which the great conglomerate mass of the mountain itself stood, until one of those sudden electric storms so characteristic of Kailas put an end to his investigations and forced him to seek shelter for the night at the nearby *gompa*, unnamed in his narrative but undoubtedly Drira Puk.

Here the authenticity of his disguise was really put to the test. It was established practice for all visitors to the *gompa* to seek an interview with the head lama. Gansser, posing as a lama of importance from a distant region, could not evade this custom without giving offence. Moreover, in the interests of complete authenticity, he should not only ask for an interview but do so with enthusiasm.

Having been schooled in his part by Paldin, Gansser duly presented himself at the head lama's chamber with bare feet and lowered head. The chamber was dark inside, lit only by the tiny and unstable flames of guttering butter lamps. The head lama was squatting 'tailor-fashion' behind a long altar.

'He had sharply cut features and an intelligent expression,' Gansser writes. Paldin having announced him, the geologist silently presented the lama with two small goblets of marbled vulcanite. The Tibetan reciprocated by hanging a red scarf around Gansser's neck, and also presented him with a bag of pills said to be good against every kind of mischance. By invoking the universal convention that among men of really deep spirituality communication by so gross a means as the spoken word is not necessary, Gansser was able to leave the chamber with his cover intact.

The next morning the weather was glorious, and Gansser took advantage of it to go out and take photographs. As he returned to the *gompa*, he saw the head lama make his daily salutations to the gods and demons of the sacred mountain. Re-entering the *gompa*, Gansser prostrated himself before the gilded images, offered up the customary butter lamp, spun the great prayer wheel, and then left to continue his *parikrama* with his porter. They ascended to the Drölma Pass then descended to 'a small sacred lake', undoubtedly Gauri Kund, where masses of rock littered the frozen surface: evidence of many pilgrims' unsuccessful attempts to break through the ice and make their ritual ablutions. 'It seems to be an unfavourable year for pilgrimages,' Ganser writes.

Moving on southwards down the eastern valley, Gansser found himself leaving the savage granite landscape of the north and once again stood immured between imposing walls of conglomerate:

> For the moment I am wholly taken up with my geological investigations. The strata of the conglomerate, which had hitherto been horizontal, are somewhat inclined, as if by pressure from the south. As we negotiate a curve in the valley, this impression is confirmed, and suddenly I come across a most interesting geological phenomenon. At a well-marked transitional line, the conglomerate strata have been covered by a number of convoluted strata sharply contrasting with the flat Transhimalayan sedimentary rocks, and the granites. Compared with the Transhimalayan rocks, this superimposed series must have undergone recent and intensive convolution. These observations show that we have to do with the northernmost vestiges of the Himalayan chain proper, which has been superimposed upon the Transhimalaya from the south – backwards, that is to say.
>
> (*Ibid.*)

'Look out, the *sadhus* [holy men] are coming!'

A warning shout from Paldin jerked Gansser from his scientific

Pilgrims' teeth wedged into the Great Rock on the Drölma La (1935)

speculations, and together they took cover in a small side valley. Later, however, they resumed their work and continued till nightfall, when they sought shelter at Zutrul Puk Gompa.

The *gompa* was comparatively uninteresting, and its running had become rather disorderly due to the absence of the head lama, who had gone on a trip to Lhasa. The following day, Gansser and Paldin visited some unoccupied hermit caves excavated in the cliffs nearby. Much to the dismay of his porter, the geologist filched a finely-carved *mani* stone to take home as a souvenir. They then proceeded back to Darchen.

While they were waiting for their pack animals and the sacrificial sheep to be got ready, Gansser and Paldin made another foray into the foothills on the southern flank of Kailas to further trace the superimposition of the rock strata first detected the day before. On their return to Darchen, they found all ready, so they could return to Kuti with their original Bhotia travelling companions. They reached the Mangshang Glacier without crisis, and found Heim waiting for them there, the Swiss flag flying over his tent. They recrossed the Mangshang Pass the following day.

Gansser subsequently published a fine, scholarly *Geology of the Himalayas*, in which he describes the geology of the Kailas region in technical detail. According to him, the northern portion of the lowlying belt separating the Himalaya and the Transhimalaya comprises a sandy alluvial plain over twenty kilometres wide, bordering the foothills of the Kailas Range. This Gansser calls the *Kailas Flysch* zone:

> The Kailas Flysch represents the last remnant of the Himalayas, thrust steeply northwards over the autochthonous Kailas conglomerate which trangresses over the Kailas granite.
>
> (A. Gansser, *Geology of the Himalayas*)

North of the thrust there is a completely different region: one characterized 'by huge fantastically shaped conglomerate mountains sitting on granites', of which Kailas itself is a beautiful example.

In 1939, the Austrian mountaineer, Heinrich Harrer, found himself in Karachi after having completed a reconnaissance of Nanga Parbat with a German expedition. The outbreak of the Second World War led to the whole expedition being interned as enemy aliens. After spending several years in various camps in India, Harrer was incarcerated in the largest of them at Dehra Dun, right beneath the Himalayas. In 1944, after various abortive attempts at escape, he and a few companions succeeded in crossing the mountains and entering neutral Tibet by the Tsangchola Pass (17,200 feet). They made contact with the local authorities and applied for asylum, but received the usual unwelcoming reception and were told to return to India. They were given a choice of routes, however, and elected to take the more westerly one by the Shipki Pass, fully intending to slip back into Tibet further along the frontier and put their request for asylum to more senior officials. They were successful and eventually arrived at Gartok, where they were granted an audience with the Garpön. He was sympathetic to their suit but could only grant them a passport to travel in his province; they could not enter the central provinces without permission from Lhasa.

On the 13th July, Harrer and his companions, Aufsnaiter, Kopp and Treipel, travelled eastwards with the intention of going to Nepal. They soon arrived at Barkha, where they caught a glimpse of Kailas. They would have liked to have made the Parikrama but the master of the 'Barkha caravanserai' (the *tarjum* perhaps?) blocked them in this and obliged them to proceed straight on their way. Gurla Mandhata, majestically reflected in the turquoise waters of Lake Manasarovar, impressed them rather more deeply than the holy Kailas, however, and also engaged their mountaineering

Heinrich Harrer

Captain R.K.M. Saker

instincts. They would have liked to have attempted to climb it, if it had been at all possible – which it was not. Harrer bathed in the icy waters of the sacred lake, though more in the interests of physical hygiene than for spiritual purification. Altogether, the beauty of the sacred region impressed him deeply. 'This is certainly one of the loveliest spots on earth,' he writes.

From Barkha, the fugitives proceeded to 'Tokchen', where they had a pleasant meeting with the new Governor of Tsaparang; then they continued on to the source of the Tsangpo/Brahmaputra, which they subsequently followed eastwards for the next fortnight.

Harrer ultimately reached Lhasa, where he eventually rose to become tutor and confidant of the present exiled Dalai Lama, then in his teens. Harrer spent seven years in Tibet all told, only leaving – and then with great reluctance – when the Chinese began to mount the final phases of their takeover of the country.

The next British visitor to Kailas, Captain R. K. M. Saker (1909–1979), was born in Aldershot of a military family. At 19, after Aldenham and Sandhurst, he took a commission in the Baluchistan Rifles but, realising he wasn't cut out for regimental life, put in a request for a secondment to the I.P.S. He was successful and in 1935 was posted to Mt. Abu., then to Gyantse as B.T.A. In 1943 he received orders to go on special duty in Western Tibet.

'I was delighted,' he later wrote. 'My wife was staying outside Simla, where I joined her to make preparations for a journey that would take me about 6 months...'

At Simla something potentially dire happened: Saker was bitten by a rabid dog. As a result, he had to undergo a course of fifteen painful injections. The tour of Western Tibet was not cancelled, though, and he was luckily able to recruit Gordon Terry, a senior doctor with the Burmah Oil Company, to accompany him. Together they made their way towards Tibet along the Sutlej, pausing every 15 miles or so at guest houses, as far as they went; later, up into the high country, they slept under canvas.

Like many of his precursors, Saker was a keen sportsman with both rod and gun. Not many days out of Simla, he branched off into the valley of the Baspa river, a tributory of the Sutlej, which was famed for its fishing. Later, having hooked and landed a very creditable trout, he reluctantly resumed the journey.

After a number of minor passes, trees became increasingly more sparse and finally vanished; then Saker and Terry found themselves 'in rugged country, virtually uninhabited.' They crossed the Sutlej for the last time by a rudimentary cantilever bridge with no guard

Nomad tent at sunset near Tirthapuri (1987)

rail. The ponies and pack animals went across happily enough, but one of Saker's orderlies, glimpsing the churning waters 200 feet below, lost his nerve and had to make his crossing on hands and knees.

At first camp in Tibet, Terry was attacked by a severe bout of altitude sickness. 'He did not tell me how ill he felt,' Saker wrote, 'and it was only later that he told me that he thought he might have to return to Simla.' Fortunately he recovered and suffered no recurrence of this painful condition, which is always incapacitating and in extreme cases can prove fatal.

They switched to yak transport now that they were on the great plateau, except for their own riding ponies. Some of the yak proved to be less than amiable and would throw their loads if vexed.

Rugged country now presented itself: mountain ranges and great plains with little vegetation except on the edges of rivers and streams. There were no settled villages, though they passed

Nomads near Tirthapuri (1987)

'occasional small monasteries and a few tents of nomads'. Food was
in short supply too, so they had to rely on their own scanty stores,
augmented by what little they could buy from Indian traders. These
hardy entrepreneurs brought cloth, kerosene, rice, barley, sugar
and other items to trade with the Tibetans for wool, borax and yak
tails:

> It was interesting to see these encampments, each tent being its owner's
> shop, while on the plain outside the sheep had been brought in to be
> clipped with much argument as to price. As soon as the Indians had sold
> their goods, the wool and borax would be loaded onto their pack animals
> to be taken back to India.
>
> (R. K. M. Saker, *Western Tibet 1943*, typescript chapter
> of an unpublished memoir.)

Wildlife, however, was abundant. There were wild asses – 'beautiful pale brown in colour with a pronounced dark stripe down their
backs and with darker manes and tails'; ovis ammon and bharral too,
'with snow leopard as their predators.' Unfortunately, there was no
time for 'proper shooting', but Saker bagged an ovis ammon for the
pot; it made good eating. A valley they passed through later was

strewn with the bleached skulls and bones of about a hundred ovis ammon. Saker surmised they must have sought shelter there one winter but been overtaken by a blizzard.

At Gartok, the local *dzongpön* proved both 'unimpressive and not very friendly', so they did not tarry in that desolate spot. Resuming, they travelled for several days 'through unchanging country, bleak and sinister.' Their supplies were running low and they lived mainly on porridge and occasional rice 'with a rare tin of meat or fish.' Famished, their mouths therefore began to water when at one camp they saw a rider approaching with panniers strapped to his pony: Saker had arranged with his wife, Angela, to have supplies sent round to meet them. However, 'a deep depression settled over us when we unpacked the panniers, one of which contained a chest with a complete dinner and tea service, while the other had a nest of folding tables. Examination of the address showed that these items were meant for the Chief Minister of an Indian hill state, who presumably received our food parcels – to the mutual annoyance of us all!'

Tightening their belts, Saker and Terry pushed on to the shores of the 'mediterranean blue' Lake Manasarovar. Despite the fact that autumn was approaching and the wind was cold and sharp, all the Tibetans in the British party leapt into the holy waters to wash away their sins. Saker, however, compromised by taking a warm bath in his tent – 'hoping that this would not destroy the efficacy of my ablutions'. Sacred water was also bottled up to provide 'valued gifts' in Lhasa, Gangtok and Gyantse.

They now encountered pilgrims. The abbot of a small monastery near Lhasa was sitting outside his decorated tent in a splendid gold *papier mâché* hat. He said he had been travelling for several months and did not expect to see Lhasa again for a year. There was also a encampment of Khampa nomads. 'They were cheerful rascals,' Saker recorded, 'earning a precarious living from their herd of yaks, periodically supplemented by armed robbery... As we outnumbered them, we felt reasonably safe...'

They also came across two memorials to the turbulent past of the region. The first was the remains of a 'pillaged and burned' monastery, which had received the hostile attentions of marauding Kirghiz-Kazaki Muslims. Gold and precious ornaments had been looted, paintings and images mutilated, and sacred books put to the torch. The monks had run off, but Saker was not able to ascertain what had been their ultimate fate. 'This desecrated building presented a grim picture,' he wrote. The other discovery was a series of caves high up in a limestone cliff, where some of Zorawar

Singh's invading Dogra soldiers had apparently billetted themselves in 1841.

Proceeding to Kailas, Saker and Terry decided to make the holy circuit. They took a leisurely three days, travelling on foot out of respect for the sanctity of the place. They found walking at that altitude over 'a very rough path' to be taxing work, so each went at his own pace. Saker arrived first at the monastery (probably Drira Puk), where they spent their first night:

> When he arrived, Gordon was in a state of exhaustion, but the monks received us with kindness and hospitality and quickly revived us with steaming bowls of Tibetan tea. I slept in a monk's cell, which, with its bare walls, was devoid of all decoration.
>
> (*Ibid.*)

Next day, pushing on towards the Drölma La, Saker found he had to pause for rest every few hundred yards.

'Kailas towered above us, only a few miles away,' he later wrote, 'a great white mass of snow; and in the clear atmosphere it looked so easy to climb the extra few thousand feet to the summit . . .' At the Gauri Kund lake, his staff went off for ritual ablution, but the good political 'was unable to pluck up the courage' to break the ice and take a dip himself. He spent a second night at Zutrul Puk monastery – and then 'we were back in our base camp, the better, I hoped, for a most moving experience.'

News arrived that a number of Austrian prisoners-of-war had escaped from internment camp at Dehra Dun. 'I was told to keep my eyes and ears open for them,' Saker wrote; 'though what I was expected to do if I found them I was far from sure.' The fugitives were of course Heinrich Harrer and his friends. Keenly appreciating the 'extreme difficulties' they must have faced, Saker confessed that he could have nothing but the highest admiration for the courage and perseverance of these men. He 'made enquiries as we travelled but picked up no news at all.'

Four months after setting out from Simla, the weather grown decidedly cold, Saker and Terry thankfully set their faces towards home. Once across the high passes, it was 'a most welcome change' to get back to lower altitudes, trees and the 'simple things of life'. Food was a special preoccupation – almost an obsession.

They had planned to meet their wives a few days out from Almora, but when the ladies duly appeared their delight at seeing them turned to disappointment when they could only muster one solitary plum cake. The reason was political. The Civil Disobedience

Mani sculptor at Kailas (1987)

Movement had closed down the local shops and transport was impossible to obtain. The cake was consumed at one sitting – could their contracted stomachs digest it? one wonders – and orders were promptly dispatched for more food to be sent up.

Saker finished his tour off with a spot of marseer fishing. He managed to bag a 12 lb. fish, though a far bigger monster broke his light tackle. He also finalized his report:

> The report I submitted speculated on the future possibilities of this region [i.e. Tibet]; gold was there for the panning, and were there other precious minerals and oil?; were the big powers ever likely to be interested, or would they continue to respect the integrity of Tibet?; The answer to the last question is all too well known to-day.
>
> (*Ibid.*)

After a few more months at Gyantse, Saker was posted back to Baluchistan. He subsequently served as Assistant Political Agent in Quetta, then for a brief time in Kalat State before gaining full status as a Political Officer in Bulsar in 1946. After Independence and Partition, he continued in the service, working for the Pakistan Government. Returning home eventually in 1959, he settled at Birdham near Chichester in Sussex, from where for the next ten years he commuted daily to a more humdrum job in the Foreign Office in London. After retirement in 1969, he was able to devote more time to his sporting interests: fishing, dinghy sailing, golf – though he never raised a gun after leaving India. He died in 1979.

The very last European at the sacred mountain prior to 1984 was a Buddhist monk and so his story rightly belongs with those of the pilgrims in Chapter Nine. His immediate predecessor, the penultiate European visitor and the last *traveller* proper, arrived at Mount Kailas in the summer of 1945. He was another distinguished mountaineer: Major T.S. Blakeney, who had begun to climb in the Alps in the early 1920s. He went to the East about ten years later and worked on tea plantations, first in Ceylon and later in the Madras district. On the outbreak of War in 1939, he joined the Army.

Blakeney's notes on his reconnaissance of Kailas were published in the *Alpine Journal*; they are brief and may therefore be quoted here in full:

APPROACH TO KAILAS. – Major T. S. Blakeney has sent us the following notes, the result of an expedition undertaken with little opportunity of preparation in August and September, 1945.

I had only a very small scale map, so I cannot give exact heights etc. As a climbing proposition, I think only the E. arete of Kailas is feasible. The W. ridge forks into a N.W. and S.W. arete, subtending an unclimbable W. face of about 4000 feet, and I could not see any way of getting on to either of these aretes. The N. face is terrific (about 5000 ft.) very sheer, and stones fall a good deal. From the Diraphuk Gompa or monastery one can approach the N. face easily enough by a small valley giving on to the moraines beneath the face. The valley lies between two peaks called, I gather, Jambyang and Chenresi, the latter being furthest west. It might be more useful for reconnaissance purposes to climb Jambyang, but as we had nothing but sleet and mist we saw nothing, whatever we did. East of Jambyang is another peak, Changnadorje, and the valley between can also be ascended, and ahead of it I got a glimpse of a pass that looked certainly easy and should, I estimate, give out on to the lower slopes of the E. arete of Kailas. Normally, pilgrims making the circuit of Kailas pass from the Diraphuk Gompa on the N. to the Zuthulphuk Gompa on the E. by the Dolma La, a pass further N. than the one I could see, but Swami Pranavānanda, author of a *Pilgrim's Companion to the Holy Kailas* etc., and of *Exploration in Tibet*, tells me that Tibetans are allowed, after they have made ten circuits of Kailas, on future occasions to short-circuit the route by what I think must be the pass I saw. If so, then a simple route to the E. arete may lie here, though I fancy it would be better approached by a climbing party straight from Zuthulphuk Gompa, without spending the time going round to Diraphuk.

The only fine day I had was on the S. side of Kailas; above the Gengta Gompa a mild ridge runs parallel to the S. face, but separated from it by a deep valley. Direct ascent of the S. face seems quite out of the question. This parallel ridge is joined by another at right angles that runs northwards to merge in the snows of the E. arete of Kailas; this looked practicable so far as I could see, and I would have liked to try, but my Tibetan guide would not hear of it, and even had he agreed I doubt if I could have braved your editorial strictures on anyone approaching a substantial Himalayan peak in unnailed boots and armed only with that invaluable asset to monsoon climbing, an umbrella. I do not recommend this route, actually, as I still think direct access is more easily obtained to the E. ridge from the E. flank; but once up on the snows of the lower E. ridge I think a camp could be pitched (we were at approximately 19,000 ft. and, I reckoned, slightly lower than the beginnings of the steep portion of the E. arête) and the summit reached next day. Probably plenty of step-cutting, but Kailas is only 22,028 ft., and there would be barely 3000 ft. to climb.

It is a grand peak; the N. face is usually considered the finest view, but my one fine day on the S. side impressed me greatly. The view from here southwards was magnificent – in the foreground, the bright blue lakes of Manasarovar and Raksas [sic] contrasting vividly with the barren hills around them; and the huge mass of Gurla Mandhata (almost a range in itself) and behind, the vast extent of the Zanskar range, from Kamet in the W. to Nalkankar and the unnamed peaks of Nepal in the E., with Nanda Devi, Nanda Kot, Panch Chhuli and others raising their heads in the background.

(*Alpine Journal*, Vol. 55, 1945–6)

Blakeney died at Chichester in 1976.

CHAPTER EIGHT

Pilgrims to the Sacred Mountain – 1

Ekai Kawaguchi

On 25th June 1897, a small group of well-wishers standing on the quay at Kobe in Japan waved goodbye to a Buddhist priest who was sailing that day on the ship *Idzumi-maru*. His name was Ekai Kawaguchi; his destination, Calcutta, and ultimately Tibet; his mission, to obtain rare Mahāyāna Buddhist texts. At least, that was the overt story. It has been alleged, however, that this pious Buddhist priest was in fact a secret agent of the Japanese government, briefed to gather information on the political situation in the Forbidden Land.

In pictures taken at the time Kawaguchi looks every inch the Buddhist priest. In one, he poses in a Japanese garden with a rosary playing through his fingers. His head is shaven to billiard-ball smoothness, he sports a whispy beard of the Chinese variety and he wears a most splendid, though heterodox, set of robes – they combine elements of the vestments of both the Nichiren and Obaku Zen sects. Then, as the eye travels downwards, it suddenly notices a discordant element: the highly polished toecaps of a pair of oxfords peeping from beneath the capacious hems. They suggest incipient European inclinations – which were subsequently to manifest themselves in the form of an interest in Theosophy.

As regards his background, Kawaguchi tells us that he was a native of Akashi and served as Rector of the Monastery of Gohyakurakan in Tokyo until March 1891, when he left to spend three years in Kyoto, living the life of a hermit and occupying himself with studying his extensive collection of Chinese Buddhist texts. It was with a view to augmenting and improving this collection that he embarked upon his epic journey to Tibet. This kept him away from Japan from June 1897 to May 1902. He left

Ekai Kawaguchi

Japan again in October 1904 for India and Nepal, hoping to make a second foray into Tibet for manuscripts.

Kawaguchi's route on his first visit to Tibet was a long and roundabout one. Initially landing at Calcutta, he went north to Darjeeling, where he spent the whole of the next year preparing himself for the Forbidden Land. He studied the Tibetan language with Rai Bahadur Sarat Chandra Das, who himself had also combined scholarship with a career as an undercover agent. As a result of one of the secret missions into Tibet that Das had made on behalf of the British, a notable lama named Sengchen Dorjechan had been put to death by drowning for having harboured him.

As the route into Tibet was known to be closely guarded, Kawaguchi decided to try to make his entry by unfrequented byways. He therefore went to Nepal, which he believed himself to be the first Japanese to visit, and where he also hoped to be able to obtain Buddhist texts. Having visited both Kathmandu and Pokhara, he eventually travelled north to a village near the Tibetan border called Tsarang, where he also lingered for many months.

'The days I spent in Tsarang,' he wrote 'were, in a sense, the days of my tutelage in the arts of living amidst filth and filthy habits.'

Here he pursued his Buddhist studies under the guidance of a lama of the Nyingma (Red Hat) school of Tibetan Buddhism, who had been obliged to leave Lhasa and live out his life in this obscure backwater because he had at sometime succumbed to 'feminine temptation', as Kawaguchi quaintly puts it. The Japanese traveller was himself something of a puritan and particularly disapproving of sexual lapses on the part of a religious. He also found the erotic symbolism of Nyingma Tantrism highly offensive, and held the founder of the sect, the Indian Tantric adept Padmasambhava, in special odium:

> Lobon [Padmasambhava] was in practice a devil in the disguise of a priest as if he had been born for the very purpose of corrupting and perverting the spread of the holy doctrines of Buddha.
> (Ekai Kawaguchi, *Three Years in Tibet*)

Naturally, such views inevitably led to heated arguments with his Nyingma lama friend, who on one dramatic occasion lost his self-possession entirely and physically attacked Kawaguchi.

While at Tsarang, Kawaguchi got himself into training for his eventual penetration into Tibet by doing a considerable amount of mountain walking, sometimes carrying heavy loads of stones on his back. He actually crossed the border in June 1900, taking a route by the northern slopes of Dhaulagiri, after which he cut straight for the Kailas-Manasarovar region. As usual, he ran the gamut of trials and tribulations – 'hunger and thirst, the perils of dashing stream and freezing blizzard, the pain of writhing under heavy burdens, the anxiety of wandering over trackless wastes, the exhaustion and the lacerations . . .'

Passing himself off as a Chinese lama, Kawaguchi seems in fact to have fared considerably better than his secular precursors. Indeed, being a Buddhist priest, he was able to command respect and get invaluable help from the people he met along the way by performing small religious services, like reading from the scriptures, preaching or divining. He also had a smattering of simple medical knowledge which he put to good use as well. No doubt his Buddhist philosophy and the depth of his faith helped him to survive. Whereas so many Westerners had gone into Tibet with loud and often violent arrogance, Kawaguchi was a consciously restrained and humble man, and while some of the philosphical beliefs that he held do not seem to have been strictly orthodox – he appears, for instance, to have believed that the Buddha was a kind of god, and that the ultimate ground of being has a personal character – his grasp of the practical, down-to-earth basis of Buddhism seems sound enough. Altogether he appears to have been a conscientious Buddhist. He was not without his human faults and failings, though: he had, for instance, to infringe the Buddhist injunction to Right Speech in order to mislead people about his true identity; and he can at times be very unBuddhist in the scathing remarks he makes about the Tibetans themselves:

> I was struck by the notion that the Tibetans are characterized by four serious defects: filthiness, superstition, unnatural customs (like polyandry), and unnatural art.* I should be seriously perplexed if I were asked to name their redeeming points; but if I had to do so, I should mention first of all the fine climate in the vicinity of Lhasa and Shigatze [!!], their sonorous and refreshing voices in reading the Text, the animated style of their catechisms, and their ancient art.
>
> (*Ibid.*)

Nor, as he comes to see more of it, does he hold Tibetan Buddhism in much higher regard. He is appalled by the decadent practices and superstitions that have crept into it, at the low level of scholarship

---

*He is referring here to the erotic imagery to be found in Tantric iconography.

Kailas Pilgrims (1986)

and the ignorance of the majority of lamas, and of their general moral turpitude. It is, however, redeemed for him by the occasional rare lama of real quality, who stands out like a precious jewel in a heap of rubbish.

Early in August 1900, when he was travelling with a group of pilgrims from Kham – the province of eastern Tibet notorious for its robbers and murderers, he reminds us – Kawaguchi had just bivouacked for the night when he chanced to look towards the north-west and saw 'a great snow-clad mountain'. It was Kailas:

> As far as my knowledge goes, it is the most ideal of the snow peaks of the Himalayas. It inspired me with the profoundest feelings of pure reverence, and I looked up to it as a 'natural mandala,' the mansion of a Buddha and Bodhisattvas. Filled with soul-stirring thoughts and fancies, I addressed myself to this sacred pillar of nature, confessed my sins, and performed to it the obeisance of one hundred and eight vows. I also took out the manuscript of my 'twenty-eight desires', and pledged their accomplishment to the Buddha. I then considered myself the luckiest of men, to have been enabled thus to worship such an emblem of the Buddha's power, and to vow such things in its sacred presence...'
>
> (*Ibid.*)

Mani stones at Manasarovar; Gurla Range beyond (1987)

Kawaguchi's pious devotions aroused the curiosity of his Khampa companions, of which he took immediate advantage, treating them to a brief but calculatedly inspiring sermon. This had an immediate and profound effect upon the hearts of these people, who belonged to a stock who 'took mens' lives with the same equanimity with which they cut their vegetables' – and Kawaguchi consequently 'blessed the power of Buddhism more than ever, and could not hold back my tears as my companions shed theirs'.

A day or so later, seeing Kailas rising in the distance across the placid waters of Lake Manasarovar, Kawaguchi thought he saw in it 'the image of our mighty Lord Buddha, calmly addressing his five hundred disciples'. He also describes it for a second time as a 'natural *mandala*', inferring thereby that the sacred mountain and its environs are a model of the order of the universe. This would also imply identification of Kailas with the mytical Meru or its equivalents. Furthermore, he goes on to identify Lake Manasarovar with the legendary Anotatta or Anavatapta of Buddhist mythology, though *buddhas* and *bodhisattvas* said to sit in lotus flowers floating upon its surface are not visible to mortal eyes. 'The real thing in the region is its wonderfully inspiring character,' he continues; 'and a wonderfully holy elevation is to be found there.' He describes his own elevated feelings in an *uta*, one of the brief (and sometimes not-so-brief) poems he composed during his travels to express his responses to the changing faces of the landscape and his own changing moods and thoughts:

> Among these mountains high here sleeps the lake
>   Serene – 'devoid of seething cares' – so named
> By native bards; its broad expanse appears
>   Like the octagonal mirror of Japan.
> The grand Kailas, majestic, capped with snow,
>   The moon o'erhanging from the skies above,
> Bestow their grateful shadows on the lake.
>   Its watery brilliant sheen illuminates me;
> All pangs of pain and sorrow washed away.
>   With these my mind besoothed now wanders far
> E'en to Akashi in Japan, my home,
>   A seashore known for moonlight splendours fair.
>   *(Ibid.)*

Kawaguchi and his companions skirted the southern shores of the lakes and then made a loop detour to the west of Kailas, visiting Gyanima, Gya Karko and Tirthapuri. This was to be a spiritually perilous phase of his journey for a young Khampa lass declared her

Tirthapuri Gompa (1987)

love for the good Buddhist priest and began to beset him with all the wiles of female cunning. He was not insensitive to her attractions either, not being, he assures us, 'a block of wood, nor a piece of stone'. He compares himself under such sweet assault to the Buddha on the eve of his Enlightenment when he was tempted by the daughters of Māra, the Deceiver – though he has to concede that little Dawa, bold though she was, was a siren of rather an inferior order. Ultimately, however, Kawaguchi was able to use skilful means to divert and defuse the girl's passion for him by reminding her of her far-away mother and her deep feelings for her. Still, no doubt, he escaped by the skin of his teeth.

Kawaguchi found Tirthapuri to be an important religious centre. He paid a *tanka** to see Padmasambhava's imprint in the local *gompa*. It was said to have been etched into the rock by supernatural means.

---

*A Tibetan coin (see p. 272).

Nyenri Gompa (1985)

Though he deplored the veneration paid to this Tantric *guru*, he found the scenery around Tirthapuri altogether delightful – in fact, 'one of nature's best essays in landscape'.

Returning eventually to the foot of Kailas, the pilgrim party broke up, each individual member apparently wishing to make his or her *parikrama* in a special way. Kawaguchi himself chose to make the outermost circuit, not concerned to break any records or subject himself to particularly gruelling austerities. He carried with him enough food to last four or five days.

His first call on his *parikrama* was at Nyenri Gompa, which he found to be dedicated to Amitābha, the Buddha of Infinite Light, and very popular with pilgrims in consequence. There was an image of Amitābha in the *gompa* made of 'white lustrous stone'; the features 'were of the Tibetan type, and looked mild and affable, awakening in me pious thoughts'. Two thick ivory tusks, five feet high, stood in front of the image, and behind them a quantity of books were arranged on shelves, though more as objects of veneration than of study. 'This use of Buddhist books is peculiar,' Kawaguchi thought, 'though it is preferable to the outrageous treatment of which these books are sometimes subjected by impious priests, who do not scruple to tear out leaves and use them for improper purposes.'

After Nyenri, he travelled up what he calls the 'Golden Valley' –

The adjective 'golden' should not be taken in a literal sense, for gold is not found near this place. Rhetorically, however, the valley deserves this distinction, the scenery all around being really magnificent. There are several fantastic rocks of great size towering far into the sky, while beyond them peeps the snow-clad summit of the peak of Tisé.

(Ibid.)

His next stop was at Drira Puk Gompa, where the head lama and he struck up such a good relationship that Kawaguchi could only conclude that they must have a spiritual affinity dating back to previous lives.* His host in fact gave up his own room to his Japanese guest. This commanded a spectacular view of the great north face of Kailas and its surroundings, the symbolism of which he explained when he brought Kawaguchi his butter tea in the evening (his precepts forbade the taking of an evening meal). The main peak of Kailas represented the Buddha, the lama maintained, while the three smaller peaks in front of it represented the *bodhisattvas* Mañjushrī, Avalokiteshvara and Vajrapāni. That night was one of the most delightful interludes of Kawaguchi's whole three-year sojourn in Tibet:

> ...it was a pleasure of an elevating kind. My mind was subdued and captivated as I looked, in that still night and in that far-off place, at the soft rays of the moon reflected on the crystal-like current that was flowing with pleasant murmur. Just as, in the holy texts, the soft breeze stirring the branches of trees in paradise is said to produce a pleasant note, that sounds to the ears of the happy denizens of that blissful abode like the voice of one reading the Scriptures, so that sweet murmur of the moon-reflecting stream deluded my enchanted ears into believing that they were listening to the divine music of Buddhism. Staying in that sacred place, and surrounded by soul-subduing phenomena, my mind soared higher and higher, till it flew up to the eternal region beyond this world of woe and care. The holy Founder tells us that the most sacred region lies in one's own pure mind, but I, sinful mortal that I was, felt elevated and chastened when I found myself in such an environment.

> *(Ibid.)*

He liked it so much at Drira Puk – he calls it 'Ri Ri Puri' – that he stayed the following day as well. Its name, he claims, means 'The Place of the Female Yak's Horn', and derives from a legend that 'Gyrva Gottsang Pa' of Bhutan was led on his Parikrama by a female yak, which he took to be a manifestation of the Buddhist deity 'Vajra'. The yak eventually concealed herself in a cavern at Drira Puk and struck her head against the rock there. This cavern was

---

*This implies mutual belief in reincarnation.

Gyangtra Gompa and and chörtens, ABOVE (1935) and RIGHT (1987)

situated beneath the *gompa*, which at the time of Kawaguchi's visit was the most prosperous of all four Kailas *gompa* and had most lamas attached to it.

When he eventually left Drira Puk, his lama friend sent Kawaguchi on his way with a yak, a guide and a supply of food and delicacies. Thus he plodded on up the 'Hill of Salvation' towards the Drölma Pass in comparative comfort. By sharp contrast, many of the other pilgrims he passed were making the Parikrama by the most arduous and painful prostration method. Kawaguchi did not feel moved to join them. He also passed a burly fellow who was 'frantically confessing to and worshipping Kailas'. This man, his guide informed him, was an especially notorious bandit from Kham: a man whose murders and other crimes were legion. While he now seriously regretted these sins and was earnestly doing penance for them, he evidently did not trust himself not to commit similar offences again, for he was also doing penance for future crimes.

'This fellow,' Kawaguchi wrote, 'was decidedly original in his conception of penance . . . . Yet, I was told that this convenient mode of repentance was universal in the robber district of Kham.'

Approaching the Drölma La, Kawaguchi could see the mountain ranges to the north of Kailas, called in Tibetan, *Gyalpo Norzin Potrang*, the Palace of King Kuvera. Recalling Kaildasa's great poem *Meghadūta* – 'Cloud Messenger' – Kawaguchi mused: 'Is it not really the mansion of the God of Wealth – that crystal abode shining in the emerald sky?' He also reflected that any 'mammon-worshipper' exploring the region would be sure to mistakenly expect to find a diamond mine there.

On the crest of the Drölma La he found the great rock, which he calls 'the natural stone image of the Mother of the Saviour'. Similarly, other stragely-shaped rocks nearby were, so his guide assured him, other images of the same person. He was now beginning to feel the effects of altitude and had to travel on the yak. On the other side of the Drölma La he encountered the Gauri Kund

Dorje Phamo (Vajravarahi)

lake, and recounts the legend that explains how the lake came to be frozen all year round. Apparently, in ancient times it did not freeze in summer, and Kuvera and his family used to take advantage of this to go there and wash their hands. One day, however, the child of a female pilgrim happened to accidentally slip into the lake and was drowned, so the guardian spirits decided that thereafter, in the interests of safety, it should remain perpetually frozen.

Kawaguchi was obliged to dismount from his yak to make the difficult descent down the eastern valley of Kailas to the Zutrul Puk Gompa. He duly notes the association with Milarepa. He stayed one night there before going on to Gyangtra Gompa, which he found to be dedicated to Dorje Phamo – 'White Thunderbolt'. He did not spend a night here, however, but travelled the mile or so on to Darchen, where he found lodging in a house.

His *parikrama* duly accomplished, Kawaguchi met up with his Khampa friends the next day and they set off together on their travels again, moving in a south-easterly direction to the west of Lake Manasarovar. The following day they passed the foot of Bönri (19,590 feet), the peak sacred to the Bön religion. Now that they were properly out of the sacred region, however, his companions returned to the unregenerate worldly ways and began, for one thing, to slaughter animals. This was offensive to Kawaguchi's Buddhist conscience, so he decided that the time for the parting of the ways had come. He subsequently set off on his own, following the Tsangpo/Brahmaputra eastwards to Shigatse and eventually reaching Lhasa itself. Again, he had to run the full gamut of misfortunes and hardships. These included two attacks by robbers. He had long before decided that he would offer no resistance should he encounter any such people: they could freely take whatever they wished of him in the way of goods or money if they would leave him his life – which, after all, was his most valuable possession. Not that he feared death if it came. As a Buddhist, he subscribed to the doctrine that all that is born must die. If he wished to prolong his life it was only that he might work for the benefit of other beings:

> Whate'er my sufferings here and dangers dire
>   Whate'er befalls me on my outward march
> All, all, I feel, is for the common good,
>   For others treading on Salvation's path.
>   *(Ibid.)*

He also nearly froze to death in a terrible blizzard: a harrowing experience that did not, however, unduly disturb his philosophic equanimity:

> Upon these plains of snow, my bed is snow,
> My pillow snow; my food also the same;
> And this my snowy journey, full of pain.
>
> *(Ibid.)*

Whatever may be asserted about Kawaguchi's possible undercover activities, there is no doubt that he was a sincere Buddhist, assiduous in his practices, which included the virtues of self-control, truthfulness (though occasionally infringed for reasons of security), compassion, friendliness and non-violence. These no doubt in the long run helped him to survive all difficulties and, after six months of hard travelling, to arrive safely at Lhasa, the Tibetan capital, a little footsore but essentially in good spirit.

Such was the benighted state of medical knowledge in Tibet at the time that Kawaguchi was able during his stay in Lhasa to win fame and fortune by employing his small medical skills. This gained him access to the highest circles of society. He met the Dalai Lama, and became a close friend of the ex-Minister of Finance, at whose home he lodged for a time. He also stayed at the great monastic university of Sera, a notable centre of Buddhist scholarship, where he sought and obtained Buddhist texts and studied Buddhism under one Ti Rimpoche, a lama of distinction.

Aside from the religious and medical aspects of his life in Lhasa, the Japanese priest was a keen observer of all aspects of the Tibetan scene. His book, *Three Years in Tibet*, contains a wealth of material on a wide variety of subjects, notably political ones. Here the sheer volume of information amassed is cited by some writers as clear evidence that Kawaguchi was in fact a secret agent. Whole chapters are devoted to such matters as Foreign Explorers and the Policy of Seclusion; the Government; Tibet and British India; China, Nepal and Tibet; and – most ominously – Russia's Tibetan Policy. This latter was at this period a highly sensitive issue among all powers with interests in Asia. The chief cause for concern was the proximity to the Dalai Lama of a Buriat lama from the Lake Baikal region of Russian eastern Siberia named Agvan Dorjiev (1854–1938), a man of high intelligence, great political acumen and iron will. Enrolling at Gomang College of Drepung monastic university near Lhasa around 1873, Dorjiev eventually rose to the exalted scholarly rank of Tsanit Khenpo: roughly 'Professor of Buddhist Metaphysics'. One of the few people in isolated and other-worldly Tibet able to give the Dalai Lama sound worldly advice, he was

*Agvan
Dorjiev*

effectively the Lama's chief political advisor for nearly twenty years, in which capacity he seems to have urged that Tibet look to Russia for support against the encroachments of China and Britain. Dorjiev himself undertook several missions to Russia. Perennial British fears that Russians were 'up to something' in Tibet were inflamed to the point of paranoia when the news leaked out that he had had four audiences with Tsar Nicholas II between 1898 and 1901.

Kawaguchi has much to say in *Three Years in Tibet* about Dorjiev's activities, which he regards as thoroughly malign. He suggests that the Khenpo circulated a pamphlet in which he argued that the Russian Tsar was about to fulfil the old Buddhist messianic myth of Shambhala by founding a great Buddhist empire. The name *Shambhala* has crept into English parlance as *Shangri-la*, the Land of Lost Content of James Hilton's novel *Lost Horizon*. It signifies a utopian Buddhist kingdom connected with the *Kālachakra Tantra* (Kālachakra = 'Wheel of Time'). Some have argued that Shambhala is purely mythical, a metaphor for an elevated spiritual state. Others, however, including the present Dalai Lama, maintain that it is a geographical reality on this planet, but one that is only visible to those with purified eyes. The messianic significance of Shambhala latterly took hold among the Tibetans and also among the Mongol nations, reaching as far as Dorjiev's Transbaikalia. It hinged around

Lhasa in the early 1930s

the notion that a great spiritual regeneration would be launched from Shambhala leading to the inauguration of a Buddhist millennium. Dorjiev's thesis was that the Tsar of Russia would become the secular patron of this buddhocracy. The Shambhala idea was also taken up and propagated in the West in modified form by the Russian artist Nicholas Roerich (1874–1947), who was a great influence on Franklin D. Roosevelt's Secretary for Agriculture, Henry Wallace. When Roosevelt built himself a retreat in the Maryland hills, he called it Shangri-la; we now know it as Camp David.

Kawaguchi also reports seeing consignments of arms arriving by camel caravan in Lhasa and the lavish presents that the Russians were bestowing on the Dalai Lama and other high Lamaist officials through Dorjiev. All of which might tend to reinforce suspicions regarding his true nature. Experts like Hugh Richardson, the last British representative in Lhasa, however, discount the possibility

Lhasa in the mid-1980s

that Kawaguchi was a Japanese spy, though there was one in Tibet at the time: Yasuteru Narita. All Kawaguchi probably did was pass on what he saw and heard to his teacher, Sarat Chandra Das, who was certainly a British agent and no doubt handed the information on to his masters. Even so, Kawaguchi's reports probably contributed to that escalating British Russophobia that ultimately precipitated the Younghusband Expedition to Lhasa (1904).

Towards the middle of 1901, the secret of Kawaguchi's foreign identity began to be leaked in Lhasa. Worse: the possibility of his being both a Japanese and a British spy was also mooted. Clearly he could not remain in the capital much longer, though when it came to the matter of flight he paused out of consideration for his many Tibetan friends. Perhaps recalling the fate of Chandra Das's protector, Sengchen Dorjechan, he realized that if he were to suddenly vanish, the Tibetan authorities might well suspect the worst and accordingly punish and torture his friends for harbouring him. He sweated on the horns of this dilemma for a long time before deciding to go to the ex-Minister of Finance and make a clean breast of everything. He told his friend who he really was and suggested that he arrest him himself and deliver him to the authorities by way of proving his own innocence in the matter. The ex-Minister would have none of it. It was entirely contrary to his Buddhist principles, he said, to deliver another person over to danger in order to save his own skin – especially a fellow Buddhist who had come to this country with the noble motive of studying Buddhism. The decision to leave was finally clinched when Kawaguchi heard a mysterious voice telling him to do just that while he was strolling in the Dharma Garden at Sera.

With his collection of Buddhist texts and other possessions packed up and dispatched to Darjeeling in charge of a Chinese merchant, Kawaguchi sadly took leave of his Tibetan friends and, accompanied only by a single porter, stole out of Lhasa. He took the direct southerly road for India, travelling fast for fear of pursuit. Ahead of him lay five serious obstacles: five 'challenge gates' notorious for their bureaucratic complications and for the extreme corruption of their presiding officers. In the best traditions of spy literature, however, Kawaguchi was able to exploit his now nationwide reputation as the 'Physician of Sera' to convince these officials – at whose merest whim he could have been held up for days – that he was in fact engaged on a mission of the utmost urgency and delicacy for no less a person than the Dalai Lama himself. He got through each of the gates without delay and was across the border without crisis.

Safely back in British India, he was still not at rest, however, for conflicting but nonetheless disquieting reports about the fate of his Tibetan friends filtered across the border to him. To settle the matter once and for all, he returned to Nepal for a second time in order to entreat the Maharaja to intercede personally with the Dalai Lama on behalf of his Lhasa friends. After initial reluctance and suspicion, the Maharaja was finally convinced of Kawaguchi's sincerity and concern, and agreed to cooperate.

And so, his conscience set at rest, Ekai Kawaguchi was able to return to his native Japan with his new collection of Buddhist texts. His ship, the *Bombay-maru*, came alongside the quay at Kobe on 20th May, 1902. He had arrived home safely, his mission fulfilled:

My heaped up sorrows and calamities
  Now all are melted like th' eternal snows
With that unfailing Beacon-light, My Guide;

The Universal Leader, Buddha Great, my Guide
Has been in all my travels in Tibet.

(Ibid.)

Bhagwan Shri Hamsa

Bhagwan Shri Hamsa

The opening scene takes place at Victoria Terminus, that extravaganza of neo-Gothic railway architecture in Bombay. On the morning of the 4th April 1908, a yogi boarded the Delhi Express. Forty-eight hours later, during which time he had changed trains three times – at Bina (where he boarded the Punjab Mail), Lucknow and Bareilly – he finally arrived at the railhead at Kathgodam. Here, with the aid of the government coolie contractor, he engaged two bearers at a rate of a rupee and a half a

Tibetans attending a religious rite at Taklakot Gompa (1926)

Tibetan monks and Indian orderlies (1926)

day, and a pony at a rate of six rupees. These were to accompany him to Almora in the foothills of the Himalayas on the first leg of a pilgrimage to Mount Kailas.

The yogi in question was one Bhagwan Shri Hamsa, and the narrative of his pilgrimage, *The Holy Mountain*, is a wonderfully exotic piece of literature, characteristically Indian and highly devotional. The style is quaintly formal, as though the author has thoroughly immersed himself not only in the writings of the Victorian masters of prose but also in the jargon of the compilers of Indian civil service regulations and railway time-tables. Purple passages descriptive of the most sublime spiritual experiences sit alongside the detailing of very precise, but very prosaic, facts – particularly facts relating to costs. The indications are that while Bhagwan was a deeply religious man, this did not preclude his also having a very keen eye for economy.

The English translation of *The Holy Mountain* from the original Marathi was made by Shri Purohit Swami, while the Introduction was penned by no less a luminary of English Literature than W.B. Yeats. Bhagwan Shri Hamsa was Shri Purohit Swami's spiritual teacher, who in turn collaborated with Yeats in the translation of the *Ten Principal Upanishads*. The Anglo-Irish poet, himself at one time a member of the magic circle known as the Hermetic Order of the Golden Dawn, other members of which included Aleister Crowley, McGregor Mathers and the poet Æ, had a great appetite for various kinds of esotericism, and it is interesting that the tendrils of his curiosity reached as far as the sacred region in Western Tibet. He seems to have had no doubt that Kailas and Meru were identical and in 1935, in the anthology entitled *A Full Moon in March,* he published a poem entitled *Meru*. With all Yeats' usual Celtic panache, this asserts that the world is an illusion, human life merely the product of mind, and man's lot a dreadful, violent struggle down the cycles of the ages to 'come into the desolation of reality'. He continues:

Hermits upon Mount Meru or Everest,
Caverned in night under the drifted snow,
Or where that snow and winter's dreadful blast
Beat down upon their naked bodies, know
That day brings round the night, that before dawn
His glory and his monuments are gone.

It seems, in short, a hymn to the transience of things.

Bhagwan Shri Hamsa's outward journey took him by the familiar

route through Almora, Ascot, Garbyang, along the Nerpani Trail
and into Tibet by the Nepalese Tinkar Pass; then on to Taklakot, the
lakes, Barkha, and finally to Darchen and Kailas. It was hard and
difficult going the whole way, beset with many perils: encounters
with lust-maddened elephants, venomous cobras, tigers, ghosts
and – perhaps most alarming for the chaste ascetic – licentious
mountain girls. His intense faith in both himself and his spiritual
master, Lord Dattātreya, added to the practice of continence and
the determination to fulfil his spiritual ideal, saw him safely
through every time. In Tibet he even fell into the clutches of a gang
of ferocious *dacoits*; his reaction –

> I cried the sweet name of my master and bowed down in mind, in
> reverent adoration before his lotus-feet, and to Shri Kailas and lake
> Manas . . . . I closed my eyes in cool and quiet meditation, with my head
> projected a little forward.
>
> (Bhagwan Shri Hamsa, *The Holy Mountain*)

When he opened his eyes –

> The man who a few moments ago stood with his naked sword drawn
> over me, now knelt down before me with his head bent, resting on his
> thumbs in a suppliant posture.
>
> (*Ibid.*)

There were other problems in Tibet besides the *dacoits*: the intense
heat of the day; the equally intense cold of the night; the inhospitable
terrain; and the people themselves, whom Bhagwan found semi-
barbaric. Moreover, what passed for justice among them was
summary and nauseatingly cruel. A young *dacoit* who had been
caught at Taklakot was sewn up in a yak-hide sack and left to roast
to death in the searing sun.

Nevertheless, the first sight of Kailas, when it came, was a
beatific revelation that thoroughly made up for all the adverse
experiences of the journey:

> I washed my hands and feet in the lake [Rakshas Tal] – and turned to look
> towards Mount Kailas, whose peak shone in a clear sky. The realization
> of my cherished object, for which I bore so much physical and mental
> suffering, seemed near at hand – the haven of my pilgrimage, Mount
> Kailas, stood before my eyes though still at a distance. The idea, the hope,
> exalted me, and soon I forgot the worry and exhaustion of the journey. I
> sat down on the beach of Lake Rakastal [*sic*] with my eyes fixed upon
> Mount Kailas, meditating upon the lotus-feet of my master. Kailas' peak
> shone clear till my meditation was over.

The peak of Mount Kailas is in the shape of a dome. At that hour the sun shone clearly upon its summit, which resembled a radiant ball of burnished silver. I was reminded of the golden dome of the temple of Shri Chidambaram, in the Madras Presidency, and its inexpressible beauty when shining in the sun's rays. There is one great difference between the two. The golden dome of the temple of Chidambaram is man-made, while the silvery peak of Mount Kailas is the work of nature.

(*Ibid.*)

Before going on to Kailas, Bhagwan took lodging in one of the *gompa* on the shores of Lake Manasarovar and performed *anushthana* – religious observance – for twelve days. This involved bathing in the icy waters in the morning and in the evening, going without all nourishment except a cup of tea in the evening, and performing meditation. Sitting crosslegged on his meditational tiger skin, he did, however, allow himself the occasional indulgence of watching the frolics of the local wildlife – hamsa duck and hares mostly – and of generally admiring the stunning beauties of the scenery through his binoculars:

Lake Manas is the home of sanctity, the abode of peace. It is the very Heart of Nature, full and throbbing. The region seems to be not of this earth, but of Heaven, and the blessed Land of the Soul. Sunrise and sunset, the canopy of the sky during the day and the shining moon and stars at night – all these are scenes of ineffable beauty.... At such a beautiful and solitary place, the mind loses itself and there is harmony full and complete.

(*Ibid.*)

Possibly as a result of the austerities practised while performing *anushthana,* he began to hear mellifluous singing and afterwards discovered footprints along the shore of the lake leading in the direction of Mount Kailas. He became convinced that these belonged to some great sage or *Mahatma,* and therefore decided that it was indicated that he proceed forthwith to the sacred mountain.

The *Pradakshina,* as Bhagwan calls the Parikrama, went uneventfully enough until he reached the eastern side of Kailas. Then his Tibetan guide pointed to a cave high up on a perpendicular ridge, bounded by glaciers, where he claimed that a Hindu *Mahātma* was engaged in contemplation. Bhagwan naturally decided that he must visit this *Mahātma* and although he could see no visible route to the cave, set off to try and reach it with his guide. Half-way up, the guide collapsed and had to be sent back down, so Bhagwan continued alone. About fifty yards from the mouth of the cave, he had to traverse a steep ice slope, and then a glacier. The final seven feet up a perpendicular precipice were climbed using minute finger- and toe-holds.

At the mouth of the cave, Bhagwan hesitated in indecision; then resolution overcame prudence and he plunged inside – only to fall headlong into a four foot pit lurking just beyond the entrance in the totally dark interior. Bhagwan groped his way on into the darkness until his head butted against something hard which, on examination, he discovered to be 'a human head with hair on it'. It was the *Mahātma*.

Friendly greetings were exchanged, and as Bhagwan's eyes gradually became habituated to the darkness he saw before him the naked body of a man in his sixties – 'a noble, full and serene figure sitting in *padmasan*' – the lotus posture – 'on a tiger skin'. The *Mahātma's* face seemed to be 'the abode of serenity, joy, peace and light, a veritable fountain of love'. There was absolutely no doubt that he was a fully-realized Master of Yoga: one who knew Brahmā. Bhagwan was also certain that this was the person whose mellifluous singing he had heard and whose footsteps he had seen along the shores of Lake Manasarovar.

Bhagwan spent three days with the *Mahātma*, during which time he slept with his head in the sage's lap and lived on water alone. Their waking hours were spent in conversation in a number of languages, ranging from perfect English to perfect Marathi. The *Mahātma* answered all Bhagwan's questions on matters relating to the spiritual life. It was, however, 'impossible to describe, even meagrely, the nature of our conversation...'. On the fourth day, having told Bhagwan to visit a fellow disciple of his own guru living at Tirthapuri, the *Mahātma* indicated that it was time for him to leave.

The coolies and the Tibetan guide were greatly relieved when they saw their employer returning safely from his perilous expedition, but more anxieties were shortly in store for them. Bhagwan's next hair-raising project was an expedition to the Gauri Kund Lake. This he undertook alone, taking all his warm clothes with him, a good supply of biscuits and a stout, metal-tipped staff. The last proved invaluable when scaling the snow- and ice-bound slopes that he had to ascend. The cold was excruciating, breathing difficult; then an avalanche swept him away. When he came to his senses, he found himself 'pitched in ice up to the waist' and 'at the very brink of death'. After two terrible nights bivouacked in holes in the ice, he managed to get back to his men.

Despite all these ordeals and the earnest entreaties of his coolies, Bhagwan determined on a second attempt to reach the Gauri Kund. This was successful, though the ascent took him nearly fifteen hours. Conditions at the lake, moreover, were arctic – 'My lips became green and blue with severe cold; my nerves seemed ready to burst, and respiration was difficult.' He broke the surface ice in order to get holy water; this stung like a scorpion's bite as he sprinkled it on his body in the prescribed manner. Then, as the sun began to set, he looked at the sky and at Kailas, and cried; '*Victory, Victory to the Lord, my Master...!*' and sat down upon his tiger skin in the *siddhasana* posture, facing north. Finally he closed his eyes and passed into profound meditation.

This was to be Bhagwan's great all-out drive to realize his spiritual ambition, which specifically was 'to have a sight [*darshan*] of the physical form of the Lord Dattātreya* Himself and to get myself initiated into the realization of the Self'. He was determined to realize this or 'die in meditation while sitting in Yogic posture'. All of which is strikingly reminiscent of that stage in the Buddha's spiritual quest when he placed himself on the 'immovable spot' beneath the Bo Tree at Bodh Gaya, equally determined to achieve his goal – which was to find a way to overcome suffering – or perish in the undertaking. By that time he had tried all the conventional religious paths and found them unable to provide a fully satisfying answer. He had also abandoned home, family, fortune, social rôle – in fact all material and emotional supports. He was in short a man *in extremis*; all that remained was his determination to find an answer to his spiritual problem.

In a similar way, Bhagwan had run the whole gamut of mental and physical sufferings. He had pushed himself far from home to an outlandishly remote and inhospitable place. All he had too was 'the intensity of my longing to realize my goal'. And realize it he did. First, he heard the voice of his Lord. This was not enough, however:

---

*According to Alain Daniélou (*Hindu Polytheism*, New York, 1964) Dattātreya is said to have been born of an emanation of Vishnu which impregnated the wife of the sage Devourer (Atri). Dattātreya protects men from evil influences; he is the originator of Tantras and Tantric rites; he likes women, drink, songs, music and the company of those of low birth. Yet he is greatly praised by the gods, who he saved from demons. He had numerous other distinctions as well. J. Dowson (*Hindu Classical Dictionary*, London, 1928), on the other hand, maintains that Dattātreya is, 'A Brahmin Saint in whom a portion of Brahmā, Vishnu and Shiva, more particulary Vishnu, was incarnate.'

Gauri Kund—The Lake of Mercy (1987)

he had to see the physical form. Accordingly, after continued meditation, the mental form which he had kept fixed between his eyebrows disappeared and, when he opened his eyes, his Master, Lord Dattātreya, was standing before him. Bhagwan prostrated himself at his Master's feet immediately; then Lord Dattātreya lifted him up, embraced and caressed him. He then gave him a *mantra* (sacred formula) and initiated him into the Realization of the Self:

> Here my Manas [mind] merged into Antahkarana [heart]; the Antahkarana with the Manas merged into Chitta [mind-stuff]; the Chitta along with Antahkarana and Manas merged into Buddhi [intellect]; the Buddhi with Chitta, Antahkarana and Manas merged into Ahankar [egoism]; and the Ahankar along with Buddhi, Chitta, Antahkarana and Manas – all merged into Absolute Brahma! I found myself reflected everywhere in the whole Universe! It was all one harmony – full of Wisdom, Infinite Love Perennial and Bliss Eternal! Where was the body, its tenements and the 'I'! It was all Satchidananda [Truth, Wisdom, Bliss].
>
> *(Ibid.)*

It was an overpoweringly blissful event; words could not adequately describe the joy which Bhagwan felt. In default of description, he proffers his reader two lines of poetry translated from the Sanskrit:

> The Master preaches through his silence,
> And all the doubts of the disciple are solved.
>
> *(Ibid.)*

Afterwards, Lord Dattātreya blessed him and, lighting a sacred fire, asked Bhagwan to perform the sacrificial ceremonies. This having been done, the Master initiated his devotee into the Giri Order of *Sannyasins** and gave him the name, 'Hamsa'. In return, Bhagwan offered his Master all he had – a single biscuit. Lord Dattātreya ate half and returned the other half as *prasad* [sacred food offering]. Finally, he told Bhagwan to request a boon. Bhagwan hesitated . . . :

'Let my heart always feel the same attachment towards Thee, though divested of its harm, that the undiscriminating soul feels in worldly objects,' he asked after a second bidding.

'*Let it be so!*' his Master replied, blessing his devotee and smiling.

Together, the two of them journeyed back to Bhagwan's camp. Although the outward journey had taken fifteen hours, in the

---

*The order of holy men who pursue the religious life in the mountains.

company of his Lord, the return journey was accomplished in a mere fifteen minutes!

After leaving Kailas and Lord Dattātreya, Bhagwan visited Tirthapuri, where he met another *Mahātma* mentioned to him by the one he had met in the cave on the sacred mountain. This second *Mahatma*:

> ... seemed a little older, but in other respects [was] much like the Mahātma on Kailas. He had the same sweet voice, the same peace and serenity beaming on his face, the same Light of the Absolute radiating from his eyes, the same full yet graceful stature. The Mahātma asked me to close my eyes and sit in meditation, saying he would do likewise. He asked me what more I had to gain. I made no reply.
>
> *(Ibid.)*

Having lived in the company of this holy man for three days, Bhagwan set out on his return journey to India. Six months and seven days after setting off on his pilgrimage, he was back in Bombay. Alighting from the train at V.T. (Victoria Terminus), he was met by three or four friends. He was justifiably proud to have attained his spiritual goal, but also rather pleased that in all the whole undertaking had cost him only 175 rupees – a mere £13. Indeed, not much to have had to pay for a glimpse of the Absolute!

E.G. Schary

Edwin Gilbert Schary

In the summer of 1918, a group of Indians were standing on the summit of a low-lying hill about half a mile from the bazaar in Gyanima. They were staring intently at something on the distant horizon. This aroused the curiosity of a travel-worn pilgrim who had arrived there three days before, and he asked a young Indian with whom he had struck up a friendship what these people found so interesting. The young Indian said nothing, merely took his friend by the hand, led him to the summit of the hill and pointed.

About fifty miles away, standing alone and isolated upon the plain, was a tremendous mountain peak of startling beauty. Its symmetrical contours were clearly defined in the rarefied atmosphere, and the late afternoon sunshine dappled it snows with subtle hues – pink, rose, purple. This was Kailas Parbat, the young Indian said: the Mecca of all the Hindus and Buddhists of the world, the sacred dwelling place of their highest gods. Moreover, this was a year of special pilgrimage to it.

The following day the pilgrim traded a robe that he had been given by a lama at Hanle Gompa and set off in the direction of Darchen with warnings against the dangers of the local *dacoits* ringing in his ears. On the afternoon of the second day, having passed no streams and consequently beginning to feel the effects of thirst, he was beguiled by a mirage into thinking that a large lake lay ahead. Finding only an expanse of desert sage and by then being too exhausted to continue, he threw a blanket over himself and fell asleep.

Continuing his journey next day, he found a stream near a nomad camp at about noon and slaked his thirst; then he followed the trail on into Darchen, where he found several hundred pilgrims encamped. While walking through Darchen, this indigent pilgrim met his young Indian friend again by chance. The Indian was delighted to see him, but told him that his sudden disappearance from Gyanima had aroused suspicions in the local lamas that he was some kind of devil. He then gave the pilgrim a few *tankas* – Tibetan coins – and took him to the adjacent *gompa*, where he instructed the attendant lama to give his friend food and shelter.

The lama took the pilgrim into a large, corridor-like room, where he left him. Time passed and the promised food did not arrive. However, whenever the lama passed the pilgrim in company with other lamas, he would make faces. The pilgrim eventually grew disgusted at this neglect and derision, and left the *gompa* to wander among the tents pitched on the plain.

Whatever his ragged, vermin-infested clothing might suggest, this penniless pilgrim did not hail from Ladakh; nor, as his disintegrating looks might lead one to believe, was he a native

Tibetan. Despite his command of Hindustani, he was not from the plains of India either. He was, in fact, a citizen of San Francisco, California, born there in 1893. His name was Edwin Gilbert Schary. He was just twenty five years old and this was his second journey to Tibet.

Schary does not appear to have had any clear notion of what precipitated him into the life of a spiritual searcher: the life that eventually brought him to Mount Kailas in the abject state described above. There does not, as in the case of the Buddha, seem to have been any precipitating crisis. It may just have been that the surroundings of his early youth 'wove the spell of romance and adventure into my life', or 'the fact that I was born with an intense imagination and the power to crystallize into fact those imaginary pictures'. His 'early longing to see what lay beyond the Farallones' led him at the age of twelve to embark upon a life of wandering. His distracted parents were even driven to employing detectives to keep track of their footloose son. All to no avail. As he grew older, the propensity merely intensified itself and became directed towards ever more exotic locations, especially when he came in contact with Oriental philosophical and religious ideas. His particular obsession became to make contact with the so-called *Mahātmas of Tibet*,* the notion of whose existence was propagated in the latter part of the last century by the Theosophical movement of Madame Helena Petrovna Blavatsky (1831–91). The *Mahātmas* were exalted beings versed in the ancient esoteric wisdom: the profound hidden teachings that underlie the more or less superficial exoteric doctrines that the religions of the world retail to the uninitiated masses. Portions of this ancient wisdom were communicated to Madame Blavatsky , Col. H.S. Olcott (1832–1906) and other of the early Theosophists by the *Mahātmas*, either directly or by occult means. Perhaps Schary himself hoped to be similarly enlightened – or at least to have the veils of mystery drawn slightly aside.

Schary set off on his first trip to Tibet on 18th December 1912, travelling first to Hawaii and then on the Australia before finally taking ship for Ceylon. He took odd jobs wherever he landed up and in this respect there is something of the classic hobo about him – something out of Jack London, perhaps, though his interest in Oriental philosophy gives him closer affinities with the hippies who were to emerge in his own native city half a century later. The experience of being down and out in many parts of the world seems to have humbled Schary, and the fact that he had as a result to live

*See also pp. 241 ff.

alongside the native people in the Asiatic countries he visited stripped him of that uncongenial arrogance that afflicted so many white men who lived or travelled in the East. He also learned to bear the vicissitudes of fortune with equanimity and to take abuse without rancour – all very useful spiritual lessons.

An interview with a Buddhist monk in Ceylon resulted in Schary's being advised to continue his search but to look for wisdom in the life of the peoples of the East rather than among priests. He journeyed on to Madras, where he tried but failed to get an interview with Annie Besant, one of the luminaries of the Theosophical Society, which had – and indeed continues to have – its headquarters at Adyar on the outskirts of Madras. After travelling and working in many parts of India, Schary eventually arrived in Kashmir on a bicycle, worked there as a schoolmaster for a short time and then proceeded to Ladakh with the intention of entering Tibet in search of the *Mahātmas*. He crossed the Tungi La and arrived on the great plateau alone, equipped only with the barest supplies and riding a horse that was totally unacclimatized to the rigours of travelling at altitudes in excess of 13,000 feet. In short, Schary was as thoroughly unprepared practically as he was psychologically for the terrible experiences that were about to beset him.

He travelled as far as Pooga before finally admitting to himself that it would be madness to continue. He turned back, but the return journey was a nightmare of thirst and fatigue that reached a horrific culmination in the sudden death of his horse. This experience had an inordinate effect upon his mind, became charged with deep symbolic significance, and haunted his nights with awful nightmares for long afterwards. He managed to stagger back over the Tungi La on foot but was only saved from almost certain death by the timely arrival of a caravan belonging to two American missionaries who happended to be on a trek up in the mountains.

Schary returned to San Francisco, but three years later he was crossing the Tungi La again. This time he had decided that he would not take a horse, or indeed any equipment or supplies beyond what he could carry on his own back. He would instead 'show a larger faith than I had on the first journey' by eschewing money and heavy sleeping robes, begging simple food from the nomads he would meet and generally living off the natural resources of the land. With formidable courage and resolution, accepting with equanimity the appalling hardships that inevitably beset him in that most inhospitable of lands, he proceeded in a generally easterly direction across Western Tibet (Ngari), passing through Pooga, Hanle,

Chimurti, Tashigong and Gyanima, until he finally arrived at Darchen at the foot of Mount Kailas.

Later at Darchen he bought and ate several large strips of cooked yak meat; then a sudden and violent hail storm drove him along with three or four hundred Hindu men, women and children to take shelter in a room in the *gompa*. While the storm raged all night long, Schary cradled two children in his arms, their mother meanwhile telling him with joy that she had accomplished the deepest wish of her heart in making a pilgrimage to the sacred mountain.

Next day, Schary went on to Barkha, where he struck a deal with a Tibetan caravan master to give him food and guidance for the next two days. As they passed Lake Manasarovar, he saw pilgrims making *parikrama* of the sacred lake. He did not join them, as he had not joined those making the Kailas Parikrama. The goal and object of his own pilgrimage lay elsewhere: not too far ahead now.

It had all fixed itself some time before. While asleep one night in the bungalow in which he had lived while working on a Malay rubber plantation during the outward journey, Schary had had a prophetic dream:

> Across my vision was portrayed a map of India and the Himalayas, also including the Bay of Bengal and the Malay Peninsula and the plantation. As I looked, I saw a finger pointing. The finger following from the plantation across the Bay of Bengal to Calcutta, on to the north-west frontier of India, up into Kashmir, and thence over the Himalayan passes, following the trail I had previously taken into Tibet itself. The moving finger continued across the place on the map representing the Tibetan Highland and stopped half-way across. Then the map disappeared from my vision and I beheld a narrow canyon through which ran a tiny stream over a terribly rocky course and walled high on each side by decaying mountains of shale and rock. On the left-hand side, about 300 feet above the stream, was a cave. Above the cave I saw the figures 9–5.

> I received the impression when beholding these numerals, that they represented September 5, and on awakening that morning I felt that I had been given direct guidance by which to reach the Mahātmas.
>   (Edwin Schary, *In Search of the Mahātmas of Tibet*)

September 5th was now rapidly approaching.

On 3rd September, Schary arrived at Todom. He was travelling faster than ordinarily. He promptly left Todom and ascended a high pass, where he met an Indian trader travelling on foot. They crossed the pass together but the Indian would not let Schary stay at his campfire that night for reasons of caste propriety and so the

American burrowed into a huge mound of wool and there slept the
night of 4th September. His sleep was terribly troubled:

> I seemed to be overcoming terrible obstacles, crossing high passes below
> which I could see great banks of clouds, and staggering over trails which
> led across endless desolation.
>
> *(Ibid.)*

When he awoke the next morning, he felt totally unrefreshed by his
night's sleep. Nevertheless, he got up and started on down the trail
through a valley under the pall of a tremendous sense of
apprehension. Nothing about his present surroundings suggested
the terrain he had seen in his dream. When the sun was well up, he
rested for about an hour beside a small stream; then, continuing for
about two miles, the stream turned into a desolate canyon:

> The stream ran over a jagged and rocky course between high banks of
> sand and shale; the ground sloped away on both sides and upward into
> strata of rock which seemed part of an ancient and decaying mountain
> range. As I entered this canyon, I suddenly looked up and beheld the
> vision of my dream.
>
> *(Ibid.)*

He found the cave. After a difficult climb, he reached its mouth and
entered.

At this point – the very climax of his journey – Schary refuses to
indulge his reader in any dramatics. This is simply because there
was no drama. He is utterly and confoundingly honest. The cave –

> . . . was just a cave – no more, no less – and no one within. . . .

> Within this cave, I sank down on my blanket and with a feeling of utter
> despondency, I suddenly realized that all my expectations of finding the
> Mahātmas of the East in this cave, living their life of seclusion, was now
> brought to naught. My dream came true in its physical aspect but that
> was all.
>
> *(Ibid.)*

For what purpose then had the dream been visited upon him? He
could only conclude that its purpose was to lead him to Tibet in
order that he might have the strange experiences of that pilgrim
journey. But the anti-climax and the disappointment were
shattering; he lay for three days in a state of total prostration,

mentally undergoing many strange experiences, and finally coming to this conclusion:

> If I learned anything at any time in all my travels, I learnt this lesson in that cave – a lesson read somewhere before in one of the writings of an Eastern sage but never until that time wholly understood:
>
> 'Within thyself deliverance must be sought. Each man his prison makes; each hath such lordship as the loftiest one. Nay, for with powers above, around, below, as with all flesh and whatsoever lives, Act maketh joy and woe.'
>
> (Ibid.)

There remained nothing now but to quit the cave and push on to the British trading post at Gyantse. Schary accomplished this in a spirit of utter hopelessness, with 'an emotional indifference which to this day, many years later, has remained with me in part'.

Mr David MacDonald, sometime British Trade Agent in Gyantse, recalls in his book, *Twenty Years in Tibet*, a strange incident that took place there in October 1918. He was in Yatung at the time, but had the story from the Gyantse men:

> One evening, at dusk, a begrimed and filthily clad figure, covered with festering sores, crawled to the main gate of Gyantse Fort. In Hindustani he asked the sepoy sentry to let him in, but the latter, taking him for a Tibetan beggar, refused and ordered him away from the post. Sinking down on a stone nearby, the man said 'I am a white man, you must let me in.' The sepoy was sceptical but the matter was taken out of his hands by an Indian officer of the Detachment, who realized after a few inquiries that the wanderer was really a white man in distress. Eventually, Schary wrote a note to Mr. Martin, my head clerk at Gyantse, to the effect that he was sick and starving, and asking for help. As soon as Mr. Martin read this letter, he of course had Schary brought in, and given food and attention. He was in a terrible condition, verminous, ill-nourished and really very ill. . . .
>
> (Quoted in Ibid.)

Thus Schary was saved for a second time by a fortunate fall into the hands of sympathetic Westerners. Having recruited his strength at Gyantse, he returned to India by way of the Chumbi Valley, Sikkim and Darjeeling. Arriving eventually at Calcutta, he took ship for Singapore and thence sailed *via* Yokohama back home to San Francisco.

This harrowing ordeal in Tibet, together with the crushing disappointment in the cave, did not put end to Schary's ambition of meeting the *Mahātmas*. He concluded, after lengthy consideration, that he simply did not yet merit the honour of such a meeting. He had therefore still to go through some 'very severe course of penance and personal sacrifice' to arrive at the required state of fitness. He also decided that he had probably failed during his second journey because he had been too indulgent with himself. The next time, he determined, he would take absolutely no provisions or equipment whatsoever but rely utterly on faith for everything. He would also consciously abstain from food and drink, 'feeling that one who wished to become a disciple of these Great Ones must show the greatest manner of personal sacrifice and indifference to physical needs. . . .' He was, in short, preparing to go back to Tibet and submit himself to a more extreme programme of self-mortification. If he met the required standards, however, he expected that someone would meet him along the trail of that 'forbidding plateau' and take him to the *Mahātmas*.

Unfortunately – or perhaps, fortunately – the British were now alerted to the fact that Schary was endowed with a marked propensity for slipping into Tibet without authorization. Consequently they were on the lookout for him, and when he tried to reach the high passes for the third time, he was caught and taken back to Kashmir, where he was imprisoned for a while before being packed off out of the country.

This was still not the end. He returned to India for a fourth time and gained employment in a caustic soda plant on the Hooghly River below Calcutta. He then wrote to his old employer in Kashmir asking for a job but promising not to enter Tibet. He had made many such promises in the past and broken just about all of them, so to anyone who knew him they could not have meant much. His old employer wrote back that the officials would never countenance Schary's return to Kashmir.

Quite suddenly and calmly a few days after receiving this letter, this strange, obsessed man Schary decided that he must put all further notion of meeting the *Mahātmas* of Tibet out of his mind, for 'to find them was not for me'. He promptly secured a berth for himself on a Standard Oil tanker sailing from Calcutta to San Francisco.

Between September and December 1924, Schary completed a circuit of the world in ninety-five days. Returning to the East Coast of the United States, he bought a transcontinental railway ticket from New York to San Francisco. He only had enough money for about two days' food. Therefore at Cheyenne, Wyoming he dismounted from the train, hoping to sell or pawn some of his clothes, buy something to eat with the proceeds, and then resume his journey. He found everything closed up in Cheyenne, however, and had to spend the night in a Salvation Army hostel; then he sold a shirt and a sweater for two dollars. He eventually arrived back in San Francisco with only five cents in his pocket.

'Thus did I consummate a 12-year cycle of pilgrimage and quest over the world's open spaces.'

And promptly the man vanishes into the mists of anonymity.

Researches in San Francisco have revealed that in 1917 an Edwin Gilbert Schary, 'foreman', was registered in official records at 1514 McAllister Street, the home of Harriett, widow of Julius Schary. In 1918 his official address was 927 Scott Street, and in the next year Lea and Muriel Schary were registered with a man of the same name at the same address. In 1921 he was registered at 2107 Bush Street; his profession is listed as 'floorman'. In 1924, he and Lea were registered at 795 18th Avenue; he was then described as a salesman. He now finally disappears from the records, for in 1925 Lea alone is listed: a saleswoman living at 415 Buchanan Street.

Is this the same man?

It is impossible to say precisely. There is a persuasive amount of circumstantial evidence, especially on the basis of the name. But on the other hand, the professions attributed to the registered Schary are rather more humble than the more prestigious 'engineer' entered in the passport of the *Mahātma*-seeker. And moreover, correlating these official dates with the few dates that Schary himself gives for his various travels does raise a few difficulties. By his own account, his first trip took him away from San Francisco from December 1912 to September 1915. He was then probably at home until March 1917, when he set off for a second time for Tibet, being away that time until early- to mid-1919, during which time the registered E. G. Schary moved from McAllister to Scott. He was at home for a few months in 1919 – the official E.G.S. then at Bush with Lea and Muriel – but left in September on his third trip, which lasted until mid- to late-1920. Between then and September 1924, when he set off on his two-month circuit of the world, he also fitted in his final and apparently brief trip to India. Lastly, if his travels did end as he says in 1924 and he then settled down in his home town, then one would have expected some record of this during the succeeding years, unless he moved elsewhere, took off again or died.

If we are to credit Schary's incredible story – and there is no substantial reason for not doing so – what is particularly striking about his spiritual search is that – unlike Hamsa's, or Kawaguchi's, for instance – it did not take place within the matrix of an established spiritual tradition. The ambitions and objectives that he was contemplating 'had possibly never before been thought of by a Westerner.* I had nothing upon which to lend me comfort, but had simply to pursue my journey with nothing but very great faith together with absolute resolve.' He was in short a total loner: not sure of what he was seeking, nor how to get it, not even of the significance of the experiences that came to him in his quest – but driven by a tremendously powerful force nevertheless; a force he could not resist.

Modern psychologists would probably diagnose Schary as some kind of obsessive or neurotic as he was prone to fits of depression, panic and nerves, and could moreover not hold down a steady job or even stay put in one place for any length of time. On the other hand, the reader of his narrative cannot help being at times awed by the sheer persistence and courage of the man. Yet the fact that these qualities were not informed by a clear sense of direction and a solid understanding of what he was about leaves one ultimately with the sad impression of a person afflicted with a desperate foolhardiness that might well have brought him to disaster. If he survived at all, it was by the skin of his teeth. Perhaps his humility and the engaging kind of innocence with which he seems to have been endowed may also have helped bring him through his terrible trials. All in all, however, Schary's story is an object lesson in the danger of embarking upon the spiritual quest without proper preparation.

Sri Swami Tapovanji Mahāraj

Swami Tapovanji (1886–1957), who was born in the south Indian state of Kerala, was a great *jñāna yogin:* one who aspired to realise the Spiritual Absolute, not by good works or ardent devotion, but through wisdom pursued within the matrix of the Advaita Vedānta system of philosophy (also sometimes called the Shankara System). He found the High Himalaya particularly conducive to his contemplation, and was especially fond of three *tirtha* or sacred sites on the upper reaches of Mother Ganga: Uttarkasi, Gangotri and Badrinath. He also wandered extensively and freely in the

---

*They in fact had – by the great Christian mystics, for instance.

Swami Tapovanji

Kojarnath Gompa (1984)

mountains, and on two occasions, in 1925 and 1930, visited Kailas-Manasarovar.

On his first visit, the good *swami* was accompanied by an Assamese *sadhu* named Anandagiri (lit. 'Mountain Bliss'). Their transparent sincerity as *sannyāsins* (renunciates) – they travelled simply, *sans* money, servants or transport – attracted much support as they passed through north-western Nepal. However, Swami-ji's strength was sapped by bouts of fever and by the time he crossed into Tibet by what he calls the Yaree or Nara Pass (17,000 ft.), he was reduced to a sorely depleted condition. Nevertheless, he pressed on, inspired by the grandeur of the scenery and by his faith in Brāhman, the Spiritual Ultimate of all Hindus.

Once inside Tibet, the two pilgrims called at Kojarnath Gompa, where they found some two hundred lamas living in commendable simplicity and seclusion from the mind-disturbing tempations of the worldly world. Although himself a devoted Hindu, Swami Tapovanji held the Buddha in high veneration, believing that, in ultimate experiential terms, both the Buddhist and the Vedāntist paths pointed towards one transcendental goal. He therefore paid his respects to the image of Lord Buddha dominating the main shrine room, and then joined the lamas in their devotions. Soon, his woes quite forgotten, he had passed into a state of *samadhi*: profound meditative quiescence.

Although his health was still declining, the *swami* and his companion afterwards proceeded to Purang Mandi, where they paused to rest and obtain supplies for the next leg of their pilgrimage. Later, however, on the way to the sacred lakes, their want of proper equipment really began to tell, for they had to spend a night out in the open, unprotected from the freezing cold, the buffets of biting winds and the onslaughts of rain and sleet. Still, their spirits were fully restored next day when, with their own pious eyes, they beheld the divine beauties of Manasarovar:

> In the *Purānas*, the lake is described as being adorned with golden lotuses and frequented by royal swans which live upon pearls, while *Apsara* beauties are engaged in perpetual water sports. On the banks stand Divine trees bending under the weight of flowers and fruits and swaying in the cool breeze, heavenly musicians meet there to pass their time in games . . .
>
> I got down into the lake and had my bath with great joy and devotion. . . .
> (Sri Swami Tapovanji. *Wanderings in the Himalayas.*)

Tapovanji and Anandagiri then spent some time resting and talking with the lamas at Trügo and Gösul Gompa. Again, while Swami-ji respected the pious lives they were leading, he did not hold the actual spiritual practises of the lamas – mostly learning and chanting religious texts – in very high regard and did not believe that they would help them penetrate very deeply into the great mystery at the core of things. The Tantric Buddhism of Tibet itself he regarded as something of a fall from the pristine standards originally set by Shākyamuni Buddha himself.

Proceeding to the Great Silver Mountain, as he calls Kailas, Tapovanji and his companion had again to spend a night out in the open, fully exposed to the elements. At an altitude of some 18,000 feet, their privations this time were excruciating and pushed Swami-ji's resolve beyond reasonable limits. Realising that he would need to conserve every ounce of energy for the return journey, he abandoned his plan to perform the Parikrama and beat a reluctant retreat. Again, helped by kind and pious people, he and Anandagiri were able to scale the Lipu Lekh and eventually to find their way safely back to Almora, where they obtained 'motor transport' to convey them on to the plains.

After such harrowing experiences, it is not surprising that, when some five years later a group of fellow *sadhus* approached Swami Tapovanji at Badrinath with a proposition to visit Kailas, he turned them down. But then came the Divine Call –

'*Start again for Kailas! Visit it once again!*'

Of course, after that there was no further debate...

Swami-ji's route this time ran from Badrinath, over the Mana Pass and into Tibet, where his first major call was on the lamas at Thöling Gompa.

This pilgrimage was an altogether less severe penance than its predecessor, for Tapovanji travelled with a large and well-funded group of holy men who had proper supplies and equipment, including tents, and animal transport to bear these burdens. However, all this material opulence proved something of a mixed blessing for, between Daba and Gyanima, it attracted the attentions of a fierce-looking *dacoit*, who was armed to the teeth:

I could [now] very well appreciate the difference between the two journeys – the freedom and joy of the first standing in sharp contrast to the dependence and fear of the second with its possessions and companions. In places like Kailas it is better to travel as a penniless mendicant, taking things as they come. During the first pilgrimage, whenever I chanced to meet highwaymen, they used to greet me and provide me with milk and food. Possessions seem a blessing, but actually they are a curse.

(Ibid.)

As things turned out, however, the wild man proved to be an imaginary *dacoit*, not a real one. Thus the mind deceives us all the time. However, he had struck a very real terror into the timid hearts of Swami-ji's companions.

Passing Tirthapuri – 'the place where the notorious Brahmasura was killed' – Swami-ji and his friends reached Darchen, where a great Khumb Mela was about to happen. As this special festival only takes place once every twelve years on the occasion of an auspicious astrological conjunction, numerous tents had been erected. Some belonged to lay people, others to lamas, a few of them from as far afield as Lhasa and Mongolia. One of the Dalai Lama's Ministers was even rumoured to be in the vicinity.

This time Swami-ji was able to succesfully negotiate the Great Parikrama – he calls it 'the holiest of penances'. He and his friends visited Nyenri, Drira Puk and Zutrul Puk Gompa as they circumambulated, and also broke the ice on Gauri Kund in order to bathe in the freezing but holy waters. Finally, returning to Darchen, the *swami* climbed the southern flanks of Kailas, from where the view southwards 'appeared not merely rare but of supramundane beauty.' Visiting Gyangtra Gompa, he was deeply impressed by the brilliance of its handsome young High Lama, surely a true *brahmin* even if not of the Hindu race. Afterwards, rejoining his fellow *sadhus*, he proceeded to Manasarovar, where he visited Chiu Gompa on this occasion.

Swami Tapovanji recorded these pilgrimages in two works written in his native Malayalam language: *Kailas Yatra* and *Himagiri Vihar*. The latter has been translated into English as *Wanderings in the Himalayas*. It is an agreeably reflective book in which travelogue is interwoven with discourse about the deepest religious matters. Indeed, in his epilogue, Swami-ji confesses that his real motive in writing was not merely to extol the physical beauties of the Himalaya but to draw the reader's attention to the sublime transcendental realities towards which those majestic mountains point. His main theme is in fact *Brāhman*: ineffable, non-dual, unconditioned, omnipresent. It is Brāhman that the true *sadhu* encounters in the Himalaya, not mere mountains. In its immanent form, Brāhman is *Ātman*: the 'I' or Self that 'dwells in the cavity of the heart of all'. It cannot be appropriated by the thinking mind, or by the physical senses; but it can be encountered in the human heart as a luminous blissful tranquillity.

Brāhman is everywhere, in all things. Brāhman is Mount Kailas. It is also the humblest and simplest of things too:

> Whether it is on the peaks of the Himalayas, on Mount Kailas or on the shores of Lake Manasa, I find the same Perfect Being. I find the same self-luminous Thing at all places, at all times, in all objects, and in all states. I find only that Object of Truth and nothing else. I smell nothing else. I do not think of anything else. I do not find my joy in any other than that Object of Bliss.
>
> (*Ibid.*)

The Maharaj of Mysore & Sadeg Z. Shah

In 1931, H.H. Krishna Radja Wadayar Bahadur, the Maharaja of Mysore, made pilgrimage to Kailas with a substantial retinue of officers, servants and coolies. This historic event was recorded by his faithful retainer, Sadeg Z. Shah, in the form of a 'Diary in Doggerel', subtitled *Nothing Better to Do*, by 'An Old Stick in the Mud.' The talented author of this unique literary gem is pictured in

The 'Old Stick in the Mud' himself

the frontispiece of his slim volume: a pukka chap indeed, striding a very small donkey, clad in an all-weather coat, authoritative switch in hand, solar topi on head.

The pilgrimage was of the standard sort: up from Almora and into the sacred region *via* the Lipu Lekh, and back the same way. There was a side trip to Kojarnath, but not one to Tirthapuri. Besides the usual catalogue of minor mishaps, nothing disasterous seems to have befallen – or anything unusual or especially adventurous either.

Here are a few sample verses from the Old Stick in the Mud's McGonagallesque masterpiece:

Kitting up at Almora:

> Posteens arrived and gillgit [*sic*] boot,
> To protect us on the mountain route.
> When the parcel was opened there was a loot;
> Sizes varied but all to suit.

The Lipu Lekh was 'awful and so intensely cold . . ./Some riders and their ponies down the khud rolled'; but later, visiting the Simbiling Gompa at Taklakot:

> The Thaklakote Monastery was fully worth seeing.
> The Chief Lama's tea cup was the skull of a human being.
> The rituals performed were supposed to be inspiring,
> But the filth and the aroma drove away all sacred feeling.

Afterwards, travelling towards the Gurla Pass:

> To walk at this height needs very good lungs.
> To show respect here, men put out their tongues.
> No fuel they have, they used dried dungs.
> A very hard life: they are called 'Bhadurjungs.'
>
> Our traffic manager still goes strong;
> In his hand he holds a stick very long;
> Like Johnny Walker he strides along:
> His memory's great and is seldom wrong.

At Manasarovar, gleaming 'like the milky way in heaven at night':

> The sight of the lake made us all take a dip,
> To wash all old sins and the new ones to nip;
> And poor Seshachar, who welcomed this tip,

Kailas: The North-west Ridge (1985)

> Now has double pneumonia, and medicine to sip.
>
> One of our syces [grooms] to-day, if you please,
> Has shot for our table two bar-headed geese.
> They will go very well with a little Kraft cheese,
> And will help the inner man to appease.

And so on the Darchen:

> From Darchen begins the circumambulation,
> A village with a headman and a small population,
> Raja Loba, Headman, in complete intoxication,
> Was attended by our doctors, who restored his respiration.

The Parikrama itself:

> Today is 26th July: 11 miles we walked.
> We had much to ponder, and so we seldom talked.
> We cross tomorrow Dolma Pass, and so our plans we chalked
> To face the crisis boldly, – for our purpose shan't be baulked.

Climbing at 19,000 was 'certainly a strain/With gillgit boots and posteens: it may affect the brain!' – but they made it and then went on to:

The Gowrikund lake was a place for a dip indeed!
One sheet of snow: a hero's heart you need!
We broke the ice for water for the deed.
I entered, and my feelings who can read?

On the way down into the eastern valley, the mount of one of the party, Karia, 'slipped on boulders', and 'rolled down half mad', leaving its hapless rider with an 'arm badly strained ... and sad'.

Having completed the circuit and returned to 'windy Barkha', the pilgrims could not restrain their joy; but the noble lyricist mused that since they had not seen any papers for eight days they were now 'truly out of date'. 'Is there a railway strike?' he wondered; 'a thought we wanderers hate.' News caught up with them at 'Lakando' (Pranavānanda's Lachato) on Rakshas Tal, however, when in their 'week-delayed mail' they read that there was cholera back at home.

Next, after a side trip to Kojarnath:

The 3rd of August, Thaklakote we reach,
Next day to Pala, then to Lepuleck [sic] breach,
Then on we go, to fight scorpion and leech.
The cook served me to-day a Melba-Peach!

Once across the pass, the pilgrims were glad to be back on 'British land', where security was assured by 'a firm ruling hand'. The idea of independence for India (*Swaraj*) was 'attractive and grand', Shah reflected, but 'self-rule needs self-discipline, firmly to stand.'

Near Garbyang, they ran into Kunwar Kharag Singh Pal, the Political Peshkar of Ascot, who had just lost his trunks (the luggage, not the bathing sort) when one of his mules slipped into the river. Apparently 'there were thousands contained in the sack', so divers had been put to work to recover them – 'but success they still lack.'

Having paid off their coolies at Almora, the pilgrims proceeded to the railhead at Kathgodam, where they caught a train for Hardwar. They bathed in the Ganges there, then caught another train to Bombay. They were finally back home in Mysore by September.

The great poetic epic finally comes to a fitting conclusion with a eulogy of the noble patron of the pilgrimage:

Our beloved Maharaja did lead all the way:
His kindness and charity, words fail to say.
Oh Lord of Kailas, to you we pray,
To guard and protect him each hour of the day.

Swami Pranavananda in New Delhi (1985)

CHAPTER NINE

Pilgrims to the Sacred Mountain –2

Swami Pranavānanda of the Holy Kailas and Manasarovar

One man deserves special homage as the Kailas pilgrim *par excellence* and unrivalled authority on all matters relating to the sacred mountain, its lakes and environs. This is Shri Swami 108 Pranavānanda Maharaj (of the Holy Kailas and Manasarovar), to give him his full religious title. In the frontispieces of his books he appears as a rather splendid Shaivite *sannyāsin* or holy man, with thick beard, shoulder-length hair (parted in the middle) and large, piercing eyes.

Swami Pranavānanda first visited Kailas in 1928, travelling there from Shrinagar in Kashmir *via* Ladakh and Gartok, and returning to India by way of the Niti Pass. From 1935, he visited the sacred region almost yearly, travelling by a variety of routes and staying for periods ranging from two to six months on the shores of Lake Manasarovar. In 1936-7 and again in 1943-4, he stayed for periods of twelve and sixteen months respectively at the southerly Trügo Gompa. In the last published account of his achievements (1959),* he claimed to have made in all some twenty-three circumambulation circuits of Mount Kailas, and twenty-five of Lake Manasarovar; he had also made one circuit of Rakshas Tal.

The main purpose of these visits was spiritual, for at the time the *swami* belonged to that particular fraternity of the devotees of Lord Shiva who pursue their *sadhana* or spiritual training in the mountains – and where better than in the vicinity of the Throne of

---

*Since this was written, a new book has been published by the *swami* : *Kailas-Manasarovar* (New Edition, Delhi, 1983).

Swami Pranavānanda in his prime

Lord Shiva itself? Swami Pranavānanda was, however, very much
more than just a religious ascetic. In his spare time he conducted
extensive scientific researches in a variety of fields and was as a
result able to amass an encyclopaedic amount of information about
the sacred region, upon which he subsequently lectured to learned
bodies, and published articles and books, both in English and the
native Indian languages. His *Exploration in Tibet* ran to two editions
(1939 and 1950), and he also produced an invaluable baedeker for
Kailas pilgrims: *The Pilgrim's Companion to the Holy Kailas and
Manasarovar*, published in Allahabad in 1938. The discovery of an
aged and battered copy of this venerable work in one of the learned
libraries of London was one of the sweetest finds during the
research for the present book.

For anyone with an interest in Mount Kailas and environs, the
Pilgrim's Companion is a truly 'sumptuous feast' of useful information

and timely advice, liberally endowed with maps and photographs, and garnished with passages of magnificently purple prose:

> The perpetual snow-clad peak of the HOLY KAILAS (styled 'Kang Rinpochhe' in the Tibetan language) of hoary antiquity and celebrity, the spotless design of Nature's art, of the most bewitching and overpowering beauty, has a vibration of the supreme order from the spiritual point of view. It is like an immediate revelation of the Almighty, which makes man bend his knees and lower his head. Its gorgeous silvery summit, resplendent with the lustre of spiritual aura, with awe-inspiring solemnity and weird grandeur, pierces the heavenly height of 22,028 feet above the even bosom of the sea.
>
> (Ibid.)

As any good guide-book should, the Pilgrim's Companion analyses some of the more-frequented routes to Kailas and Manasarovar, and both the circumambulation routes of the sacred mountain and the sacred lake, stage-by-stage, giving exact specifications of distances and times of travel between the various stages. It also provides copious ancillary notes on places of interest or of special religious significance that the pilgrim will encounter either along the way or by making side-trips. That the swami has so much information to impart bears able testimony to his close acquaintance with the various routes as well as with the sacred region itself. It moreover demonstrates the high degree of development which the great Hindu institution of pilgrimage to Mount Kailas had attained over the centuries.

Arguably most interesting to the general reader is the mass of general information which the Pilgrim's Companion contains. Right at the beginning, for instance, Swami Pranavānanda discusses the significance of tirthas or places of pilgrimage. These, he maintains, are pervaded by 'magnificent spiritual vibrations' as a result of various kinds of highly-evolved holy men having lived and performed tapas [spiritual practices] in them. Subsequently aspirants are drawn to the great tirthas precisely because they hope, by exposing themselves to these subtle vibrations, to gain spiritual enrichment. There are many tirthas in the Himalayas, but almost undoubtedly the holiest are Kailas and Manasarovar:

> In the surroundings of the Holy Kailas and Manasarovar, even the most wandering mind – to whatever religion he may belong... becomes concentrated and irresistibly, unknowingly and unconsciously feels the Divine Presence that seems hidden behind the apparently vast universe, as if propelled by some one from behind, and a good sadhaka may even

enter into sublime ecstacies involuntarily. But, just as a man, the
mucous membrane of whose nose has become dull, cannot perceive the
scent of an article, so it is no wonder if a person devoid of any spiritual
tendencies cannot perceive or feel the effect of the spiritual vibrations
existing in a particular place.

(*Ibid.*)

A little further on, in a section designed to orientate the would-be
pilgrim to conditions generally prevailing in Tibet at the time, he
deals with the evocative matter of *mahātmas* and mystics:

Several sensational articles are freely published both here and in the
west about the Mahātmas and *Siddhas** in this little seen and less studied
part of the world. Most of these stories, gaining currency here, are more
of the nature of stunts than anything else. I may mention that I visited
altogether about 50 Monasteries and not less than 1500 monks. During
these visits I came across a Lama (from Lhassa) in the year 1936, and
attended some *tantric* rites he conducted in the Simbiling Monastery [in
Taklakot] for three days; and another *Tulku*† Lama aged sixteen in the
year 1928 whom I felt to be an elevated soul. These are the only notables
who I happened to meet. This is not to say, however, that really great
Mahātmas and yogis do not exist. . . . The simple fact remains that really
spiritually advanced Yogis or Lamas are as rare a phenomenon here as
everywhere else. . . . *There is no doubt however that the surroundings of the Holy
Kailas and Manasarovar are surcharged with spiritual vibrations of the supreme order
which make one exhilarated and elevated.*

(*Ibid.*)

As regards who is capable of undertaking the rigours of a
pilgrimage to Kailas, Swami Pranavānanda maintains that 'any
person who has not got very weak lungs or affected heart' could go.
If he were an Indian, he would need no passport, but he would be
well advised to take with him a fair amount of clothing, a stock of
medicines and a number of miscellaneous other items, all of which
the *swami* is kind enough to list. That the list of medicines runs to
some twenty-one items is explained a little later when the *swami*
discourses upon the 'general ailments of the way':

Dysentery, diarrhoea, cold, cough, fatigue and feverishness due to
tiresome ascents [*sic*] and descents. . .and reeling sensation or headache
during high ascents. . . .'

(*Ibid.*)

*Tantric Masters
†Incarnate Lama

Among the other exigencies of pilgrimage are the ruthless *dacoit* bandits that infest the areas about a day's travel beyond Taklakot. For protection against these desperadoes, the good *swami* advises the pilgrim to travel within a group, which should also be armed. Guns or armed guards could be hired from the Bhotia traders in Taklakot. If guards were hired, they would also act as guides and interpreters. One final stratagem that the *swami* urges as beneficial for deterring *dacoits* is to fire two or three warning shots into the air about an hour or two after sunset when stopping at places known to be scenes of *dacoit* attacks.

The pilgrim should also be prepared to meet with all the extremes of weather known to meteorology:

During the pilgrim season – July and August – very often, the Holy Kailas and Mandhata peaks would be under cloud and be playing hide-and-seek with the visitors. When the sky is clear the sun is scorching. During the cloudy party of a day and during nights it would be very cold. The weather changes like the weathercock. Now you will be perspiring profusely in the scorching sun; in a few minutes a cool breeze gently blows; the next moment you will have clouds with terrific thunders and lightnings followed by drizzling rain or downpours of water in torrents; sometimes you will see a rainbow, shortly after, you may have a hailstorm followed by showers of snowfall.... Here is perfect calmness, the next moment there break out whizzing, tempestuous winds.... Here on a conical peak the ice is glittering in the sun like a silver bar, there on a dome-like peak are hanging golden canopies, the far-off mountain ranges are enveloped in thick wreaths of inky black clouds, there a belt of amber clouds or the seven-coloured semicircular rainbow encircles the Kailas dome, or the nearby Mandhata's giant heads are ablaze in scarlet flames when the sun begins to dip in the west or the meagre snow-capped Punri peak raises its head into the pitch-black messengers of Indra.... Sometimes it seems that day and night, morning, noon and evening and all the six seasons of the year have their sway simultaneously.

(*Ibid.*)

Against all these exigencies, the pilgrim would not be without the benefit of what Swami Pranavānanda calls 'help and popular persons'. He reports on the noble efforts of the 'Shri Kailas-Manasarovar Kshetras Committee, newly constituted in Almora and Provincial Branches at Lahore, Rawalpindi, etc.', to provide food, blankets and accommodation for pilgrims and to generally look after their 'comforts and conveniences'. On the whole it would seem that there were numerous *dharmasalas* (rest-houses) and other places where the pilgrim could find lodging on the Indian side of the passes. Once across into Tibet, however, they were virtually non-existent and Swami Pranavānanda therefore recommends the pilgrim to hire himself a tent or to bring one with him from the Plains. He also gives the names of various people – Bhotia traders, post masters, schoolmasters – to whom the pilgrim may apply personally for help at various specific places. Mail could also be forwarded *via* Bhotia traders from the final post office on Indian territory: at Garbyang.

Regarding the best time for commencing a pilgrimage, Swami Pranavānanda is of the opinion that one should start from Almora around the middle of June if one wishes to avoid the rains, though most pilgrims in fact set off at the end of that month. The full round trip *via* Almora may be accomplished in some fifty days, though an extra three or four days should be allowed if the pilgrim wishes to make a circumambulation of Lake Manasarovar, and a further week if he wishes to visit Tirthapuri and Gyanima. The largest *mandi* (market) in Western Tibet is to be found at the latter place; others at Darchen, Taklakot and Trügo on Lake Manasarovar. Food might be bought at these places, though 'articles of any special liking' should be brought from Almora. The *swami* enumerates the various kinds of food that might be obtained along the route, but warns that in Tibet it becomes less plentiful, and the pilgrim is well-advised to stock up at Taklakot with enough provisions to last both the outward and return journeys from Kailas. In Tibet, transactions might be made either in Indian rupees or Tibetan *tankas* (*see below*), though Tibetans preferred the former.

Tibetan tankas (coins)

Finally, the brave pilgrim having, with the noble *swami's* advice and the guidance of his itineraries, successfully negotiated the fraught route to the Holy Kailas and duly made the prescribed

circumambulation of the sacred peak, he is sent on his way home
with the following inspiring remarks:

> Return journey should be done, taking proper rest wherever needed,
> following the route of the outward journey. As this pilgrimage cannot
> be undertaken easily, or often, one should spend some days leisurely in
> quiet meditation either at Kailas or preferably on the shores of the
> Manasarovar, where one can enjoy the *darshan* [sight] of the Holy Kailas
> and a bath in the Manas. Whether one be a pilgrim or tourist one should
> not fail to derive full benefit of these holy and grand places by staying
> there at least for a few days, but not run on in indecent haste. Pilgrims
> should make it a point to devote sometime daily for peaceful meditation
> and contemplation, by the side of the turquoise-blue surface of the
> charming lake. One breathes more happily and with greater ease; one
> feels a real pleasure in life, and yearns to remain sailing indefinitely on
> the fascinating blue depths and the sacred waves... (T)he inner joy
> which one feels when one is faced with an object of superhuman beauty
> and eternal charm, such as is presented by this summit under a cupola of
> perpetual snow... is certainly better described by one more gifted
> poetically and aesthetically disposed than myself. How can Manasarovar
> and Kailas be the objects of divine honour from two religions so
> different as Hinduism and Buddhism unless it be that their over-
> powering beauty has not only appealed to, but made an indelible
> impression on, the human mind, that they seemed to belong rather to
> Heaven than to Earth? Even the first view from the hills on the shore
> causes one to burst into tears of joy at the magnificent landscape; and a
> more intimate association undoubtedly throws one into a deeper mystic
> trance wherein one feels nearer the Divine Presence than anywhere
> else. The author feels that if he has stimulated interest in any of the
> numerous prospective readers of his book, to undertake this very
> wholesome journey to this Abode of Bliss in the Abode of Snow and to
> feel that inner joy and enjoy that peace of mind which he is sure every
> mortal is bound to share with himself, his labours will have been more
> than amply rewarded. If in addition any one devotee, having been
> inspired by the August Presence himself, can hand on this Torch of
> Illumination to his fellow brethren, the gratifying reflection of having
> originated and perpetuated this chain of inspiration will fill the author
> with that supreme satisfaction, which the fulfilment of a noble and self-
> imposed mission of serving humanity naturally yields as its most
> legitimate consequence.
>
> (*Ibid.*)

The writer of that fine panegyric was born Kanakadandi Venkata
Somayajulu in East Godavari District in south India in 1896. After
graduating from the D.A.V. College in Lahore in 1919, he worked
in the Railway Accounts Office in the same city for a short period

before resigning and becoming a political activist. He joined the non-Cooperation movement and between 1920 and 1926 was an active Congress worker in West Godavari district. Then he 'had a call from the heights of the Himalayas in consequence of an internal urge for search after Truth'. In plain language, he took to the religious life.

Swami Pranavānanda's guru or spiritual mentor was H. H. Shri 1108 Dr. Swami Jñānânanda, D.Sc., Ph.D., F.Inst.P., M.S. Sigma XI, who 'after attaining Realization took to Scientific Research with the aid of his intuitional knowledge'. Swami Jñānânanda's scientific research took him to places as far afield as Dresden, Ann Arbor (Michigan) and Liverpool, and ranged from the study of X-rays to that of nuclear physics. According to Dr. Paul Brunton, who met Swami Pranavānanda in the 1930s, it was the fact that Swami Jñānânanda had already made a Kailas pilgrimage, and whetted his disciple's appetite with vivid descriptions of the journey and its goal that prompted Swami Pranavānanda to make his own initial Kailas journey, along with an unnamed companion, in 1928. His guru, the great 'Swami-Scientist', also whetted his appetite for things scientific.

Among his own scientific achievements (mainly attained in the Kailas region), Swami Pranavānanda lists the following:

> I discovered the sources of the Four Great Rivers of this region from all points of view, namely tradition, quantity of water, length and glacier. I negotiated four new passes... reached the northern, southern and eastern bases of the Kailas peak; ascertained the number of islands in the Rakshas lake (two); discovered Tso Kapala; studied the lakes cursorily when they were frozen in winter; sounded Gauri Kund and Manasarovar; collected some fossils; and undertook some minor expeditions to the 'Deserted Cave City' [Pangtha] and other places.
>
> (Swami Pranavānanda, *Exploration in Tibet*, 2nd Edition)

In claiming to have discovered the true sources of the 'Four Great Rivers' he is, of course, challenging the claims of Sven Hedin, the Swedish explorer. Naturally, any great river will have many tributary streams at its headwaters, and it will be a matter of debate as to which can with most justice be cited as the true source. Various criteria may be invoked: local tradition, for instance, or length, or volume of water. Pranavānanda contends that Sven Hedin's sources for the Sutlej, Indus and Brahmaputra 'would not satisfy any one of the above three criteria . . . in its entirety; and as such he cannot claim to be "the first white man and European" to discover the sources of these rivers finally, unless one accepts his fixing of the sources at random, applying different criteria for different rivers, to suit his own convenience, whim and taste.' (*Ibid.*)

(Incidentally, there is a slight whiff of contentious nationalism about both this and about Swami Pranavānanda's challenges of other European commentators, Charles Sherring, for instance – residues, perhaps, of the old political activism. Nevertheless, he must also have been deeply fascinated by things European to have dabbled so deeply in scientific research, though he subsequently seemed obliged to prove that native Indians could outdo the Europeans at their own games.)

The *swami's* researches at the sacred lakes apparently began during his twelve-month sojourn at Trügo in 1936–7, when he studied their freezing and thawing. It must have been exceedingly chilly work, for at one time the thermometer sank to 50.5° below the Fahrenheit freezing point. He was able to use the ice, however, to cross to the two islands of Rakshas Tal and survey them both. Later, in more benign weather conditions, he continued his researches with the aid of two boats. The first, a three-seater rubber boat called *Janma-Bhoomi*, was presented to him by a Bombay well-wisher; he sailed it on Manasarovar in 1946 and also used it to take soundings of the Gauri Kund lake. Meanwhile, the Maharaja of Bhavnagar, Sir Krishna Kumar Sinha, had presented him with a four-seater sailing-cum-motor-boat called *Jnan Nauka*. This was made of galvanized steel and had airtight compartments fore and aft to make it unsinkable. It was not, however, a simple matter to have this craft transported across the Himalayas for, although he had got it as far as Almora by 1942, he had to wait until mid-1947 before he had mustered sufficient funds to have it taken to its destination. It was eventually launched upon the sacred Mañasarovar on 17th August 1947, with, so far as can be judged from his own account, no sense of sacrilege on either Swami Pranavānanda's part or on that of the spectators watching the event from the shore:

With the 𝟑𝓈 and Tri-coloured Cakra and Charkha flags proudly fluttering side by side on the deck, the 'Jnan Nauka' rushed into the turquoise-blues of the celebrated celestial Lake amidst deafening cheers of pilgrims, Tibetans and Bhotia traders. A few soundings were formally taken.

(*Ibid.*)

Times must indeed have changed. A century earlier, heads would surely have rolled!

In 1949–9, the Government of U.P.* made a special grant towards an outboard motor. The *swami's* main ambitions with these boats was not only to take soundings but also to locate the thermal springs situated in the bed of Lake Manasarovar and to reach the centre of the lake, said by Tibetans to be inaccessible. When his work was done, Swami Pranavānanda planned to leave *Jnan Nauka* at Manasarovar 'for the benefit of future pilgrims and tourists'. In a similarly public-spirited way, he is reputed to have donated many of the Tibetan curios and other items from his 'Kailas-Manasarovar Museum' to the Provincial Museum at Lucknow.

Swami Pranavānanda must indeed have been a unique individual, apparently able to combine Eastern spirituality and the Western scientific outlook without experiencing any kind of internal conflict. One moment he is detailing cold, empirical data or giving precise numerical specifications, the next he is quoting Walter Bagehot or soaring off into a giddy effusion about the aesthetic delights or the mystical power of the landscape. Then he can abruptly come down to earth again and dispassionately debate the possibilities for the future commercial development and exploitation of the sacred region. He can look forward with equanimity to a day when a 'Kailas-Manasarovar Air Company' begins operating flights from airfields on the plains of Barkha, and when an 'All-India Kailas-Manasarovar Club' inaugurates boat and launch trips on the sacred lakes. He can even go so far as to moot a mountaineering expedition to the Holy Kailas itself – 'if such a venture be at all allowed by the conservative, superstitious and suspicious Tibetans'.†

Although those who kindly write in his favour in the introductions and forewords to his books naturally claim that Swami Pranavānanda was well-known and even loved in the sacred region on account of his high spirituality and the fact that he also maintained a 'Free Travelling Dispensary' through which he gave medical aid to rich and poor alike, it may well be that he was not in fact without his critics, as Lama Govinda suggests in the following letter to the author, dated 11th January 1981:

> I met Swami Pranavānanda in Almora and Calcutta, but he refused to come to my camp, though we sent a messenger to him. But he did not

*Uttar Pradesh.
†Note: The *swami's* predictions look increasingly as though they will soon be realised – see *Kailas Reopens*, pp. 339–40.

dare leave the monastery, because he was afraid of robbers. He was not much appreciated by the Tibetans, for whose religion and tradition he had not much understanding. He even planned to make the holy-Manasarovar-lake into a pleasure resort with motorboats and the like. The Tibetans regarded this as a desecration and his discovery of the sources of the Brahmaputra, Indus and Sutlej were already forestalled by Sven Hedin, who described the Manasarovar in glowing terms.

As regards the *swami's* more recent whereabouts, Shri Uma Prasad Mookerjee of Calcutta, who himself made and filmed a Kailas Parikrama in 1935, met him that year and from time to time again during the following years. In a letter to the author dated February 1981, however, he reports that he has had no news 'for the last two or three years'. Dr Sálim Ali of Bombay*, who made an 'ornithological pilgrimage' to Kailas in 1945, meanwhile writes:

> I met Swami Pranavānanda for the first time since 1945 at an official ceremony in New Delhi in 1976, where both he and I were receiving civil awards from the President of India. Unfortunately, there was little time to talk, and I don't know where he is now. In all my travels in Western Tibet, he was the only rational and science-orientated man I came across!
>
> (Letter to the author; March 1981.)

Reports that the good *swami* was still alive and well continued to filter through, however. In the early 1980s, we heard that he was living in a retreat somewhere in the Kumaon region. Efforts to reach him by letter failed. Then in 1988, Hugh Swift, the Berkeley mountain-walker, confirmed that he was alive 'as of circa 1985. I have a colour slide of him taken in 1985 by an acquaintance. He was living in Pithoragarh . . . but I understand that he has been strongly requested by the Indian authorities to keep a low profile. Michael

---

*Dr. Sálim Ali, a self-confessed materialist, sceptical of all religion, writes in the same letter of his own reasons for travelling to the Kailas region and his responses to the sacred mountain: 'My chief motive for visiting Mt. Kailas and Lake Manasarovar was to study the ecology, behaviour, breeding and biology of the birds of that high elevation, many of which we know only as winter migrants in the Indian subcontinent. I must confess that the sight of Mt. Kailas produced no different spiritual response to what I feel at the sight of any other, maybe less holy, Himalayan giants – for example, Nanda Devi or Kanchenjunga – a mixed feeling of ecstasy at their supreme majesty and indescribable grandeur.'

Prof. Giuseppe Tucci and unidentified Tibetan grandee (1935)

Henss, a principal of Indoculture Tours, Zürich, has met the *swami* and also has a photograph . . .' Disappointingly, letters dispatched to the Pithoragarh post office again evinced no reply - so the rest is silence . . .

Professor Giuseppe Tucci

In the summer of 1935, the distinguished Italian scholar, Professor Giuseppe Tucci (1894-1984), visited the sacred mountain during an expedition to Western Tibet; he was accompanied by Navy Medical Captain Eugenio Ghersi.

Tucci, arguably the foremost Tibetologist of modern times, was a man whose deep knowledge of the history and prehistory of the land, its art, culture and languages, was informed by an equally deep sympathy with the spiritual life of the place. According to the distinguished Anglo-German scholar, Dr. Edward Conze, who worked with him, Tucci was 'also a believing and to some extent even practising Buddhist'. Dr. Conze adds that Tucci believed that he had been a Tibetan in a former incarnation, and that this fact accounted for his friendly reception by the 'normally suspicious Tibetans'. Whatever the substance of these matters, it is certain that Tucci came to Kailas as something very much more than a mere scholar. The fact that there was spiritual sympathy and sensitivity there too enabled him to accumulate invaluable information about the sacred mountain during the latter phase of its religious heyday, information which no other Kailas pilgrim or traveller with the possible exception of Lama Govinda could have acquired. Tucci understood the iconography he encountered; he knew what ascetics were trying to achieve in their particular practices; he could read sacred texts; he could detect in remains and ruins the residues of political and religious traditions that were current long before the Lhasa authorities brought this corner of Western Tibet under their control, or even before Buddhism became the prevalent religion - residues, in fact, of the times when this part of the world fell within the domains of independent kings and when Bön shamans and the luminaries of the folk religion were the arbiters in matters spiritual.

Just how Tucci managed to make himself *persona grata* with the Tibetan authorities is not clear*, but evidently, between 1927 and

---

*Hugh Richardson has since informed me that Tucci received help from the British Indian Government.

1949, he did travel extensively in Tibet with their cognisance and even their co-operation, and was able to bring away large quantities of texts, art objects and artefacts for later study. Sherpa Tensing, the conqueror of Everest, who was with Tucci on a later expedition to Lhasa and Central Tibet, maintained that he had purchased 'whole libraries' and altogether came away with a total haul amounting to some 40 *maunds* – 3,300 lb. – of books. Clearly expeditions on this scale were a costly proposition. His work was indeed generously financed at one stage by the Mussolini Government, though beyond photographing his porters making the Roman salute, Conze does not believe that Tucci helped to forward the cause of Fascism to any significant extent.

Tucci's party reached the shores of Rakshas Tal on 7th July, having set off from Almora on 6th June and travelled by way of the Lipu Lekh, Kojarnath and Taklakot. He duly noted the characteristic atmosphere of depression haunting the western lake, and did not prolong his stay there but was soon travelling over hillocks and ridges in the direction of Manasarovar. The sight of the rippling turquoise waters of the eastern lake formed a contrast and relief to the unremitting desolation prevailing all around. He observed, however, that few Tibetan and Indian pilgrims were still prepared to undertake the lengthy and difficult business of a Manasarovar Parikrama, most being satisfied to take a brief dip and leave the matter at that. This struck Tucci as highly significant. It indicated to him a shift of pre-eminence away from the Lake of Brahmā, the Creator, to the Mountain of Shiva, who is many things in Hindu mythology: Destroyer, Great Ascetic, and the Lord of the Dance. Esoterically this shift signified a move away from preoccupation with the creative energies of the universe to one with death and the cycles of continual renewal. Indians and apparently a little less so Tibetans, had come to despise rebirth in the Paradise of Brahma – or indeed in any heaven or hell, because like all other forms of existence they are subject to the Law of Impermanence and must pass. Peace, ultimate peace, could only be found in the deathless: in Nirvāna.

Tucci decided to resist latterday laxness, however, and to make a Manasarovar Parikrama. Arriving at Chiu Gompa, which he found built over a cave associated with Guru Rinpoche, he left the bulk of his baggage there before setting off. He visited all eight of Manasarovar's *gompa* but found their contents and inmates unimpressive in the main, and the *gompa* themselves of unexpectedly recent provenance. None seemed more than two or three hundred years old, indicating that Buddhists had only recently to come to live

Yaks emerging from Manasarovar at Trügo Gompa (1986)

on these shores permanently. Indeed, it was probably the fact that the sacred lake had for so long been venerated by Hindus that had ultimately prompted Buddhists to add it to their roster of sacred places. Certainly pilgrims from India had been making their way to Manasarovar at least since the Heroic Age, for the great epic, the *Mahābhārata*, repeatedly sings in praise of its sanctity.

But Tucci's *parikrama* was not a sedate spiritual-scholarly progress. For two days his party was attacked by violent storms that delayed its progress. Mighty winds brought monsoon rains lashing down upon their heads, the waters of the sacred lake were whipped up into violent waves, and the summit of Kailas was shrouded in thundercloud, while deep, ominous rumbles broke constantly near its southern side and resounded along the valleys and ravines of the Gurla Range.

And then *dacoits*. They had first been reported at Bönri and then confirmed at Seralung. The band, reputedly led by a man of noble birth, had been raiding extensively in the vicinity. A little perversely, Tucci found the prospect of an encounter exciting: offering a welcome relief from the boredom that had set in as he had travelled in the monotony and silence of that lakeside wasteland. The herders, merchants and pilgrims camped around Trügo (*lit*: 'Door to the Bath') Gompa were not so unperturbed, however. They spiritied all their possessions inside the *gompa*, confident that the *dacoits* would not wish to invoke the wrath of the unseen powers by violating that sanctuary. Even a high official retired inside the monastery walls for protection. As confrontation-hour inexorably approached, preparations were made. Tucci's party had a number of weapons but only Tucci and Ghersi knew how to use them.

At six o'clock on 17th July, the *dacoits* appeared over the horizon. There were about thirty of them, wearing sheepskin coats and long pointed hats. Mounted, they drove before them the herds of yak, sheep and horses they had seized during their recent depredations. They were armed with the usual long muzzle-loaders that are fired by lighting a fuse and retiring.

At the crucial moment, it was the expedition's cine camera that proved to be their decisive weapon. When Ghersi mounted it upon its tripod, took aim and began to turn the handle, the hearts of those formidable desperadoes were filled with abject terror and they took to headlong flight. Tucci put this down to the same superstitiousness that would have prevented the *dacoits* from invading a *gompa*. Indeed, to any ordinary Tibetan of this and earlier periods, the world was suffused with demonaic, divine and semi-divine powers in which they lived in fear and awe. The advent of Buddhism did little to change this disposition; indeed, in Tibet as elsewhere, Buddhism accommodated itself very largely to such beliefs and the practices of exorcism, divination, and propitiation that they spawned, and absorbed many of them. There was a similar complementary process on the other side: Buddhist elements entered and modified the other, older religious traditions of Tibet. Thus in his definitive work, *The Religions of Tibet*, Tucci is able to identify three separate living religious traditions, all fruitfully interacting: Buddhism, the Bön religion, and also a folk religion practised very largely by the ordinary people, varying from place to place, and liberally endowed with 'multifarious and all encompassing pre-Buddhist beliefs'. It was undoubtedly the deep-seated fears rooted in the superstitious pre-Buddhist folk religion that manifested themselves when the *dacoits* saw Ghersi's cine camera. Here was probably a piece of magical apparatus capable of enslaving the vital spirit – thus exit the *dacoits*, frantically pummelling their horses' flanks.

The *dacoits* were not the only ones to be impressed by the quasi-magical 'powers' apparently possessed by the Europeans. There-

Bhumānanda (1935)

after, Tucci's party attracted numerous timid souls from among the ranks of the Indian pilgrims, some of whom had already suffered at the hands of the *dacoits*. Subsequently, he was never without an entourage craving protection.

One Indian who did not lose his nerve was the celebrated *sadhu* [holy man], Bhumānanda, who instead of bolting into a *gompa* had sedately retired to a grotto on the shores of Manasarovar, where Tucci later encountered him, seated on his vocational tiger-skin and attended by two devotees. Instantly on meeting, the Italian became aware of a deep affinity: a sympathy emanating from the subconscious level – far more than ordinary friendship. Thereafter they would travel together, and Tucci looked forward to learning a great deal from this living repository of the ancient spiritual traditions of India.

Back at Chiu to recover his baggage, Tucci witnessed the cremation of a Nepalese woman pilgrim who had just died. There were no tears, no lamentations; she had merely quit one life for another and had been fortunate to do so on this most auspicious of grounds. The sounds of sacred songs filled the silence of the infinite wastes; the reflection of red flames glimmered on the sacred waters.

Tucci's Manasarovar Parikrama had taken him ten days to

complete, though he noted ruefully in his journal that practitioners of *lung gom*, an esoteric yoga endowing its adepts with the power to cover enormous distances by means of long, floating strides while in a state of trance, could accomplish as much within a single day.

Thereafter the Italian turned northwards and began to traverse the great grasslands beyond the sacred lakes. Increasingly he was made aware of the vast spiritual resonance of the place. Here surely the Divine – call it by what name you will – had left its signature. The prevailing desolation and immensity somehow had a unique capacity to put man in contact with the eternal. The earth was an altar, the sky a vault, and the pillar of the sacred mountain joined them. It was not hard for him to appreciate on this evidence why so many great mystics had been produced from among the nomadic herders who grazed their beasts on these grassy plains. Notable among them had been Dromton (1008–64; *see below*), the pupil of the Indian master, Atiśa, who had founded the seminal Kadampa school and played a vital part in the second diffusion of Buddhism in Tibet.

Dromton

Tradition maintains that Buddhism was originally introduced to Tibet around the seventh century A.D., simultaneously from Nepal and China, during the reign of King Songtsen Gampo. However, in the ninth century it was all but obliterated during a savage persecution waged by King Langdarma, and it was not until the eleventh century that a new generation of teachers, translators and proselytizers appeared to restore and reform what had in the interim fallen into decadence as well as decline. This decadence, Professor Tucci maintains, set in due to the teachings of the

Tantras having been 'taken in a grossly exoteric and literal sense, not according to the esoteric interpretation'. Atiśa, along with Rinchen Zangpo and Marpa (Milarepa's teacher) were of this new generation, and indeed the Kailas area was the scene of great activity during this period of Buddhist regeneration.

At Darchen, the general spiritual fervour began to intensify. There were all manner of people here: folk from India and the foothills, nomads from distant provinces of Tibet, rich merchants from Lhasa, ascetics, brigands, Bön-po, Hindus and Buddhists of every school. Equal faith and devotion had brought them thither and united them in a single spirit that transcended all divisions and controversies.

Having called on the local Bhutanese official, Tucci pitched camp near the Hindus. Their numbers were growing all the time, and although they looked undernourished, poorly dressed and emaciated, Tucci clearly saw the power of their faith in their eyes, which had obviously fortified them against all hardships. The need for sleep also seemed to have left them, for they chanted together until the early hours of the morning. All seemed to have a guide – not a guide to show them the geographical route but one conversant with the uncharted depths of inner space. These were not the phoney, degenerate *sadhus* so often encountered on the Plains, but men of genuine spirituality. Each was the spiritual centre of the small group with which he travelled and by his devotees was regarded as an embodiment of spiritual truth – in a sense, as cosmic consciousness itself. Such men knew the true significance of the sacred mountain – as Bhumānanda explained to Tucci:

> God is here within us … and not there on the mountain: the mountain is no more than a heap of stones. But people cannot raise themselves instantly to the heights of our contemplation: the life of the the spirit is an ascent – some begin from a long way off, some from nearby; but though the paths are various – and must of necessity be various, since men think, understand and feel in varying ways – though the paths are various, the point of arrival is one alone.
>
> (G. Tucci, *Santi e Briganti nel Tibet Ignoto*)

Each evening, dressed in orange, Bhumānanda would sit on his tiger skin before his devotees as they sang their sacred songs to accordion accompaniment and recited rhythmic litanies in which the name of a god was repeated over and over again with accumulating exaltation until all were intoxicated with religious feeling. By contrast, Bhumānanda would remain immobile, eyes focussed inwards in meditation, breath almost imperceptible. He seemed to have passed out of his body into another world. Tucci realised that for him the spiritual world was as real as the material world is for other people, and just as they would think him mad to throw away what small time was allowed him on earth in pursuit of spiritual goals, the ascetic would equally pity those who traded their chance of the bliss that can only be attained by following the spiritual life for the vain pursuit of worldly desires.

And so to his own Kailas Parikrama, during which Tucci visited all of the *gompa* of the sacred mountain, catalogued their libraries, studied their statuary and pictures and himself collected a large number of Buddhist and Bön-po artefacts and manuscripts.

His first port of call was Gyangtra Gompa, one of the two *gompa* on the southern side of Kailas. Cloud obscured the surrounding mountain heights and snow fell as he climbed the steep ridge to the *gompa*, which was set in a spectacular amphitheatre of rock and seemed part of the single upthrust of the earth that had produced the eminence upon which it was situated. Within, amid the usual Tibetan artefacts and arms and armour said to have been taken from Zorawar Singh's Dogra soldiers, he found memorabilia of Indian *sadhus* who, apparently, had a special predilection for the place. The keepers spoke with deep respect of two in particular: Ananda Singh, who had for many years lived there, like the guru-poet Milarepa taking no other food than herbs and nettles; and a nameless ascetic who had lived entirely naked at the foot of the *gompa* practising *tumo*, the yoga of the psychic heat. This produces great inner warmth in the practitioner, even in the coldest of climates, and may be tested by placing wet cloths on the body and noting how long it takes for them to dry through.

Prof. Tucci's second *gompa* was Nyenri; the weather was freezing and cloud again obscured the surrounding mountain heights, though just before midday the wind tore a rent in them through which the sacred cone of Kailas was momentarily visible, sparkling in sunlight in the upper air. The library and paintings at Nyenri Tucci found to be of little significance, and only one lama was in attendance, his confrères having descended to Darchen. Tucci reflected that with the onset of the bitter Tibetan winter, the lamas would have to shut themselves off within the well-protected walls of the *gompa* and hug closely to the fire till summer. They might do nothing, or study the life of a great saint . . . or just while away the long hours of boring solitude with dice. Clearly many of them were lesser men, not capable of maintaining the high standards of religious practice set by their ancient mentors.

Tucci found Drira Puk to have been built over a cave where

Coxampa, one of the masters of the Drugpa Kagyu school, had pursued the austerities in which he had been initiated by Naropa, the teacher of Marpa – who in turn was the teacher of Milarepa. At one time this *gompa* had been the seat of an incarnate lama as well. In ancient Tibet, certain distinguished lamas, including the Dalai Lama, were thought to be *bodhisattvas* – highly evolved spiritual beings who had elected to forgo their own spiritual liberation in order to work for the good of other beings. Thus they would return time and time again to the world of suffering to continue their altruistic and compassionate endeavours. Continuous lineages from one birth to another could be traced, and special oracles and divinations had been developed to help locate each new incarnation. Those seeking a reborn *tulku* (incarnation) might, for instance, go to a place indicated by the oracle priests and there begin to look for particular signs. Finally, when they had located the possible new incarnation, they would apply tests – such as showing the child candidate personal objects used by the previous incarnation. Often children would select the correct objects and discard spurious ones introduced to try to trick them. They might even recognize old acquaintances and begin to behave generally as though they knew who they were and what was expected of them. The Tulku of Drira Puk had, however, apparently become tired of the endless cycle of incarnations in which he had found himself locked and, renouncing his Bodhisattva Vow, had eventually failed to return. A substitute had therefore been sent from Lhasa: a very humble and devout man who received Tucci in his cell and spoke with him.

Tucci also found a printing shop at Drira Puk. Tibetan books consist of long unbound sheets of coarse paper printed from hand-carved wood blocks and stored between heavy wooden boards in silk wrappings. The Italian scholar was particularly delighted to locate the blocks from which a guide to the sacred region could be printed. This outlined the history, geography, religious and mythological associations of the sacred region: a kind of spiritual baedeker. He carried paper with him and so was able to commission a copy for his own study purposes.

The final *gompa* which Tucci visited during his *parikrama* was Zutrul Puk, which he found to be also attached to the Drugpa Kagyu sect. It was a modest building of comparitively recent origin and owed its importance to the association with Milarepa. It contained a stucco statue of the great *guru*, who was posed in characteristic fashion, hand to ear, singing one of his myriad songs. Silver lamps and votive objects had been placed upon the adjacent altar; also copper and bronze goblets, which the monks changed

ABOVE, Drira Puk Gompa in 1935 and BELOW as it has been rebuilt and looked in 1985

religiously every day. These lamas were not, in Tucci's view, men of the same spiritual calibre as their mentor; the Italian noted that their religious ardour had atrophied to the cold conventionality of monastic life −and they eyed his money offering with unseemly keenness.

Tucci entered fully into the spirit of the Parikrama and was clearly moved by it. He noted the places of auspicious association and also observed the palpable piety of his fellow circumambulators, Buddhist, Hindu and Bön-po alike. Even the dogs, regarded as spiritually-endowed beings themselves, followed their masters around. The whole landscape surrounding the sacred mountain was clearly not of this world but a thoroughly spiritualized landscape: an earthly projection of the cosmic *mandala*, no less. As he stood in the blast of the wind at Drölma La, amid the great rock and the various prayer-flags and relics, he reflected upon the truth of Radhakrishna's dictum that it is good to kneel where others have knelt before because the Divine is present in those places. Academically, his tour drew him to the conclusion that Kailas must have been a sacred mountain since the dawn of history. Long before the advent of Buddhism, it had been venerated by the Bön-po, but its importance in more recent times was certainly due to the influence of the Kagyu school and the association with Milarepa, who had succeeded to the leadership of the school, after the death of his own teacher − Marpa −the founder of the school. As regards its Tibetan name, *Tisé*, he was of the opinion that this derived from an ethnic substratum of great antiquity, possibly from the ancient languages of Gu-gé, the vanished independent kingdom which had once had its capital at Tsaparang in the Upper Sutlej Valley to the south-west of the Kailas region.

A fresh influx of pilgrims arrived in Darchen from India on the night that Tucci completed his circuit. The echoes of their ecstatic hymns to Lord Shiva filtered through the canvas of his tent. Rising to the sky in one concerted sound, they seemed to express the universal cry of an anguished humanity: a cry of pain and dissatisfaction with this impermanent life, and a consequent longing for the bliss of the eternal. Of course, by and large ordinary religious are not able to grasp the notion of a purely formless Absolute so they need the tangible symbol of the god with his topknot, trident and ash-smeared body. Behind the symbolic form, however, lurks that great formless reality:

I bow to the most exalted Lord, God made manifest, the total cessation of all activity, who is everwhere, who pervades all things. He is Brahmā,

Lama Govinda and Li Gotami in London

he is the sacred revelation. Hail to Him, the essence of the Absolute, free of attributes, beyond imagination, beyond all desire; pure mind, filling infinite space.

Hail to him who is without form, but who is the source of all that has form, the fourth dimension of the Spiritual. Hail to the King of the Mountain, who transcends speech, understanding and the senses. In his fearful aspect he spells death to the king of death; in his merciful aspect, by making himself accessible to us through his attributes, he takes us beyond phenomenal existence.

(Ibid)

On 26th July, Tucci's party left Darchen to pursue its journey to Ladakh by way of Dulchu and Tirthapuri. They were in Gartok on 1st September and reached Leh just over a month later.

Just two years before his pilgrimage to Kailas, in 1933, Tucci had founded IsMEO: the Instituto Italiano per il Medio Estremo Oriente, which is housed in the Palazzo Brancaccio in Rome's via Merulana. There he held court, the prototypical autocratic Italian *professore*, until his death in 1984.

Lama Anagārika Govinda

E.L. Hoffmann (1898–1985) was a multi-faceted, talented and cosmopolitan character of German-Bolivian extraction. Early interests in architecture and archaeology – he was also an accomplished artist – took him to the East in 1928. In Ceylon [Sri Lanka], he discovered Theravāda Buddhism, and in Burma he received lay ordination as an *aragārika*, literally a 'homeless one'. A decisive change of direction came in 1931, however, when he discovered Tibetan Buddhism for the first time in Darjeeling and met his main guru, Tomo Geshe Rinpoche. The somewhat idiosyncratic title he subsequently adopted, Lama Anagārika Govinda – lama being the Tibetan equivalent of guru or teacher – proclaimed his connection with both the Theravāda and Tibetan Tantric traditions, though the latter enjoyed his main loyalty thereafter. His path was also somewhat freewheeling one, lying somewhere between that of the monk and that of the lay person. In his own words, it was 'the way of individual experience and responsibility, inspired by the living contact between Guru and Chela [Disciple] through direct transference of power in the act of initiation.'

His spiritual wanderings took Lama Govinda several times to Central, Southern and Western Tibet. He was able to convice the authorities of the sincerity of his wish to study Tibetan Buddhism, for he was not a covert traveller but carried proper authorization papers (*lamyiks*). He regarded all his Tibetan journeys explicitly as *pilgrimages* rather than ordinary travels, for a pilgrimage –

> does not follow a laid-out plan or itinery ... does not have a fixed inner or outer purpose, but ... carries its meaning in itself, by relying on an outer urge which operates on two planes: on the physical as well as on the spiritual plane. [It is] a movement not only in the outer, but equally in inner space, a movement whose spontaneity is that of the nature of all life, i.e. of all that grows continually beyond its momentary form, a movement that always starts from an invisible inner core
> (Lama Anagārika Govinda, *The Way of the White Clouds*)

A great expositor of Tibetan Buddhism to the West, Lama Govinda's special interest to our present field of study lies in his capacity to trace the underlying esoteric aspects of the sacred mountain and its lakes, and of his pilgrimage to them. He visited Mount Kailas in September 1948 in company with his wife, the Parsi photographer Li Gotami. The principle objective of that journey was, however, to visit the abandoned city of Tsaparang in the Upper Sutlej Valley, once the capital of the Kings of Gu-gé, and study the remains of the temples and monasteries founded there by Rinchen Zangpo (958–1055).

In the account of his pilgrimages to Tibet, *The Way of the White Clouds*, Lama Govinda splendidly elucidates the special qualities of sacred mountains in general. Some mountains are just mountains, he maintains, but others are more: they have personality, and hence the power to influence people. *Personality* in mountains consists in the qualities of consistency, harmony and one-pointedness of character. When personality occurs in a human being it can result in his becoming a great ruler or a sage like the Buddha; when it occurs in a mountain, then it is recognized as a vessel of cosmic power and elevated to the status of a sacred mountain. There is never any need to point this out or argue the case; it is usually quite obvious, and the sole response available is one of worship. To the truly spiritual man, the whole notion of climbing a sacred mountain would be utterly unthinkable. He would want to be conquered *by* the mountain rather than conquer the mountain himself. To achieve his goal he will open himself to the mountain, contemplate it from every point of view and in all its moods and aspects, and thereby approach the very life of the mountain – 'a life that is as intense and varied as that of a human being. Mountains grow and decay, they breathe and pulsate with life. They attract and collect invisible energies from their surroundings.'

But even among these spiritually-charged colossi there are some that soar even higher than the rest to become symbols of the highest aspirations of humanity. They are 'milestones' in the 'eternal quest for perfection and ultimate realization'; 'signposts that point beyond our earthly concerns towards the infinity of a universe from which we have originated and to which we belong...'. And the greatest of them all, since the very dawn of time, has been Mount Kailas.

Why has Kailas attained this position of pre-eminence among the world's sacred peaks? For one thing, it lies at the intersection of two of the most important cultures of the world: those of China and of India. It is also the highest point on the great Tibetan plateau: a kind of spire to the Roof of the World. There too arise the four great rivers that, flowing off in the four directions, symbolize the cultural and religious links between India and Tibet. Moreover, two of them – the Indus and the Tsangpo/Brahmaputra – clasp northern India like the great embracing arms. Then there is the noble isolation of Kailas in the sequestered Transhimalayan range: and finally the regular, architectural quality of its form that irresistibly reminds the beholder of a great temple.

Govinda does not fail to remind us of the spiritual associations of Kailas to both Hindus and Buddhists. To the latter it is the gigantic *mandala* of the *Dhyāni Buddhas* and *Bodhisattvas* 'as described in the famous *Demchog Tantra*: the "Mandala of the Highest Bliss"'. He also equates Lake Manasarovar with the Anotatta (or Anavatapta) lake of Buddhist mythology. Finally, just as every Indian temple has its water tank in which the pious may bathe, so also Kailas has its pair of lakes. Govinda ascribes solar and lunar symbolism to these respectively: Manasarovar is solar, light and masculine; Rakshas Tal is lunar, dark and feminine.

When he deals with the significance of the Kailas Pilgrimage , Lama Govinda clearly shows how the trials of the outward trek across the Himalayas and the crossing of the high passes into Tibet all represent a kind of chastening preparation for the ultimate experience of Kailas itself: a kind of grinding down of the pilgrim's ego – his sense of separate (and special) individual identity; his sense of 'I' – so that he is brought to a state of sufficient receptivity. There is an initial visionary glimpse when at last the high passes are crossed: a look into a 'country of eternal sunshine' where everything is totally different from that which the pilgrim has so far experienced. Then comes the actual descent into Tibet itself, where 'the vivid colours and chiselled forms of rocks and mountains stand out in brilliant clearness, divested of any trace of vegetation, like the

Akshobhya

world on the first day of creation, when only heaven and earth were facing each other in primal unity'. Indeed, the journey through Tibet could actually be seen as recapitulation of earlier phases in the evolution of the world: after bare but beautiful desolation, the pilgrim encounters small patches of green pasture and small fields of yellow barley, followed by the first simple habitations of primitive men – cubiform and cave dwellings. A great obstacle then stands in the pilgrim's way in the shape of the great swastika massif of Gurla Mandhata. He must cross a high pass surmounting one of its arms, and thereby go beyond the zone administered by the Dzongpön of Taklakot into the lawless zone of *dacoits*. The pilgrim may well begin to feel apprehensive at this stage – and with good reason – but as though to dispel his anxieties and send him forward with refurbished faith and confidence, he is given a second visionary glimpse: this time of the shining ice-cone of the sacred mountain itself 'like the full moon in the dark blue sky'. This is just a prelude, a foretaste of greater things yet to come. When he actually reaches the summit of the Gurla Pass all his expectations are exceeded.

Who can put into words the immensity of space? Who can put into words a landscape that breathes this immensity? – where vast blue lakes set in emerald-green pastures and golden foothills, are seen against a distant range of snow mountains, in the centre of which rises the dazzling dome of Kailas, the "Jewel of the Snows"...

It certainly is one of the most inspiring views of this earth, a view, indeed, which makes the beholder wonder whether it is of this world or a dreamlike vision of the next. An immense peace lies over this landscape and fills the heart of the pilgrim, making him immune to all personal concerns, because, as in a dream, he feels one with his vision. He has gained the equanimity of one who knows that nothing can happen to him other than what belongs to him already from eternity.

(Ibid.)

A deep bond of brotherhood unites all those who have been fortunate enough to have had these experiences. It is the brotherhood of Kailas pilgrims, and in Lama Govinda's description it almost amounts to a religious order, though one devoid of vows, rituals, dogma and the like. It is shared experience that bonds them; experience that they will carry back with them when they return to the ordinary world and which will be a constant source of strength and inspiration to them throughout the remainder of their lives, 'because they have been face to face with the eternal, they have seen the Land of the Gods'.

Initial excitement gives place to 'exalted serenity' as the pilgrim proceeds to the shores of Lake Manasarovar. The waters of the sacred lake grade from emerald blue near the shore, through deep blue to purest ultramarine at the centre. Wonderful sunsets take place here when the world is aflame 'with all the colours of fire'. Indeed, everything is bewitchingly beautiful and awe-inspiring, animals know no fear because men do not commit the sacrilege of killing them, and health-giving herbs as well as other salubrious gifts of the gods abound, also precious metals.

In contrast to the benign Manasarovar, which is endowed with many temples, none have been built on the shores of the neighbouring Rakshas Tal. (According to Swami Pranavānanda, Rakshas Tal has one *gompa*: Tsepgye, situated near its north-west corner.) Evidently, the uncannily sombre, even sinister atmosphere that haunts the dark lake has deterred people from building them.

Then Lama Govinda describes how the subtle but irresistible force draws the pilgrim on towards the goal of his pilgrimage: the

Tarpoche, the great flag pole near the start of the Kora Circuit (1985)

sacred mountain itself. At most times during the day its ice-dome is obscured by cloud, but it is usually clearly visible in early morning and in the evening, and at those times the pilgrim will reverently bow down to it and repeat his sacred *mantras*. He keeps both eye and mind fixed one-pointedly upon it as he approaches it across the wide, grassy plain that occupies the space between sacred mountain and sacred lakes. When at last he reaches Darchen, the last outpost of civilization and the place where he will begin his *parikrama*, he begins to feel a joyful tension brewing up inside him. Will he, he wonders, be up to the tremendous mental and physical demands of the great circumambulation?

> Nobody can approach the Throne of the Gods, or penetrate the *mandala* of Shiva or Demchog, or whatever name he likes to give the mystery of ultimate reality, without risking his life – or perhaps even the sanity of his mind. He who performs the *Parikrama* . . . with a perfectly devoted and concentrated mind goes through a full cycle of life and death.
>
> *(Ibid.)*

So the pilgrim knows that during the course of his *parikrama* he will have to confront death. In Zen Buddhism there are traditionally two deaths: ordinary death and the Great Death. The latter is by far the more significant from the spiritual point of view. It is the death of 'I': the individual ego consciousness, the root of all our delusions and consequent woe and loss of Eden. The pilgrim experiences the 'joyous tension' of which Lama Govinda speaks precisely because it is quite on the cards that he may encounter either or both of these forms of death during the course of his circumambulation.

Ekai Kawaguchi referred to Kailas as a 'natural *mandala*'; Lama Govinda talks of it in similar vein: as the 'Mandala of Highest Bliss according to the teachings of the *Demchog Tantra*'. He expounds the mandalic significance of the sacred mountain in wonderful detail, elucidating the esoteric import of the landscape and its colours, and the mythological and religious associations attendant at every stage. As a whole, the Parikrama represents one turn of the Wheel of Life (see p. 46) during which symbolic death and rebirth will be experienced.

The pilgrim sets off from the golden plains of the south in the prime of life. He proceeds into the red western valley, the Valley of Amitābha (the fourth of the Dhyāni Buddhas, the Buddha of Infinite Light, personification of Compassion), where the sun is setting. Here the architectural quality of the ruddy rocks makes him feel as if he is passing between rows of gigantic temples adorned with all manner of wonderfully carved ornaments. From above, the ice-dome of Kailas seems to look down upon him from two deep hollows reminiscent of the empty eye-sockets of a skull – and skulls, Lama Govinda reminds us, adorn the terrible aspects of both Shiva and Demchog, reminding us of the transiency of all things. The northern valley of Kailas is dark and full of intimations of mortality. Here, however, the pilgrim is presented with a magnificent view of the great northern face of the sacred mountain: a sheer rock wall five thousand feet high and flanked by attendant peaks symbolic of Mañjushrī, Vajrāpani and Avalokiteshvara.* Here:

The mountain is so near that it seems to the pilgrim as if he could just walk over and touch it – and at the same time it is intangible in its ethereal beauty, as if it were beyond the realm of matter, a celestial temple with a dome of crystal or diamond. And indeed, to the devotee, it is a celestial temple, the throne of the gods, the seat and centre of cosmic power, the axis which connects the earth with the universe, the super-antenna for the influx and outflow of the spiritual energies of the planet...

What the pilgrim sees with the naked eye is only the substructure and emanation of something much more grand and far reaching. To the Tibetans the mountain is inhabited and surrounded by thousands of meditating Buddhas and Bodhisattvas, radiating peace and bliss, and sowing the seeds of light into the hearts of those who want to liberate themselves from the darkness of greed, hatred and ignorance.

(Ibid.)

The pilgrim passes through the portals of death when he crosses the Drölma La Pass: the highest point on the Parikrama and dedicated to Drölma (Skt: Tara, the Goddess of Mercy). The ascent to the pass is, according to Lama Govinda, the greatest trial that the pilgrim has to undergo. Here he must shed his 'I', his ego; here too he will encounter the Mirror of Yama, the Lord of Death, in which all his past deeds are reflected. Here too are a couple of rocks between which he must lie in the posture of a dead man to receive the judgement of Yama. He should also think with gratitude of all

---

*Mañjushrī: Bodhisattva of Wisdom; he is often shown carrying the Sword of Wisdom in his right hand, and a volume of the Prajñāparamitā literature in his left hand (see p. 397). Vajrapāni: another bodhisattva, the Wielder of the Diamond Sceptre. Avalikiteshvara, Tib: Chenrezi; Chin: Kwan Yin (female aspect): 'the greatly compassionate', a bodhisattva who became the chief Protector and Patron Deity of Tibet and who manifests in the Dalai Lama.

who have helped him in life but who are now dead, and leave some relic of them behind him before he proceeds on his way towards rebirth. The new man who proceeds down the other side of the Drölma La into the green valley of Akshobhya (see p. 294) can celebrate his resurrection from the dead by bathing in the Gauri Kund Lake – the 'Lake of Mercy', as it is known to the Tibetans. The eastern valley is redolent with associations of the guru Milarepa, who composed at least some of his hundred thousand songs while he was pursuing his religious practices there. The place most strongly connected with him, according to Lama Govinda, is the cave at Zutrul Puk, where there is what is reputed to be a print of his foot in the rock of the roof. Legend has it that when he first went to live in the cave, he found it too low and cramped, so he used his occult power to raise the ceiling. Not knowing the full extent of that power, he pushed too hard and in consequence made the cave too large and draughty, so he had to go above and press it down again – presumably with rather more closely regulated force – until it was just right for comfort.

The rocks in the eastern valley are a 'fairyland of colours', a recapitualtion of all the other rocks encountered during the circular route: flaming red, dark blue, vivid orange, bright yellow. Having run the chromatic gamut, the pilgrim finally returns to his starting point, Darchen, on the margin of the open, sunny plains of the south. The symbolic colour of these plains is gold and their association is with Ratnasambhava, another of the Dhyāni Buddhas, known as 'The Jewel Born' or 'The Compassionate Giver'. Here too there are many *mani* walls, which are composed of stone tablets upon which the sacred *mantra, Om mani padme hum,* has been carved. The pilgrim should rightly add a tablet of his own to one of these as a token of his gratitude for the blessings conferred upon him during his *parikrama.* If he has been especially fortunate, he may not only have seen the various aspects of the sacred mountain itself, all of them stunningly beautiful in their various ways, but he may also have been treated to a splendid vision of the deity or ideal of his heart, 'be it in the divine forms of Shiva and Pārvatī, or of *buddhas* and *bodhisattvas*, or any other significant symbol connected with this place and its compelling atmosphere'. He also adds a stone for the benefit of those who will come after him.

Finally, Lama Govinda concludes (a little strongly, some might say):

Only he who has contemplated the divine in its most awe-inspiring form, who has dared to look into the unveiled face of truth without being overwhelmed or frightened – only such a person will be able to bear the powerful silence and solitude of Kailas and its sacred lakes, and endure the hardships and dangers which are the price one has to pay for being admitted to the divine presence on the most sacred spot on earth.... It is as if their individual consciousness, which obscured or distorted their views or their conception of the world, were receding and giving place to an all-embracing cosmic-consciousness.

(*Ibid.*)

When, many months after setting off on their final pilgrimage to Tibet, of which their visit to Mount Kailas formed part, Lama Govinda and Li Gotami crossed the high passes back into India and so 'returned to the world', they did not realise that 'Tibet's hour of fate had struck' and that, except in their dreams, they would never see that magical land again. A year later, Chinese troops invaded eastern Tibet. By 1959, their takeover was complete and the Dalai Lama, capitulating to the inexorable, fled to exile in India.

Latterly, Lama Govinda lived at his *ashram* in the hills near Almora, which was the headquarters of Arya Maitreya Mandala, the order he founded in posthumous honour of Tomo Geshe Rinpoche. In the early 1980s, his health began to deteriorate and he moved to Mill Valley near San Francisco for medical reasons. He passed away there in 1985.

Sri Swami Satchidānanda

In 1958, Swami Satchidānanda (b. 1914), a handsome south Indian holy man with a large and luxuriant beard, set off for Kailas from Sri Lanka. His devotees, who a few years earlier had established an ashram for him on the island, were reluctant to let him go. They knew full well that the popular phrase 'departure for Kailas' was a metaphor for death itself, so there was a very real danger that their beloved guru might not return to them. Swami-ji resolved the debate by pointing out that all would ultimately be resolved according to His will: that is the will of Shiva, the Lord of Kailas.

Travelling north, Swami Satchidānanda first visited Rishikesh, a holy place situated near where Mother Ganga disembogues from the mighty Himalaya. There he received the blessings of his own guru, Sri Swami Shivānanda Māharaj, the founder of the Divine Life Mission, who had himself made pilgrimage to Kailas in 1931 in the company of Sri Swami Advaitānandaji and Sri Suratkumari Devi (Rani of Singhai). In a very real sense, therefore, Satchidā-

Swami Shivānanda (LEFT) and Swami Satchidānanda (RIGHT) at Shivānanda Ashram, Rishikesh

Swami Satchidānanda and friends in camp en route for Kailas (1958)

nanda was following in his master's footsteps.

By the time he had reached Almora by way of Delhi, Swami-ji had met up with the other four members of his party: Sri Swami Premānandaji, the initiator of the pilgrimage; his factotum, the 14-year-old Kunthan Singh; Mr Praveen Nanawathi of Bombay and Mr Ramdas of the Punjab. Further on, at Bhageswaram, they hired a cook named Divan Singh, two porters and four mules to carry their food, utensils, clothing and camping equipment. All in all, then, this was not by any means an ascetic pilgrim band conforming to Swami Tapovanji's most rigorous requirements, but materially a very well provided one.

Trekking *via* Milam, Swami-ji and his friends crossed the Unta Dhura Pass into Tibet, then struck north until they intersected with the Sutlej near Khyunglung. After that they followed the river south-eastwards through Tirthapuri to the Kailas region.

The first view of the holy mountain, vouchsafed to the *swami* on July 11th, was overwhelming. His heart bursting 'with joy beyond expression', he threw himself on the ground in pious prostration and a joyful prayer bubbled to his lips:

The new Gurugem Gompa with Bön-po cave temple in the cliff beyond (1987)

Swami Satchidānanda and friends crossing the Milam Glacier (1958)

'I have seen my Father! How could I want for more? You have
appeared before me. You have rid me of all pain. My heart is full. *Oh
Lord Shiva, prostrations unto Thee! Jai Shiva! Jai Shiva! Jai Shiva!'*
    A little later, visiting what he calls Gurgiyang Gumfa (which is
probably Swami Pranavānanda's Gurugem Gompa), he discovered a
statue of the Buddhist deity Demchog, entwined with his consort
Dorje Phamo, on the main shrine. He had no hesitation in equating
the divine couple with Shiva and his consort (*shakti*) Pārvatī. In
terms of Tantric symbolism, however, there are certain important
differences. In the Hindu system, the male deity stands for the
unmanifested aspect of Ultimate Reality and the female for the
powerful creative aspect. In the Buddhist system, on the other
hand, the male stands for the power of skilful means (*upāya*) and the
female for the passive quality of wisdom (*paññā*).
    This is not the place to go deeply into the meaning of Tantra, but a
few words about its Buddhist manifestations might not come amiss.
Basically Buddhist Tantra is about transforming one's body speech

and mind into those of an enlightened buddha by special yogic means. These are highly powerful and can engineer spiritual transformation very quickly; but they are also very dangerous, especially if misused, so are traditionally hedged around with all sorts of protective devices: veils of secrecy, initiation ceremonies, grave oaths, etc., etc. It is also always emphasised that Tantra is not for the raw beginner but only for the person already well-advanced in spiritual practice, thus morally impeccable, deeply compassionate and, through proficiency in meditation, fully aware of the basic ground of Emptiness (*Shūnyatā*).

In Tantric practice a strong magical element comes into play. Through various rituals, like worshipping or visualising or identifying with a particular Tantric deity (*yidam*), uttering words of power (*mantra*), making special symbolic hand movements (*mudrā*), visualising or constructing *mandala* and so forth, great powers of concentration are forged and mighty spiritual energies generated. These are then mobilized to the great project of spiritual realization.

In the Buddhist system, there is a hierarchy of Tantras, with the most elevated, Highest Yoga Tantra (*Anuttara Yoga Tantra*), strictly reserved for the most adept practitioners. Here again there are two component stages: the Generation Stage and the Completion Stage. In the former, which is essentially preparatory, the practitioner learns to conjure the deity and his/her *mandala* out of the primal Emptiness of his own mind or out of a seed syllable (*bīja*), to visualize the deity in fine detail and dissolve him/her back again into Emptiness, and so forth. At the Completion Stage, on the other hand, the esoteric view of the human body as a system of very subtle channels (*nādi*) and vital centres (*chakra*), which we have already mentioned, comes into play. A subtle 'wind energy' (*prana*) circulates through this system, though in the spiritually undeveloped person this is vitiated. Using the virtuoso powers of concentration and energy arousal developed at the Generation Stage, the adept will seek to arouse and direct the wind energy into the minute *bindu* or 'droplet' situated in the heart *chakra*. If he succeeds, all conceptual thought cuts out immediately and he is precipitated in *Mahāmudrā:* the Primordial State.

But to return to Swami Satchidānanda ... Coming to Tirthapuri, he visited the local hot springs and recalled what he termed the legend of Basmaasura, which must be identical with Swami Tapovanji's Brahmasura, mentioned above. According to legend, Lord Shiva once bestowed upon a pious *asura* a special power whereby he could turn anyone whose head he touched to ash. The *asura* at once decided to test his new accomplishment – on Lord Shiva himself! – who instantly took off in flight. Lord Vishnu, seeing all this, presented himself to the *asura* in the form of a beautiful girl, with whom the base creature promptly fell in love. When it came to marriage, however, he found he lacked the necessary water for his prenuptial ablutions, but Vishnu materialized a jar of water and told him to slick his hair down with that. The *asura* fell into the trap. The moment he touched his own head, he reduced himself to a pile of ashes that remains at Tirthapuri, a memorial to his folly and to the power of the great gods.

Arriving at Kailas, the *swami* again reflected on the spiritual significance of the sacred mountain. To him it was no mere symbol: it *was* Lord Shiva in one of his many 'guises and

Swami Satchidānanda (RIGHT) and Swami Premananda (LEFT)

appearances', specifically the 'simplest possible form': the *Viswa-lingam* or universal phallic form. Furthermore, although the great god is worshipped as a manifestation of Ultimate Reality, there is also a hermaproditic form of Shiva (*Ardhanārīsvara*), in which 'the god has literally become one with his consort', Pārvatī or Umā Devi. This is also, according to Swami Satchidānanda, apparent at the sacred mountain, 'the eastern wing of Kailas, which appears on the left being the Holy Mother and also 'the *sanctum sanctorum* of the River Ganges.'

Seen through the eyes of intense faith, therefore, the mere *darshan* [sight] of Kailas is a living experience of Ultimate Reality and as such is profoundly transformative, generating a kind of holistic or cosmic consciousness in which all duality is expunged: 'The mind passes effortlessly beyond the bounds of time and becomes immersed in the boundless grace of God. That joy of knowing that the seer, the seeing and the seen are One is experienced . . .' The Swami elsewhere adds:

> One who treads the soil of Kailas knows that he is a blessed soul. No-one could possibly reach this place on his own. Only those who have done great penance can win the grace of the Lord's strength which enables one to achieve such a goal. Once he has seen his beautiful person, . . . the inner divine power that has lain dormant begins to function. The mind concentrates effortlessly . . .
>
> (Swami Satchidānanda. *Kailash Journal*)

Swami-ji and his friends circumambulated the great Viswalingam, pausing at each of the *gompa* on the circuit to pay their respects to the resident lamas. At Drira Puk, Satchidānanda took special advantage of the splendid view of the great north face to sit and deeply absorb the vision of his Lord as He manifested Himself anew from moment to moment in the ever-changing play of light. When he tried to take a photograph, however, the Lord vanished – an example of His playfulness perhaps? But the good *swami* resolved to have one more *darshan,* and this indeed, by the Lord's grace, was vouchsafed him.

Next day he climbed to the Drölma La, repeating the name of Shiva all the way. Going then to Gauri Kund, he and his friends broke the sheet of glass-like ice covering the surface of the tarn in order to take a sacramental dip. Each emerged glowing, 'as if he was coming out of the ocean of love of the Divine Mother', though one lost consciousness and some of the rest, perhaps cautioned by this, merely performed their ablutions 'mentally'. The serried peaks surrounded them, meanwhile, one of which, attributed to Pārvatī, shed a 'giant ice crystal' while they watched that smashed through the ice sheet.

The way down to Zutrul Puk proved a cold and steep descent across hard snow. When they eventually got there, the party gathered an aromatic herb which, when dried, would serve as 'Incense of Kailas'. The next day some of his companions went up to visit Gyangtra Gompa, but Swami Satchidānanda returned directly to Darchen, where he was visited by Swami Mukthānāndaji of Rishikesh, a resident of the Shivānanda Ashram. Together they shared a delightful cup of tea with milk.

Having himself paid a visit to Gyangtra the following day, the *swami* and his companions then set out for Manasarovar to purify body and mind further. In Swami-ji's eyes, Manasarovar was Shakti to Kailas's Shiva, it was Gauri to the mountain's Shakaran: in more prosaic terms, the female component of the basic Tantric duality. He saw snow-white swans 'contentendly pecking at the lotus flowers' that grew on the beautiful green waters. His party's actual *parikrama* was no charmed affair, however. They had to cross many rivers, one of which was unbridged, and were tormented by mosquitos. To cap it all, their mules also absconded – but they were later found and everything turned out well in the end.

Beyond the lakes rose the imposing bulk of Gurla Mandhata. Mandhata, Swami-ij recalled, had been a great king who had renounced his throne and all its perogatives in order to pursue the holy life. It was at the mountain that he had finally achieved realization. Another Purānic legend maintained that Ganesha and Muruga, the sons of Shiva and Pārvatī, had first appeared in a cave at the summit of this majestic peak.*

The return route ran *via* Taklakot, the Lipu Lekh, Garbyang, Bukti, Malpa, Jipthi, Sardhaan, Pangu, Yela, Dharchula, Askot, Dhal and Bijapur to Bhageshwaram and finally Almora. There were more ordeals and difficulties to be weathered, and the *swami* himself suffered a heavy fall and was later struck by a falling rock. Fortuitously, Dr Krishnan of Bombay happened along almost at once – he was going to Kailas with a group of pilgrims himself – and was able to confirm that no serious injury had been sustained.

'Here is matter for thought for those who do not believe in the grace of God.' the *swami* reflected.

---

*Swami-ji also recounts the legend of a 'Southern Kailas' near Trincomalee in Sri Lanka, created by order of Lord Shiva himself following the chaos caused by the competitive antics of the gods Vāyu and Adisesha.

Later, having made an additional pilgrimage to the Amarnath cave in Kashmir and also put in an appearance at Rishikesh for Swami Shivānanda's 72nd birthday celebrations, Swami Satchidānanda arrived back in Sri Lanka on 29th September. His Kailas Pilgrimage – the real foot-slogging part of it – had begun on 8th June 1958 and ended on 8th August, during which time he had covered over 800 miles. Though he felt some sense of achievement afterwards, he knew these feats could not have been accomplished without the help, care and guidance of the Lord of Kailas.

A few years later, in 1966 to be exact, having spent in all some thirteen years with his devotees in Sri Lanka, Swami Satchidānanda departed for the United States. There he established a Satchidānanda Ashram at the appropriately-named Yogaville in Virginia. Ancillary Satchidānanda Ashrams and Integral Yoga Institutes have since been established in many other parts of the world.

Tibetan pilgrim at Mt. Kailas (1985)

Tibetan Pilgrims

It is regrettable that we have been unable to include here any accounts of pilgrimages to Kailas-Manasarovar by native Tibetans. The reason for this is mainly cultural: most of the accessible accounts we have are written by Westerners and, to a lesser extent, by Indians (Kawaguchi is the great exception).

It should, however, be emphasised that the absence of Tibetan accounts does not in any way imply a lack of respect for the Tibetans. In the great matter of Kailas pilgrimage, they remain preeminent, having visited the sacred mountain and its lakes and circled them in far greater numbers than any other category of pilgrim.*

---

*Since going to press we have repaired this deficiency – see pp. 431-3.

CHAPTER TEN
Kailas Reopens

Since the foregoing was written, there has been a dramatic thaw in mainland China's relations with the rest of the world. China itself was opened to foreign tourists in the late 1970s and in 1979 organized tour groups were allowed to visit Lhasa and a few other selected sites in Central Tibet. Then in 1981, a harbinger of exciting things to come, Indian pilgrims were given permission to visit Kailas-Manasarovar by the classic pilgrimate route *via* Almora and the Lipu Lekh pass for the first time since 1962.

Indian Pilgrims

In August 1981, it was announced that some sixty Indian pilgrims divided into three groups would be leaving for the sacred region in September and October. Applications had to be in within a week. They poured in – in thousands – so that lots had to be drawn to decide who would go. The first party of twenty pilgrims was led by Pundit Kishen Singh's grandson, S. C. Rawat.

According to Raghubir Singh, a member of one of the first parties, as the Indian pilgrims passed through the high Himalayan villages, the enthusiastic Bhotias garlanded them and showered them with presents, shouting, '*Kailas yatra, safal ho!*' ('May the Kailas pilgrimage be successful!'); to which the pilgrims responded with a hearty, '*Victory to Shiva!*' Further up at the Lipu Lekh, which was swathed in snow and cloud, five Tibetans with ponies 'loaded our baggage and led us into their country.'

The Indian pilgrims were accompanied throughout their time in Tibet by members of the militia that patrols the Tibetan borderland. They were driven in Chinese jeeps over the Gurla Pass to the sacred

Indian pilgrims at the Lipu Lekh (1986)

Indian Pilgrims' Guest House (I.P.G.) at Taklakot (1986)

lakes and were eventually offloaded at Darchen, 'the much-damaged Buddhist monastery at the southern base of Kailas.' Some pitched their tents there; others went off to perform the *parikrama* in deep devotion to Lord Shiva. As one explained to Singh:

> "The shape of Kailas is in the form of a *Viswalingan* [universal or world-phallus] as if installed in a *yoni* [female sex organ]. It is in the *stula* form: that is, for the naked eye. Only after great penance, in this life, can one see Kailas in the *sukshana* form, that is, as the divine light after closing the eyes. This light is the inner eye. If the inner eye is opened, we can have ultimate worship of the mighty Shiva. The *darsham* [sacred view] of is an attempt to find the light of god. This is the holiest, the final and the ultimate truth.'
>
> (Raghubir Singh, 'Pilgrims Return to Kailas, Tibet's Sacred Mountain.' *Smithsonian*, Vol. 13, No. 2)

It became painfully apparent on this and subsequent visits that the religious structures of the Kailas region had been heartlessly

Images desecrated during the Cultural Revolution.

White Temple, Tsaparang (1986)

desecrated and destroyed during the Cultural Revolution (1966–
76). The crucial year seems to have been 1966. The dominant
Marxist ideologues of the day then unleashed their Red Guards on
Tibet with an open mandate to expunge the old order and
inaugurate a brave new world. The great irony is that Tibetans
seem to have been talked into, or forced into, the actual physical
hard work of destruction. Many of them, it has been suggested,
were still faithful to their Buddhist traditions but somehow
managed in their minds to separate the religion from its material
structures. At Kailas itself, the six monasteries were mostly
reduced to rubble and, among lesser structures, the Gateway to
Kailas (Gangi-ni or 'Two Legs') was destroyed, as was the great
prayer flag (Tarpoche), where in the old days Tibetan Buddhists
would gather to celebrate their numerous festivals; also the line of
stūpas enshrining the remains of the leaders of the Drigung Kagyu
school of Tibetan Buddhism below the southern face of Kailas. The
story was similarly sad at Manasarovar.

But on the positive side, Singh found that spiritual life still went
on to a degree at Kailas. At Darchen, 'we conversed with four
monks in halting Hindu ... The herders, other lamas and devout
Tibetans came daily through Darchen to walk around Kailas.'

Indian pilgrims have been going to Kailas regularly by the

Lake Pangong in the Aksai Chin

Almora/Lipu Lekh Route every year since 1981. The season seems to run from May or June until the full moon of October. Apparently in 1986 5000 candidates from all over India applied to the Ministry of External Affairs (Government of India) in New Delhi to go. The lottery was again employed to reduce that to 300, and then, after stringent medical checkups, the figure was further whittled down to 200. These were organized into groups of 25–30 individuals, each of whom paid about Rs. 10,000/– (c £385) to the Indian and Chinese governments for the privilege.

The usual pattern seems to be that the pilgrims are driven up directly from New Delhi for the first 600 odd km.; they then dismount and trek the final 100 km. or so across the Himalayan foothills. This leg of the journey is superintended by the government of the state of Uttar Pradesh and takes several days. Many of the pilgrims will be armed with the new paperback edition of Swami Pranavānanda's *Kailas-Manasarovar*, which was re-published in New Delhi in 1983 by the author. At the Lipu Lekh, one group of pilgrims is exchanged under the eyes of the Chinese and Tibetan border guards for another that is just returning, so there is only one group on Tibetan soil at any one time. The Chinese provide ponies at the Lipu Lekh to take the pilgrims down to where lorries are waiting to drive them along a very rough road to the bus that eventually takes them into Taklakot.

By the time that they reach Taklakot (alt. Purang, Pulan), the pilgrims are mostly exhausted, so they are allowed to rest and acclimatize for a day or so at the Purang Guest House, which has been specially built to cater for their needs. Then they are loaded into the bus again:

> It's quite a moving event to be travelling in the bus with these pilgrims, all singing songs to Shiva and Kailas and Manasarovar, and to be with them as they cross the final pass on the side of Gurla Mandhata and see this beautiful lake, Rakshas Tal, stretching out before them, and across from that, on the other side, is the sacred mountain, standing out like a white dome on the skyline. And they immediately break out into cheers and call, '*Jai! Jai! Jai Kailasa! Jai Shiva!*' And they stop the bus and get out and perform a little *puja* [religious ceremony] to Agni [the God of Fire]; and they're crying and weeping, and it's such a joy in their hearts, because Kailas is the greatest object in the Hindu tradition of pilgrimage and there it is before their very eyes ... and it's as beautiful as they may ever have dreamt.
>
> (Brian Beresford; recorded interview with the author, 5th June 1988)

Choying Dorje (LEFT) and Subhu Sengupta of Indoculture Tours (RIGHT)

At Manasarovar, each group is split into two sub-groups. One makes a circuit of Manasarovar while the other goes on to Kailas. Special facilities, including permanent guest-houses and standing encampments, are provided at both places as well as at Taklakot, and an official named Choying Dorje has been posted at Darchen by the Ali Tourist Service to look after the Indian pilgrims' welfare. Afterwards the two sub-groups change over before joining up again to return to the Lipu Lekh and be exchanged for the next group coming up from India.

Western Pilgrims & Travellers

Though organized parties of well-heeled tourists were allowed in earlier, independent Western travellers were first allowed to enter Tibet in 1984. Of course, movement was tightly controlled and at first limited to showcase sites in Central Tibet. But soon the 'porous' nature of the modern Chinese Empire became apparent.

Communications between the authorities in one area and those in another are often poor – and there are all kinds of other cracks and chinks in the official armour through which the resourceful traveller can wriggle or creep.

Very soon, therefore, tough, ingenious and determined Westerner travellers of both sexes were again getting through to Kailas. In doing so they inaugurated a whole new era in the history of the mountain.

The caravans of yaks and ponies, not to mention the small armies of porters and servants, that had accompanied the intrepid Kailas travellers of old were replaced by trail bikes, Toyota Landcruisers, jeeps and Isuzu busses. There were even some hardy souls who walked and/or hitch-hiked.

They found great changes in Western Tibet. There are now rudimentary roads along which ply robust motor vehicles. The army is much in evidence too, for the sensitive – and much disputed – border with India lies nearby. The military are apparently particularly concentrated in the Rudok area and down the Sutlej, while further north at Lake Pangong, high up in the Aksai Chin, the Chinese Navy is ensconsed. Attempts are also under way to exploit the mineral riches of the area – coal, gold, uranium – and a new provincial capital has been built: Shiquanhe, also known as Ali, which is the best the Chinese tongue and palate can do with the old Tibetan name for the region, Ngari. It lies on the Indus, near the old Tibetan settlement of Tashigong. A big radar mast dominates it. It has numerous Chinese compounds and two and three storey concrete buildings with metal roofs, very boring architecturally. The population is around 50,000, consisting mostly of off-duty Chinese troops: the town seems to serve as an R & R centre for the military camps in the area. It is also a way-station used by truckers coming down from Sinkiang and, in consequence, is far better supplied with food than any other town in Western Tibet. There is now a new tourist hotel there, the Ali Hotel, and several restaurants.

The most influential person in Shiquanhe as far as Western travellers have been concerned has been the famous Mr Li, Vice-Director of the Foreign Affairs Bureau. He is an intelligent and friendly man, very keen to promote tourism in his area and helpful to travellers. It's a sign of the times that Mr Li has two video players and a generator to run them.

There are nowadays three main routes in and out of the Kailas area:

Firstly, there is the Northern Route, which is basically a rough dirt track running at an average of 15,000 feet, mostly across gentle

The tracks of the Southern Route to Kailas, with running kyang (1987)

Deaf-mute pilgrim at Shiquanhe/Ali (1984)

undulating plains, though it does traverse the Kailas Range a couple of times, once dramatically. This is the main trucking route between Central and Western Tibet and can be accessed from either Lhasa or Kathmandu (*via* Zhangmu). It starts at Shigatse, and runs from there to Lhatse, Raga, Tsochen (Coqen) and Gertse (Gerze) to Shiquanhe. From Shiquanhe, various dirt roads lead to Tsaparang, Thöling, Purang/Taklakot and Kailas-Manasarovar.

Secondly, there is the Southern Route. This parts company from the Northern Route at Raga. From then on the going is said to be relatively good between the large military township of Saga and Zhongba, a minimal town where there is just one store, and reasonable from there up to Parayang (alt. Paryang, Payang), which is little more than a collection of huts with one poorly provisioned shop and a compound where travellers can stay. However, from Parayang to the Maium (or Maryum) La, the going gets very tough. The problem is the Yarlung Tsangpo river. This splits into many channels which are fed by tributories pouring down from the mountains to the north and south. These generally wash out the road in summer, and in winter it simply turns to ice, so it is only passable for one or two months of the year – and then with difficulty. Bradley Rowe says: 'The road is literally just tyre tracks across savannah scrubland. It's very sandy in places. It's quite possible to get stuck in the sand, or in summer in mud. In fact, our bus got stuck in a marsh and we had to spend one night rebuilding the road . . . It's liable to take longer than going the northern way.'

Finally, there is the Kashgar Route, which runs north-west through Rudok, up past Lake Pangong, through the Aksai Chin, a remote and sparsely populated region seized from India some years ago, and over the Kun Lun Mountains to Yechen (Khargalik), where the roads from Kashgar and Khotan converge. Travellers report that this is much harsher than the Northern Route. Though there are spectacular vistas, especially in the Aksai Chin stretch, the landscape is mostly very bleak and there are many passes, which are difficult to negotiate when the bitterly cold winter weather sets in. Furthermore, truck stops are very few and far between, and supplies are virtually unobtainable.

The most accessible route to Kailas-Manasarovar, the one up from Almora and over the Lipu Lekh, is off-limits for Westerners due to Indian rather than Chinese official sensitivities. North-western Nepal is also off-limits by order of the Nepalese Government, though some people have got in and out through there, usually passing through Simikot.

Bradley Rowe in the Kun Lun Mountains on the Kashgar Route (1987).

1984

No-one is quite sure who can claim the honour to have been the first Westerner at Kailas since Lama Govinda in 1948. There is a vague rumour that a New Zealander got there during the Cultural Revolution (1966–76), crossing into Western Tibet from the west and leaving *via* Nepal. There is another vague rumour that an Italian went across with one of the first parties of Indian pilgrims in 1981. Of course, those parties were strictly reserved for Indian nationals, but, so the story goes, this man was able to pass muster, having lived the life of an Indian *sadhu* or holy man for 15 years.

However, neither of these shadowy figures is known by name, nor have they published anything. By default then, and until evidence to the contrary is forthcoming, the accolade must fall to Bradley Rowe.

I first met Bradley at a small gathering of Tibetophiles in a flat in north London in 1986. Ironically this was only about half a mile from the house in which I had written *The Sacred Mountain*. He was a squarely-built, cleancut young man, wearing a loose shirt open to display a T-shirt with the flag of Free Tibet emblazoned on it. He dazzled us with dozens of vivid slides taken on his various epic treks through Tibet, where he'd ranged widely for months on end, visiting many exceedingly remote monasteries, shrines, mountains, lakes and valleys, some never before seen by Western eyes. What struck me them most forcibly – it's always trivial details that hook the attention – was the thickness of his spectacle lenses. This did not suggest scholarly myopia or a vague weakness of the eyes so much as a kind of concentrated vision: that of a man who would blank out all peripheral matters to direct his whole attention onto his central interests.

Bradley comes of Devonian stock, though he was born in the Midlands in 1955. He was educated at Sherborne and Bristol University, where he read Economics. Afterwards, he worked for five years as a chartered accountant in London before throwing that up in favour of what he calls 'travel as a way of life'. That was in 1982. But there were dangers in just wandering the world promiscuously, he realised, so he gave himself a central theme: 'To explore sites that have been religiously used, and only religiously used, since ancient times; and, most essential, the actual routes between them. Which paths did the pilgrims take when visiting these sites; what spiritual practises did they perform *en route*; what special geographical features did these sites possess; what were the legends associated with them?' Now religious structures made of

Victor Chan

wood and other light materials can be moved or destroyed quite easily. Stone, however, tends to endure and to stay in place. Thus was born the Stone Routes project.

Having carefully researched his subject for many months, Bradley eventually set off on his travels in August 1983. He had intended to make Stone Routes a worldwide study and had plans for linking India up with South America (which he had already visited) *via* Easter Island. But he was deflected into China when it opened up in 1984. It was while he was there, walking around the various Buddhist and Taoist sacred mountains, that he heard that it was now possible for individual travellers to go to Tibet.

Arriving in Lhasa with the first batch of tourists in September 1984, he at once set about trying to get to Kailas, which was quite central to the Stone Routes brief. It would, he decided, be quite foolhardy to try to go it alone, however, knowing neither Tibetan nor Chinese and having no proper maps; so he looked around for a suitable companion. All the other Westerners in Lhasa at the time were totally fascinated by the holy city and so quite uninterested in venturing elsewhere. But Bradley kept trying and eventually did find his man – and a remarkably well-qualified one too.

Victor Chan is a Canadian of Malayan-Chinese extraction. Although by training an atomic physicist, he became a businessman after going to Hong Kong, where his Canadian wife had substantial family business interests. For a time he edited a financial journal, but his affluent lifestyle soon began to pall; his marriage ended too. So he decided to go to China to write a guide book. Victor possessed one invaluable asset: a Hong Kong passport of the kind issued to Overseas Chinese, which enabled him to travel more or less anywhere in China and Tibet. Bradley, of course, had only a British passport and in 1984 Kailas was not open to Western tourists. Being with Victor, however, he could pass himself off as a British historian – 'which effectively is what I am' – acting as Victor's assistant.

As it was now late in the season and Bradley was ill equipped to winter at high altitudes, he was anxious to push on to Kailas as quickly as possible. Victor, however, insisted that they first visit the Everest Base Camp – the remote north-east one accessible only on foot through the Kharta and Karma valleys. This bit a hefty chunk out of their available time and left then with barely $200 in Chinese currency and severely depleted food supplies. Nevertheless, sixteen days later they got to Lhatse, a few hours from Shigatse, where the Northern Road to Western Tibet begins. There they began hitching

ABOVE the Citadel at Tsaparang and RIGHT, the Stupa of King Yeshe Ö. Tsaparang (1984)

lifts on the open backs of trucks.

Unfortunately, Bradley had no down or wool clothing with him, only cotton. Surviving arduous truck drives exposed to the elements at 13,000 feet plus in October so attired was, on his own testimony, 'no fun'. Also he and Victor were unable to get a single through ride, so had to kick their heels for two days in each of the one-yak towns *en route*. They encountered no problems from local officials, however; in fact, they gave Bradley permission to continue. The delays did further erode their diminishing resources, however, and – more importantly – their time. The upshot was that be the time he got to Shiquanhe Bradley's visa had run out.

'Then I did a very wrong thing,' he admits. 'I forged the extension to my Chinese visa, for which I was later arrested and had to pay a substantial fine. I am very sorry for this, but at the time I could see no alternative if I was to get to Kailas.'

But for the time being, at any rate, luck was on their side. Despite the official Lhasa embargo on Westerners travelling in Western Tibet, the Ali [Ngari] region bosses, far from being hostile to foreigners, were actually seeking to devise ways of luring them in large numbers to the region. Indeed, the main theme of a high level conference in progress at the very moment that Bradley and Victor reached the new provincial capital was – the opening up of Western

Tibet to tourism. They also met the famous Mr. Li. He was a little suspicious at first, but Victor's Hong Kong passport reassured him and, perhaps to get them out of town for the duration of the official meeting, he agreed to hire them a jeep at a concessionary rate for nine days to take them to Mt Kailas. He also supplied a driver who had recently come out of the Red Army but was reluctant to return to China for reasons of his own.

Bradley and Victor managed to talk a third traveller into going along and sharing the cost of the jeep with them. This was Minoru Kishipa, a virtuoso Japanese *suchi* chef, who was also a veteran of various epic journeys. His routine was to work periodically in places like New York, Paris and London, 'earn pots of money' and then take off to places like the Himalayas and South America. He had also spent three years as a Buddhist monk at the foot of Adam's Peak in Sri Lanka. Minoru was very unusual for a Japanese; for one thing, he carried no camera.

Mr Li's ex-Red Army driver jeeped our three travellers on diabolical dirt roads past Gartok and on down to Tsaparang and Thöling, the lost cities of the long-defunct Kingdom of Gu-gé.

Then, having spent two days exploring those remarkable ancient sites, they roared up along a stretch of road newly built by a Chinese Army roadworking gang to Menjir (alt., Mencir, Moincêr, Missar), a coal-mining town very near the Guru Rinpoche *gompa* and hot springs at Tirthapuri. Menjir is reputed to be the highest coalmining town in the world, but climatic conditions are so extreme there that the open caste pits can only be worked at certain months of the year. The travellers also passed several nomad camps of fifteen to twenty tents, some of which had herds of as many as 500 or 600 yaks and sheep.

The jeep driver dropped Bradley and his friends at Kailas with only two days to make the *parikrama* or *kora*. It therefore had to be something of a whistlestop tour. They all set off separately though Bradley arranged to meet up with Victor Chan at Drira Puk, the northern *gompa*, that evening. At that stage Minoru Kishipa's plan was to go only half-way round and then return to Darchen before nightfall.

Bradley set off bright and early, determined to go at his own pace and do his own thing:

> I had a very deep feeling for Kailas. It had been a long lifetime wish of mine to get there – it's obviously central to the things I'm studying – and so I was doing all sorts of little antics, like adding stones to almost every cairn (and there's a significant number of them), which kept me way behind Victor. And I was so astounded at the first view of Kailas that you get from the south-west corner that I sat there, gazing at it, for quite a while.
>
> (Interview with the author, June 4th 1988)

Suddenly he noticed a group of about twenty pilgrims nearby. They obviously knew the place very well and also what rituals needed to be performed, for they were going round in a very expert way, making prostrations, adding stones to particular cairns – the men and the women doing different things. Bradley thought they hadn't noticed him but as they prepared to go on, two of the men came up to him.

'Come on, time to go,' they said.

So he ended up 'trucking along with those pilgrims', one of whom was weighed down by a whicker rucksack containing many *mani* stones which he had carried for hundreds of miles. They paused to enjoy a sustaining cup of Tibetan butter tea below the ruined remains of Nyenri Gompa. Opposite, the sheer western face of Kailas reared up against the cloudless sky, a truly astounding sight and also the closest that the pilgrim gets to the actual summit on the whole circuit. Then on, past the start of the path that leads to the source of the Indus – Bradley cast a whistful glance at that – and so to Drira Puk Gompa, which was just a pile of ruins at that stage, with no attendant monk.

The Tibetan pilgrims prepared to pass the night at Drira Puk. They only had blankets, but they huddled against the ruined walls of the *gompa* for what scant protection they might provide. Victor, however, was nowhere to be seen. He had in fact completely missed the ruined *gompa* and gone on towards the Drölma La. Bradley, not knowing this at the time, decided that he had better push on and look for his friend.

He found Victor and Minoru up within about a hour's climb of the summit of the pass. They had managed to find some high-altitude yak herders who had generously agreed to let them spend the night in their tent. It was a bitterly cold night. Bradley, with no protective clothing, nearly froze to death in his flimsy polyester sleeping-bag. Minoru, with no sleeping-bag at all, was in a far worse plight. Eventually, around 3 a.m., the prospect of imminent death from hypothermia forced him out of the tent and he began walking in a desperate effort to generate bodily heat. Fortunately he had a down jacket, but in the dark he lost his way and it was only by dint of great good fortune that he finally got safely back to Darchen.

Bradley was intensely glad when the sun hit the walls of the yak herders' tent next morning. He and Victor then went up to the Drölma La, which was littered with innumerable cairns, yak hair, pieces of cloth, broken cups, safety pins and other detritus left behind by pilgrims. Then they proceeded on down the eastern valley to Zutrul Puk, which, unlike the other *gompa* on the circuit, had received some reconstruction work.

However, they did not have time to linger as they could see the headlights of their jeep. Mr Li's driver, back from two days amid the heady delights of the coalmining town of Menjir, had returned and was eager to get on to their next destination. He even began to try to cut across the scrubland at the south-east corner of the mountain to intercept them. Had he reached them, it would have technically meant that they had not fully completed their *parikrama*. Bradley, determined as ever, was not going to be cheated of that prize; so he forged on to Darchen – and got there. At that time the damaged *gompa* was partly used for private housing, but had no attendant monks.

Having achieved a great ambition, Bradley's feelings were intense:

I felt a magnificent sense of relief somehow. It was as if something had changed; but it was an unchanging feeling too... A sense of achievement – a real sense of privilege... I've walked round many holy mountains now, but there's something particular about that one. It's the altitude, the way it stands out, the unique drainage pattern of the area, the whole structure, little pebbles you find around and, I suspect, the fact that it's been spiritually used for so long by numbers of different pilgrims... Also, many other religious sites have seen commercial activity over the years but this hadn't and that was somehow detectable in the atmosphere. I didn't see any particular visions or hear bells, but there were sounds: the streams, the wind, birds – and sights: unassailable crags, shrines, cloudless views of the majestic dome of Kailas itself....A great accomplishment in my life, I felt.

(ibid.)

His next destination was Manasarovar. He was not able to bathe in the lake because it was beginning to freeze over, so – 'it was a quick sip – a kiss and a promise to come back...' Chiu Gompa was wrecked like all the rest, but there was a slightly reconstructed shrine there and a few attendant monks. Nearby, the old gold workings were still being operated, and the Ganga Chu, the connecting channel, had water in it. Bradley tested the current and found to his amazement that it was flowing both ways. The channel did not, however, connect up fully with Rakshas Tal, so he concluded that there must be substantial underground drainage.

Driving down between the lakes, he and his friends crossed the flank of Gurla Mandhata and arrived at Purang (Taklakot to the Indians, Pulan to the Chinese). The local authorities here came under Mr. Li's jurisdiction, so, as the travellers had Mr. Li's driver with them, they were treated very well. They were put up in the new Chinese compound and to their delight were served an excellent meal of Nepalese food.

Bradley found Purang to be a bustling commercial centre and a unique cultural mix. In the bazaar, ordinary Tibetans and nomads rubbed shoulders with Nepalese traders and Indians masquerading as Nepalese, coolies, off-duty Chinese troops on the lookout for bargains and even a few Kashgari truckers. It also has an ancient cave village cut into the mountainside, though as now most of the caves are incorporated into private houses they cannot be inspected. A monastery is situated nine levels up the cliff too, Tsegu Gompa, where Sudhana, who features in the *Gandavyuha Sūtra*, is said to have lived. The old hill-top fortified monastery, Simbiling, was destroyed in 1966.

From Purang, the jeep took them on a short day trip to Kojarnath

Hot springs at Khyunglung (1987)

monastery, which lies in the Karnali valley, near where the river crosses into Nepal. Bradley and his friends found the attractive *gompa* being lovingly restored by a dedicated group of monks. Then it was a lightning trip back to Shiquanhe, where Mr Li arranged for them to visit the thermal springs that provide Ali's electricity while he arranged for a truck to take them to Kashgar, one of the ancient waystations on the Silk Road in Sinkiang.

After five bleak and comfortless days in the back of a truck, exacerbated by a minor bug, Bradley and Victor reached Kashgar, where they were rewarded with their first shower in two months. Bradley then returned to Central Tibet and spent several months there before going on to Eastern Tibet, where he spent several more months following old pilgrimage routes. He then returned briefly to the West.

1985

Charabancs of Western tourists at Mount Kailas! Preposterous? But it had to come – and it did in August 1985.

Again, it is hard to say exactly which was the first organized tour to the sacred mountain, but the strongest contender is a private Californian expedition organized in association with CITS (China International Travel Service) by Peter Overmire, which snatched the prize from the Mountain Travel company by some two weeks. Overmire's party of 'fourteen adventurous Californians' included William Forbes and Sue Burns, both then working at the Lincoln School in Kathmandu; Lorri Lockwood, another teacher; a Marine Ranger (retired); a doctor; and a Chinese-American named Bob Hong'who was also there to see whether the contributions that the Chinese community in America makes to the régime for the reconstruction of temples destroyed during the Cultural Revolution was having effect in Tibet.'

Starting from Kathmandu, the tourists drove up to the Tibetan border, where the vehicle that CITS was providing was waiting: a luxury coach with red corduroy seat covers – hardly the most appropriate vehicle for traversing some of the most remote and rugged terrain in the world. The Chinese crew were equally ill-equipped, it seems: they wore city clothes, had never been to Western Tibet before, spoke no Tibetan and did not know the roads. What ensued then, if we are to believe the testimony of the American participants, was a surrealistic picareque 'that can be played two ways – comedy *à la Airport* or its flip tragedy.'

Having paused at the new tourist facilities at Zhangmu, the bus crossed several high passes and then, descending into the treacherous Yarlung Tsangpo valley, lit out for Kailas at a remorseless pace, driving 14 or 16 hours a day to conform to an inexorable but probably fictitious schedule. Behind crawled a back-up truck, carrying a heavy cargo of 'beer, Coke, canned mandarin oranges, spam', etc. This was driven by the hero of the journey, a cheerful Tibetan who was the one person around who did seem to know the roads. One passenger wrote:

We were expected to cover between 300 and 400km. each day driving over dirt roads which became quite extinct during the second day, across rising rivers which were not bridged (it turns out that there is a Monsoon in Tibet, this year's being particularly profuse). One of their prime objectives, it seemed, was to make sure that we spent our nights in walled compounds run by the Chinese, like army barracks, road maintenance stations or rest camps for nomads. We could sleep anywhere but . . . in the grasslands, raised up so close to the enormous Tibetan sky: a landscape of incredible appeal to us, which the Chinese imaginitively filled with 'lions, bears and bandits' – a paranoia fit for an invader, a guilt-complex in a bear suit.

(Photocopied letter from William Forbes, dated June 2nd 1986.)

Late on the evening of the fourth day, the battered party came in sight of Lake Manasarovar. Some then opted to go down to Purang, but six, chaperoned by two of the Chinese, camped at the lake for two days and bathed in the 'legendary sin-cleansing waters'. William Forbes walked as far as Gösul Gompa, noting sadly the ruined remains of the monasteries that had once ringed the lake.

At Darchen, the tourists met Choying Dorje, the highly educated and intelligent young Tibetan who is now the principal guide at Kailas and looks after the welfare of the Indian pilgrims with genuine solicitude. Born in the shadow of the sacred mountain and into a family that has lived in the region for generations, Dorje naturally imbibed the lore and legend of Kailas with his mother's milk, and is perhaps today the leading expert on such matters, though he has been abroad and widened his horizons too. Between 1960 and 1969 he lived in refugee camps in India and there picked up good Hindi and rather more rudimentary Indo-English. A small, slight, camera-shy man, he is an employee of the Ali Tourist Service, a local body with headquarters in Shiquanhe and a good reputation for helpfulness towards foreign travellers.

And so to Kailas Parikrama, which took 'three glorious days'. Ten yaks herded by 'weather-worn, gaucho-like men' and four porters carried the tents and supplies. Forbes and his wife hired a lama guide, who proved a sound investment, for he knew the whole circuit like the back of his hand and made sure they gathered all the special items that it is customary to bring back from Kailas. Forbes wrote:

Each face of the mountain was different . . . The South Face: snow-pillowed, gentle and inviting; deep regular striations forming a stairway to the top (for a giant or a god). The West Face: misted and floating strangely beneath its waterfalls. The remote North Face: shaped like a pyramid, full of natural power . . . It rained, snowed, hailed . . . We flew, floated, strolled upon the ancient path. At times it felt as if Kailas was propelling us around itself in a mystical game of peek-a-boo from behind its cloud-shroud, revealing, then concealing its majestic faces . . . We arrived back in Darchen aglow, almost not believing that we had done what we had done – somehow feeling we could just go on and on, around and around, again and again.

(Ibid.)

There is an old proverb about pilgrimage: 'It's your good Karma that helps you get there; it's your bad Karma that impedes your getting back...' The grim truth of this made itself all too apparent on the return journey. The Tsangpo had by then risen and the 'roads' turned to mud. The luxury coach and its attendant truck stuck and stalled many times and eventually ground to a halt axle-deep in a quagmire on the wrong side of the river. A further complication was that Peter Overmire had aggravated his hernia trying to push the vehicle clear and there were fears that peritonitis might set in. Eventually two of the Chinese went to get help.

Despite the fraught situation, this was the first time that the travellers had been relatively free to do what they liked, so they made the most of their 'two day camping respite from bus captivity.' Meanwhile, the party's paediatrician was busy looking after Peter and two other invalids, one suffering from suspected pulmonary oedema, the other from a chest condition.

Finally, an ancient ambulance appeared on the opposite shore. The sick were ferried across to it on a makeshift raft of oil drums and air-mattresses and taken to hospital in the army camp at Zhongba. The other tourists followed in an army truck. To their immense relief, the Chinese doctor announed that peritonitis was not about to strike Peter Overmire and an emergency operation was not necessary. He eventually received surgery in Japan in September and made a good recovery.

The journey was afterwards resumed by truck, though later the hapless bus reappeared, its interior soaking: it had been dragged across the Tsangpo by army trucks. It carried the jaded tourists on to Lhasa for 'another week of hardships'. William Forbes and Sue Burns did not go on that leg of the tour, however, having returned directly to Kathmandu by Land Rover and bus. True pilgrims, they had no regrets:

> For Billie and Sue, all these misadventures were 'no sweat', as we were still riding the high vibe of having been taken to the holiest of all Himalayan shrines, the Abode of Shiva, the Center of the World, the Radiant Crystal Jewel of Snow Mount Kailash. We are still riding it – and it feels like we will from now on...

(ibid.)

The Swiss firm, Indoculture Tours, operated by the Zürich book dealer Michael Henss, also brought its first organized tour parties to Kailas in August and September/October '85.

These were set up in association with CMA (China Mountaineering Association) and led by Subhu Sengupta, who as an Indian national had already made the Kailas-Manasarovar pilgrimage with the Hindu pilgrim parties in 1983 and 1984, and Henss himself. Another two tours were organized in 1986, three in 1987 but only one is scheduled for this year (1988). Henss reports: 'Bönpo and Buddhist pilgrims have been more frequent in 1987 than 1985.'

Other highly significant visitors to Kailas in August 1985 included a five-strong Swiss-German party that came in by Toyota Landcruiser. It included the well-known mountaineering athlete, Reinhold Messner, who specializes in scaling the world's 18,000+ meter peaks without benefit of oxygen.

It will be highly disconcerting to all those who hold Kailas in reverence as a sacred mountain to know that Messner, the 'notorische Tabubrecher' ('notorious breaker of taboos'), has set his sights on the summit. So far the Chinese authorities, hoping among other things to be able to lure the Dalai Lama back to Tibet, have not risked offending Tibetan feeling by permitting a mountaineering assault on Kailas; but this embargo is strictly provisional. The CMA has in fact given Messner a guarantee that, as soon as political circumstances are propitious, he and his friend, the Zürich heart specialist Prof. Dr. Franz Rhomberg, 'will receive first permission' to climb the sacred mountain.

The moral issues bearing upon an assault on Kailas were hotly debated by the five members of Messner's party before setting out on their journey. According to his ex-wife, the Munich journalist Ursula Demeter, Messner, then aged 41, argued his case on the grounds of the individual's right to freedom; he also added that taboos are only for those who create them and if nobody was watching, nobody would be insulted if he climbed the mountain. Ms. Demeter and another member of the party, Beat Curti, 47, a Zürich entrepreneur and editor, defended the sanctity of symbols and argued for respect of other peoples' values and beliefs.

'One should not trample in mountain boots on gods turned to stone,' argued Mr. Curti.

Dr Rhomberg, 57, and the fifth member of the party, Christian Hardmeyer, 49, remained silent.

And so to Kailas, which Ms Demeter approached with Rod Stewart pumped into her ears by her Sony Walkman, at the same time reflecting on the humour implicit in the fact that she, a woman, should be travelling towards the largest phallus in the world.

Although at this stage not permitted to climb Kailas, on July 28th Messner set off before dawn to sprint round the *kora*. This 'fastest pilgrim on earth' accomplished one complete 45 km. circuit in some twelve hours. 'He tells us of much newly fallen snow, of a risky river crossing and a female corpse at the foot of the pass,' reports Ms. Demeter. Next day, he was up early again to set out on an even more gruelling 80 km. solo marathon around Manasarovar, which he completed by 22.30 hours. He had taken with him a beaker to draw drinking water from the lake and obtained food from wayside nomads: 'For payment, they cut a lock of my hair.'

On July 31st, the whole party performed a more leisurely three-day *kora* together. On the day they finished, August 2nd, Messner received the sad news that his brother, Siegfried, had fallen to his death in a climbing accident in the Dolomites. This meant an expeditious departure.

A year later, drawn together by their shared adventures in Tibet, the five travellers met from time to time in their favourite restaurant in Zürich, the Kronenhalle. There, over sumptuous meals, they recalled past privations and projected new plans. Each confessed to be toying with the idea of returning to Tibet once more. As for Reinhold Messner, 'that man of action is already on his way to Tibet . . . to find out why the Sherpas left Kham and moved to Nepal . . .'

Messner is clearly a brave spirit who has achieved many almost unbelievable mountaineering feats. It would indeed be a great pity if he sullied his fine reputation by profaning the peak of Kailas. To do so would not only deeply offend millions of devout Hindus and Buddhists across Tibet and India, but millions more of their co-religionists and sympathizers in other parts of the world too.

Besides Ms. Demeter's German-language record of the Messner excursion, two other books have appeared describing visits to Kailas in 1985: one by Peter Somerville-Large, the other by Sorrel Wilby.

The Tibetan foray of the Anglo-Irish writer, Peter Somerville-Large, was a somewhat dodgy one, for he went in on a doctored passport and without proper permits. Consequently he lived and moved under the shadow of apprehension by the dreaded Public Security Bureau. One invaluable asset, however, was his companion, a young photographer named Caroline Blunden, whose fine black-and-white photographs adorn his book, *To the Navel of the World*.

Peter Somerville-Large

Caroline possessed a smattering of Mandarin Chinese and thus was able to talk the two of them out of many tight corners.

Peter and Caroline's journey took them along the Northern Route to Shiquanhe, then down to Kailas, the lakes and Purang, and out *via* north-west Nepal. At Kailas, they met Chöying Dorje and stayed at his rest-house at Darchen. A fellow guest was a Japanese scholar, 'Dr Kazuhiko Tamanura, Professor of Tourism from Doshisha University, Kyoto, Japan', who was compiling data on the pilgrims at Kailas. 'Kazi' was attached to the Chinese-Japanese Friendship Mountaineering Expedition that successfully climbed Gurla Mandhata in 1985. A Chinese television crew was also in the area: 'big, burly men wearing tracksuits emblazoned HIGHER PERFORMANCE GORTEX.' The Irish couple performed the Parikrama and also witnessed the raising of the great flag-pole for the Spring Festival. Unfortunately, the pole fell, broke and had to be spliced for a second (successful) attempt. Finally, it was interesting to know that many children in the area were learning English and could greet the travellers with text-book phrases.

There is much that is interesting, entertaining even in the Somerville-Large book. Occasionally the writer is capable of inspired impressionistic passages that vividly evoke a scene or situation, as when he describes the dust and discomforts of a ride in the back of a truck to Sinquanhe: 'Imagine a pitted, dusty road on which the wild driver is going at sixty miles an hour behind a comrade who is throwing up dust, which pours down your throat to combine with your thirst..', etc., etc. And at Kailas: 'Above us was still the steep line of corrugated brown peaks that guarded Kailas, and from time to time the holy mountain would emerge from a cauldron of clouds with snow running down its shoulder like a Christmas pudding...' Fine writing like this, plus its quirky observations and dry humour, in fact make *To the Navel of the World* an English travel book of the archetypal sort.

'I was worried about you,' Choying Dorje told Peter when he at last arrived back at Darchen at the end of his *parikrama*. 'Such an old man walking the round.'

Sorrel Wilby is something else altogether. She recounts her amazing Kailas adventures as she might have told them to a gang of fellow Australians with the aid of an Esky-full of tinnies. Her book is gutsy, over the top, souped up with modern pop imagery, shrill ejaculations, jokey asides, and numerous unretouched references to basic realities, including physical functions – 'Awakened by a sudden attack of the Chinese food greasies I only just reached the compound toilet in time'... 'What a wonderful piece of New Zealand slang, 'piss-bolt'. It sounded like something one of Jigme's famed yaks would do. Piss – then bolt!'...

To think that this stands in the great tradition of Kailas literature: alongside such masters of the English language and paragons of decorum as Captain Rawling and Charles Sherring! It was with a great condescension that I read on... only to find, despite myself, that I was fascinated. Here, against all the auguries, was a real adventure story that achieved completely new and original things. A book of depth and sensitivity too, animated by the presence of a very engaging narrator. Indeed, something else altogether!

Sorrel is a middle-class girl from Sydney. After dropping out of art school, she drifted for a while before a disasterous relationship spurred her to carve out a new career as a photojournalist specializing in adventurous travels with a bicycle. Cycling epics on Mt. Fuji and along the Great Wall of China won her a reputation that had reached Tibet by the time she first got there in 1984 – and gained her both a warm welcome and tangible help from Jigme Surkhang of the Tibetan Sports Federation.

Jigme initially suggested a cycle ride to Shigatse.

Sorrel Wilby milking goats in a nomad encampment (1985)

'No, Jigme,' Sorrel replied. 'I want to walk across Tibet.'

Jigme eventually arranged for Sorrel to drive out to Purang, where she could begin her walk, with a convoy of Toyota Landcruisers bearing the first Indoculture tour party and a four-man film crew on assignment for a West German TV station. Sorrel promply fell in love with the crew's tall, blond leader, Hyo Bergman, and they held hands as they cruised westwards. By that time Sorrel was also beginning to have qualms about the daunting project to which she had committed herself: to walk back to Lhasa along the Southern Route and then proceed to Qamdo.

Unlike her male precursors, she is always perfectly honest about her feelings:

'Fear and doubt had suddenly spread throughout my mind, grabbed my stomach and knotted it into a hundred bow-lines and half-hitches. But it was too late now...'

At Purang, having purchased a donkey, which she now

christened Budget, Sorrel reluctantly said goodbye to Hyo and his friends, and set off alone for Kailas. Budget carried her baggage as far as the lakes, then bolted. With a little help from her friends, however, Sorrel forged on to the sacred mountain and performed the *parikrama*. Rain, hail and snow flailed down upon her as she went round, but she found warmth and companionship with some Tibetan pilgrims. Back at Darchen, she slept in late and then successfully treated thirteen cases of 'Kailas-knee' with tooth-paste, sunscreen and other unlikely remedies.

By now it was clear that Sorrel would have to modify her original plan. Flooding ruled out a pedestrian return to Lhasa by the Southern Route; she also gave up the notion of going to Quamdo. Instead, she decided to return to Shiquanhe, then to loop round through the Kailas (or Gangdisê) Range to intersect with the Southern Route lower down, at Parayang. This meant a detour of 1,500 km., making the total distance to be walked some 3,000 km.

In her engaging innocence, Sorrel had put herself in the way of the whole catalogue of ordeals and disasters. She lost her pack; had her money stolen; suffered from almost continual sickness, particularly bowel complaints (about which she is *never* reticent); broke her fingers; received advances from lecherous Chinese officials (which she successfully repulsed); was locked up; was violently attacked by a drunken Yarka horseman, etc., etc. But all this was tame stuff compared with the culmination of her Sven Hedinesque journey: an epic dash with a group of nomads across the trackless wastes of the Gangdisê Range in Arctic conditions, during which she and her companions got themselves well and truly lost. It was only with immense good fortune that she eventually reached Parayang; but even then her problems were not over. Before she was back in comparative civilization, she had undergone a strange Kafkaesque interlude during which she seemed to falter on the brink of insanity.

That Sorrel managed to survive at all was not only due to her own immense courage and resilience, but also to the fact that she went out of her way to learn the local dialects and so could communicate with the Tibetans, particularly the nomads, and recruit their help. Indeed, she is rare among Kailas travellers in that she did not look down upon the denizens of the black tents of Western Tibet as backward and insanitary primitives. On the contrary, she respected them and happily mucked in with them: eating their food, playing with their children, even trying her hand at milking their goats. In her book, *Tibet: A Woman's Lone Trek across a Mysterious Land*, individual nomads really come alive as people with loveable quirks and characteristics – and very great human qualities, particularly kindness and generosity. Deeply moved by these, Sorrel could see that they arose from their ancient Buddhist traditions, and, although spiritually undecided herself, *in extremis* she found herself invoking the aid of the Buddha as well as the Christian God of her own culture. The Tibetan nomads, for their part, clearly warmed to Sorrel too and respected her for the gruelling pilgrimage that she was making. Some of them assumed that she was some kind of nun! As for Sorrel herself, by the end of her journey she felt she qualified as a true-blooded Tibetan herself. . . .

Another independent journey in 1985 recaptured something of the flavour of the old Kailas journeys. This was made by a British watercolourist, Charlie Foster-Hall, and Chris Langridge, a photographer, who reached Kailas in late October/early September by the Soutern Route. The two hitched as far as Parayang and then, because a flooded branch of the Tsangpo a little further on prevented motor traffic going any further, they decided to buy a yak to carry their stores and baggage and to trek the rest of the way to Kailas on foot along unfrequented byways. The yak, like Sorrel Wilby's Budget, proved to be a cantankerous beast, with definite ideas of its own and a repetoire of contrary tricks to implement them. Eventually Charlie and Chris sold it to some willing nomads and went on under their own devices – with a definite sense of lightness. They then wandered across the vast, featureless tableland, staying with nomads, often at a loss to know precisely where they were:

> We had out doubts about Samsang, possibly, like Horbo, only the name of some pastures: a moveable place made of tents when it did exist . . . Our valley got larger and, subsequently emptier, the mountains on either side rising higher, the feeling of bleakness even greater. We scanned the horizon. Was that dark speck in the distance a tent – or just a stone a few hundred yards off? Did it move? Perhaps a herdsman – or just a bird . . . ?
>
> (Letter from C. Foster-Hall to the author, 14th July 1988)

Eventually, however, they met up with a jeep and back-up truck combination that drove them into the sacred region. Catching view at last of Kailas and its attendant panoramas, Charlie reflected:

> I felt privileged . . . but to whom I knew not. There were so many things that could have stopped us, so many adverse possibilities; so many valleys that we could have entered, lost our way and never been heard of again . . . I looked at Chris in the back of the jeep . . . and without saying

anything we both knew that the elation had arrived.

(Ibid.)

They rested for a few days at Barkha, where they were given hospitality by a 22-year-old teacher from Lhasa who was operating a small live-in school for the children of the local nomads: 'He was well-paid, got 6 months holidays every year and even in this extreme corner seemed content.' Then they went on separately to Kailas, where Charlie performed two *koras* and would have made a third had Chris and he not by now been deeply exhausted, as well as depleted of food supplies and unable to get more. Winter was advancing too. They therefore found a truck heading for Shiquanhe/Ali and bade farewell to the sacred region.

Of the other independent travellers who were at Kailas in 1985, probably the first and the immediate successor of Bradley, Victor and Minoru Kishipa, was Masao Endo, a Japanese photojournalist and war correspondent with experience in Lebanon, Central America, Vietnam (where he was slightly wounded), Afghanistan, etc., who made an epic winter trip to the sacred region. He is said to have bought a horse and walked most of the way, which must have been extremely gruelling.* Then Naomi Duguid tells of one Mel Goldstein and his son; and a German lady of 65 and her son. Charlie Foster-Hall met a Yugoslavian girl and a Frenchman called Stephan. But there are undoubtedly many, many more. In fact, probably more Westerners visited Kailas either independently or in tour groups in 1985 than had done so in all the years between 1812 and 1984 put together.

1986

One day in the spring of '86, Brian Beresford picked up the phone in his North London flat. The metallic voice at the other end belonged to Daniel Adams, a Los Angeles TV cameraman whom he had met in Ladakh ten years before.

'How would you like to go to Mt Kailas?' Daniel asked. 'Some people got through last year. I have enough money saved up. Let's go *via* the Silk Road.'

It was the kind of offer you can't refuse. Brian had been fascinated by Kailas ever since reading Govinda's *The Way of the White Clouds* many years before. He had just six weeks to get ready. He started at once.

---

*For more about Masao Endo, see pp. 425–6.

Brian Beresford, Sean Jones and Daniel Adams (1986)

Brian is New Zealander, with one of those open Antipodean faces and brown curly hair. He's amiable, creative – and notoriously vague. Born in Auckland in 1948, he dropped first out of university to train as a photographer and then out of photography to go travelling. He and his wife Marie eventually joined the crowd of Western expatriates who in the 1970s gravitated to Dharamsala, the north Indian hill station where the Dalai Lama lives in exile. Dharamsala is a kind of little Tibet set on the slopes of the scrubby Himalayan foothills, a poor substitute for the majestic Land of Snows itself, but to Brian and Marie arriving there felt like a spiritual homecoming. Not only did they instantly warm to the Tibetans themselves but they became quickly convinced that in the teachings of Tibetan Buddhism they had found a rare jewel. Brian therefore set himself to learn Tibetan at the newly-opened Library of Tibetan Works and Archives so as to have access to the vast treasury of Buddhist texts available in the language. He and Marie quickly developed a deep devotion for His Holiness and the other Tibetan masters that they met.

About a week before he left, Brian mentioned the Kailas trip to one of his friends, a London travel agent named Sean Jones. Sean,

A Lama of one of the Tantric Colleges in Lhasa chanting for the success of the Beresford-
Jones pilgrimage to Kailas (1986)

once voted himself onto the party. 'I'm coming with you whether you like it or not,' he told Brian with his native Lancashire bluntness – he was born in Preston in 1944.

Taller and more squarely built than Brian, Sean today looks every inch the successful businessman he has become; but back in 1967, he dropped out of his accountancy studies to take the Hippie Trail to India. He trekked and travelled widely, sometimes with horses, in remote parts of the Indian Himalaya as well as in the high regions of Pakistan and Afghanistan. He also worked on the Tarbela Dam project in Pakistan and built himself a house in the Swat Valley. Around 1973 he too gravitated to Dharamsala and developed a deep devotion for the Dalai Lama. There he met Brian Beresford, but it was not until they were both back in Britain – Brian and Marie returned in 1978, Sean the following year – that they became friends. What brought them together was a mutual friendship with Kevin Rigby, with whom Sean had made his first journey to India. Kevin had ordained as a Tibetan Buddhist monk in Dharamsala, where Brian had met him. He had been a talented artist in the Tibetan tradition of religious scroll painting (*thangka*), but later gave up the monk's robe and returned to lay life, only to die tragically in Pakistan in 1978.

The fourth member of the party was Richard Gayer, an English friend of Daniel Adams, who makes a hobby of adventurous travel. Brian and Sean, both dedicated and practising Buddhists, had strong spiritual reasons for wanting to go to Kailas; Daniel and Richard, though interested in the teachings, were more in it for the adventure.

Using the newly-opened Karakoram Highway that links Pakistan and China, the four travellers reached Kashgar in Sinkiang without hitch and on the very first day had the good fortune to run into Naomi Duguid and Jeffrey Alford, who were just about to set off to cross the Kunjerab on trail bikes and pedal on south down the Hunza Valley to Gilgit. They had recently been at Kailas and told the new arrivals all about their adventures

Jeffrey (b. 1954), a veteran Asian traveller from Wyoming, met Naomi, (b. 1950), a Toronto lawyer, in Lhasa in October 1985. Hiring a Toyota Landcruiser from the Tibetan Taxi Co. on Beijing Dong Lu in Lhasa, they left for Kailas in mid-April 1986. Reaching Shiquanhe/Ali 'after six extremely uncomfortable days driving' and fearing they might run into trouble with local officialdom, they tried to bypass the new city but were run to ground by the famous Mr. Li. He at first told them they would have to turn back and that there would be a fine to pay; later he revised his views and gave them a permit for Kailas, though he empounded Naomi's passport *pro tem.*

Purang/Taklakot they found 'distinctly uncolourful', for heavy snows blocking the high passes were preventing foreign traders and pilgrims from coming in and livening up the bazaar. Afterwards, though Rakshas Tal was frozen over, they were able to wade into Manasarovar for chilly ablutions. 'The landscape and light were magnificent,' Naomi later wrote. 'We saw a very unhurried fox by the lakes, a number of eagles, and a wolf . . . There were two monks at Chugu [Trügo] Gompa, as well as a woman and child and a very fierce mastiff . . . The *gompa* had been rebuilt and was very clean and new looking . . .'

Although Kailas would not officially 'open' until June, they found accommodation in a dirt-floored room of the new guest-house. For food, they had to make do with what they had brought, none being available locally. It was snowing heavily too, but they nevertheless climbed up behind Darchen and headed north along the ridge that runs between the valleys of the Lha Chu and the Serlung Chu. Gaining a height of about 17,500 feet, 'the clouds slowly lifted and we then had sparkling views of Kailas and neighbours, as well as of the whole wonderful landscape across to a snowy and ethereal Gurla Mandhata . . . And then we walked on back down at dusk and spent another cold night at Darchen before heading back.'

Returning to Lhasa, the proprietors of the Tibetan Taxi Co. were so appalled at the state of their Landcruiser that they vowed never to send a vehicle to Western Tibet again. Naomi and Jeff did not linger; they retrieved the trail bikes that they had left behind and travelled north by bus and train to Kashgar.

Despite this fortuitous meeting, Kashgar was not an auspicious city for Brian, Sean and their friends. The local authorities obdurately refused to sanction travel through to Western Tibet, so they were obliged to make a long and circuitous journey – almost a kind of extended semi-circumambulation of Tibet itself. They flew with their gear (which included a lot of film and video equipment) to Urumchi, then caught a train to Dunhuang, and from there bussed up onto the Tibetan plateau, an arduous haul from 1,500 to 14,000 feet. Then they traversed, firstly, the edge of the Tsaidam Basin, an enormous shallow saucer of land in the trough of which lie salt marshes, and later a vast, perfectly flat plain that apparently freezes in winter and then, by the action of the spring thaw, is churned up into ridges that make it look uncannily like a gigantic ploughed field stretching away to the blue horizon in an uninterrupted 360° sweep.

'These sights gave us a taste of the vastness of northern Tibet,' Sean remembers. 'Our Japanese bus was flying along a good metalled road at a steady 60 m.p.h. for hour after hour, and there was hardly a change of perspective. It was quite a strange experience.'

After spending a night at Golmud, they finally arrived at Lhasa, where they again encountered official obstacles in the way of their pilgrimage. They were eventually able, however, to talk a Tibetan truck-driver into carrying them along the Northern Route – for a price.

The journey was not without its tense moments. They had not been on the road long, when the police stopped the truck. They were, however, able to go on after the driver had paid a fine. Later, arriving in Shiquanhe and putting up in a third rate truck-stop after some eleven rough and dusty days on the road, they received an official visit from Mr. Li, accompanied by his translator, Mr. Shui, and a full supporting cast of uniformed policemen.

'It is illegal for foreigners to stay in this place,' Mr Shui translated.

Ominous words...But then Sean conceived a stroke of genius. He proclaimed himself a London travel agent intent on helping open Western Tibet up to tourism – and produced an official letter from CITS, written in best Mandarin, to prove his *bona fides*. Mr Li's attitude at once became immensely benign.

'Mr Li says this is very good,' Mr Shui said. 'You must come to Ali Hotel, the fine hotel in town. Mr Li will give you good rooms – *and make sure you get a special rate.*'

A business deal was eventually negotiated between Reho Travel (Sean's company) and the Government of Western Tibet. Mr Li would lend the travellers every assistance to see the sights of Western Tibet and in return they would give the GOWT a copy of the videos they shot for tourism promotion purposes. The happy arrangement was consummated at a series of splendid banquets, during which there were many fullsome speeches and toasts.

'Mr Li says, you know, now we are working in cooperation together, you do not worry, there is not any difficulty,' Mr Shui announced. 'And next year, next year we will do our best to improve the facilities.'

From then on the tour went very smoothly according to a detailed schedule that they worked out with Mr Li. A Toyota Landcruiser and a jeep took them to Menjir, then on to Purang and from there

*Sean Jones (CENTRE) and Brian Beresford (SECOND RIGHT) being toasted by Mr. Li
and associates in Shiquanhe/Ali (1986)*

directly up to Darchen, where they arrived on July 24th. Lodgings
were found at the Indian Pilgrims' Guesthouse and they met
Choying Dorje before setting off on a three-day *kora*. Their party
now included a young French woman named Rafaelle Demandres;
Joe, a *Nisei* or Japanese-American; Thapgye, a Tibetan boy pilgrim
from Kham, the son of a *ngakpa* [shamanistic priest]; and an Anglo-
Brazilian couple, Clare and Juan, who travelled along with them
now and again. Altogether, a good sense of comradeship prevailed.
The weather was highly turbulent, however: cloud obscured the
summit of the sacred mountain and, at the outset, they
encountered, by turns, rain, sleet and glorious sunshine. The
omens were that things might be worse further north – at least if
the reports of a rapidly retreating Indian pilgrim were to be
credited.

'*It has been terrible!*' he cried above the prevailing tumult, a bizarre
figure in a pink woollen balaclava under a plastic Trilby, puffy down
jacket and *dhoti*. 'Our tents were ripped to shreds, so we have been
all night standing up in a blizzard! Forty-five miles in such
conditions! I cannot go on. Today I have seen a helicopter over

there, so perhaps my companions will be saved. I am wishing you the good luck . . . ' And he stumbled off.

On the first evening, they erected their tents beside a row of ruined *chörtens* on a flat patch of tussocky grass near the ruins of Nyenri Gompa. Below the *gompa* lay the legendary Hidden Elephant's Cave, associated with Padmasambhava, and on the far side of the river, Pema Puk, a cave associated with the historical Buddha. Behind that rose a line of towering red rock buttresses said to symbolize the Sixteen Arhats of Buddhist hagiography.

It poured uninterruptedly all night, so when Sean awoke just before dawn next day, his ears were assaulted by a phantasmagoria of sound: the patter of rain on his tent, water cascading from the surrounding heights, the rushing of river and stream, steady *drip-drip-drips* and the occasional crash of avalanching rocks swept down the rock walls by the ubiquitous meltwater – all reverberating round the enclosed valley.

'I thought the whole mountain was falling down,' he recalls. 'It is an elemental place – I felt that very strongly.'

After dawn, however, an atmosphere of wonderful clarity prevailed: the sky became clear and blue, and the brilliant sunlight of the new day struck the South Face of Kailas obliquely. This was their first view and – a dramatic touch – a plume of high altitude vapour streamed from the summit.

At Kailas, Sean and Brian saw scores of pilgrims, mostly from the eastern Tibetan provinces of Amdo and Kham, who had come the equivalent of several thousand miles across the plateau on foot, sometimes bringing their families, livestock and even their pets – animals are blessed by a circuit of Kailas too. Modern Tibetan pilgrims often visit the Jokhang (or 'Central Cathedral') in Lhasa as well as Kailas-Manasarovar, and sometimes even slip illegally across the high passes into India to pay their respects to the Dalai Lama in Dharamsala before going on to the Buddhist holy places. They can be away for two or three years at a time.

Inspired by such devoted pilgrims, who were already cir-cumambulating, the travellers resumed their progress up the Western Valley. They were treated to spectacular but always changing views of the mountain as it appeared through gaps in its curtain wall of crags, now bathed in benign sunlight, now wreathed in lugubrious cloud, sometimes even lashed by lightning. The going was not easy. They had to jump across many pools and rivulets and clamber over tangles of boulders and tussocks. Though the wind remained steadily favourable, they were alternately soaked by rain and dried out by the sun, but it was 'all quite acceptable – inspiring even.'

Towards its extremity, the Western Valley begins to close in. The Western party passed the solitary pinnacle known as Guru Rinpoche's Torma – a *torma* is a cake used in Tibetan religious ceremonies – and there were other imposing rock formations on the opposite (western) side of the valley, notably the group symbolizing the Longevity Triad of Vijaya, Amitayus and Tara. Further up, near the confluence of the Lha Chu (lit. 'Water of the Gods') with the river that gushes down from the Drölma La, they veered off to join some nomads who were grazing their flocks on a patch of grass. There were also tents pitched throughout the season for the Indian pilgrims. The nomads welcomed the weary travellers to their fire, and, after eating, some of the party gratefully crashed out in their black tent.

The first thing that Brian did next morning was to perform a *puja* [religious ceremony] as a token of gratitude for having been allowed to safely reach this unique place. He and Daniel Adams then went off by themselves to explore the side-valley that leads to the foot of the North Face. They did not see the summit: the mountain dissolved away above them into swirling morning mists.

Now several hours behind schedule, they hurried up the steep ascent to the Drölma La in the footsteps of their companions, who had gone on ahead. Altitude and gradient now began to tell. For respite, they allowed themselves to stop for a few moments at the Mahasiddhas' Cemetery (sometimes also called the Vajrayoginī Cemetery), a desolate and eerie spot just below the pass, yet appropriate for spiritual reflection:

Tantrically, Mount Kailash can be considered a symbolic manifestation of the Mandala of Chakrasamvara (Tib. *'Khor.lo.bde.mchog* or *'Khor.lo.sdoms. pa*). The twelve arms of Chakrasamvara, the embodiment of compassion, represent the twelve links in the Chain of Dependent Origination (Skt. *Pratitya Samutpāda*: the Buddhist doctrine of endless cyclic causation, roughly cognate with the Wheel of Life). Here at the eleventh link, so to speak, at the northernmost point of the circuit, one was both symbolically and also in a very real physical sense encountering the experience of death. The force of this was driven home to me by the fact that the eviscerated torso of a young girl was lying amidst the debris of discarded items at the cemetary. It had been gnawed by dogs. We found out later that she had drowned in a swollen torrent – the rivers at Kailas are quite treacherous; you can easily be swept away by the current – while making

the circuit and her family had brought her body back here...
(Brian Beresford. 'Pilgrimage to Mount Kailash
The Middle Way, Vol. 62, No.2)

When Brian at last reached the head of the pass and Daniel asked
him how he felt, '*Dead!*' was his reply: dead from sheer physical
stress and exhaustion – and dead to his old self too. Yet,
paradoxically, he also felt more alive than ever: something had
opened up at depth. He offered up prayers of gatitude.

But after any experience of intense exaltation, there is always the
inexorable deflation. So it was, after passing the Gauri Kund lake
and tumbling down the cyclopean staircase of rocks and boulders
that leads to the verdant eastern valley, there was a downing sense
and, more ominously, of moving forward to the next link in the
Chain of Dependent Originaton: that of ignorance.

'Our egoism had lulled us into a false sense of security,' Brian
later wrote; 'that all would be well, no matter what. We had
seriously misjudged...'

Night was now closing in fast and Zutrul Puk, their destination,
was still far away; their companions were furthermore nowhere to
be seen. Fortunately, they found shelter for the night in a tent with
two Tibetans, but Sean and Rafaelle were less lucky. They
wandered off the main path onto the wrong side of the river that
cascades through the Eastern Valley and spent the whole night in
the open, on the move most of the time because, whenever they did
lie down to doze, the 'chill factor' would strike them to the bone.
Nevertheless, Sean recalls, 'all this time I didn't feel there was any
danger. I felt the mountain was friendly, was watching over me...'
It was altogether a night of strange and marvellous experiences. For
instance, towards dawn, crouching for shelter beneath a concave
slice of rock, Sean found himself serenaded by other-worldly
whistlings and what seemed like bird calls mixed with the sounds of
rocks and water falling.

'Am I really hearing all this?' he asked himself; then realized that
the rock was a kind of natural acoustic dish that gathered all the
sounds of mountain and river, then amplified and transformed
them into a kind of celestial music...

When the dispersed pilgrims finally straggled into Zutrul Puk
around noon next day and compared notes, they found out that
they had all in some way or other falled prey to the Link of
Ignorance. Fortunately, there were no casualties – but it was a
warning...

Zutrul Puk is of course inextricably associated with Milarepa and

Cairns on the way to Drölma La (1987)

Wintry conditions on a summer's dawn at Kailas (1986)

his contest of magic with Naro Bön-chung. The old *gompa* that used to enclose the famous miracle cave was destroyed during the Cultural Revolution, but it has since been replaced by a 'mud-walled shrine', now supervised by a dour old Tibetan couple, devotees of Milarepa's Karma Kagyu school. The slopes behind are screed with millions of carved *mani* stones, Buddhist and Bön-po, as well as the shards of blown-up *stūpas*. Higher up the mountainside, there are abandoned cells and caves, cleverly fashioned out of hollows in the rock, that were once obviously used for retreat purposes. Nettles grow around them in abundance, setting a seal on local associations with Milarepa and the legend of his subsistence on an austere diet of nettle stew.

'When Milarepa subjugated the Bönpo, he invoked the force of Chakrasamvara [Demchog], who was his personal *yidam* [Tantric deity], at Mount Kailash,' Brian later explained. 'It's hard to say whether he brought in this force or not, because of course the mountain had always been identified as the abode of a deity. Hindus had long regarded it as the Abode of Shiva – Chakrasamvara is the Buddhist transformation of Shiva – and in the preBuddhist Bön tradition, the founder, Thönpa Shenrab, is said to have come to earth there. But when Milarepa overcame Naro Bön-chung, the power of the mountain changed hands in a sense and the association with Chakrasamvara was forged. The presence of the deity still

Retreat cave with nettles above Zutrul Puk (1986)

pervades the mountain and its environs, giving pilgrims the opportunity of entering the *yidam's mandala* of sacred power and wisdom. In terms of the sheer power of the place, just being present there opens up the heart in a quite extraordinary manner.'

Next day, they were back at Darchen in a mere five hours – back to mundane consciousness and everyday activities; but changed immeasurably too. Following their prepared schedule, they then drove south to Kojarnath, the temple in the Karnali valley south east of Taklakot, where they met a 23-year-old lama from Amdo named Lobsang Samten Gystso, a graduate of Drepung monastic university near Lhasa. Though himself a member of the Gelugpa school, his purview presently includes all monasteries and sacred shrines in Western Tibet, even those of the Bönpo, for in these troubled times the Tibetans are more concerned to keep their religious traditions alive than with nurturing old sectarian differences.

Consignment of religious artefacts returned by the Chinese (1986)

Lobsang Lama reconsecrating returned images (1986)

Having witnessed the colourful spectacle of a ritual Lama Dance at Kojarnath, Brian and Sean returned to Purang, where on August 1st a festival was held to celebrate Peoples' Liberation Day. The following day they ascended the Lipu Lekh to video the arrival of a party of Indian pilgrims. Then on August 6th they began a three-day circuit of Manasarovar.

In terms of metaphysical sumbolism, Brian and Sean regard Lake Manasarovar as a perfect foil to Kailas. If the mountain stands for power and majesty, both physical and spiritual, the lake is contrastingly a place of beauty, tranquillity and spaceousness. Brian maintains:

> In a sense you could say that the quality of the lake is delight. It is tremendously sensual in that the senses are constantly filled with beauty: the flowers are wafting scents to the nose, you hear the beautiful sound of the birds and the geese as they fly across or float on the lake. It has that quite overpoweringly.
>
> (Recorded interview with the author, June 5th 1988)

Their starting point was at Huoré on the north east corner, where they were lodged in a gloomy mud-walled room that contained just three beds and a poster of Chairman Mao greeting Deng Xiao Ping. At the lakeside the following day they met up with a party of pilgrims from Amdo who were scouring the pebbly shore for the pellets of polished jet that are associated with the Karmapas, the patriarchs of the Karma Kagyu school. For the pilgrim, everything strange found in these auspicious settings takes on an awesome religious significance, including the egg-shaped balls of grass created by the natural action of wind and water at the lake.

Trekking southwards, the crystal shimmering waters of the 'Invincible Jewel Turquoise Lake' gently lapping the multi-coloured pebbles of the shore, they came at last to Seralung (lit. 'Hailstone Valley'), the eastern gateway of the Manasarovar Mandala. Prior to 1950, around a hundred monks had lived here; all that remained were a few ruined walls that served as sheep and goat pens, though a small new *gompa* had been built a short distance away. Ensconced in a bright yellow and blue American tent nearby was their friend Lobsang Lama. He was repairing and reconsecrating a consignment of Buddhist statues that the Chinese had previously looted but were now returning. Few of these ancient and venerable relics had been spared the destructive attentions of the Red Guards.

A delightful day's trek on horseback with Lobsang Lama and his acolytes across lush grasslands studded with tiny flowers brought

Sean and Brian to the rebuilt Trügo Gompa, the southern gateway lying at the foot of Gurla Mandata. They found six monks in residence there. Then they pushed round to Tseti in the west, the place where a portion of Mahātma Gandhi's ashes are said to have been consigned to the sacred waters and where, appropriately, Hindu pilgrims make their ritual ablutions.

A little to the north lay Chiu Gompa, a place of powerful association for Sean and Brian, for Tibetan Buddhists claim that here Guru Rinpoche (Padmasambhava), the founder of the

Gateway to Kailas: the new Chörten Gang-ni financed by Sean Jones (LEFT) and its predecessor destroyed in the Cultural Revolution (ABOVE) (1987 and 1926)

Nyingma or Old School, 'took Rainbow Body' (alt. Body of Light); that is, departed this world leaving only his clothes, nails and hair behind. Auspiciously, Sean and Brian found a 'broad torrent' of water freely flowing in the nearby Ganga Chu, though it had previously been dry for many years. For the Tibetans, this was a splendid omen, portending a change of fortune for both their country and its religious traditions – possibly even that their subjugation beneath the Chinese yoke might be coming to an end.

An opportunity for expressing their gratitude for this supreme pilgrimage presented itself just before they left. Choying Dorje asked Sean if he would contribute towards the rebuilding of the Chörten Gang-ni, the Gateway to Kailas. Returning later from other sites, including the ruined splendours of Tsaparang and Thöling, Sean made a generous offering and Brian sketched out a new design in which the old square top was replaced by a *stūpa*-like structure. The Gang-ni is now rebuilt to this design.

As a grand finale of their trip, Mr Li had promised to lay on a cruise on Lake Pangong in a Chinese naval gun-boat, but this had to be cancelled.

In case their many videos and films should arouse suspicion at an official exit point, Brian and Sean – Daniel and Richard had left earlier – decided to leave on foot by the ancient trading route linking Western Tibet with Nepal. They soon ran into difficulties. At the insignificant police-post of Munchu, they were detained by hostile police, who tried to send them back. They appealed to Simikot and Kathmandu for permission to proceed, but nothing came.

Growing desperate as the days passed without any outcome, they wired a final plea to Kathmandu. At the same time, they organized a grand day-long *puja* on Guru Rinpoche Day, in which the power of Buddhist 'protectors' (benign spirits) was invoked. The local Tibetans turned up in force, and some lamas. A two-foot high *torma* was made; and there was a riot of noise from drums, cymbals, bells and thigh-bone trumpets, plus chanting.

Uncannily, permission came through almost at once. Free at last, they trekked on to Simikot and caught a light 'plane at the local airstrip, which lifted them to Kathmandu and the comforts of (comparative) civilization in less than a day after $4^{1}/_{2}$ months of hard travelling.

1987

In the summer of 1987, Naomi Duguid and Jeffrey Alford were back in Lhasa, intending to ride their trail bikes eastwards into Sichuan. However, serious fighting on the Indian border south-east of Lhasa caused them to decide instead to take their bikes out to Western Tibet. They now had a Canadian friend with them, Anthony Southam, and in Lhasa ran into other fellow cyclists whom they had met on earlier trips. These included Lee Day, a freelance photographer from New York who had tried to ride to Kailas in 1986 with two friends but had been turned back by bad weather and awful road conditions; Wendy Baylor and Jeremy Schmidt, an American couple from Wyoming; also Pat and Baiba Morrow from Alberta. Jeremy is a travel writer and Pat a photographer; together they had already landed a contract for a book.

These eight decided to join forces to get to Kailas. However, it initially proved difficult to find transport. The authorities had clamped down on foreigners travelling by truck – drivers taking them were fined heavily – in an effort to force them to use the 'expensive and ill-informed services of the China Travel Service.' However, a driver was eventually located who was able, through a brother with clout in the Public Security Bureau, to obtain a permit to transport them; there was no problem getting individual travel permits for Shiquanhe and Kailas.

Supplied with enough food to last six weeks, they set off for Kailas along the Northern Route in early July. Their bicycles were lashed to the sides of the truck and heavily padded to protect them from the unmerciful jostling that they would inevitably undergo. Their driver, Gyaltso, knew the road well, and brought them to Shiquanhe without hitch. They found the new town 'full of traders from Sinkiang and of the wilted but somewhat fresh produce they had brought to sell. The market was more lively than it had been 14 months before . . . There were [also]— four or five little restaurants in the market area, two run by Uighurs from Sinkiang, the rest by Chinese . . .'

Turning south, they were dropped about ten kilometres west of Darchen, and the next day four of the party began walking around Kailas. That night they camped just south of the confluence of the Belung Chu with the Lha Chu. A monk was camped nearby; he was on his ninth *kora*. The following morning, as the weather had begun to close in, they paused at a small tent just across the river from Drira Puk Gompa that was doing business as a *chai* (tea) stall. Few pilgrims seemed to be around: 'we concluded that they were probably sensibly waiting for better weather.' The mist now turned to 'wet, clinging snow' that was pasted onto their bodies by a strong wind as they struggled up towards the Drölma La. At times visibility was virtually down to nil. Reaching the pass at last, they gave thanks and then, forging on, pitched camp on the first piece of level ground they could find. Their third and last day was 'clear and brilliant'. As they finished off the circuit, they were pleased to see more pilgrims hurrying around – and noted that the clockwise Buddhists seemed to be matched by 'an almost equal number of Bön pilgrims heading around counter-clockwise . . .'

Returning to their campsite, they waited while the rest of their party went off to do their circuit. Only then did they begin riding their trail bikes east and then south past the lakes towards Taklakot/Purang:

We had no problems with the authorities; instead the headache was the riding conditions. Grim hills of soft sand and the heavy glacial rubble around Gurla Mandhata and near Rakshas Tal made riding a real struggle. Each bicycle was loaded with 50 to 75 lbs of 'stuff': tent,

sleeping-bag, food, stove, spare parts, clothes for every temperature and
weather (we used them all!!). We spent two nights by Manasarovar and
another by Rakshas Tal, where we were joined by a group of nomads and
their herd of yak and horses. They were travelling back north from
Purang after doing business, although what business we never
discovered. We thought we'd make it to Purang in a day from Rakshas
Tal, but the riding was painstakingly slow, inching over and around
double-fist-sized rocks – *bump-bump-bump* – and occasionally getting a
tyre caught between two rocks – *crash!* – pick up the bike (slowly, it's not
light!) and wobble up/down the road.

(Naomi Duguid. Letter to the author, July 19th 1988)

They spent eight days exploring the Purang area on their bikes – 'all
was green with ripening barley and a few vegetables.' There was
the rare novelty of yak yoghourt to savour too. Many Nepalese
traders were this time in evidence, 'selling everything from fabric to
Nescafé to trinkets,' and themselves buying wool. Daily, huge
flocks of sheep were driven into enclosures and sheared, their wool
being then roughly carded and twisted into chunky yarn which was
wound into large balls for transportation over the mountains.
There was also some Transhimalayan traffic in salt, brought from a
mine east of Shiquanhe, though as the Chinese had tried to restrict
this, the traders had to find skilful ways of circumventing the
regulations.

In Purang, the bikers met two other Westerners but, after
making inquiries, they concluded they were the first to bring bikes
to the region, though they did meet a young Japanese who had
pedalled up the Tsangpo valley and was making for Sinkiang but
who did not visit either Purang or Kailas.

Deciding not to cycle back to Shiquanhe, Naomi and her friends
got a lift on a truck. Passing through Darchen, they met a German
group travelling under the auspices of China Travel Services. They
also heard the details of a tragedy of which they had already picked
up fragments:

An Englishman had travelled up from Nepal in May or June 1987 and,
because he had good rides, had reached Kailas in a week or so. He set out
to walk around the mountain and became ill somewhere near Drira Puk
Gompa. Some foreigners came upon him the following day and helped
him down to the river, and then rushed off to get help. He apparently
died the following day. Then the locals at Darchen had the problem of
deciding what to do with his body. The foreigners who had brought him
down said that because he was a practising and believing Buddhist he
should be disposed of as the local Buddhists would do. He was therefore

Naomi Duguid on trail bike at Kailas (1987)

given a 'sky burial' near the bridge across the Drölma La Chu, just across and up a bit from Drira Puk. There was apparently a huge fuss when the Chinese authorities in Ali found out what had happened. But the consensus among those involved in Darchen was that they had handled the situation correctly and as the Englishman would have wished. I'm sorry I'm not able to tell you his name.

(*Ibid.*)

The Big Bus to Kailas (1987)

Boiling a kettle, Western Tibetan style (1987)

This is the first record that we have of a Westerner dying while on the Kailas Parikrama. The actual cause of death is unclear, but it may have been pneumonia, or pulmonary oemeda – a dire condition brought on by altitude.

After Darchen, the truck took Naomi and her friends to Shiquanhe in some fourteen hours of hard, cold, dusty travelling disagreeably enlivened by the fact that some of their Khampa pilgrim fellow travellers, in a mood of post-*parikrama* celebration, were hitting the bottle. They then caught another truck north, which finally dropped them off in the Kun Lun Mounains, where they spent a number of days cycling over the last passes and down into the desert. Naomi recalls: 'The heat was a shock after the cold nights at high altitude. But we luxuriated in fresh tomatoes and green peppers...'

Another veteran Kailas traveller was back in 1987: Bradley Rowe. This time he was determined to get there by the Southern Route up the Yarlung Tsangpo valley: broadly the route used by Ryder and Rawling's Gartok Expedition of 1905. Things were easier this time. Bradley was armed with an official permit and, learning from his former experiences, had a good down sleeping bag with him, warm clothing and a Gor-tex tent. As it was also possible by now to hire vehicles, he got involved in the organization of what became known in Lhasa as the 'Big Bus to Kailas.' A Japanese Isuzu bus was hired from the Lhasa Bus Company – 'an excellent machine that required no servicing on the way', according to Richard Lanchester, another of the passengers. There was a back-up truck as well, to carry all the fuel needed for the round trip, plus the baggage of 33 people. The contract specified a trip lasting 26 days, covering some 3,100 km., including sidetrips to Purang and, if possible, Tsaparang and Thöling, with a longer diversion to Shiquanhe if necessary. The cost worked out at around a very reasonable £120 per head.

It was exceedingly tough going along that waterlogged route, but there were compensations, notably glimpses of the great herds of *kyang* (wild asses), twenty to thirty strong. At times they tried to outrun the Big Bus to Kailas, which lent the flavour of a wildlife safari to proceedings. There were also marvellous views of the Himalayan giants on the southern skyline: Annapurna, the Dhaulagiris, and the mountains of Mustang and Dolpo.

Bradley's travelling companion this time was a slender, energetic and highly independent young Swiss woman of 26 named Lisi Kaiser, with whom he had already trudged hundreds of miles of stone routes. Able to function well at high altitude even when

Lisi Kaiser on trek in Central Tibet (1987)

burdened with a heavy backpack, Bradley believes that Lisi's 'tireless, uncomplaining attitude and her ability to quickly establish rapport with even the most reticent Tibetan' contributed significantly to the success of his expeditions to central and eastern Tibet.

The Big Bus to Kailas dropped Bradley and Lisi at Chiu Gompa, from where they trekked to Huoré on the north-east corner of the lake, not far from the Bön-po sacred mountain of Bönri. Then, after a brief bathe for the good of their souls, they proceeded to Kailas. There had been significant changes at the sacred mountain since Bradley's previous visit – and not all of them were for the good.

Certainly, the *gompa* had been rebuilt – and incredibly, due to strange properties of the local materials or climate, or both, they overnight took on the appearance of great antiquity. They were also catering energetically to the needs of the Indian pilgrims, who pay a substantial amount for a 'package pilgrimage'. Rudimentary guest-houses had appeared at Drira Puk and Zutrul Puk, while the IP (Indian Pilgrims') Guest-house at Darchen had been substantially upgraded and now possessed a new wing containing four-bed dormitories. Priority to stay there was being given to Indian pilgrims. The Gateway to Kailas (Gang-ni) was back too, thanks to Sean Jones' generosity; and a road had been built right up to the flag-pole, Tarpoche – also restored – on the south-western corner of the circuit, so pilgrims could drive up in style to start their circumambulation.

Furthermore, although by the time Bradley arrived they had departed, Kailas had been visited that year – and indeed in 1986 and 1985 as well – by comparatively large numbers of Westerners, both organized groups and independent travellers. The result was that Kailas was being afflicted by that most insidious of modern evils: pollution. The areas around the *gompa* were more or less open air latrines with scraps of toilet paper much in evidence. Naomi Duguid had also noted as much at Darchen: that it was difficult for she and her friends to find a patch of ground to camp on that was not covered with filth, and the stream was a running sewer. 'If the weather had been warmer,' she writes, 'the whole area would have stunk!'

This was not all, however. Though the groups tended to be self-sufficient, bringing their own tents and supplies, the independents were affecting the local environment in other adverse ways:

> They force themselves on the Tibetans, which will either make the
> Tibetans resentful or commercial. For instance, there were a few people

who spent a couple of months in the area, hanging out mostly in caves.
They were members of the *ganja*-smoking [i.e. hashish or marijuana
using] community – peace, love and Hare Krishna, almost. This has put a
strain on the economy. It's driven up the price of *tsampa* and butter...
(Bradley Rowe. Recorded interview with the author, June 4th 1988)

In short, an insidious commercialism was infiltrating the sacred
region. All kinds of supplies and services were on offer – at a price,
and usually an inflated one. Some travellers – though admittedly not
those in 1987 – even reported that they had been required to pay a
fee to make the holy *parikrama* itself. These developments had
altered the *tone* and atmosphere of the place. That freedom from the
values of the marketplace that Bradley had so prized in 1984 was
definitely being eroded. Even the monks in the monasteries no
longer greeted Western travellers with the warmth and friendliness
they had displayed three years before. They were becoming
decidedly blasé.

Gil Levey (Mangalānand)

Bradley and Lisi had five days at Kailas this time, which meant that they could go round reasonably slowly, climbing lesser hills and exploring other interesting side aspects. On the *kora*, they met several athletic circumambulators intent on completing the circuit in a single day, and one kindly monk from Kham who insisted on carrying Bradley's rucksack up the final ascent to the Drölma La, pointing out special sites on the way. Just before the pass, he paused to grind a stone in the hollow of Milarepa's Medicine Rock, producing a little stony powder in the process. This he promptly ate for its legendary health-giving properties, and then invited Bradley to do the same, a courtesy that was graciously accepted. The Drölma La itself had a new presiding spirit: 'an amazing dreadlock-covered dog that lives at 18,600 ft. at the pass off donations of food from pilgrims, who realise that they have met an unusual beast of great character and show it due respect!' (Richard Lanchester).

A couple of days were also spent investigating the interior, including the Inner Kora, the special circumambulation route immediately below the Southern Face strictly reserved for those who have performed a statutory thirteen rounds by the usual route. The Tibetans maintain that certain spiritual masters are actually hurt in some way if this rule is broken. In deference to this tradition, Bradley did not perform the Inner Kora but he did go up to where it begins and scrutinized it through binoculars.

'There's a grey-brown rock, which looks exactly like a cathedral, placed directly below the southern face and you have to go round this *via* a pass,' he told me. 'The last bit looked a dangerous scramble. You go past two minor lakes. There are some shrines but no ancient *chörtens*. [These had of course been destroyed during the Cultural Revolution.] There are also a few long-term retreat caves up there with people in them.'

He and Lisi also visited the two *gompa* on the southern side. Gyangtra had been reconstructed, Serlung only partially so. These can be easily taken in on a day trip from Darchen. The *gompa* at Darchen remained closed, however, but rumour had it that negotiations were in progress between the Chinese and the Bhutanese to reopen it.

The Big Bus to Kailas, with its tighter schedule, had long since gone on its way by this time. Several of the passengers did not return to Lhasa but walked out of Tibet to Simikot in Nepal. As for Bradley and Lisi, after Kailas they travelled through difficult by-ways to the long-abandoned cave city of Khyunglung, the capital of the ancient kingdom of Zhang Zhung. The desiccated mountainside

Nomads (1985)

there is honeycombed with literally thousands of dug-out caves deserted long before Buddhism took hold in the region – perhaps even, Bradley hypothesises, before the Bön religion. A fascinating place, begging for proper archaeological investigation. There were also meetings with the *dogpas*: the nomads. Of course, they could not be approached directly. They still have fierce mastiff guard-dogs, for one thing, though in fact these can usually be discouraged merely by stooping and pretending to be pick up a stone. Bradley evolved a very effective strategy for establishing contact and getting himself invited to stay in their tents:

The camps were always off the main trail. About an hour after sunset, they'd be bringing in the yaks. I'd aim to hit them about then. I'd walk 5 or 10 yards. towards the tents, then stop and wait until someone noticed me. I might have to wait half an hour or an hour, but finally someone would arrive who considered himself in charge or of a high enough position. He'd get some of the kids to look after the dogs and he'd walk towards me, at which stage I'd begin walking towards him. We'd meet and he'd ask me what I was doing. We spoke in mime with a few local dialect words thrown in – they're very receptive to that. I'd normally say, 'I'm going on pilgrimage', and tell him where I'm headed. He'd say, 'Oh, that's a long way away. You can't get there tonight.' With a bit of luck, after a few minutes I'd get invited into a tent for a cup of tea, and then I'd have a place for the night. If I wasn't offered a cup of tea, I'd have to look for alternative accomodation. I have slept in caves . . .

(Ibid.)

The nomads, Bradley guessed, had benefitted greatly from modern political changes in Western Tibet. There was no question of their devotion to Tibetan Buddhism or their love of the Dalai Lama, but new economic developments implemented by the Chinese had made many of them – and many village Tibetans too – positively wealthy by Tibetan standards. The real victims of the new system are the people in compound settlements along the roads, in the new towns and working in what few industrial developments have been set up.

The winter was by this time closing in fast and night temperatures had plummetted far below zero. Bradley and Lisi therefore made their exit from Western Tibet by the Kashgar Road and spent the ensuing winter following stone routes in northern Pakistan.

In 1988, I met Bradley in north London. His room was as austere as a monk's cell. Apart from piles of maps (many of them hand-drawn by himself), a few books and the folders containing the material gleaned for his Stone Routes project, it was almost bare: the room of a man who does not put down roots or develop attachments. He was already planning ambitious new journeys along ancient pilgrim routes in remote parts of the world.

'I believe that there is a kind of geomantic or *feng-shui** type of relationship between man and the earth, which has not been adequately explained,' he said, staring intently from behind thick lenses. 'I don't know whether I can do it, but I'll give it a good few years trying to find out.'

1988

The opening of Tibet, which facilitated the fascinating new forays into the Kailas region recounted here, received a savage setback in 1987 and 1988 when the frustration of the Tibetans finally erupted and there was open rioting in Lhasa. The police station was set on fire, as were cars and busses, and sadly many people were killed, mostly on the Tibetan side, for the Chinese authorities retaliated with draconian ferocity. Since then, there has been a clampdown on tourism. Some organized parties are allowed, but the freedom of independents – 'disorganized travellers' as an official sign in Lhasa quaintly calls them – has been curtailed.

However, the total embargo of the pre-1980 era is unlikely to be reinstated. China, moving away from her old hardline Marxist ideology, is now well on her way towards developing a consumer society and needs her contacts with the West. Also the 'porous' nature of present-day China is too well-known and understood for the ingenious traveller to be entirely thwarted. Right now, though, the situation is far more difficult than three or four years ago, but there are signs for optimism.

For instance, as we go to press we hear that Brian Beresford has left for the Kailas region with an organized party of 73 Western pilgrims. They enjoy the complete blessing and cooperation of the Chinese authorities. The culmination of the journey will be a spiritual retreat at Kailas lasting from 10th to 22nd August 1988, led by Namkhai Norbu Rinpoche, the well-known married Dzogchen master from the Dergé district of east Tibet who currently teaches in the Instituto Orientale of Naples University.

'We'll set up camp at different locations and people will live in

---

*Geomancy is the mystical science of the energy currents and power-points in the earth itself. *Feng shui* (lit. 'wind and water') is the Chinese equivalent. It amounts to a kind of geophysical acupuncture system.

Namkhai Norbu and his Dzogchen group (1988)

their tents doing different practises and perhaps exploring particular areas before moving on to the next camp,' Brian told me before he left. 'It's also quite likely that Namkhai Norbu may take this opportunity to transmit to us teachings that he's never transmitted to his disciples before.'

Three days will also be spent at Lake Manasarovar and then, after returning to Purang to rest, the party will go on to Tirthapuri in the Sutlej Valley to the north-east of Kailas. This site is associated with Guru Rinpoche and his consort, Yeshe Tsogyel. There are hot springs there, a cave where Guru Rinpoche meditated and strange rock formations that look like natural *stūpas*.

Namkhai Norbu (b. 1938) is a large, aristocratic man, unusual in that he is about the closest one is likely to come to a free thinker among Tibetan lamas, who are mostly very bound by tradition. Generally highly regarded, he has nevertheless rather unconventional views on many issues. For instance, though agreeing that

Dzogchen (lit. 'Great Perfection') is a teaching within the repetoire of Nyingma school of Tibetan Buddhism, where indeed it is regarded as the highest teaching, Norbu propagates it as 'a wholly self-sufficient path in its own right': the pure essence that underlies all authentic religious teachings. There are even non-Buddhist Dzogchen traditions, he maintains, notably in the Bön religion This links up directly with his critique of those historiographers who assert that Tibet derived its culture and spirituality entirely from India. By contrast, Norbu stresses the importance of strong indigenous and non-Indian cultural and spiritual traditions that flourished notably in the ancient preBuddhist kingdom of Zhang Zhung before it was incorporated into the centralized Tibetan state in the 7th century.

Norbu's interest in Kailas, then, and the reason that he will be leading a retreat there, stem from the deep importance of the mountain and its attendant lake within both the preBuddhist Bönpo Dzogchen traditions of ancient Zhang Zhung and also the Buddhist Dzogchen traditions of the Nyingma school. As we have already seen, numerous sites in the Kailas-Manasarovar area are spiritually associated with the seminal Nyingma master, Guru Rinpoche (Padmasambhava), and he finally departed this life, or in Dzogchen terms, took Rainbow Body, near Chiu Gompa.

Norbu's Dzogchen 'is a teaching concerning the primordial state of being that is the individual's own intrinsic nature from the very beginning'. Once perceived, the aim of practice is to remain steadfastly in this state amidst all the vicissitudes of life. This is *Presence*: the fact of being unfalteringly awake in the *here/now*: so simple to talk about, so difficult to achieve.

> There was once a great master of Dzogchen living in Tibet and at one point a very learned scholar visited him, saying, 'You practitioners of Dzogchen are always meditating – that's it, isn't it?'
>
> 'What is it that I'm meditating on?' asked the master.
>
> The scholar replied, 'Ah – so you aren't meditating, then?'
>
> The master replied: 'When am I ever distracted?'
>
> (Namkhai Norbu, *The Crystal & the Way of Light*)

NOTE: *For more information on this new wave of Kailas pilgrims and travellers, see Appendix 5.*

Shenrab Miwo, the systematizer of Bön

The Pilgrim trail along the Lha Chu valley (1985)

CHAPTER ELEVEN

The Heart of the Matter

Of course, the world knows many other sacred mountains besides Kailas, and indeed there is a whole panorama of religious and semi-religious associations that may become attached to mountains. As J.A. MacCulloch writes: 'There are few peoples who have not looked upon mountains with awe and reverence, or have not paid worship to them or to gods or spirits associated with them in various ways.' And he concludes: 'Sporadically we find no cult of mountains or mountain-spirits, but that is generally where no cult of nature exists, or, of course, where no mountains exist.'

This powerful capacity to sound the deepest resonances in the heart of man must in part at least stem from the large and imposing qualities that mountains possess. 'Their height, their vastness, the mystery of their recesses, the veil of mist or cloud now shrouding them, now dispersed from them, the strange noises which the wind makes in their gorges, the crash of a fall of rock, or the effect of the echo, their suggestion of power, their appearance of watching the intruder upon their solitude – all give them an air of personality, and easily inspire an attitude of reverence and eventually of worship....' – MacCulloch again. In short, mountains may impress themselves upon the human imagination as *beings*, necessarily great beings at that, with spiritual properties akin to or even greater than those of man. They may come to be regarded, in fact, as *gods*.

An outstanding example of such a mountain is *Fuji*, that beautifully balanced volcanic cone rising from sea level to rather over 12,000 feet which has become the symbol of Japan. The subtle and various moods of Fuji have inspired many Japanese artists. The *haiku* poet, Bashō*, for instance:

---

*Matsuo Bāsho (1644–94), a Zen layman who lived an ascetic life and was prone to wandering off to remote parts of Japan where he could commune with unspoiled nature: He pefected the 17-syllable *haiku* form of poetry.

A day when Fuji is unseen
Veiled in misty winter showers –
That day, too, is a joy.

And Mushinarō:

Lo! There towers the lofty peak of Fuji
From between Kai and wave-washed Saruga
The clouds of heaven dare not cross it,
Nor the birds of the air soar above it.
The snows quench the burning fires,
The fires consume the falling snow.
It baffles the tongue; it cannot be named.
It is a mysterious god.

Arguably most evocative of Fuji's visual moods in the way it sometimes appears to hover suspended in the middle air, severed from the earth by engirdling mists.

Although declared as a god by Mushinarō, Fuji is also looked upon as the abode of a god (*kami*), to whom there is a shrine on the summit where Shinto priests annually hold religious rites connected with the opening and closing of the mountain. This may exemplify a shift or development that may take place in the religious connotations of mountains, whereby the divinity of the mountain somehow becomes detached from the mountain proper and takes on a connected, but partially autonomous, life of its own. Thus a mountain may cease to be regarded as a god and come to be seen as the abode of a mountain god.

Mountains may also be seen as the dwelling places of sky or rain gods, or of the great gods in general. Their height and consequent proximity to the skies or heavens, traditionally the dwelling places of 'higher' spiritual beings, naturally invites this kind of role. The most famous example of this to be found within our European heritage is *Mount Olympus*, a 9,551 foot peak spanning the borders of Thessaly and Macedonia which, so classical Greek mythology informs us, was set aside to be held in common by the gods when the sons of Cronos drew lots for the partition of the empire of the world. And on Olympus the immortals passed their days in merrymaking and laughter, feasting, supping ambrosia, serenaded by Apollo and the Muses, savouring the aromas wafted upwards from the altars of the world below . . .and eventually, at the end of each day when the torch of sun was doused, retiring for repose in houses built for them with woundrous craft by Hephaestus.

Olympus soars in a single sweep above a deeply-flanked plateau. Below, fall wooded slopes furrowed by many torrents – hence 'Olympus of the thousands folds'; above, meanwhile, the main line of the peak is curved in the form of a kind of amphitheatre, the upper tiers of which, often hung with shreds of cloud, have the appearance of gigantic seats out to accommodate the gods in council under the presidency of geat Zeus. When thunder and lightning were loosed about the summit, mortals in the world below knew that the gods were wrathful.

Marco Pallis, however, argues that such classical Greek fancies were strictly for exoteric consumption only. The relationship between the gods and Olympus, he maintains, was essentially symbolic: 'The true Olympus is only discernible by those "who have eyes to see".'

Their capacity to bridge the gulf between the twin spheres of earth and heaven also makes mountains convenient halfway stations where men and gods may meet. Numerous such vital encounters are reputed to have taken place and been duly recorded in the annals of the world's great religions:

> And the Lord said unto Moses, Come up to me into the Mount and be there and I will give thee tablets of stone, and a law and commandments which I have written, that thou mayst teach them.... And Moses went up into the Mount and a cloud covered the Mount. And the glory of the Lord was upon *Mount Sinai* and cloud covered it six days; and the seventh day the Lord called Moses out of the midst of the cloud. And the glory of the Lord was alike a devouring fire on the top of the Mount in the eyes of the Children of Israel. And Moses went into the midst of the cloud and gat him into the Mount; and Moses was in the mountain forty days and forty nights....
>
> (Exodus, 24)

Indeed, the Jews of old seem to have been highly impressed with the spiritual power of mountains. 'I will lift up my eyes to the hills, from whence cometh my help,' sang the Psalmist, David, who himself spent a lot of time at the heights, at first as a shepherd boy and later when he was on the run from King Saul. *Horeb, Nebo, Zion, Carmel* and *Moriah* are other mountains accorded religious veneration in the Bible; *Jerusalem*, meanwhile, is *'God's Hill*, and the *Dome of the Rock* is venerated by Jews and Muslims alike.

Christians, on the other hand, venerate their 'Skull Hill', *Golgotha*, where Christ was crucified; esoterically it is to them the spiritually 'highest' place on earth and hence, by virtue of the homology of the material and the spiritual, must logically also be the physically highest one too. A similar status, backed up by similar thinking, is accorded by the followers of Islam to the black rock known as the *Ka'ba* in the city of Mecca, which is kissed as part of the orthodox *Hajj*, the great pilgrimage that every true Muslim is required to make to the holy city. Another Hajj rite involves circling two small mountains or beacons of God called *Safa* and *Marwah*, upon which heathen idols were situated until dethroned by the prophet Muhammad. It was to the mountains adjacent to Mecca that Muhammad began to withdraw for meditation and prayer around the year 610A.D., the direct result of which was his fateful encounter with the Angel Gabriel in a cave upon *Mount Hira*, when he felt himself seized by the neck by an overpowering force and given dictation of the *suras* of the Holy *Koran*. Finally, mention should be made of a popular Muslim belief that the world is bounded by an outer range of curtain mountains: the *Qāf*.

Somewhat further east, the *Elburz Mountains*, which rise in Iran just north of the capital, Teheran, and run for some 600 miles in extent, have long been spiritually significant for local peoples. They were identified with *Haraberezaiti*, an axial mountain lying at the centre of the world and linking earth and sky. 'The sun and stars revolved around it; light came from it and returned there; on it, was no light or darkness, no cold, no wind, no sickness; on it, Amesha Spentas built a dwelling for Mithra, and he looks upon all the material world from it; below it was the Chinvat bridge. . . . 'According to Zoroastrian belief, on the other hand, all the mountains of the world sprouted from the Elburz – rather like runners, one presumes. It was on one of their peaks that the avatar Ahura Mazda revealed the law; indeed, Ahura is 'him who goes to the lofty mountains', and the mountains vivify his creation and oppose the antithetical forces of Ahriman ranged against him. The highest peak of the Elburz is the 18,600 foot *Demavend*, itself liberally endowed with all manner of religious and mythological associations. The epic writer of the *Shahnama* records how the tyrant Zohak was overthrown by Feridun and allowed to die in chains in a cavern on the slopes of the mountain. The heroes Jemshid and Rustem are also reputed to have been habitués of Demavend, and legend even associates the mountain with the final settling of Noah's Ark after the subsidence of the waters of the Great Flood – though this claim would be challenged by the partisans of the none-too-distant *Mount Ararat*, a fine, symmetrical peak rising gracefully from the arid floor of the earth in the north-east corner of Turkey, not far from where the frontier converges with those of Iran and the USSR.

The capacity of mountains to link earth and heavens, the twin spheres of men and gods, also serves to make their summits ideal situations for altars, shrines and temples. Many a mountain-top monastery in modern Greece, for example, stands where once an old mountain-shrine was located. Indeed, in places where suitable eminences do not naturally occur, man has repaired the deficiency himself – with his own hands. The *ziggurats* of ancient Babylon were nothing less than man-made mountains seven storeys high, with an apartment on the summit reserved for the local deity. On festive occasions the god might descend from here to his city to receive worship and petitions and to dispense benefits. The *teocalli* of ancient Central America are another example of the same sort of phenomenon, and we have already elsewhere mentioned the great *stūpa*-temple at Borobodur, which is a man-made Mount Meru. Many another – and far less spectacular – mound or tump may have been created for similar purposes, perhaps even our own enigmatic Silbury Hill. Mention has also been made elsewhere of the fact that certain buildings (as opposed to solid constructions like pyramids or mounds) are endowed with mountain symbolism: the Hindu temple, for example.

Mountains are also universally associated with the dead – again perhaps in the first instance because they were buried upon their slopes and summits, from where it was thought they might most directly rise to world above. In time, however, negative associations might set in: fear of the presence of ghosts or of monsters, or even of the forces of the powers of evil – responses that the ominous moods of mountains and their darker, heavier characteristics might well tend to compound. Many a European mountain is disgraced with a diabolical name – *Eiger* (Ogre), *Teufelsberg, Monte Disgrazia, Les Diablerets* – and there was once a time when the regular falls of rock from the summit of the *Matterhorn* were thought to be direct action by the Devil himself. A sinister 'Grey Man' haunts the mists of the Scottish *Ben McDhui*, while the *Himalayas* will never again be free of the unsettling presence of the huge-footed *yeti*,* which at any time may come charging from the snowy heights to carry off some forlorn Sherpa maiden in its great hairy arms, or beat to death some hapless traveller caught out at the heights with no means of escape.

The dead need not always arouse the fears of the living, however. Indeed, in the noblest of them the deepest hopes and aspirations of a people may reside. In many traditions – the Celtic, Teutonic,

---

*There are, apparently, two types of yeti: the larger yak-eating variety, and the smaller man-eater.

Slavic – a great hero like Arthur, Fionn, Merlin or Bruce, lies asleep in the heart of some hill or mountain, whence to re-emerge sometime in the future to 'renew all things sublunar'. In Hindu tradition, on the other hand, the souls of the sainted dead are thought to go and live on *Himavat*, while ancient Chinese Taoist mythology maintained that they repaired to the dwelling place of the immortals, one of two Chinese heavens, which was situated in the *Kun Lun Mountains*. Here the Lady Queen of the West held court in a fabulous nine-storey palace of jade, around which were magnificent gardens in which the peaches of immortality took their 3,000 years to ripen. Needless to say, these were forbidden fruit to any but those who had lived thoroughly virtuous lives. As on Olympus, the denizens of this Chinese heaven enjoyed a continual round of banqueting and pleasure.

The Chinese have traditionally displayed themselves highly sensitive to the natural world and keenly aware of the deeper qualities and dispositions inherent in natural phenomena like features of landscape and climate. The accumulation of their wisdom in such matters is systematized in their geomantic doctrines (*feng shui*), where the special effects of the presence or absence of a mountain in a landscape are delineated, and in the *I Ching* or *Book of Changes*, where the hexagram associated with *Mountain* is *Kên*, subtitled *Keeping Still* by the great German Sinologist Richard Wilhelm. The symbolism of *Ken* is full of intimations of meditation. It is a state of strong immoveability; of perfect balance, male above and female below; a state in which all motion hangs suspended, not in death or inertia but in the great stillness that is the origin and resolution of all things. Like a great meditating sage, a mountain sits with strong solidity upon the surface of the earth, quietly accumulating massive protean energies. Within the context of the old Chinese state, furthermore, the Emperor was seen as discharging a function analagous to that of the *axis mundi* of world mountain. He mediated with Heaven on behalf of his people. Not surprisingly, therefore, the axial mountain formed an essential decorative feature of the border of the robe he wore on ritual occasions.

Old China abounded with sacred mountains and every year hordes of pilgrims resorted to them, often journeying together down the pilgrim roads in groups under the banner of the pilgrim club to which they belonged. In their hands they clutched little bundles and ritual bags; also the obligatory thermos flasks and unbrellas. The old Chinese term for pilgrimage was in fact 'journeying to a mountain and offering incense'. The hallowed slopes and cloud-hidden summits of the sacred peaks were liberally endowed with wonderful temples and shrines, guest halls, pagodas, and rock-cut statues and inscriptions, which the pilgrims toured in appropriate order, mounting the particularly steep places perhaps by means of specially cut stairs or chainways. The poor travelled under their own devices; the better off might be carried in slings or *palanquins*, or borne in the arms of stout-hearted porters. Their motivation for making these pilgrimages might not seem very high-minded to us: to gain good luck, or secure an improvement in health or fortune, or to discharge an old penance. A genuine religious element was rarely lacking, however; and the practical disposition of the Chinese enables them to mingle the mundane and the spiritual with greater flexibility than Westerners.

Among the Taoists, five 'official' peaks were venerated in particular: *Tai shan, Wu yueh, Hua shan, Heng shan and Sung shan*. They were guarded by five Taoist emperors, the most exalted of which was the Great Emperor of the Eastern Peak (Tai-yueh ta-ti), who resided upon *Tai shan* in Shantung province. He was a maifestation or appointee of the Jade Emperor, with special powers over the lives and deaths of mortals, the dispensation of fate and fortune, and so forth. In these onerous functions he was assisted by a sizeable and complicated spiritual bureaucracy. Richard Wilhelm, was deeply impressed on a visit to Tai Shan that took place earlier this century.

It spreads itself with majestic calm over the region, and at its foot springs flow together from various directions. The clouds brood about its summit and it dispenses rain and sunshine over a wide area, because when its head is covered with clouds, which brood above it, then it draws more fog towards itself and the humid winds drive the clouds into cracks and hollows and rain descends upon the land. When it disperses the mists again, exhaling them, in tiny delicate clouds, so that they float gently away and disappear in the blue, the people know the grey days are over. The sun shines again over the fields and at night the great stars flicker in the deep black sky.... The vital forces innate in these proceedings, the mysterious clarity of these powers, have always attracted me....

(Richard Wilhelm, *The Soul of China*)

Chinese Buddhists, on the other hand, bowed their heads in special awe to four 'famous' mountains, each of which was associated with a particular *bodhisattva*: *Omei* in Szechuan (Samantabhadra), *Wu tai* in Shansi (Mañjushrī), *Chiu-hua* in Anhwei (Kshitigarbha) and *P'u-t'o*, an island in Chekiang (Avalokiteshvara). Legends and stories flourished in all these places of the presiding *bodhisattva* presenting himself in some unlikely guise to a pilgrim or visitor, so pilgrims tended to be on their guard and to treat all whom they encountered from the most elevated down to the most lowly with special care. Indeed, in all these places, a vivid atmosphere of wonder and magic must have asserted itself in the popular imagination, and in consequence it is not surprising to find reports of all kinds of marvels. John Blofeld, in a captivating account of a visit to *Wu tai shan*, records seeing 'fluffy balls of orange coloured fire, moving through space, unhurried and majestic – truly a fitting manifestation of the divinity!' The *bodhisattva* associated with Wu tai shan was Mañjushrī, he who wields the sword that slices away delusion; he had often appeared on the sacred mountain in the guise of a monk.* Many of these marvels would today of course be accountable in terms of natural phenomena, however. Beyond the great precipice at *Mount Omei*, for instance, a figure might appear in the golden mists of sunrise which the ardent would take to be an apparition of the *bodhisattva* Samantabhadra. Moving forward to meet the *bodhisattva* in a state of exaltation, however, they would plunge into the awful abyss below with fatal results. What they had in fact witnessed was their own shadow, projected with subtle atmospheric trickery.

The religious associations of at least some of the spiritually significant peaks of the world must derive, not so much from the qualities of the mountains themselves, as from the fact that they are associated with particular and noteworthy mystics. In this connexion, one thinks especially of *Arunachala*, a hill near the town of Tiruvannamalai in southern India which in modern times was the home of the great Ramana Maharshi. Maharshi seems to have identified the mountain with the Highest Principle:

> Nandi Said: 'That is the holy place! Of all, Arunachala is the most sacred! It is the heart of the world! Know it to be the secret Heart-centre of Shiva! In that place He always abides as the glorious Aruna Hill!'
> (A. Osborn (ed.), *The Teachings of Ramana Maharshi*)

In fact, mountains have always and everywhere been regarded as ideal places for religious retreats. There, at least, far from the hurly-burly of the everyday world, the solitude necessary for the

---

*On a pilgrimage to Wu tai shan in 1883/4 the greatest modern Ch'an (Chinese Zen) Master, Hsu Yün (1840–1959, – indeed, he lived to be 119!), was helped by a beggar named Wen-ji, whom he later believed was Mañjushrī in disguise.

cultivation of the contemplative life may be found. Thus not only have hermits and yogis retired to lonely caves and cells in the high places, but the members of great orders have also gone there to found secluded monasteries. We have already in this book encountered innumerable Asian instances of such things, but they are not lacking elsewhere – even here in homely Europe. We have our *Mount Athos*, our *Monte Cassino*, the high *Mount St. Bernard* monastery, the lofty retreats of the beleaguered Cathar heretics in southern France, *Mont St. Michel* and *St. Michael's Mount* – and a great many others besides.

Moreover, mystical experience is not necessarily the monopoly of dedicated mystics. Even modern-day mountaineers, as a breed not particularly noted for their spirituality, have reported all kinds of mystical or semi-mystical encounters on the heights. These may be incidences of what might be called Nature Mysticism, where exalted states of consciousness are encountered amid sublime natural surroundings, in situations of great solitude, often when in a hyper-oxygenated or physically stressed condition. Or they may be incidences of Danger Mysticism, where the possibility of sudden death serves to trigger off heightened states. Perhaps indeed, subconsciously, many mountaineers venture into the hills half in search of such experiences. It is at least comforting to know that, even in our spiritually barren age, the mountains are still there, still endowed with a capacity to free the spirit. When in his baleful *Waste Land* T. S. Eliot intoned, *'In the mountains, there you feel free'* – it was as though he were appealing to a last hope.

Mention of Eliot brings us into the ambit of literature, and here we also find testimony to the spiritual power of mountains. The ominous presences of *Popocatepetl* and its 'wife' *Ixtaccihuatl*, both spiritually resonant peaks in Mexico, loom over the pages of Malcolm Lowry's anguished religious novel, *Under the Volcano*. There the connotations are distinctly hellish, redolent with forebodings of death and damnation, but literature also has its great redemptive peaks. The *Montsalvat* of the Grail literature, for instance, where the golden chalice that is the end and object of the heroic spiritual quest is guarded by dedicated knights; and in Dante's *Divine Comedy*, after the terrible descent into the pits of Hell, spiritual regeneration begins with an ascent of the *Mountain of Purgatory*, upwards, cornice by cornice, from the nether realms of the excommunicate and the late repentant *via* St Peter's Gate to the Earthly Paradise itself, situated, most significantly, upon the summit.

This is not the first time that we have encountered the graduated stages in the development of the spiritual life likened to the stages of an ascent of a great mountain. It is a powerful metaphor. Lost amid the open places of the world, buried in minutiae, unable to see further ahead than our own noses, we are tossed hither and thither by every random event and can attain no lasting sense of who we really are or where we are going. When we begin to climb a mountain, however, things become clearer. We disengage from the pressures and pulls of the world, which recedes below us, becoming smaller and hence less threatening. We then reach a stage where we have a wider perspective: when the full scope and scheme of things can be grasped as a whole and our own place in it identified. Finally, there is a growing sense of having triumphed over confusion, and of the possibility of real growth and transcendence.

But is this really the case? There are in fact objections that may be levelled against the vertical model of spiritual development. To rise to the heights is certainly to reach a privileged position and there one may feel suitably superior to those caught up in the turmoil of the world. The vital question, however, is whether we are truly transformed. Have true wisdom and compassion arisen – or are we merely enjoying a blissful vacation from the harsh realities of the human condition? In orthodox Buddhist mythology, the fortunate denizens of the cloud palaces on the summit of Mount Meru may enjoy great pleasure and freedom from pain for a very long time, but inevitably the sad day must come when the beautiful flowers in their hands begin to wither and their armpits to give off odours that make them uncongenial to their *deva* playmates. Then the bitter season will soon arrive when they too must die. A true leap from the Wheel of Life may not in fact be made from the heights of Meru but only from a human situation, down upon the terrestrial plane, where the passions may be properly encountered, engaged and transformed.

The theme which we have undertaken to investigate here is one of truly vast proportions, and we could range on expansively over the whole surface of the earth accumulating fresh evidences. We could trace the significances of *Adam's Peak* for the people of Sri Lanka, investigate why *Mount Abu* has become such a great place of pilgrimage in Rajasthan, note how the Masai of Africa regard *Mount Kilimanjaro* or the North American Indians *Mount Shasta* or the Aborigines of Australia *Ayer's Rock*; we could unravel the mysteries of the volcanoes of the Hawaiian isles, travel on to New Zealand, the islands of south-east Asia. . . .

All of which would merely disperse and break up our theme

rather than bring its elements together and into focus for an attempt at a solution of the problem posed in the beginning: namely, what, in its highest, fullest manifestations, does the great universal symbol of the sacred mountain represent, what great mystery does it enshrine . . . ?

The matter of the sacred mountain reaches its consummation in the concept of the *axis mundi* or world mountain – a great manifestation of which was *Mount Meru* or *Sumeru*, the linch-pin of the Hindu, Jain and Buddhist world-views, which in past centuries held currency extensively in Asia. The axial mountain crops up in other traditions too: there is the *Haraberezaiti* of the Iranians, the *Himingbjör* of the Germans, the *Tabor* of the Israelites and the *Golgotha* of the Christians. In fact, according to the great historian of religion, Mircea Eliade: 'it is even found among such "primitives" as the Pygmies of Malacca and seems also to be part of the symbolism of prehistorical monuments.' In other traditions again the axis is not represented by a mountain but by a great tree, such as the Sacred Oak of the Druids, the World-Ash of the Scandinavians and the Lime-tree of the Germans. Or by a navel or *omphalos*, as at Delphi in ancient Greece . . . and indeed as is indicated in the etymology of Tabor, *tabbur* meaning 'navel'. All in fact are representations of that profound and potent reality which may be called *the Centre*.

When initially discussing the significance of the Centre, it is useful to distinguish an outward, exterior or macrocosmic aspect (the way it occurs in a cosmos or cosmic system) from an interior, microcosmic aspect (the way it occurs in man). The old traditions were able to identify fine correspondences or homologies between the microcosmic and the macroscosmic, between man and the universe: 'as above, so below'. As we shall see, however, this is really an artificial distinction, at worst downright misleading, at best merely pragmatic; that is, useful insofar as it allows us to approach the heart of the matter, where ultimately we will find all distinction and dichotomy resolved – for in essence the Centre is the place of unity *par excellence*.

Externally, in any world system, the Centre represents that one great fixed point against which all measures may be taken and relations drawn. It is like a great surveyor's rod at the heart of things, by its very presence giving coherence and form to that which would otherwise be incoherent and formless. It has the power, in short, to make cosmos out of chaos. It is also the most *spiritual* of places: indeed it is here that divine or spiritual reality impinges upon profane or mundane reality. This being so, it is the 'place' where the gods or higher spiritual realities may be most readily encountered.

Finally, it is the place where creation began – as is suggested by the navel associations. In Tibetan depictions of the cosmos, Mount Meru appears to be the spearhead of what looks like a massive downward thrust of spiritual power or energy. This congeals into matter at the summit of the mountain, and thence proceeds downwards, diminishing as it goes, until it hits the terrestrial level, where it suddenly spins outwards, whirling a vortex of oceans and continents as far as the outer limits.

Paradoxically, while there is and can be only one Centre, there may also be innumerable other 'centres'. This is possible by virtue of its essentially spiritual nature. Being omnipotent, the spirit is splendidly free to manifest itself as and where it wills, even in apparent defiance of normal laws. As Mircea Eliade points out, any vital location may be a 'centre': a temple, a shrine, a palace, a city, the place where some crucial event took place. It is easy to see why this should be so in the case of temples and shrines. Earlier we discussed how the Hindu temple was built upon the model of Mount Meru and hence penetrated by the *axis mundi*, spiritual 'power' being thereby drawn into the place and concentrated at its heart. Eliade extends the argument still more widely and asserts that any construction – not just the palace of a great World Emperor or *Chakravartin* but even the simple *yurt* of a humble Mongolian nomad – insofar as it imitates the created world, is theoretically penetrated by the *axis mundi* and constitutes a 'centre.'

Internally, in man, on the other hand, the Centre represents the spiritual essence, which goes by many names in the various traditions. Hindus call it simply *That* or *Ātman*. In Buddhism it is the Buddha Nature, the Heart; 'the Unborn, Unoriginated, Uncreated, Unformed'. Christians might call it the Christ Nature. To the great German mystic, Meister Eckhart, it was 'the little point' – an apt term, for really the Centre is not a thing, a place, a substance, or indeed anything that may be grasped in a concrete way at all. It is essentially conceptual – Eliot's *'still point of the turning world'*. Yet for all its elusiveness, it is the origin and goal of all our life and energy; 'the place of creative change', in Jung's account; the great home in which we all dwelt before self-consciousness drove us out of Eden and set us ranging through the ten thousand things on our desperate search for that lasting rest and resolution that can only be attained by returning whence we originally came.

Nostalgia for the lost Centre initiates the heroic spiritual quest – and here the threads begin to draw together, paths converge and run increasingly in parallel. The way that the aspirant must travel is notoriously difficult, fraught with all manner of difficulty and danger up to the most extreme. Death is always very much on the cards. And casualties are legion: the margins of the path are said to be lined with the bleached bones of those who have fallen by the wayside. But this is all necessarily so; only the most intense of pressures can secure the most exacting of transformations: initiation from the profane into the spiritual. Finally, for the few who penetrate that far, all paths coalesce in a single goal and realization. *He who reaches the Centre of the World reaches his own Centre and finds them one.*

Pilgrimages in general, and pilgrimages to sacred mountains like Kailas in particular, might be fairly regarded to a greater or lesser extent as conventionalized re-enactments of the heroic spiritual quest. As such they combine an outward physical journey through concrete space to a geographically-defined centre, with a concomitant inward spiritual progress. The goal itself – in our case, Kailas – is of little real importance in itself. It may at first *seem* charged with vast significance, be overwhelmingly beautiful, endowed with wonderful supernatural energies and generally replete with all manner of exotic association, but all these qualities merely serve the essentially pragmatic function of providing a focus for the spiritual aspirations of the pilgrim. As Bhumānanda told Professor Tucci, Kailas is really just a heap of stones. What is really important from the spiritual point of view is the journey itself. With its inevitable exposure to hunger, the exigencies of climate, its very palpable dangers (*dacoits*, wild animals, precipitous falls), its constant demands to endure the unendurable with patience and to accept the unacceptable, to curb self-indulgence and face hazards with equanimity, its all-pervading insecurity – with all this, and with its mitigating joys and diversions, the classic Kailas Pilgrimage no doubt amounts to a very effective course of spiritual training such as might elsewhere be applied in a monastery, though there less dramatically and intensively, and thus taking rather longer to achieve similar results.

In her book, *The Catalpa Bow*, Dr. Carmen Blacker describes elaborate mountain pilgrimages to peaks named Haguro and Omine in Japan. They are still enacted each year, though nowadays with considerably less rigour than in times past. Here pilgrims are put through what is clearly a carefully worked out programme of

Kailas from just east of Barkha (1987)

spiritual training, being deliberately subjected to a succession of ordeals and endurance tests in a context replete with esoteric Buddhist symbolism and ritual. Unrelenting discipline is applied, and the threat of death is exploited extensively and deliberately. Pilgrims are, for instance, dangled head-downwards over yawning precipices; and in the past they were left in no doubt that, if they fell by the wayside, they would be left to die. Clearly, the ultimate fears need to be invoked in order to bring about that pitch of seriousness that spiritual change requires. Only the man who has been driven to an extreme, in fact, who has lost or let go of everything and has nothing left to lose, is ready for the final awakening.

There is no doubt that, if fully realizing its potential, pilgrimage to Kailas could result in a full spiritual awakening. On the other hand, it would be naive to suppose that anything like a constant procession of enlightened beings came tripping back over the Himalayas from there. The failure rate among those undertaking the spiritual life is notoriously high: 'Many are called, few are chosen'. Nevertheless, it is also inexorably the case that in the spiritual life nothing short of the ideal is really good enough. One cannot be partially enlightened: it is one thing or the other.

Finally, may we hazard a guess at what lay at journey's end for the rare few among Kailas pilgrims who achieved some sort of spiritual illuminaton at the sacred mountain?

Here we tread upon especially treacherous ground. The nature of that which lies at the end of the spiritual quest is, in all traditions, said to be beyond the power of words to convey. Indeed, even to attempt to do so is to run the risk of throwing up new proliferations of misleading pictures and ideas, thereby obscuring rather than clarifying the matter. What confronts us here is a great mystery that cannot be grasped by the mind – and thereby appropriated to the province of 'I': of the self-aggrandizing ego. The best that we can do therefore is to attempt some general indications – and then chop them ruthlessly away....

The most complete account of an actual spiritual event of some considerable profundity is given us by Bhagwan Shri Hamsa. He describes encountering the physical form of his spiritual master, Lord Dattātreya, on the Gauri Kund lake, and receiving initiation into the Realization of the Self. Although he maintains that words are inadequate to describe the joy he experienced, he is in fact quite specific as to what happened technically. His various faculties merged one with another until finally all merged with Absolute Brāhman:

It was all one harmony – full of Wisdom, Infinite Love Perennial and Bliss Eternal! Where was the body, its tenements and the 'I'. It was all Satchidananda (Truth, Wisdom, and Bliss).

(Bhagwan Shri Hamsa, *The Holy Mountain*)

This is clearly a description of a state of consciousness from which all sense of a separate, individual 'I' had vanished, leaving nothing less than – Totality. One could call it a state of holistic or cosmic consciousness.

Bhagwan was, of course, an orthodox Hindu. Orthodox Buddhists might well aspire to something similar.

Many who pursue the spiritual life do so in despair of the sufferings of *samsāra*, the world of illusion, aspiring instead towards some kind of transcendence. And indeed, by the practice of spiritual techniques, it is possible to attain certain spiritual states in which both personal suffering and the suffering of the creation as a whole seem safely transcended. The Jains, for instance, aimed for such a rarefied state of consciousness, one beyond all sensation, thought and feeling. The problem with such beguiling states is that they are, like everything else, subject to the Law of Impermanence. They must pass, and in consequence cannot constitute a complete and lasting solution to the problem of suffering, which in Buddhism is axiomatic.

Buddhist practice is in fact centrally concerned with *clear-seeing:* with seeing things *as they really are.* The chief impediment to clear seeing is the delusory notion of 'I' that seeks to establish itself in the temporary and unstable combination of elements that comprise what we know as a human being. These elements are undergoing changes all the time, though the greatest and most dramatic is their dispersal at death. Fuelled by the energy of the passions (greed, hatred, delusion), 'I' is forever devising new schemes for securing and substantiating itself upon the shifting sands of existence. Thus when Mañjushrī, the Bodhisattva of Wisdom (see p. 397), wields his enlightening sword, he summarily slices away the accumulations and encrustations of self-promoting pictures and notions that 'I' has thrown up against its own eclipse, and reveals the true face of things. Nothing at all is added; in fact, a great deal is taken away. What remains is true *wisdom*, which in basic Buddhist thought is invariably accompanied by *compassion* – and therein lies an end of suffering. As the great Sixth Patriarch of the Zen school, Hui Neng, said:

The idea of a self and of a being is Mount Meru. . . .When you get rid of

Mañjushri

the idea of a self and of a being, Mount Meru will topple....
(trans. Wong Mou Lam, *The Sūtra of Hui Neng*)

Or equally, Mount Kailas will topple....

And what remains after that mighty falling: after the thunder has reverberated away and the dust begins to settle?

Just a heap of stones – a mere mountain, in fact: nothing more or less than that. The great miracle is our ordinary, everyday lives – as Layman P'ang, the great Chinese Zen man, said:

How wonderful, how miraculous!
I fetch wood; I carry water.

The writing – and perhaps also the reading – of this book have been a kind of literary pilgrimage to the sacred mountain, pursued in

A nun at Kojarnath Gompa (1986)

studies, in correspondence, in the learned libraries of London, with here and there the vivid high-point of an actual meeting with a real-life Kailas traveller. There has been the commercial side too: the meetings and negotiations with producers and publishers. There has been the endless accumulation of papers: notes, photocopies, drafts.... And the writing itself: the conjuring of veritable mountains of words – and then the honing and the fining....

Just a heap of stones – just a heap of papers....

This is in fact what seems to lie at the heart of all matters, not merely the matter of the sacred mountain: the simple reality of the here and now, so basic and yet so very hard to face, accept and fully grasp. There never was anything particularly special about that silver mountain shining against the indigo sky up on the dizzy heights of Tibet.... Nothing more special in fact than anything I encounter on the way to work each morning through remorselessly unromantic London N.W.10: down past the council flats; on by the crash repair garage with its acrid fumes of paint spray....

CHAPTER TWELVE

Epilogue

So, with a new wave of pilgrims and travellers at Mt. Kailas, a pattern has repeated itself. The wheel has turned through another cycle...

But what are we to make of these latest developments?

For the present writer at any rate, an essential value is beginning to be lost. What was, when I first wrote this book, so striking and fascinating about Kailas was its majestic solitude up there on the Roof of the World, safely protected by the snowy ramparts of the Great Himalaya from the excesses of modern secular society. It seemed a sanctuary for the spiritual values that have been so sadly lost elsewhere in our world.

Following in the wake of the Western travellers and pilgrims, however, come the tourists and they will no doubt hasten the advance of secular and materialistic values, which the post-Marxist Chinese are intent on propagating anyway. Ironically, tourism will probably in the long run far more effectively undermine the spiritual grandeur of this 'remote and remarkable' peak than all the iconoclastic activities of the Red Guards of the Cultural Revolution. There is furthermore the very real threat that mountaineers will soon assault the peak: a gross violation by any token.

But, however much it is lamented, it probably had to come. The star of secular materialism, whether of the capitalist or the communist variety, is rising inexorably in the East at the moment. The trinkets of techno-consumerism possess an alluring magic that makes them irresistible to the people of underdeveloped countries like China and Tibet. And, if we Westerners were ourselves unable to resist them, how can we expect of others a degree of wisdom and restraint of which we previously were not capable.

But just as the East now falls victim to the black magic of techno-consumerism, so many of us in the West grow weary of it all and begin to long for that elusive spiritual jewel that we have lost in the mad scramble to indulge our materialistic and sense cravings.

As we have noted, Kailas has for millennia stood as a colossal symbol for the great spiritual mystery at the heart of things. But that mystery is not limited to Kailas – or indeed to any other sacred mountain. Its ultimate abode is the human heart, and there each one of us may encounter it if we look with proper diligence. Traditionally, in Buddhism, that mystery is approached through the practice of morality, through the cultivation of wisdom (study of the sacred texts, keeping company with the wise, etc.) and through meditation.

In meditation, we let go of all our usual obsessions and preoccupations – we give the thinking mind time off. Then, becoming fully awake to the fact that we are present *here, now*, we gently turn the eye of awareness inwards and observe our inner mechanisms of thought, feeling, bodily sensation...

Gradually, bringing the errant mind back time and time again to awareness in the here-now, we explore inner space: a process similar to descending into the waters of a deep, dark lake. On the surface, there may be turbulent currents and waves; but below, in the depths, there is unshakable calm. So, passing beyond the province of me and mine, with all its flotsam and jetsam of superficial mental and emotional activity, our awareness at last opens out into a vastness that is much greater than our petty mundane selves. There is peace there, clarity, and something that transcends the dualities of existence and non-existence, good and bad; something that is not touched by evil or by pain – or even by death itself...

But what is it?

That is the central question: one we can usefully ask ourselves over and over and over again.

If we ask it often enough, we might find we are not who we once thought we were – but something infinitely more wonderful...

APPENDIX 1

Kailas-Manasarovar Travellers' Guide

Compiled in 1988 in consultation with Bradley Rowe;
and with help from Brian Beresford, Sean Jones, et al.

'People go to Kailas thinking, 'Oh, it's just another journey.'
But it's not like that. It's a very rigorous undertaking.
Whether you go by jeep or bus or in the back of a truck,
It's a very, very difficult journey to make.'

We begin with this wise caveat from Brian Beresford. A journey to Kailas is a long, difficult and hazardous one: one not to be lightly made, and certainly not without proper preliminary research and preparation.

We have compiled the following notes from information culled from recent travellers, notably Bradley Rowe. They apply mainly to individual travellers, not members of organized groups, who would hopefully be properly looked after by their tour operators.

It must be emphasised, however, that conditions and regulations are changing all the time, and travellers would do well to invest a fair amount of time in careful research before embarking on a journey/pilgrimage to Kailas-Manasarovar.

General Information on Travel in China & Tibet

The actual mechanics of getting to China/Tibet and many other basic matters relating to tourism are dealt with in various standard guide-books. The most acclaimed of these is *The Tibet Guide* by Stephen Batchelor (London: Wisdom Publications, 1987. 466 pp. Copiously illustrated in colour, with numerous maps and diagrams. £13.95/$26.95).

This book, which was the winner of the Thomas Cook Guide Book Award in 1988, gives essential information on tour groups, individual travel, visas and permits, customs, weather, currency,

postal services, what to bring, photography, transport, accomodation, food, health (including altitude sickness), etc. It also has a
comprehensive glossary and list of useful words and phrases, plus a
wonderful guide to the iconography of Tibetan Buddhism
illustrated by Robert Beer, an accomplished *thangka* painter. It is
indeed rare among guide books in that it is based on an informed
and deeply sympathetic understanding of the Tibetans, their
religion, culture and language – Stephen lived with Tibetans as a
monk for many years – and so is the ideal baedeker for the pilgrim as
well as for the tourist.

Most importantly it includes a comprehensive guide to travel in
Western Tibet by Brian Beresford and Sean Jones, which of course
includes substantial surveys to the circuits of Kailas and Manasarovar.

As we have already pointed out, official Chinese policy on travel
to Tibet is unclear at the moment (1988) following the disturbances
of 1987 and 1988. A solid embargo hasn't come down, but it is much
more restricted than, say, in 1985-7. This applies even more so to
Western Tibet.

Useful Addresses for Sounding Out the Current Official Climate

U.K. China Travel Service Ltd.,
24 Cambridge Circus,
London WC2H 8HD
tel. 01 836 9911

China National Information Centre
4 Glentworth Road,
London NW1
tel. 01 935 9427

Embassies and consulates of the Peoples' Republic of China should
also be approached. What you will be told, however, is likely to vary
greatly and you are in fact unlikely to get 'straight' information.

Visas

Visas are issued by embassies and consulates of the P.R. of China
for three months, six in some countries. They give access to all
places in China open to tourists at the time of entry. Visas were not
available in Kathmandu until about 1986, though could always be
very readily obtained in Hong Kong.

Travel Permits

Visas only give entitlement to visit 'open' places, of which there are now perhaps around 300 (Beijing, Shanghai, Xining, Golmud, etc.). In addition there are 'permit places', for which an additional travel permit is necessary; and also 'closed' places, requiring a special travel permit. The latter are only granted to organized (and usually expensive) tours operating in association with CITS (China International Travel Service) or CMA (Chinese Mountaineering Association). These permits are issued by offices of the Gongangju, a special police arm of the Foreign Affairs Bureau, in Lhasa, Shigatse, Kasa, Shiquanhe/Ali, etc.

At the moment (1988), Lhasa is a 'permit place' and Western Tibet a 'special permit place'. However, as a general rule, setting aside a few strategically sensitive areas, it's possible, by paying enough money, to get a permit to go anywhere in China.

Though things were and still apparently are bureaucratically quite straightforward for well-organized groups, they have always been more difficult for individual travellers. In 1986 and 1987 there was a temporary period or relaxation, but since the troubles things have tightened up considerably. At present, reports indicate that permits for travel anywhere in Tibet are *only* issued to organized tour groups – and even then with discouragement – though these need not necessarily be large groups. Individuals who managed to slip into Lhasa in mid-1988 were reported to have been subject to large fines and explusion.

Another complication is that, in modern China, local authorities in each area seem pretty much a law unto themselves and do not always synchronize regulations with each other. Thus, until 1987, as far as the Western Tibet officials themselves were concerned, their region was fully open to tourism. The Lhasa authorities, on the other hand, were at first giving it out that Western Tibet was closed, then later permits were issued, but even these were subsequently discontinued.

However, in all our researches into recent travel in Western Tibet, we have heard of no traveller being arrested or fined. Even when people have been stopped, officials have seemed reluctant to take responsibility for dealing with them. In modern China, passing the buck is an honoured convention.

Routes to Western Tibet

The Kashgar Route:

Some travellers have come south to Shiquanhe/Ali from Kashgar, but usually by stealth. The Kashgar authorities have never issued permits to travel to Western Tibet. Bradley Rowe in any case advises Kailas travellers against using this route, because 'you have a significant rise onto what is the highest road in the world quite quickly' – thus there is a special danger of altitude sickness, to which at least one traveller has succumbed (1985). It is also a very bare, bleak route, passing through very underpopulated regions, like the Aksai Chin. That, added to the fact that there are very long distances between truck stops, means that, if you are hitching rides, 'you should certainly not accept a lift for anywhere but Shiquanhe or perhaps Rudok' – that is, if you don't want to find yourself alone and forlorn in a barren wilderness with no help or human contact for many miles around. Bradley also adds: 'Actually, all traffic leaves from Yecheng (Khargalik), not Kashgar: that's where the roads from Kashgar and Khotan meet.'

Travel in the opposite direction is rather easier. Bradley says: 'From Shiquanhe to Yecheng, most trucks are empty and happy to take paying passengers, although they may have room for only one in the cab. Travelling in the back can be particularly dangerous on this road.'

The Kashgar Route runs (cumulative distances in kilometers in brackets):
Kashar (0) – Yecheng (249) – Mazar (498) – Xiadulla (600) – Rudok (1239) – Shiquanhe (1356) – Menjir (Moincêr, Mencir, Missar; 1616) – Darchen (1674) – Kailas.

Through N.W. Nepal and N. India:

The old trade routes in through north-west Nepal are proscribed to Western travellers by the Government of Nepal. A few have entered and/or exited without official visas, going through Simikot and Yari; some encountered difficulties with local officialdom.

Others have come up from Kathmandu and, travelling *via* Zhangmu and Tingri (Dingri), where there are tourist hotels, have got onto the Southern Route along the valley of the Yarlung Tsangpo (Brahmaputra); and gone out that way too.

We have not heard of any Westerner passing either way by the classic Lipu Lekh route down to Almora and the plains of India, however. This would be the shortest and quickest route – the plains of India are only about 120 miles from Kailas as the lammergeier flies – though one that would have to be negotiated on foot or horseback across the mountains, for there are no metalled roads for much of the way. In this case, the Indian Government restricts access. Traders sometimes cross *via* the Tinkar Pass, which is just inside Nepal.

Via Lhasa:

Most individual Kailas travellers in recent years have gone first to Lhasa, usually taking the train from Beijing to the great terminus of Lanzhou, then on to Xining and Golmud, where road transport is available. Others have arrived by road or 'plane from Kathmandu and Chengdu. A few have travelled by road and rail *via* the Karakoram Highway from Pakistan to Kashgar, Urumchi, Dunhuang and Golmud.

Once in Lhasa, travellers wishing to hitch-hike have negotiated rides to Western Tibet at one or other of the various truckstops around the once holy city. According to latest reports, this is no longer possible. Most truck convoys going to Western Tibet start from Shigatse, where there are several depots.

The Northern and Southern Routes:

Assuming of course that whatever formalities are currently in force have been fulfilled, the traveller starting from Lhasa has the choice of either the Northern or the Southern Routes (see pp. 321–5). In either case he/she will have to first go to Shigatse – a journey of at least eight hours – and then on to Lhatse and Raga.

The Northern Route runs (cumulative distances in km. in brackets): Lhasa (0) – Shigatse (340) – Lhatse (492) – Raga (727)* – over the Kailas Range to Tsochen (Coqen; 969) – Gertse (Gerze; 1244) – Getsai (Gyegyai, Gê'gyai; 1649) – Shiquanhe/Ali (1741) – Menjir (Moincêr, Mencir, Missar; 2001) – Darchen (2062) – Kailas.

The Southern Route runs Lhasa (0) – Shigatse (340) – Lhatse (492) – Raga (727) – Saga (785) – Zhongba (Drongba; 930) – Paryang (Parayang, Payang; 1037) – Maium/Maryum La (1157) † – Huoré (1289) – Barkha (Barga; 1317) – Darchen (1327) – Kailas.

---

*The distance cited is to Raga crossroads, not to the Chinese compound, which is 14 km before.

†There are also several other passes to be crossed besides this one.

As we have already dealt fairly thoroughly in the main body of the text with these two main routes, it's unnecessary to go into them in greater detail here, save to emphasise that both are extremely rough, unmetalled roads; also that the Northern Route is the main link between Central and Western Tibet, and though longer, is the faster option. According to Bradley:

> It's possible to go from Shigatse to Shiquanhe very fast in three days, though I'd recommend taking four. Flat out in a Toyota Landcruiser you could do it in two, but that would be nightmarish. If, at the other extreme, you accept short lifts [in trucks] and get stuck in between as I did on my first journey, it could take you as much as eighteen days.

Beyond Shiquanhe, the road to Purang, which goes past Kailas and between the two sacred lakes, is, according to Bradley 'relatively OK'. The authorities try to keep it open most of the year but there may be a few months – late December, January, February – when it might be difficult. Certainly there would be minimal traffic then – 'but that is not so much the condition of the road as the fact that it's so cold that even blowtorches won't get the vehicles' engines to work...'

The Southern Route along the valley of the Yarlung Tsangpo is altogether more problematical than the Northern Route, even at the most clement times of year. Due to the rains, the dirt track (which is all it is) gets washed out and travellers have had to turn back because of impassable floods and mud. In any case, even if things go well, 'it is liable to take you longer than going the northern way.'

Possible Means of Transportation

Depending on the affluence of the individual traveller, it has been possible to hitch rides on the backs of trucks, to get a group together and hire a bus from Lhasa, and, lastly, to either hire a Toyota Landcruiser or buy a seat on one going to Western Tibet at a price based on mileage (which worked out around $350, one way). The Toyota option is therefore strictly for the well-heeled, though by far the quickest and most comfortable way.

We have heard of several brave spirits cycling to Western Tibet. One is a Japanese, who apparently knew nothing of Kailas and pedalled right past it; another is Cecilia Neville, who made an epic solo journey on two wheels from Hong Kong to Kashgar *via* Chengdu, Lhasa and Western Tibet. Then in 1987, two Germans reached Kailas by pedal power, though they trucked out. Others have brought in trail bikes and ridden them in the area, though the going can be difficult, particularly on the sandy stretches. We have also mentioned people travelling for stretches of the way to Kailas on foot, staying with the nomads, etc. Bradley has provided some useful tips on obtaining an *entrée* with these fine people, who can be very hospitable – though beware their mastiff guard dogs!

There have finally even been cases of people buying yak and donkeys to carry their supplies and equipment. Lacking the necessary expert know-how in handling these often refractory animals and finding food for them – grazing is scarce and fodder difficult to buy – their experiences have invariably been untoward.

Food & Accommodation

In 1987, a meal worked out on average around 5 *yuan*, i.e. less than US$2.

Accomodation (i.e. a bed) was about the same per night – more in the Ali Hotel and at Purang and Darchen.

Best Times of Year to Travel to Kailas/Manasarovar

Bradley Rowe says:

> Unless you're seeking extreme endurance conditions à la Scott of the Antarctic, certainly December, January, February and March are out – even April and November. So that leaves May to October; this is the main season. I've always tended to go at the very end – late October/early November – because the skies tend to be clear [and hence good for photography]. But at night it is then getting critically cold to the extent that you have to break ice to get water and even then it will still freeze in your pan. But I had the right equipment last time [1987], so it didn't really bother me.
>
> In July and August there can be substantial amounts of cloud and you may not catch more than a few fleeting glimpses of Kailas. But really summer months are probably the best time.... May I would imagine would be quite a good time [i.e. after the cold and snows of winter; before the rains set in].

Facilities

There are rough-and ready truck stops in some of the small towns on the Northern Route; also a truck stop just outside Shiquanhe/Ali, though foreign travellers have been officially permitted to stay only at the Ali Hotel, the Hilton of Western Tibet. There are restaurants in Shiquanhe too.

In the Kailas region there are now facilities for Indian pilgrims: permanent guest houses at Taklakot/Purang and Darchen. Foreign travellers have been permitted to stay at these but priority is given to Indians. Also, during the pilgrimage season, there are standing encampments of tents where pilgrims and travellers can stay; some serve as tea stalls too. We also hear there is now a 'restaurant' of sorts at Darchen. It is unlikely to receive Egon Ronay's seal of approval.

There are police posts at Shiquanhe/Ali, Taklakot/Purang, Thöling and Barkha. The officials at the latter have apparently in recent times been *au fait* with the latest tourist regulations.

The key man to get to know at Darchen is Choyling Dorje, an employee of the Ali Tourist Service, who is now in charge of the mountain and looks after the interests of pilgrims. He speaks English and is by all accounts a mine of information on the mythology and lore of Kailas.

Supplies

Food can be bought at Shiquanhe/Ali and Taklakot/Purang: tinned fruit and meat, noodles, chocolate bars, etc. Some basics (e.g. *Tsampa*: roasted barley flour) are said to be on sale at Darchen too. But little or nothing is available elsewhere.

Hazards

Among the particular hazards that face the Kailas traveller, and especially the individual one, are:

1. *The Problem of Altitude.* This besets almost everyone, including young and fit people, particularly if they fly into Tibet. If the symptoms (e.g. dizziness, blurred vision, coughing up blood, etc.) persist and are ignored it can become acute and even fatal. Extreme physical effects include pulmonary or cerebral oedema, the only solution to which is a rapid descent to lowlying ground – something that is not possible from Western Tibet,

where there are no airfields or rapid communications with the lowlands. As a general rule, altitude least afflicts people who come up onto the plateau of Tibet gradually and slowly; this allows time for acclimatization.

2. *Extremes of Climate.* Intense heat and cold can be experienced in comparatively quick succession at Kailas, even in summer. Those travelling on the backs of trucks report conditions well below freezing at night.

3. *Specific Diseases.* We hear of three varieties of dysentry being brought up fron Sinkiang *via* the Kashgar Route; remedies for dysentery can be obtained and carried. A highly virulent new strain of hepatitis has also been reported, which killed over 1,000 people in Khotan in the autumn of 1987, causing the city to be quarantined. Bradley advises: 'Care should be taken eating with Kashgaris in Shiquanhe and all fruit should be peeled. Beware watermelons, which are porous enough to pick up diseases.'

4. *Lack of Hospitals* – and even basic medical facilities outside the main centres.

5. *Lack of Food Supplies* – outside Purang/Taklakot and Shiquanhe/Ali.

6. *Shortage of Drinking Water.* At Kailas itself there is much running water, but with the growing pollution problem it's hard to know how pure this will be. The Tibetans themselves only drink river water in emergency, preferring to boil up salt tea. Bradley says, 'Springs, if you can find them, provide some of the best water in the world.' *En route* for Kailas, however, water can be hard to come by.

Things the Independent Traveller Should Take

1. *Basic Medical Supplies.* Bradley Rowe carries a very comprehensive medical kit put together on the advice of the Institute of Tropical Medicine in London. It includes antibiotics, antiseptics, specifics for dysentery, moleskin bandages and elasticated bandages for sprains, etc.

2. *Food Supplies* – including high protein rations. Bradley carries muesli bars, soup cubes, instant noodles, grains, powdered milk and other energy-giving beverages, dried fruit, nuts, sugar, salt

and tea. He recommends carrying extra items for giving to locals who provide hospitality.

3. *A Good Water Container* – plus sterilizing tablets or else a multi-fuel stove for boiling water (for at least 10 minutes). Also a tin cup since boiled water is available in thermos flasks at most truck stops.

4. *A Range of Clothing for all Weathers* – particularly warm clothing, including a down jacket and down sleeping bag; strong footwear; sunglasses and a hat; a waterproof. Ideally some sort of lightweight tent should be taken too.

5. *Good maps and compass.* Available from Stanfords in Long Acre, London, etc.

General Rules of Thumb for the Independent Traveller

Bradley recommends the old trekker's maxim: 'Walk high, sleep low.'

He too adds that, as dehydration – which happens at altitude – can lead to acute kidney pain, 'Rest often, drink a lot.'

And: 'Test yourself – acclimatize . . .'

Brian Beresford says that, on the high passes, 'the only solution is to BREATHE DEEPLY!'

Short Checklist of Sites to Visit in the Sacred Region:

Kailas Parikrama or Kora – circa 32 miles/51 km. Six *gompa*: Nyenri, Drira Puk, Zutrul Puk and Darchen, Gyangtra and Serlung. Numerous sacred sites. Start and finish at Darchen.

Manasarovar Parikrama or Kora – circa 54 miles/86 km. Presently five *gompa* standing: Langpona, Seralung, Trügo, Gösul (Gossul) and Chiu (gold workings and Ganga Chu nearby).

Rakshas Tal – west of Lake Manasarovar (now litle visited by Western travellers). Tsepgye Gompa on the north-west side now fully operational.

Dulchu – 14 miles/22 km. south-east of Tirthapuri (no road). Unattended *gompa* at the traditional source of the Sutlej.

Tirthapuri – 3 miles/5 km. south of Menjir, on a feeder of the infant Sutlej. Guru Rinpoche cave, *gompa* and hot springs.

Gurugem – c. 6 miles/10 km. west of Tirthapuri. Small active Bönpo cave temple and ruined *gompa*. Many caves.

Khyunglung – abandoned cave city; one time capital of the ancient kingdom of Zhang Zhung. Two days walk 18 m/29 km. WSW of Tirthapuri on the Sutlej itself. No road access. Small Gelugpa *gompa* in village before cave city.

Tsaparang and Thöling – ancient capital and spiritual centre (main monastery) of the long-defunct kingdom of Gu-gé. West of Kailas. Access from Shiquanhe/Ali: 136 km. on the Barkha road to Naburu military camp, then 144 km. to Thöling; *or* 189 km. from Menjir. Many cave cities and ruins nearby, including Daba (Dapa, Dawa) and Dongpo. Tsaparang and Thöling are 20 km. apart.

Taklakot/Purang (Pulan) – ancient cave dwellings and bazaar; great centre for the wool trade; Tsegu Gompa. Taklakot is 104 km. from Barkha (Barga).

Kojarnath – a site sacred to the Hindus where there is now one (reconstructed) *gompa*; 15 km. south-east of Taklakot in the Karnali valley.

Sources of the Great Rivers – especially that of the Indus (north of Drira Puk) and the Yarlung Tsangpo/Brahmaputra (east of Manasarovar). Again, no modern Western traveller seems to have visited these.

Bönri – sacred Bönpo mountain. Near Huoré, north-east corner of Manasarovar.

Pollution

Bradley and other recent travellers have expressed concern at the contemporary blight of pollution that is beginning to afflict Kailas now that Western travellers are beginning to arrive there in large numbers. He has been particularly offended by the fact that people defecate in the environs of the *gompa*, and often leave toilet paper there too, which does not degrade in the dry atmosphere. Litter is also beginning to accumulate.

Travellers are therefore urged to respect the environment of Kailas by answering the call of nature in secluded places, and, if possible, burying or covering their waste products and burning their litter or carrying it away.

Bradley says: 'Many groups will be able to take away their litter and dump it in Shiquanhe, etc., with minimal inconvenience. I carried my tins, plastic containers, etc., in my pack.'

Respect for the Sanctity of Kailas

Kailas is a holy mountain, Manasarovar a holy lake.

Even if the Western visitor to Kailas does not share the Buddhist or Hindu beliefs of the people for whom Kailas is sacred, he/she should sensitively respect their beliefs. This means honouring the inviolability of the peak of Kailas and observing time-honoured practice and decorum at other specific sites, like the Inner Kora, which should not be circumambulated until thirteen circuits by the orthodox route have been accomplished.

It is also, strictly speaking, inappropriate to kill *any* sentient being in such holy places: even small, irritating insects, etc., let alone larger animals. The consumption of alcohol, tobacco and, to a lesser extent, the eating of meat are also out of place here. Sexuality should be regulated, harsh or false speech avoided and commercial activity suspended. Loud noise, whether natural but especially electronic, is also out of accord with the spirit of the place...

What is called for is an attitude of respect: that in these places humans sense the presence of a reality larger and more significant than themselves. This great transcendent mystery does not have to be recognized in Buddhist or Hindu terms. The Christian, Jew or Moslem could discern here equally well the presence of their own God – and the unbeliever, humanist or atheist could regard this as a place to contemplate their highest ideals...

Useful Addresses

Brian Beresford has set up a travel agency and can provide advice and information about new tours/pilgrimages:

Kailash Travel
Flat 5, 118 Haverstock Hill
London NW3
tel.: 01-586 7372
Telex: 268018 REHO G (Attn. Brian Beresford)

Jeff Hann is trying to arrange tours *via* India with the Indian pilgrims. He has contacted the Government of India but so far has not yet received permission. He hopes to have Kailas tours operating by 1989:

Hann Overland,
2nd Floor,
268-270 Vauxhall Bridge Road,
Victoria, London SW1 1EJ
tel.: 01-834 7337
Telex: 914846 HANNOVG

Organized tour companies – they can be *very* expensive – include:

Indoculture Tours AG (Michael Henss)
Weinbergstrasse 102
CH-8006 Zürich
Tel.: 01-363 01 04
Telex: 815 029 ict ch

Sierra Club,
Dept H-528
P.O. Box 7959, San Franscisco
CA 94120, USA

Mountain Travel
6420 Fairmount Ave
El Cerrito, CA 94530, USA

Some Kathmandu trek and tour operators are also in the Kailas business. The biggest is:

Dawa Norbu Sherpa,
Rovers Treks & Expeditions (P) Ltd.,
Naxal Nag,
Pokhari, P.O. Box, 1081,
Kathmandu, Nepal

They took 30 sherpas to Kailas in 1986 and are on good terms with the Chinese. They are very useful in getting visas, organizing individuals into groups, etc.
Also:

Tiger Mountain Travel Int. Ltd.,
P.O. Box 3989,
Durbar Marg,
Kathmandu, Nepal
Tel. 221379
Telex. 2216 TIGTOP NP
Fax. 977-1-221379

Indian Nationals

Indian nationals may join organized pilgrimages to Mount Kailas and Lake Manasarovar, arranged by the Government of India in collaboration with the Chinese government. These run from May or June through to October. Travel is by the classic route *via* Almora and the Lipu Lekh Pass. In Tibet there are rest-houses at Taklakot/Purang and Darchen (where the man is in charge is Choying Dorje, who speaks both English and Hindi); elsewhere there are standing encampments of tents. Travel is in groups of about 25/30 pilgrims.

Application to join should be made well in advance to the Ministry of External Affairs of the Government of India in New Delhi. Thousands apply, but only about 300 are accepted, so lots have to be drawn. Cost is around Rs. 10,000/-.

The G.o.I. Ministry of External Affairs in New Delhi will no doubt supply further information and briefings.

Stop Press

As we go to press it is clear that travel to Tibet is still very restricted. In April 1989, Martial Law was declared in Lhasa, the focus of recent troubles. This, allied to internal trouble in China itself, made travel to Tibet very difficult. Martial Law was lifted in April 1990, and though travel is still not what it was in the years 1984 to 1988, it is slightly easier. Travellers have to be in groups, though these can be quite small (three is apparently enough), and are not subject to too many impositions. Generally observers see a pattern emerging. During periods of political unrest and subsequent repression, travel is restricted. Then, when things relax, travel becomes a bit easier, but at the same time political dissent also breaks out again, initiating another phase of repression and travel restriction. Things are therefore changing all the time. We have not heard of Western travellers at Kailas since 1988.

NOTE. While every effort has been made to ensure the comprehensiveness and accuracy of the foregoing information, which has been collected from recent travellers to the Kailas region, it is tendered for what it is worth and no guarantees can be given or liability accepted in respect of it. It must be again emphasised: a journey/pilgrimage to Mount Kailas is a high risk venture and each individual embarking upon it must fully satisfy themselves personally that they are adequately provided and informed to make it, as well as physically fit.

APPENDIX 2

Hyder Hearsey's Journal of his 1812 Expedition to Manasarovar with Wm. Moorcroft

One of those most interesting developments following the publication of the first edition was the location of the manuscript of the journal kept by Hyder Hearsey (1782–1840) during his journey to Lake Manasarovar with the remarkable William Moorcroft (1767–1825) in 1812. This was then in the possession of one of Hearsey's descendents, John Hearsey, who at the time was living at Angmering in Sussex. It naturally cast a deal of new light on this pioneering expedition.

One fact that emerges most forcefully from Hearsey's journal is Moorcroft's indomitable spirit, especially the manner in which he coped with the distressing and debilitating bouts of sickness that beset him during the expedition. Just two days after the 54-man party had set off, he was hit by the first attack of a 'bowel complaint', which brought on 'a cold, shivering fit, caused by frequent evacuations.' Heasey noted on 13th May:

> Mr Moorcroft felt himself very weak and proceeded very slowly. Nothing but an extraordinary firmness of character and resolution of mind in the condition he was in could have carried him on. The way tho' pretty good, required the attention of the eye at almost every step, even to the person in health and spirits. This plainly shows how much control the mind has over the body and what benefits accrue to the person possessed of that advantage, going through the vicissitudes of human life in a very active sphere.
>
> (Hyder Hearsey, *A Tour to Eastern Tartary*, etc)

Praise indeed, for Heasey was no wimp himself. Born the wrong side of the blanket of an British infantry officer and a 'Jat lady', he had been schooled at Woolwich and then, deprived of the channels for advancement open to his legitimate half-brothers, had to carve out a career for himself as a mercenary. And a colourful, picaresque career it was too – but then, he *was* named after Hyder Ali of Mysore, the scourge of the British . . .

At 16 this 'very ingenious but uneducated man' entered the service of the Nawab of Oudh. After that he became A.D.C. to the French adventurer General Perron and at a mere 17 was in deputy command at Agra Fort. Subsequently, he transferred his allegiences to Perron's rival, the Irish adventurer George Thomas. (Both Perron and Thomas were out to carve kingdoms for themselves from the ruins of the Mughal Empire.) After Thomas's demise, Hearsey offered his services to the British, bringing with him a regiment of cavalry, the remnant of a larger force he had raised on his own account. He led this irregular horse against the Mahrattas under the overall command of Lord Lake.

On his marriage to Zuhur-ul-Nissa, a native princess of Cambay, Hearsey was given an estate at Kareli near Bareilly in Rohilkhand as a present by the Mughal Emperor himself. But he didn't settle down there. Soon new opportunities were emerging for his driving, energetic spirit, this time in the new field of exploration and survey-work. In 1808, he joined Raper and Webb in their quest for the source of the Ganges. As we have already noted, he gained a bad name for himself, possibly unjustly, but what he learnt on that expedition of the skills of surveying and map-making made him the perfect man to go with Moorcroft to Tibet in 1812. Moorcroft himself reciprocated Hearsey's good opinions; the Anglo-Indian, he believed, possessed 'courage, spirit of enterprise, acquaintance with language, manner and habits of the natives of Hindoostan and its borders, decisiveness of character and fertility of resource.' Moorcroft's biographer, Garry Alder, believes that the two men probably met at Bareilly when Moorcroft was *en route* for Hardwar in the spring of 1812.

On the first leg of their journey, Moorcroft and Hearsey had of course to run the gauntlet of the martial Gurkhas, then in control of the Kumaon and Garhwal regions. Clearly they needed some kind of cover. What that could be occurred to them when some nautch girls – one or two of them quite good looking – visited them as they sat down to a 'frugal meal' one evening quite early on. The girls said that they had heard that 'some great Mehunts' had arrived and they wished to sing to them. The travellers tossed them a few *timashas* to be gone but 'This gave us the hint of representing the characters of Mehunts or Goseins' and that 'ever afterwards served us very well'.

Gosains were a species of holy men who in those days wandered freely in the mountains of India and Tibet, visiting the holy places and supporting themselves by dabbling in trade. Sometimes they also acted as spies and secret agents. After Moorcroft had disguised himself as one, Hearsey found that he cut 'a most ludicrous appearance, a large patch of lamp black round each eye, and his face and neck stained with the Juice of Walnuts, then smeared with the ashes of burnt Cowdung.' However, his 'gravity of countenance' had an 'irresistable effect on the Eye of his beholders, who take him for Sanctity itself.'

Despite their superficial sanctity, Heasey and Moorcroft were in fact a lecherous pair, apparently quite ready to attempt to seduce any likely women that they came upon. Indeed Moorcroft had something of a reputation. According to the Frenchman, Victor Jacquemont, his 'principal occupation was making love'. He and Hearsey didn't always get their oats, however:

> Among the Boojeahs were many females, three or four had some claim to beauty, but two decidedly were handsome. Much credit must be allowed to their Chastity as offers were made very liberally to persons in their station, which either want of language or management on our part prevented having the desired effect.
>
> *(Ibid.)*

Of the hardworking women of Niti:

> They smoke Tobacco, drink Spirits and have no reserve. They are great beggars, but tho' tempted very much, would not swerve from their duty to their husbands. From being constantly employed, their inclination to venery is much curbed.
>
> *(Ibid.)*

Having been delayed at Niti and again in Daba, Moorcroft and Heasey finally contrived to bribe and bluster their way through to Gartok, and then to 'Gaunguree or Durchun', which to Hearsey's disappointment was not the place of consequence that he had imagined. 'There are only 4 houses,' he lamented, but it did have a number of merchants, mainly Indians from Johar and Darma, and of course two Chinese tea merchants, but none from Lhasa. The day, August 4th, was mainly devoted to commercial transactions:

> Halt this day at Gaunguree in expectation of being able to dispose of some of our articles. The people are anxious to sell us shawl wool unpicked for 27 niygahs per rupee ready money and we would procure

to the amount of 2 or 300 rupees worth. There are no merchants here of any consequence and of course no purchases of our articles to any large amount; the few purchasers there are mostly Lamas who offer no more than 2 phitauks of gold for 3 yards of my orange broad cloth, which is only equivalent to 18 Rs. or 6 Rs. per yard. This I rejected. There are an amazing number of hares in the vicinity of this place and they are very tame.

(Ibid.)

One persistant question is of course how both Moorcroft and Hearsey could have been so close yet so unresponsive to Kailas, surely one of the most spectacular mountains in the world. 'The Kylass Mountain appears very plain, distant and detached,' is just about all that the swashbuckling Anglo-Indian adventurer has to say. One reason perhaps is that both he and his companion were pre-Romantics. Wordsworth and his poetic ilk had not yet fully awakened the Western consciousness to the spiritually-uplifting beauties of unspoiled nature. Indeed, nature had not in 1812 been significantly spoiled – certainly not in the Himalayan region and Western Tibet. What is abundant and freely available is often not valued. Moreover, it is clear that Moorcroft and Hearsey were highly *practical* men, whose attentions were foscussed very closely, perhaps obsessively, on mundane matters. They gathered mountains of data on just about everything – so much so that one commentator was prompted to write in the catalogue of Moorcroftiana published by the Indian Office Library:

The Manuscripts give an account of Moorcroft's journeys, of his multifarious investigations into commerical affairs, his relations with the ruling authorities, and any matter even remotely connected with such matters. The *adventitous matter predominates and often obscures the personal record.* [My italics]

Then appears a list of topics, which range from Rhubarb to Asafoetida, from Agricultural Implements to Liver Rot, from Painting in Kashmir to Prangos.

On August 5th, our redoubtable adventurers crossed the plain of Barkha, and on August 6th and 7th they were at Lake Manasarovar. As Heasey's record of August 6th, a crucial day, has not to date been published in full, we will do so here:

THURSDAY, AUGUST 6th. Halt on borders of Lake Mansurwur. Morning early, raining and very cloudy. Therm. 47°. [*In Hearsey's record there now appears a sentence containing an almost illegible word which Charles Allen, transcribing it as 'Amamus today at 11 AM,' cites as evidence that Hearsey's efforts at seduction were not all fruitless. However, to the present writer that reading, though undeniably adding spice up the story, is far from conclusive.*] It was my intention to have bathed and got shaved; however, after breakfast altered my mind and we got our fishing tackle ready and went along the shore. Mr. Moorcroft had set off about half an hour before me and I followed his footsteps, looking for a place proper to throw in my tag line, but could not find one, the surf being so very high and the shore stony. I proceeded about 3 miles when I gave up all ideas of fishing. Here I saw several Poland Wild Geese with their young ones unable to fly. I waited here nearly 3 hours for the return of Mr. Moorcroft, to make use of his gun. These animals came grazing within 30 yards of me. I made my servants lie down and they would have come closer had we not started up to catch the young geese. We had a smart run for it and the youngsters were obliged to crest their legs for it and beat us hollow. From this spot I commenced my survey of the Lake. To the left we saw a picturesque little hill with a building upon it. From this Station 1 I made my first bearing. From thence to our encampment was 2 m. 5 f. 146 yds. Going and coming I had gone near 6 miles. There were many gulls. I collected some small pieces of crystal and some curious stones. The lake on this side throws up an amazing quantity of grass and very fine shells, which are small. On my return, which was just after sunset, I found it very cold. The wind was very high and the surf rolled in huge waves. This side I have surveyed has the appearance of a circle. The Therm. at 7 p.m., 59°. This morning we were obliged to call Dusrut and the two Horsemen, who it appears had been telling the Tartars not to sell us anything; this they denied and after some little explanations they promised to us their endeavours to sell our property and buy us everything we wanted. Dusrut, the rogue, is at the bottom of this because we took a Darmee [i.e. from the Indian village of Darma] interpreter into service, who has procured us some wool. There are vast numbers of black gnats along the side of the lake and on the spot we are encamped I have killed 3 centipedes and many large black spiders. In the dry grass and small pebbles on the lake's side are also vast numbers of small red spiders. Mr. Moorcroft did not return until near 11 o'clock p.m., almost starved with hunger and cold. He had gone a great distance but had not come to the nuddee [i.e. stream] which issues from the lake into Rawan Radd [Rakshas Tal]. The surf was too high to fish. He saw many geese and fired some shots at them but could not get near them. The distance he went along the shores of the lake might be 12 miles and he had to return the same, altogether 24 miles. He was dreadfully fatigued. On returning before sunset, I saw an enormous large animal or fish like a porpoise. It kept a considerable time upon the surface, was of a brown colour and had apparently hairs. I first mistook it for a dead chowhur [yak] until I saw it in motion, when it disappeared. There are two species of gulls, one the small white one with red beak who skims the surface for his prey, the other as large as a duck, marked with black.

(Ibid.)

The next day rain and hail fell to the accompaniment of thunder rolling across the lakes and mountains. 'The climate here varies very much,' Hearsey wrote; 'the nights are generally clear with high wind till near morning, when the wind dies away and it becomes cloudy and warm, attended by rain; the middle time of the day is at one time hot, then cold, then raining and cloudy; this continues with the wind going all round the compass till near sunset, at which time the wind sets in with violence from the SW and very cold. The new moon and the sun entering Leo may in some measure affect this . . .'

At 11.30 that night, two native *pundits,* Hurruck Dao and Kurrukpooree, returned, having been sent off after breakfast 'to ascertain whether there was any communication between this lake and Rawan Rudd Lake, or if there was any outlet.' They were exhausted from walking a punishing 36 miles in all 'as far as the Krishna river', but had found nothing, thus confirming Moorcroft's (erroneous) thesis that 'this extensive lake, to which sanctity is given by the Hindoo shastras, has no connection by exit with any river or even with Rawan Rudd.' If there ever had been a channel of the kind old Harballabh had described to Moorcroft, 'it has dried up and the bed risen considerably above the height of the lake.'

After breakfast next morning, Moorcroft and Hearsey finished cutting their names and the date into a stone beside the lake. Then they took a last bathe before commencing 'our Return towards Hindoostan.' As they travelled, they cast the occasional backward glance at the sacred region now receding behind them. 'Kylass has altered his appearance very much,' Hearsey recorded.

The main details of the somewhat disasterous homeward journey are set out in the earlier part of this book. Suffice it here then to set out the lineaments of Hearsey's subsequent career. In keeping with the character of this turbulent man, there was more fighting . . . more trouble . . .

To begin with, when he got back to the plains he found himself again in ill odour with the British authorities: this time they were accusing him of having made preparations to invade Gurkha-held territory. There was also a long-standing legal wrangle over the Dehra Dun region, which Hearsey claimed to have fairly purchased but to which the authorities never recognized his title.

He did not go with Moorcroft on the fatal expedition to Bokhara: apparently, they could not agree on the best route to follow. Instead, when the British eventually decided to curb the expansion of the bellicose Gurkhas and to restrict them east of the Kali River,

Hearsey forgot former frictions and rallied to the flag. Unfortunately, he got himself severely wounded in the thigh and taken prisoner to boot. He would certainly have been beheaded had he not been recognized by Hasti Dal, the Gurkha commander, whose own life Hearsey had himself saved during the Ganga Mission. Though never fully recovering from the effects of the wound, he lived for another fifteen years. The Siege of Bharatpore (1826) was his last campaign. After that he lived peacefully with his wife on their estate at Kareli until his death in 1840. He left behind him two sons and a daughter. Touchingly, one of the sons was named William Moorcroft Hearsey...

APPENDIX 3

Ryder, Rawling and Bailey: Additional Biographical Details:

Captain C. H. D. Ryder (1868–1945) was educated at Cheltenham College and entered the Survey of India, then 'a carefully picked service', in 1891. For a few years from 1894 he served in China, then between 1903 and 1905 was Chief Survey Officer in Tibet, where, 'He maintained a triangulation under most difficult conditions and made a good survey of all this new country, with large-scale maps of Lhasa and Gyantse.' His work in Tibet of course culminated in the Gartok Expedition, which took him and his colleagues into the Kailas region.

Afterwards, between 1906 and 1913, Ryder was in charge of surveys in the North-West Frontier from Baluchistan to Chitral, then was attached to the Turco-Persian Boundary Commission. The outbreak of World War 1 caught him in the Middle East, and he had to cross Russia to Archangel in order to return to India *via* England. He later worked in India and Iraq until 1919, when he became Surveyor General of India, a post he held until his retirement in 1924.

According to his obituarist, he was a fine character: 'For in addition to brains and physique, Ryder's mere presence inspired confidence... Though full of quiet humour, he was a man of few words and very reticent about his own exploits, only showing his outstanding ability by the ease with which he got things done in the simplest possible way.'

Captain Ryder's colleague, Captain Cecil Rawling, was a Devonshire man, born 1870 and educated at Clifton, after which he joined the Somerset Light Infantry. His geographical work began with a foray across the Lanak-la into Tibet in 1902, followed by a more abitious but equally unauthorized journey the following year when, with Lieutenant Hargreaves, he surveyed some 38,000 square miles of Western Tibet. This naturally led on to service with the Younghusband Expedition and the subsequent Mission to Gartok. While *en route* for Mount Kailas, he saw Mount Everest from the north and this inspired in him the ambition of exploring the approaches to the great mountain and later of climbing it. But his service career now drew him away to England, and then he went with an expedition ('largely ornithological') to Dutch New Guinea. At the outbreak of World War 1, he commanded a battalion of his regiment in France, seeing much fierce strife on the Somme and around Ypres. He was killed by a shell while standing outside his Brigade HQ on the Western Front.

According to his obituarist, Rawling would 'Always seem the *beau ideal* of a British soldier. He had no taste for heroics or fine talk; but he had a heart as tender as a woman's, and a loyalty in friendship as impulsive as a boy's.'

Finally, Lieutenant Frederick Marshman ('Eric') Bailey (1882–1967), was one of the greats of Central Asian exploration. Educated at Edinburgh Academy, Wellington and Sandhurst, he served first with the 17th Bengal Lancers and, from 1903 to 1905, with the 32nd Sikh Pioneers. His participation in the Younghusband Expedition to Tibet inaugurated a lifelong fascination for that country and its people. He became a Tibetan speaker and, having joined the Indian Political Service (I.P.S.) in 1905, was appointed British Trade Agent (B.T.A.) at Gyantse, the large town in southern Tibet where a vital engagement had been fought during Younghusband's advance on Lhasa. Later, as a private individual, he made an epic journey from China to India *via* Tibet. His daring exploration work in south-east Tibet and the Mishmi Hills won him the Royal Geographical Society's Gold Medal in 1912; then in 1913 he resolved one of the great geographical riddles of the day when, with Captain H.T. Morshead, he discovered the dramatic gorges through which the Tsangpo of Tibet pierces the formidable Himalayan barrier to become the Brahmaputra of the plains of India.

During World War 1 Bailey was an undercover agent in best

Richard Hannay style in Bolshevik Turkistan. His cover having been blown, he led a desperate fugitive existence, only managing to escape to safety in the end by the skin of his teeth. By contrast he was also a keen natural historian and is perhaps best remembered as the discoverer of the famous Himalayan Blue Poppy, which bears his name: *Meconopsis Betonifolica Baileyii*.

Subsequently Bailey saw service as a Political Officer firstly in Sikkim (1921-28, during which time he made an official visit to Lhasa in 1924), then in Central India. He was Resident in Baroda (1930-2) and in Kashmir (1932-3), and finally Envoy Extraordinary and Minister Plenipotentiary at the Court of Nepal (1935-8). He retired in 1938, but during World War II was a King's Messenger in Central and South America, as well as being in the Home Guard. He died in Stiffkey, Norfolk, in 1967.

APPENDIX 4

Note on the Darchin Monastery Dispute

by F Williamson
Political Officer in Sikkim.

Darchin is a monastery of insignificant size in a desolate and miserable spot under Mount Kailas in Western Tibet.

2. The Darchin area, including Kailas, appears to have been granted to the Bhutanese some hundreds of years ago by a king of Ladakh. The grant was confirmed by one of the earlier Dalai Lamas, perhaps the fifth. The confirming document is in the possession of the Maharaja of Bhutan. Tibetan dates go in cycles of sixty years and it has not been found possible to ascertain the date of the document, as the particular cycle in which it was written is not stated. Copies of such of the documents as are available are now on record in my office, having been obtained during my recent visit to Bhutan.

3. Apart from its importance as a holy place of pilgrimage, the Darchin area is not worth quarelling about and a more unattractive

spot I have seldom seen. Feeling about Darchin, between Bhutan and Tibet, has been high since about 1921, when the Sonam Lekhung, the agricultural department of the Tibetan Government, began to register some of the residents of the area, who are chiefly pastoral nomads, as Tibetan subjects, and to tax them accordingly. They claimed that, as their families had not been settled there at the time when the former Dalai Lama confirmed the grant, they could not be considered as 'subjects' of the Darchin Labrang (monastery). This, of course, raises the question as to whether Darchin is Bhutanese territory, as His Highness of Bhutan would claim, or whether it is merely an estate in Tibetan territory held by him, as the Tibetan Government would claim. This point has, however, been avoided by both sides. In practice, the taxes, etc., on the local residents are collected by the Head Lama, and a very small portion of them is remitted to Bhutan, the remainder being retained by the Lama.

4. The late Maharaja of Bhutan had a certain amount of acrimonious correspondence with the Tibetan Government on the subject and the matter came to a head in 1930 when, no suitable Lama being easily available, the present Maharaja sent a layman named Tobda La as his representative. The Garpöns, with the approval of the Tibetan Government, objected strongly to this. Tobda La took back as Darchin 'subjects' a number of people who had been previously registered by the Sonam Lekhung. A tense situation followed, the Garpöns forced these 'subjects' again to give up their so-called Bhutanese nationality and beat a number of them severely. They made it so uncomfortable for Tobda La that he had to return to Bhutan. Tobda La was egged on to take 'subjects' back by one of the factions of Johari traders, who appear to have acquired a more or less recognised right to be the sole British subjects to trade with Darchin 'subjects'.

5. When I was about to go to Western Tibet in 1932, the Maharaja of Bhutan asked me to do what I could about the dispute. After Tobda La's departure, a Tibetan, formerly Barkha Ta-tsam (or Tarjum), was appointed by the Garpöns to be in charge of Darchin, and he is still there. I found him uncommunicative and far from helpful to my enquiries. I discussed the matter with the Garpön, there being then (and now) only one instead of two at Gartok. He was friendly and promised to do nothing to aggravate the situation but said that the trouble all took place in the time of his predecessor, that he knew little about it, but that all the people taken by the Sonam Lekhung were really Tibetan and not Bhutanese subjects.

6. When I was in Bhutan in the summer of 1933, the Maharaja

asked me to make an effort at Lhasa towards a settlement. I spoke to the Kashag about it and found that it concerned the Sonam Lekhung Department under Kusho Kunphel La. So I discussed it with him and with the Dalai Lama also, taking up the attitude that, as a friend of both parties, I desired to do all that I could to help them to reach a settlement satisfactory to both sides. The attitude of everyone in Lhasa was very friendly. They agreed that, if the Maharaja would send a responsible Lama as Den Dzin, or head of the monastery, he should discuss in detail with the Garpön the case of each house or family claimed by both sides and try to reach an agreement. They said that they had no desire to deprive the Maharaja of the Darchin area or to encroach on his rights there, but that their information was that nothing unreasonable had been done by the Garpöns. The Kashag have since written a letter to this effect to His Highness. It is couched in friendly and conciliatory language, very different from that used in previous correspondence, and it is to be hoped that, even if both sides do not agree in every detail, nothing serious will again occur. The Maharaja has not yet sent a new Den Dzin, but I hope he will do so next summer.

7. Although the foreign relations of Bhutan are under us, direct correspondence between Bhutan and Lhasa is carried on in questions of this kind. The matter is really a religious one and I think that we should intervene as little as possible. I only took any part at all because the Maharaja was extremely pressing that I should do so and because I saw that the atmosphere at Lhasa was favourable to the receipt of friendly suggestions from me.

Dated Gangtok,
The 6th January 1934.

APPENDIX 5

Stop Press

Since going to press, the following information has materialized:

Masao Endo

The Japanese photojournalist Masao Endo specializes in assignments that deal with 'religious conflicts, wars and cultural minorities.' He first visited Tibet in 1982, when he actually walked all the way from Chengdu to Lhasa: a memorable experience. He has since been back several times, travelling in the central, eastern, western and northern parts of the country. Some of his journeys have been to off-limits areas.

Masao Endo's first two attempts to reach Mt. Kailas by the Southern Route – in 1983 and 1984 – were abortive. He did, however, manage to get there in January 1985 – a harsh time of year by any token. Setting out from Lhasa at the tail end of 1984 along the Northern Route, temperatures had plummetted to –22° C and in consequence he encountered 'a bleak, desolate land'. He bought a horse at Tingri to carry his equipment, which included a Dunrop (*sic*) tent, a specially-made sleeping bag, gas heater, emergency food supplies (including dried mutton), compass and a NASA Landsat map. He was unfortunately obliged to abandon the horse at Camp 21 'due to the severe cold and the overburden'. He then continued on foot from Camp 21 to Camp 22, where he luckily met some road construction workers who gave him a lift on their truck into Ali district.

'Our trip was frequently interrupted by bad road conditions,' he recalls in a letter of 11th September 1988. 'It took us ten days to get to Gerze instead of the normal five. Then I continued my trip on foot from Shiquanhe to Mt. Kailas accompanied by a local guide. It took six days. All the rivers were completely frozen at the time. After I had stayed three nights at Mt. Kailas, I headed for Lake Manasarovar on foot, which took two days. When I got back to Mt. Kailas, I could hardly see the mountain because of a heavy blizzard. My impressions of it were therefore rather disappointing. Truly it was a beautiful snow mountain, contrasting with the blue sky. However, if I am honest, it was not quite as spectacular as I expected. I wonder if this is attributable to my lack of religious mind, brought up in a 20th century materialist world...Fortunately, I was able to get a lift again in a truck from near Mt. Kailas.'

Gilbert R. Levey (Mangalanand)

Inspired by his adventurous grandfather's world travels, Gil Levey left Calfornia back in 1969, straight after high school, on a world tour. After seeing Europe, he travelled overland to India and by the summer of 1970 was living in Kashmir and had been given the religious name of Mangalanand by his guru, Sri 1008 Sri Swami Nirmalanand Saraswati of Ram Mandir, Shrinagar. He had just turned the tender age of eighteen. Since then he has spent many years in India, 'doing yoga, going on pilgrimages, serving *sadhus* [holy men], playing music – and enjoying this unique experience of life.'

In 1986, after passing six weeks in the edifying company of holy men at the great Khumb Mela* gathering at the Hindu religious centre of Hardwar, Gil and his wife Ariane (Saraswati Puri) proceeded to Kathmandu, where they met their old friends William Forbes and Sue Burns, who told them all about their trip to Kailas the previous year. Inspired by the story, Gil and Ariane procured Chinese visas, picked up supplies (tent, food, camping stove, etc.) and headed for Tibet themselves. Getting off their bus at Lhatse, they managed – 'by luck and the blessings of Lord Shiva' – to get a lift all the way to Kailas in a truck carrying a party of Chinese road surveyors. The journey, along the Northern Route, took about ten days as the surveyors had to pause from time to time to do their work.

Gil writes in a letter of 11th September 1988: 'In all, it took us two and a half days to circumambulate Mt. Kailash. We did our *puja* at Drölma La on June 22nd 1986. It was full moon *and* summer solstice. Afterwards, we proceeded to Manasarovar for a bathe, and then returned to Lhasa *via* Darchen and Shiquanhe.'

Gil and Ariane, as good devotees of Lord Shiva, stocked up with rocks from Kailash, water from Manasarovar and other assorted *prasad* [sacred gifts], which they distributed to the 'Hindus, Buddhists and believers' they met in Nepal and India. 'People were very happy to receive *prasad*,' Gil recalls.

In February 1987 their six-month Indian visa ran out, so Gil and Ariane returned to Nepal for the Shivaratri Festival at Pashupatinath. Gil had no plan to return to Kailas at this juncture, but now he started to see the sacred moutain in his meditations and feel its presence growing stronger and stronger every day. His stock of *prasad* was also running out.

'I decided that Kailash was calling me to return to do more *pujas* and collect more *prasad* for distribution,' he writes.

As Ariane decided that it was not propitious for her to return to Kailas yet, Gil set out alone at the end of April. This was earlier than the previous year and conditions were much colder; all the lakes *en route* were frozen. However, he could console himself that this year he would be in time for the Kailas Mela, the celebration of the Buddha's Birthday, which in Tibet falls on the full moon day of May.

Hitching a lift at Lhatse on a truck with some Khampas, Gil reached Kailas in twelve days, arriving on May 8th. There were few

---

*Khumb Mela – a great religious festival held on auspicious dates arrived at by special astrological calculations.

people there at the time and it was not possible to perform the
circuit; also, because of some quirk of the Tibetan calender, the
Buddha's Birthday would not be celebrated until the full moon of
June. All the pilgrims at Kailas therefore jumped into another
available truck and went to circumambulate Manasarovar, which
took four days. Gil then went back to Barkha and in three days
managed to get a truck to take him south to Taklakot, from where
he went on the Kojarnath Gompa. He was now travelling with two
Americans whom he had first met in Shiquanhe and three of the
original Khampas. They later returned to Kailas and this time were
able to do the circuit on the new moon day at the very end of May. It
was the opening of the season. Again, they all performed *puja* at
Drölma La.

Gil had hoped to be able to stay till the full moon of June, but the
chance of a lift with some trucking nomads along the Southern
Route as far as Saga was too good a chance to miss. Again his bags
were bulging with Kailas/Manasarovar/Tirthapuri *prasad*. He finally
arrived back in on June 7th.

On his first visit to Kailas, Gil reports meeting no Westerners
beyond Lhatse. On the second trip, however, he met an American
devotee of H.H. the late Karmapa named Ward Holmes (Yongdu)
and a girl named Penny at Shiquanhe; also a Swedish tour group
which included the curator of the Tibetan Museum in Stockholm,
who were making a film about Kailas. Along the Southern Route he
met two Frenchmen who were travelling on foot, two Swiss men
and a German girl.

Peter Overmire

Peter Overmire, who organized the trailblazing first tour to Kailas
in 1985, is a former Wells Fargo Bank official from San Francisco.
Now in his sixties, he devotes his retirement to his lifelong passion
for mountains and travel. When we met in September 1988 (his
wife Rozell was with him), he proved to be an energetic,
enthusiastic and very convivial person, with very vivid memories of
his Kailas trip.

Peter first saw a picture of Kailas in the *Alpine Journal* around 1946
and was then struck by its 'magic shape', so when in 1985 his friend
Dawa Norbu Sherpa of Himalayan Rover Travel in Kathmandu told
him that the border between Nepal and Tibet would open that year,
he replied, 'That's wonderful, Dawa. Tell me when it happens.' On
April 15th he received a telex from Dawa: YOUR PERMIT FOR
KAILAS IS IN HAND. YOU LEAVE KATHMANDU AUGUST

1ST.

Peter would have preferred to have taken a small group, but the financial terms dictated by China Tibet Travel Service (CTTS) necessitated that he organize a larger group to share the cost. Originally, $15,000 was quoted for a minimum group of one or two vehicles and a staff of ten. Finally fifteen people went for a total cost of $40,000, taking in not only Western Tibet but Lhasa as well. Among the co-travellers that Peter recruited were three of his old Wells Fargo Bank colleagues, Jim Dutcher, Andy Grimstead and Mary Wikstrom; William Forbes and Sue Burns of the Lincoln School in Kathmandu; Kitty Reichart from Massachusetts; Lorri Lockwood; Nancy Shanahan and Kevin Donlan from San Francisco; the Chinese-American Bob Hong; also Shirley Adyani, Rainer Arnhold, Beanie and Dick Wezelman, and Deena Wynne.

Peter was shocked at the cultural devastation in Tibet, but Kailas itself was no anti-climax:

> I think it would be impossible for anyone to go to that mountain and walk around it in any sort of a blasé fashion and say, 'Well, it's a mountain.' It's *not* a mountain. I mean, geology just doesn't work that way. There must be something, some force . . . And to see the evidence of perhaps a couple of thousand years of pilgrimage: the incredibly worn spots, the *shapjes*, the Buddha's footprints, absolutely glistening black with butter . . . A number of the people I work with say, 'Why did you do this? Are you a Buddhist?' No, I'm definitely not a Buddhist . . . [but] the manifestations of any true religion can be incredibly beautiful even to one who is not of the religion.

The high point of his circuit had to be the Drölma La:

> We were fairly well-acclimatized by that time, so the climb was not that bad at all . . . There again it was a party, although it was snowing lightly. Much sharing of *tsampa* and we had typical mountain climbers' mixed dried fruit and nuts and chocolate. I confess I like dried fruit and nuts and chocolate better than *tsampa* but the sharing had to be both ways. It was a very emotional hour I guess we spent at the pass – and a very free, warm interchange. And that was our experience all the way round the mountain once we got rid of our Chinese Big Brothers and were able to meet the Tibetans.

After returning from Kailas, Peter went to see H.H. the Dalai Lama in Dharamsala. His Holiness asked him a few questions – whether there were still fish in Manasarovar; whether he, Peter had caught any fish (a trick question?) – but altogether he did not seem to place an especially high value on the sacred mountain, and Peter felt he looked upon pilgrimage there as a somewhat fanatical practice. More importantly, he asked Peter to make known what he had seen in Western Tibet to the rest of the world – a request that he intends to honour to the best of his ability. The Dalai Lama also assured his American visitor that he had committed no sacrilege in leading a tour party to Kailas.

Peter has already done some research into changes in the sacred region. From an old native of the Darchen-Barkha region now living in exile he has heard that prior to 1950 there were Government-employed caretakers to see that the ducks coming up from India to breed on the lakes were not troubled by predators and that the fish did not swim so far up the tributory streams to spawn that they couldn't return.

He hopes to return to the Kailas, but only if he can walk from India or Nepal as a true devotee of the sacred mountain.

Alan Nichols and Hugh Swift

Peter Overmire told me about two other Americans who had been at Kailas in 1985.

One of them, Alan Nichols, a San Francisco attorney in his sixties, was at Kailas perhaps in April, so was probably the first Westerner there that year and the immediate successor of Bradley Rowe. When the opportunity came to go in early 1985, he dropped everything and set off for Hong Kong with no visas. It proved to be a very expensive undertaking. When he got to Lhasa, CITS required that he take two Toyota Landcruisers and, to his horror, made him sleep in the Chinese compounds along the road. He has since written a rather unusual book called *To Climb a Sacred Mountain*. What makes it unusual apparently is that he describes ascending or visiting various sacred mountains around the world as a devotee of the particular religion or cult with which each is associated.

Hugh Swift, 'the Berkeley mountain walker', on the other hand, was at Kailas a little later, in early September. He has since written in a letter:

> In 1985, I went to Mt. Kailas from Kashgar, travelling on my own. That time I only did one *kora/parikrama* and I found, as have many pilgrims, that the difficulties in reaching the mountain far exceeded the rigours involved in circling it. After continuing on to Lhasa and Kathmandu, I returned home. But something kept gnawing at me and in 1986 I returned to Kashgar by plane and went overland again to Mt. Kailas (not without some difficulty, either year). Then I did two more *koras*, the

second being a very special one with Choying Dorje, a man who lives there and assists pilgrims of all nationalities. [30.ix.88]

Hugh Swift has set down 'some of what I learned and experienced' in *Trekking in Nepal, West Tibet and Bhutan*, to be published in 1989 by Sierra Club Books (British publisher as yet undecided). Another Kailas book will be published in Britain by Thames & Hudson in 1989: photographs by Kerry Moran, text by Russell Johnson.

The 1988 Dzogchen Pilgrimage

For a long time after the pilgrim party left, we heard little of its progress. Then news began to filter through that there had been a major setback. The party were unable to cross the Tsangpo at Lhatse due to floods. Having been held up for several days, the bold decision was then made to withdraw to Lhasa and from there travel all the way round to Kashgar in order to home in on Kailas from the north-west.

Although some of their colleagues had dropped out along the way, a core of travel-battered pilgrims eventually reached Kailas but spent a shorter time than scheduled there. In early October, I received this postcard from Brian Beresford:

Dear John,
Yes, it's still *so* difficult! To enter the realm of the sacred mountain as a pilgrim automatically brings internal and external obstacles into play. Yet somehow, despite everything, we did manage to take the largest group ever to Kailash and Manas...but *via* the Silk Route! An extraordinary voyage. In future years we will go again. You must come then. Thank you for your maps. They led to special discoveries. Much to tell you.

Best Wishes,
Brian

(Much love too. Judy)

Lopön Tenzin Namdak

After we went to press, I met the noteable Bön-po lama, Lopön Tenzin Namdak, senior tutor at the Bön monastery of Smar-ri near Simla in northern India. He was at pains to dissociate his tradition, 'Swastika Bön', disseminated by Thönpa Shenrab (who the Lopön said was born in Shambhala), from early or unsystematized Bön to which many macabre and low religious connotations have become attached. He also denied that any record of Naro Bön-chun or his famous contest of magic with Milarepa occurs in Bön texts. What he did emphasise was the association of the sacred mountain in Bön-po tradition with the *yidam* Meri (lit. 'Fire Mountain' or 'Volcano') depicted in wrathful form with nine heads, several of them black, and eighteen arms. Meri is thought to be identical with the Zhang Zhung deity known as Ge-khod (lit. 'Subduer of Evil'), who has a retinue of some 360 lesser emanations—the *ge-khod* described earlier by Professor Tucci. Our interview proceeded thus:

L.T.N.: What the Bön-po think is that Kailas was the centre [*dewa*] of the kingdom of Zhang Zhung. Now, the people of Zhang Zhung particularly practised the *sadhana* of the *yidam* Meri, who blessed Mount Kailas, Lake Manasarovar, their rivers and adjacent mountain ranges. A *yidam* is not a mountain god; it is an emanation of the Buddha. Therefore we make pilgrimages to Mount Kailas to expunge our defilements.

J.S.: *Did you ever go to Mt. Kailas yourself?*

L.T.N.: Yes, I went there once, carrying my things. Of course this place is not very easy to reach, so the journey was difficult.

J.S.: *Did you meet any Bön-po masters there?*

L.T.N.: No. There was a new Bön-po monastery and solitary caves at Khyunglung three days to the west of Mt. Kailas, but I didn't go there.

J.S.: *Did you find Mt. Kailas very beautiful?*

L.T.N.: 'Beautiful' doesn't mean anything. The mountain is only significant to us because it has been blessed by Meri. This means that the *yidam* has consecrated it, endowed it with spiritual power. Because of this, a pilgrimage can cure disease or repair misfortune.

J.S.: *Did you make a kora [parikrama] around the mountain?*

L.T.N.: Yes, six times, anti-clockwise.

J.S.: *Where did you stay?*

L.T.N.: We just stayed at night in the rocks or in empty or open places—anywhere.

J.S.: *Were there ever any Bön-po monasteries at Mt. Kailas?*

L.T.N.: Yes, several. In the east there was Pawé and in the south [or south-east] there was one a very big monastery called Lingur Lhatse, which existed before the kingdom of Zhang Zhung. But those and all the others were destroyed. In the early morning you just see traces of their ruined buildings in the ground. And there were also places where you could dig up Bön-po *tsa-tsa* [small stamped clay tablets] and figures.

J.S.: *Did you perform puja [religious ceremonies] to the yidam Meri?*

L.T.N.: It is not necessary to perform *puja* there because the *yidam* doesn't reside there always. We can make *puja* anywhere—even in England! Mt. Kailas is only a place blessed by the *yidam;* it's only for that reason that we go there.

J.S.: *So the important thing is to make the kora?*

L.T.N.: Yes, of course. The main thing is to remember when you see the mountain that it was blessed by the *yidam,* otherwise it means nothing—it just makes you tired!

J.S.: *Were there many other Bön-po at Mt. Kailas when you were there?*

L.T.N.: Yes, quite a lot.

J.S.: *Do many Bön-po texts mention Mt. Kailas and Lake Manasarovar?*

L.T.N.: Yes, several texts. We also have two *karchak* [guide-books] which tell about auspicious locations: caves, *shapjé,* and so on.

Inner Kora

One fact that has recently come to light is that the cathedral-shaped rock to the south of Kailas around which the Inner Kora runs is associated with Yenlagjung, one of the Sixteen Arhats, also known as Angi Raja or Ingada (? Lit. 'The Limb-born One'), whose special field of activity is Kailas. L.A. Waddell claims that he went as a missionary there; also that iconographically he is depicted as holding an incense-censer and a cow-tail fly whisk.

The Sixteen Arhats are luminaries of the Mahāyāna pantheon. They are not *arhats* in the true sense of the term, for some fault detains them in *Samsāra* and will continue to do so until the coming of the Future Buddha, Maitreya. Like certain *bodhisattvas,* they serve as protectors of the Dharma.

BIBLIOGRAPHY

Primary Sources

Books

Chang, Garma C., *The Hundred Thousand Songs of Milarepa*, New York, 1962

Gansser, A., *The Throne of the Gods* (With Heim, A.), London, 1939
—— *Geology of the Himalayas*, London, 1964

Govinda, Lama Anagārika, *Bilder Aus Indien Und Tibet*, Haldenwang, 1978
—— *Psycho-Cosmic Symbolism of the Buddhist Stūpa*, Emeryville, 1976
—— *The Way of the White Clouds*, Berkeley, 1962

Govinda, Li Gotami, *Tibet in Pictures*, Emeryville, 1979

Harrer, Heinrich, *Seven Years in Tibet*, London, 1953

Hamsa, Bhagwan Shri, *The Holy Mountain*, London, 1934

Hedin, Sven, *Transhimalaya*, 3 vols, London, 1910
—— *Southern Tibet*, 9 vols, Stockholm, 1917

Kawaguchi, Ekai, *Three Years in Tibet*, Adyar, 1910

Landor, Arnold Henry Savage, *In the Forbidden Land*, 2 vols., London, 1898

Longstaff, Dr Tom, *This My Voyage*, London, 1950

Pranavānanda, Swami, *Pilgrim's Companion to the Holy Kailas and Manasarovar*, Allahabad, 1938
—— *Exploration in Tibet*, 1st ed., Calcutta, 1939; 2nd ed., Calcutta, 1951

Rawling, Capt. C. G., *The Great Plateau*, London, 1905

Schary, Edwin, *In Search of the Mahātmas of Tibet*, London, 1937

Sherring, Charles A., *Western Tibet and the British Borderland*, London, 1906

Tichy, Herbert, *Tibetan Adventure*, London, 1938

Tucci, Giuseppe, *Santi e Briganti nel Tibet Ignoto*, Milan, 1937
—— *The Religions of Tibet*, London, 1980
—— *Transhimalaya*, London, 1973
—— *The Theory and Practice of the Mandala*, London, 1969
—— *Tibet*, London, 1967

Webber, Thomas W., *In the Forests of Upper India*, London, 1902

Articles

Blakeney, Major T. S., *Approach to Kailas*, in *Alpine Journal*, Vol. 55, 1945–6, pp. 316–7

Hedin, Sven, *Journeys in Tibet, 1906–8*, in *Geographical Journal*, Vol. XXXIII, April 1909

Kapur, Chatter Bhuj, *A Pilgrimage to Mount Kailas*, in *The Modern Review* (India), Vol. LX, No. 2, August 1936

Longstaff, T. G., *Notes on a Journey through the Western Himalaya* in *Geographical Journal*, Vol. XXIX, Feb. 1907, pp. 201 ff.

Moorcroft, William, *A Journey to Lake Manasarovar in Undes, a Province of Little Tibet*, in Asiatick Researches, Vol. 12, 1818, pp. 375 ff. (see also *Geographical Journal*, August 1905, pp. 180 ff.)

Ruttledge, Hugh, *Notes on a Visit to Western Tibet in 1926*, in *Geographical Journal*, Vol. LXXI, May 1928, pp. 431 ff.

Ryder, Capt. C. H. D., *Exploration and Survey with the Tibet Frontier Commission and from Gyangtse to Simla v[a Gartok*, in *Geographical Journal*, Vol. XXVI, Oct. 1905, pp. 369 ff.

—— *Sven Hedin's Expedition in Tibet*, in *Geographical Journal*, Vol. XXX11, Oct. 1908, pp. 585 ff.

Smith, Capt. H. U., *A Trip to Thibet, Kylas, Source of the Sutlej and the Manasurwur and Rakhas Lakes*, in *Proceedings of the Royal Geographical Society*, Vol. XI, 1866–7, pp. 119 ff.

Stoll, Eva, *TISE–der Heilige Berg im Tibet*, in *Geographica Helvetica*, Bd. 4, Berne, 1966

Strachey, Lieut. Henry, 66th Bengal N.I., *Narrative of a Journey to the Cho Lagan (Rakas Tal), Cho Mapam (Manasarovar) and the Valley or Purang etc.*, in *Journal of the Asiatic Society of Bengal*, July, August and September 1848

Strachey, Lieut.-Gen. Sir Richard, *Narrative of a Journey to the Lakes Rakas-Tal and Manasarovar in Western Tibet, Undertaken in September 1848*, in *Geographical Journal*, Vol. XV, February 1900 (pp. 150 ff.), March 1900 (pp. 248 ff.), April 1900 (pp. 394 ff.) and *On the Physical Geography of the Provinces of Kumaon and Garhwal in the Himalaya Mountains, and the Adjoining Parts of Tibet*, in *Journal of the Royal Geographical Society*, Vol. XXI, 1851, pp. 57 ff.

Wilson, R.C. *Kailas Parbat and Two Passes of the Kumaon Himalaya* in *Alpine Journal*, Vol. 40, 1928, pp. 23 ff.

Archives

The India Office Library and Records lodges much material of interest. The records of the Political and Secret Department contain the following in particular:

Report by W. S. *Cassels,* Assistant Commissioner, Almora, on a visit to Western Tibet in July 1907 (L/P&S/7/207/No. 1873)

Report by N. C. *Stiffe,* Deputy Commisioner of Almora, on his visit to tibet of July 1911. (L/P&S/11/21/No. 2476)

Narrative of Personal Experiences in Western Tibet in 1929 by E. B. *Wakefield.* (L/P&S/12/4163)

Report on a visit to Western Tibet in October 1932 by F. *Williamson,* Officer on Special Duty in Sikkim. (L/P&S/12/4163)

Original Texts

i.–Dewang, N. Norbu, *mTsho Mapham dKarchag – History of the Sacred Mountain Tise and Blue Lake Mapham'.* To be published by ISMEO, Rome.

ii–*Two Rare Bonpo Dkar-chag of the Sacred Kailash and Manasarowar written by Ye-ses-rgyal-mtshan and Dkarru Grubdban Bstan-'dzin-rinchen, reproduced from rare manuscripts preserved at Baam-glin Monastery in Dolpo, by Tashi Dorji* – Tibet House, New Delhi (1979)

iii–De Rossi Filibeck, Elena, *Two Tibetan Guide Books to Ti-se and La-phyi.* Bonn, 1988.

Secondary Sources

Ali, S. M., *The Geography of the Puranas,* New Delhi, 1966

Avalon, Arthur (Sir John Woodroffe) (trans.), *The Tantra of the Great Liberation,* London, 1913

Beal, Samuel, *A Catena of Buddhist Scriptures from the Chinese,* London, 1871

Blacker, Carmen, *The Catalpa Bow,* London, 1975

Blofeld, John, *The Wheel of Life,* London, 1959

—— *The Tantric Mysticism of Tibet,* New York, 1970

Brunton, Dr. Paul, *A Hermit in the Himalayas,* London, 1975

Burckhardt, Titus, *Sacred Art in East and West,* London, 1967

Daniélou, Alain, *Hindu Polytheism* New York, 1964

de Filippi, Filippo (ed), *An Account of Tibet: The Travels of Ippolito Desideri of Pistoia, S.J., 1712–21,* London, 1937

Ekvall, Robert V., *Religious Observances in Tibet,* Chicago, 1964

Eliade, Mircea, *Patterns in Comparative Religion,* London, 1958

—— *The Myth of the Eternal Return,* Princeton, 1974

Gombrich, Richard, *Ancient Indian Cosmology,* in Blacker, C. and Loewe, M (ed.) *Ancient Cosmologies,* London, 1975

Hardy, Spence, *Manual of Buddhism*, London, 1860
—— *Legends and Theories of the Buddhists*, London, 1881
Hastings, James (ed), *The Encyclopaedia of Religion and Ethics*, Edinburgh 1921 – articles by L. de la Vallée Poussin, *Buddhist Cosmogony and Cosmology*; by H. Jacobi, *Hindu Cosmogony and Cosmology*; and J. A. MacCulloch, *Mountains and Mountain Gods.*
Havell, E.B., *The Himalayas in Indian Art*, London, 1924
Hoffmann, Helmut, *The Religions of Tibet*, London, 1961
Hori, Ichiro, *Folk Religion in Japan*, Tokyo, 1968
Huc, M., *Travels in Tartary, Thibet and China*, Chicago, 1900
Keay, John, *Where Men and Mountains Meet*, London, 1977
Lauf, D. I., *Tibetan Sacred Art*, Berkeley and London, 1976
MacGregor, John A., *Tibet – A Chronicle of Exploration*, London, 1970
de Nebesky-Wojkovitz, R., *Oracles and Demons of Tibet*, The Hague, 1956
Olschak, B. and Wangyal, G. T., *Mystic Art of Ancient Tibet*, London, 1973
Osborn, Arthur (ed), *The Teachings of Ramana Maharshi*, London, 1971
Pallis, Marco, *The Way and the Mountain*, London, 1960
Rooke, G. H. (trans.), *The Meghaduta of Kalidasa*, Oxford, 1935
Sandberg, Graham, *Exploration in Tibet*, Calcutta and London, 1904
Schmid, Toni, *The Cotton Clad Mila. The Tibetan Poet-Saint's Life in Pictures*, Stockholm, 1952
Sircar, D. C., *Cosmography and Cosmology in Early Indian Literature*, Calcutta, 1967
Snellgrove, D., and Richardson, H., *A Cultural History of Tibet*, Boulder, 1980
Stevenson, Mrs. Sinclair, *The Heart of Jainism*, Oxford, 1915
Takakusu, J., *Essentials of Buddhist Philosophy*, Delhi, 1975
Tripathi, Maya Prasad, *The Development of Geographical Knowledge in Ancient India*, Benares, 1969
Waddell, L. .A., *Lamaism or the Buddhism of Tibet*, Cambridge, 1967
Ward, Michael (ed), *The Mountaineer's Companion*, London, 1966
Warren, H. C., *Buddhism in Translations*, Cambridge, Mass., 1896
Welch, Holmes, *The Practice of Chinese Buddhism*, Harvard, 1967
Wilford, F., *The Sacred Isles of the West*, in *Asiatick Researches*, Vols. VIII, IX and X, Calcutta, 1808
Wilhelm, Richard, *The Soul of China*, London, 1928
—— *I Ching*, London, 1975
Zimmer, Heinrich, *Myths & Symbols in Indian Art & Religion*, Princeton, 1974

ADDENDA 1988

Primary Sources

Books

Alder, Garry. *Beyond Bokhara. The Life of William Moorcroft, Asian Explorer and Pioneer Veterinary Surgeon, 1767–1825*, London, 1985

Allen, Charles. *A Mountain in Tibet. The Search for Mount Kailas and the Sources of the Great Rivers of India*, London, 1982.

Baumann, Bruno. *Tibet, Kailas, Seidenstrasse: Die Diamantene Weg*. Austria, 1988.

Demeter, Ursula. *Kailas. Die Reise zun Heiligen Berg*, Zürich, 1987

Ghersi, E. *Secrets of Tibet*, London, 1935

Kopp, Hans. *Himalayan Shuttlecock*, London, undated.

Large, Peter Somerville – see Somerville-Large

Pearse, Col. Hugh. *The Hearseys. Five Generations of an Anglo-Indian Family*, Edinburgh and London, 1905

Satchidānanda, Swami. *Kailash Journal. Pilgrimage into the Himalayas*, Yogaville, Virginia, 1984

Shah, Sadeg Z. *A Visit to Kailas in Tibet in 1931. A Diary in Doggerel*, Mysore, 1931

Shivānanda, Swami. *Pilgrimage to Badri and Kailas*. Date and Place unknown.

Snelling, John – *see* Williamson, Margaret D.

Somerville-Large, Peter. *To the Navel of the World. Yaks & Unheroic Travels in Nepal & Tibet*, London, 1987

Tapovanji Mahāraj, Shri Swami. *Wandering in the Himalayas*. Bombay, 1984

Wakefield, E.T. *Past Imperative*. London, 1966

Wilby, Sorrel. *Tibet. A Woman's Lone Trek Across a Mysterious Land*. London, 1988

Varma, Rommel and Sadhana. *Ascent to the Divine. The Himalaya Kailasa-Manasarovar in Sculpture, Art and Thought*. Switzerland, 1985

Williamson, Margaret, in collaboration with John Snelling. *Memoirs of a Political Officer's Wife in Tibet, Sikkim and Bhutan*. London, 1988

Articles

Ali, Dr. Sálim, *An Ornithological Pilgrimage to Lake Manasarowar and Mount Kailās*, in the *Journal of the Bombay Natural History Society*, Vol. 46, 19??, pp 286–308.

Anon, *The Pilgrimage & Retreat at Mt. Kailash. August 14 24, 1988*, in *UK Dzogchen Newsletter*, February 1988.

Beresford, Brian, *The Lost Kingdom of Gu-gé*, in *The Middle Way*, London. Vol. 62, No. 1, May 1987, pp 37–42. With colour photographic supplement, *Art Treasures of Tsaparang and Thöling*, photographs by Brian Beresford and Sean Jones.

—— *Pilgrimage to Mount Kailash*, in *The Middle Way*, London. Vol. 62, No 2. August 1987, pp 111–116. With colour photographic supplement, *Kailash Mandala*, photographs by Brian Beresford, Sean Jones and Richard Gayer.

—— *Pilgrimage to Manasarovar, The Invincible Jewel Turquoise Lake*, in *The Middle Way*, London. Vol. 62, No 3, November 1987, pp 187–192. With colour photographic supplement, *Manasarova*, photographs by Brian Beresford, Sean Jones and Richard Gayer.

Cunningham, J.B., *Notes on Moorcroft's Travels*, etc., in *Journal of the Asiatic Society of Bengal*, Vol. XIII, pt. 1, 1844

Das, Sarat Chandra, *Dispute between a Buddhist and a Bönpo Priest for the Possession of Mt. Kailas*, in *Journal of the Asiatic Society of Bengal*, Calcutta, Vol. 5- (1), S.206.

Govinda, Lama Anagārika, *The Mystic Mandala of Kailas and its Sacred Lakes*, in *Maha Bodhi*, Calcutta, July 1951

Pearse, Col. H., *Moorcroft and Hearsey's Visit to Lake Manasarovar*, in *Geographical Journal*, Vol. XXVI, 1905

Raper, Capt. F., *Narrative of a Survey with the Purpose of Discovering the Source of the River Ganges*, in *Asiatick Researches*, Vol. XI, 1810

Singh, Raghubir, *Pilgrims Return to Kailas, Tibet's Sacred Mountain*, in *Smithsonian* magazine, Washington, D.C. Vol. 13, No. 2, May 1982

Tucci, G., *Il Manasarovar, Lago Sacro del Tibet*, in *Vie Italia e Mondo*, Vol. III, 1936

Wakefield, E.B., *A Journey to Western Tibet, 1929*, in the *Alpine Journal*, Vol. LXVI, Nos 302/3, May and November, 1961

Watson, Francis, *The Passion of William Moorcroft* in *The Listener*, February 11, 1960

Unpublished Journals & Letters

Forbes, William, *Greetings from Kailash!* Cyclostyled letter, 1985

Hearsey, Capt. H. Y. *A Tour to Eastern Tartary performed in 1812 by William Moorcroft Esqr Supt Hon Compy Stud & Capt H Y Hearsey disguised in the Character of Gooseins with an acct of the intervening Country of Kumaoon& Gurhwal taken from Capt Hearsey's Minutes*. Coll. late John Hearsey.

Longstaff, Tom, *The Manasarowar-Sutlej Problem. A note on the channel between Manasarowar and Rakas Tal, on the source of the Sutlej*, (1909) Royal Geographical Society (London) Archives.

Saker, R. K. M., *Western Tibet 1943*. Coll. Mrs Angela Saker.

Wakefield, E. T., *Journal (1929 Tour of Western Tibet)*. Coll. Lady Wakefield.

Williamson, H., *Western Tibet 1932*. Williamson Collection, Cambridge University Museum of Archaeology and Anthropoloy.

Also letters from Naomi Duguid, Charlie Foster-Hall, Richard Lanchester, Lorri Lockwood et al.

Secondary Sources

Avalon, Arthur. *The Serpent Power* (Revised Edition), Madras, 1931

Batchelor, Stephen. *The Tibet Guide*, London, 1987

Batchelor, Stephen (ed). *The Jewel in the Lotus. A Guide to the Buddhist Traditions of Tibet*, London, 1987

Bedi, Rahul Kuldip. *Kailas & Manasarovar, After Twenty-two Years in Shiva's Domain*, New Delhi, 1984

Cammann, Schuyler. *Trade Through the Himalayas. The early British Attempts to Open Tibet*, Westport, Conn., 1970 (reprint)

Conze, Edward, *Memoirs of a Modern Gnostic*, Two parts. Sherborne, Dorset, 1979

Dowman, Keith, *Sky Dancer. The Secret Life & Songs of the Lady Yeshe Tsogyel*, London, 1984

Evans-Wentz, W.Y, *Cuchana and Sacred Mounains*, Chicago, 1982

Fletcher, Dr. Harold, *A Quest of Flowers*, Edinburgh, 1976.

Gould, Basil, *The Jewel in the Lotus. Recollections of an Indian Political*, London, 1957

Henss, Michael, *Tibet. Die Külturdenmäler*, Zürich/Freiburg, 1981

Holditch, Sir Thomas, *Tibet the Mysterious*, London, 1908

Hopkirk, Peter, *Trepassers on the Roof of the World*, London, 1982

Kramrisch, Stella, *The Hindu Temple*, Calcutta, 1946

Lamb, Alastair, *British India & Tibet, 1977–1910*, London, 1986 (Revised and expanded edition of *Britain & Chinese Central Asia. The Road to Lhasa, 1767 to 1905*, London, 1960.)

Lehrman, Fredrick (ed.). *The Sacred Landscape*, Berkeley, Cal. 1988.

O'Flaherty, Wendy Doniger, *Asceticism & Eroticism in the Mythology of Shiva*, London, 1973.

Pearse, Col. Hugh, *The Hearseys. Five Generations of an Anglo-Indian Family*, Edinburgh and London, 1905

Norbu, Namkhai, *The Crystal & the Way of Light*, London, 1986

—— *The Necklace of Gzi*. Dharamsala, 1981

Roerich, Nicholas. *Himalayas – Abode of Light*. London and Bombay, 1947

Swinson, Arthur. *Beyond the Frontiers. The Biography of Col. F. M. Bailey*. London, 1971

Woodcock, George. *Into Tibet. The Early British Explorers*. London, 1971

Film & Video Material

Frederick Williamson took b/w cine film on his 1932 visit to Kailas with Frank Ludlow. Quality poor. This is now lodged in the National Film Archive.

R. K. M. Saker took some colour footage of his 1943 visit with Gordon Terry. Quality again poor. This film is still in the possession of the Saker family.

Brian Beresford and Sean Jones directed a 1½ hour video of their 1986 Kailas Parikrama. Entitled *Kailash: The Sacred Mountain*, this is available, cost £31, from the Medidian Trust, The Buddhist Film & Video Archive, 330 Harrow Road, London W9 2HP. Two companion 1½ hour videos, *Shanshung: The Artistic Treasures of Tsaparang & Thöling* and *Into the Heart of Asia: A Buddhist Pilgrim in Central Asia*, are available from the same source, at £25 add £31 respectively.

Much other film and video material has been taken since 1985. There are reports, for instance, of a network Japanese TV film of Kailas.

******

Note:

The author is compiling a new work on Kailas-Manasarovar which will include much new material not included for reasons of space in the present work. This is projected to contain a definitive guide (*Karchak*) to the sacred sites on the *parikrama* circuits. Anyone with relevant or new information is invited to contact *Empty Circle Press, Sharpham North, Ashprington, Totnes, South Devon TQ9 7UT*

INDEX

(NOTE: An M in brackets (M) after selected general items indicates that they are of specifically contemporary relevance.)

ACKNOWLEDGEMENTS

TO THE FOLLOWING:

Messrs. Macmillan, for permission to quote from *Transhimalaya* by Sven Hedin

Theosophical Publishing House, for permission to quote from *Three Years in Tibet* by Ekai Kawaguchi

Messrs. Faber and Faber, for permission to quote from *The Holy Mountain* by Bhagwan Shri Hamsa and from *Tibetan Adventure* by Herbert Tichy

Messrs. Frederick Warne, for permission to quote from *In Search of the Mahatmas of Tibet* by Edwin G. Schary

Messrs. Edward Arnold, for permission to quote from *In the Forests of Upper India* by Thos. W. Webber and from *Western Tibet and the British Borderland* by Charles A. Sherring

Messrs. Heinemann, for permission to quote from *In the Forbidden Land* by A. H. Savage Landor

Mrs. Margaret Shinnie, for permission to quote from articles by Captain H. U. Smith, Major C. H. D. Ryder and Hugh Ruttledge, originally published in *The Geographical Journal*

Edward Pyatt Esq., for permission to quote from articles by Major T. S. Blakeney and Colonel R. C. Wilson, originally published in *The Alpine Journal*

Lama Anagarika Govinda, for permission to quote from his book, *The Way of the White Clouds*

Messrs. A. P. Watt Ltd., for permission to quote from the poem 'Meru' by William Butler Yeats

Central Chinmaya Mission Trust for permission to quote from *Wandering in the Himalayas* by Sri Swami Tapovanji Maharaj

Swami Satchidananda for permission to quote from *Kailash Journal*.

AND TO THE FOLLOWING FOR OTHERWISE HELPING OR LENDING ENCOURAGEMENT:

Lama Anagarika Govinda, Herbert Tichy, Esq., John Knight, Esq. of the B.B.C (who produced the Radio 4 programme, *Pilgrimage to the Sacred Kailas*, broadcast in August 1980), C. B. Kapur, Esq., Miss

Martha Patrick, Dr. Irmgard Schloegl, Mr. Christmas Humphreys, Phiroz Mehta, Esq., Dr. Carmen Blacker, Edward Henning, Esq., M. Hookham, Esq., S. Hodge, Esq., John Blofeld, Esq., John Hearsey, Esq., Alpo Ratia, Esq., Shri Uma Prasad Mookerjee of Calcutta, Dr. Sálim Ali of Bombay, Messrs. Gyatso Tsering (Director) and Samphel of the Library of Tibetan Works and Archives (Dharamsala), Mr. Werner Leonhard, Mrs. Jean Warren, Dr. G. Alder, Geoffrey Marshall-Taylor Esq., Prof. Corrado Pensa, Stephen Batchelor, Charles Foster-Hall, Richard Crane, Peter Overmire, Hugh Swift, Gil Levey, William Forbes, Bradley Rowe, Masao Endo, Brian Beresford, Sean Jones, Lorri Lockwood, Eva Hookway, Richard Lanchester, Lopön Tenzin Namdak and H.H. the Dalai Lama of Tibet.

Unpublished Crown-copyright material in the India Office Records reproduced in this book appears by permission of the Controller of Her Majesty's Stationery Office.

PICTURE CREDITS

Bradley Rowe/Stone Routes: front cover, 2, 3, 28b, 33, 38, 42–3, 44, 62–3, 66b, 68–9, 78, 100–1, 114–5, 116, 140–1, 164–5, 168–9, 174b, 178, 190–1, 195, 198–9, 208, 209, 222–3, 225, 228–9, 244–5, 258, 304–5, 318, 322–3, 324, 328, 330, 331, 335, 347, 356, 368b, 370, 379, 394

Brian Beresford & Sean Jones: 61, 66a, 92, 176–7, 180, 193, 212–3, 221, 281, 314, 315, 316, 317, 348, 352, 358, 359, 360a, 360b, 362, 398

Brian Beresford: viii, 32, 147, 294, 377

Hugh Swift: back cover, 18–19, 34b, 117, 320, 380

Michael Henss: 40–1, 156–7, 288, 296–7

Chris Piper: 4a, 4b, 5, 6–7, 8a, 8b, 14, 15

Hugh Ruttledge/Major David Ruttledge: 28a, 70, 72b, 74, 76, 84b, 120, 124, 150, 152, 158, 174a, 238a, 238b, 363

Dr. André Herold: 47, 64, 84a, 126–7, 142, 226, 264

Masao Endo: 374a, 374b

William Forbes & Sue Burns: 39, 311, 368a

Hugh Clift/Tharpa Publications: 26, 46

Prof. G. Tucci/IsMEO (Rome): 34a, 204, 278, 283, 288

Sven Hedin: 112, 132, 136, 145

Lady Wakefield: 160a, 160b, 162
Mrs. M.D. Williamson: 170, 171
Mrs. J.M. Jehu: 72a, 234
Mrs. Vera Sherring: 121
Mrs. Charmian Longstaff: 129
Lisi Kaiser: 326
Naomi Duguid: 367
Stephen Batchelor: 235
C.B. Kapur: 184a, 184b, 186
Museum of Ethnology, University of Zurich: 20
India Office Records & Library: 80-1
Library of Tibetan Works and Archives: 230
Royal Geographical Society: 89
Lahore Museums: 81b
A. Breslavetz: 233
Central Chinmaya Mission Trust: 257
Todd Mitchell: 266
Swami Pranavānanda: frontispiece, 268, 272
Buddhist Society (London): 290
Swami Satchidānanda: 302, 303, 306, 308
Robert Beer: vii, 397
Hamish Hamilton: 341
Macdonald/Queen Anne Press: 343
Gilbert Levey: 372
Government of India Tourist Office: 23
Captain John Noel: 13
Alpine Journal: 153
A. Gansser/A. Heim: 201a, 201b
Heinrich Harrer: 206a

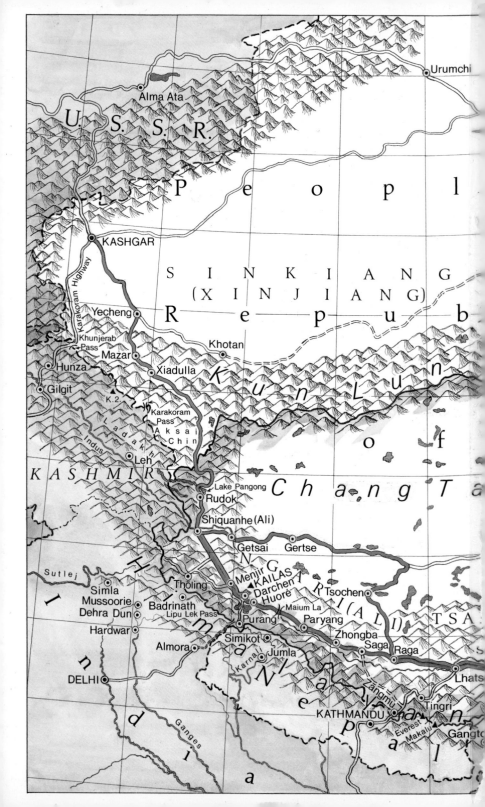